The Cloud Computing Journey

Design and deploy resilient and secure multi-cloud systems
with practical guidance

Divit Gupta

BIRMINGHAM—MUMBAI

The Cloud Computing Journey

Group Product Manager: Niranjan Naikwadi
Publishing Product Manager: Surbhi Suman
Book Project Manager: Arul Viveaun S
Senior Editor: Aamir Ahmed and Nathanya Dias
Technical Editor: K Bimala Singha
Copy Editor: Safis Editing
Proofreader: Safis Editing
Indexer: Hemangini Bari
Production Designer: Aparna Bhagat
DevRel Marketing Coordinators: Namita Velgekar and Nivedita Pandey

First published: December 2023

Production reference: 1071223

Published by Packt Publishing Ltd.
Grosvenor House
11 St Paul's Square
Birmingham
B3 1RB, UK

ISBN 978-1-80512-228-9

www.packtpub.com

To my mother, Shashi Gupta, and the memory of my father, Pritipal Gupta, for their sacrifices and for exemplifying the power of determination. To my sons, Yash and Darsh, who made me understand true love.

– Divit Gupta

Foreword

It is both an honor and a pleasure to contribute a foreword to this remarkable technical book penned by my esteemed colleague, Divit. Having had the privilege of working alongside Divit during our tenure at Oracle and being a guest on his insightful podcast show, I can attest to the depth of his expertise, the breadth of his vision, and the unwavering passion he brings to the IT industry.

Divit's unique ability to seamlessly integrate his profound knowledge of the IT landscape with a keen understanding of optimizing narratives for search reflects his commitment to delivering excellence. This book stands as a testament to his insatiable thirst for data, experimentation, and the relentless pursuit of knowledge – an endeavor that has undoubtedly enriched the technological discourse.

Throughout our shared experiences, I have witnessed Divit's exceptional leadership qualities firsthand. He not only possesses impressive technical acumen but also embodies the attributes of a visionary leader. Divit's capacity to absorb diverse ideas, coupled with his decisiveness in making bold and strategic choices, sets him apart. In the complex realm of Oracle, he serves as a results-oriented architect, leading by example and demonstrating an unparalleled dedication to overcoming challenges.

As you delve into the pages of this book, guided by Divit's expertise, I encourage you to absorb the wealth of knowledge and insights he imparts. It is a journey led by a seasoned professional who not only understands the intricate nuances of our dynamic industry but is also committed to sharing that understanding for the benefit of all. May this book be a beacon of enlightenment and inspiration for technologists, architects, and enthusiasts alike.

Rohit Rahi

Vice president of Customer Success Services, Oracle America

Contributors

About the author

Divit Gupta, a seasoned IT professional with 20 years of industry expertise, excels in driving strategic architecture initiatives and providing leadership in multi-pillar sales cycles. With a global impact, he spearheads technical partnerships, defines team vision, and champions new strategic endeavors.

As the host of popular podcasts such as *Tech Talk with Divit*, *Live Labs with Divit*, and *Cloud Bites with Divit*, he showcases technological initiatives and leadership. In 2022–2023, he served as Oracle TV's correspondent for CloudWorld. A recognized expert, Divit presented on Oracle database technology at Oracle CloudWorld FY 2023.

His passion for knowledge sharing extends to international conference talks, technical blogs, and multiple books on emerging technologies. Divit has been featured in several prominent newspapers and technology magazines worldwide. Holding over 40 certifications from Microsoft, Oracle, AWS, and Databricks, he remains at the forefront of technology.

I want to thank my friends and family who have been close to me and supported me.

About the reviewers

Anushree Srivastava is a customer engineer at Google USA. She is a data and analytics architect with 15+ years of experience in designing and implementing data-driven solutions for a wide range of industries, including digital advertising, transportation management, banking, life sciences, insurance, and healthcare.

She has a proven track record of success in data platform modernization, data integration, and cloud analytics. She has expertise in Google Cloud Platform, Informatica PowerCenter, Oracle, Teradata, Salesforce.com, SAP HANA, BusinessObjects, and OBIEE.

As well as the aforementioned, she is skilled in data analysis, data modeling, and ETL development. She is also experienced in managing and delivering complex data projects on time and within budget.

Anushree is passionate about using data to solve real-world problems and improve business outcomes. She has strong interpersonal and communication skills, with the ability to work effectively with both technical and non-technical audiences.

Venkata Ravi Kumar Yenugula is an **Extraordinary Ability** (**EB1-A**) *Einstein Visa* recipient from the United States, an Oracle Certified Master, a co-author, and a technical reviewer. He is TOGAF-certified, has published 100+ technical articles, and is an Oracle Open/cloud speaker (x3). He is an IEEE Senior Member with 26+ years of multinational leadership experience in the United States, Seychelles, and India in **Banking, Financial Services, and Insurance** (**BFSI**) verticals.

Venkata has co-authored four books – *Oracle Database Upgrade and Migration Methods*; *Oracle High Availability, Disaster Recovery, and Cloud Services*; *Oracle GoldenGate with MicroServices*; and *Oracle Global Data Services for Mission-Critical Systems*

He was the technical reviewer of four books – *Oracle 19c AutoUpgrade Best Practices*, *Oracle Autonomous Database in Enterprise Architecture*, *End-to-End Observability with Grafana*, and *Maximum Availability Architecture (MAA) with Oracle GoldenGate MicroServices in HUB Architecture*.

He is an **Oracle Certified Professional** (**OCP**) in Oracle 8i, 9i, 10g, 11g, 12c, and 19c, and he is also an **Oracle Certified Expert** (**OCE**) in Oracle GoldenGate, RAC, Performance Tuning, Oracle Cloud Infrastructure, Terraform, and Oracle Engineered Systems (Exadata, ZDLRA, and ODA), as well as being Oracle Security- and **Maximum Availability Architecture** (**MAA**)-certified.

He has published over 100 Oracle technology articles, including on **Oracle Technology Network** (**OTN**), in *ORAWORLD* Magazine, on UKOUG, in *OTech* Magazine, and on Redgate. He has spoken three times at **Oracle Open World** (**OOW**) in Las Vegas/San Francisco, US.

Oracle Corporation has published his profile on their OCM list and in their *Spotlight on Success* stories.

Table of Contents

Part 2: Compute, Storage, and Networking

3

Compute   55

4

Storage   81

5

Networking   107

Part 3: Security, Compliance, and Databases

6

7

8

Preface

This book provides an overview of cloud technology, covering everything from the basics to the more advanced concepts and allowing you to design and build cloud systems that can stand the test of time through practical examples and information on the latest trends.

This book helps to solve the problem of a lack of expertise in cloud computing by providing a comprehensive guide to cloud architecture and best practices for using different vendors and tools. It also covers security and compliance considerations and provides guidance on how to design and build scalable and resilient cloud systems. This can help businesses avoid costly mistakes, ensure their cloud systems are secure and compliant, and build cloud systems that can adapt and grow with their business.

By the end of this book, you will have an understanding of how to leverage different vendors and tools to build robust and secure cloud systems. This knowledge can help businesses and professionals leverage the power of cloud computing to achieve their goals more efficiently and effectively.

Who this book is for

The book is targeted at anyone who is interested in understanding cloud technology, including business leaders and IT professionals who want to learn about the benefits, challenges, and best practices of cloud computing. It will be useful for those who are just starting to explore cloud technology, as well as those who are already using cloud technology but want to deepen their understanding and optimize their usage.

Overall, the book is ideal for anyone looking to build and manage robust and secure cloud systems efficiently and effectively.

What this book covers

Chapter 1, Fundamentals of Cloud Architecture, discusses the history, present state, and future of cloud computing architecture. This chapter delves into the origins of cloud computing, tracing its roots from time-sharing to the commercialization of services.

We will then explore the pervasive influence of cloud computing today, discussing its models, benefits, challenges, and real-world implementations. Understanding cloud architecture becomes the focal point as we unravel the components, deployment models, and key concepts such as virtualization and load balancing. Finally, we will turn our attention to the future, exploring emerging trends such as edge computing, serverless computing, and quantum computing, while contemplating the challenges and opportunities that lie ahead.

Chapter 2, Components of a Cloud Infrastructure, begins by exploring the foundation of a cloud infrastructure, which includes physical data centers, networking, and storage systems. It discusses the importance of server virtualization and hypervisors in enabling the efficient utilization of computing resources. The chapter then delves into the concept of virtual networks and their role in facilitating communication between different components of the cloud infrastructure. It also explores storage technologies such as block, file, and object storage. Additionally, the chapter discusses the importance of load balancers, firewalls, and security mechanisms in ensuring the integrity and protection of the cloud infrastructure.

Chapter 3, Compute, provides a comprehensive exploration of the essential components and concepts related to compute and storage in cloud computing. The chapter delves into the various compute options available in cloud computing. It covers the concept of **Virtual Machines** (**VMs**), which allow users to create and run multiple instances of operating systems on a single physical server. The advantages of VMs, such as resource isolation and scalability, are discussed in detail. Additionally, this chapter explores the concept of serverless computing, where users can run their applications without needing to manage the underlying infrastructure.

Chapter 4, Storage, provides a comprehensive exploration of the essential components and concepts related to storage in cloud services. This chapter introduces you to the fundamental role of storage solutions in cloud computing. It covers a range of cloud storage types, including object storage, file storage, block storage, and hybrid storage, discussing their unique characteristics and use cases. This chapter also discusses essential considerations for selecting and managing cloud storage, such as security measures, performance factors, data transfer and migration strategies, data durability, availability, and scalability.

Chapter 5, Networking, presents a comprehensive exploration of networking's vital role in cloud environments. The introduction lays the groundwork by explaining the significance of networking in facilitating seamless communication and data transfer among cloud resources. This chapter covers various networking types, including **Virtual Private Cloud** (**VPC**), subnetting, load balancing, **Content Delivery Networks** (**CDNs**), and **Virtual Private Networks** (**VPNs**), providing insights into their functionalities and benefits.

Chapter 6, Security and Compliance 1 – Cloud Perspective, delves into the best practices for cloud security, offering you a comprehensive toolkit to strengthen their defenses. Encryption, a fundamental pillar of data protection, will be explored in depth, and we will examine its role in safeguarding sensitive information from unauthorized access. Additionally, you will discover the significance of **identity and access management** (**IAM**), secure API usage, network security, and secure coding practices for cloud-native applications.

Chapter 7, Security and Compliance 2 – Cloud Perspective, is the second part of the previous chapter. In this chapter, you will explore critical aspects of security in cloud computing, gaining insights into compliance and legal considerations, cloud security best practices, incident response, cloud forensics, managing cloud security at scale, and the evolving threat landscape.

Chapter 8, Database Services – Part 1, is dedicated to exploring the various database offerings available in the cloud. You will learn about managed database services provided by major cloud providers, such as **Amazon Web Services** (**AWS**), Microsoft Azure, and **Google Cloud Platform** (**GCP**). This chapter will delve into different types of databases, including relational databases, NoSQL databases, and data warehousing services.

Chapter 9, Database Services – Part 2, is dedicated to exploring the various database offerings available in the cloud. You will learn about managed database services provided by major cloud providers, such as AWS, Microsoft Azure, and GCP. The chapter will delve into different types of databases, including relational databases, NoSQL databases, and data warehousing services.

Chapter 10, Monitoring and Management, delves into the critical aspects of overseeing and maintaining database systems in the cloud. This chapter provides a comprehensive understanding of the tools, practices, and techniques required to monitor databases in real time, track resource utilization, and respond to potential issues promptly.

Chapter 11, Backup and Restore Mechanisms, serves as a practical guide, providing a step-by-step walk-through of essential procedures for data backup and restoration within cloud environments. We'll unravel the complexities, providing you with the skills to navigate and implement these critical operations seamlessly.

Chapter 12, Backup and Restore Procedures, delves into the critical aspects of data protection and recovery in cloud computing. In this chapter, you can expect a thorough exploration of various backup and restoration strategies, techniques, and best practices tailored to the cloud environment.

To get the most out of this book

Before delving into this book on cloud computing, it's beneficial for you to have a foundational understanding of basic computing concepts, networking principles, and general IT infrastructure. Familiarity with operating systems, particularly in a server environment, is advantageous. Additionally, a grasp of fundamental security concepts and practices will enhance your comprehension of the book's discussions on cloud security. While the book strives to explain concepts comprehensively, a basic awareness of traditional IT operations will aid in drawing parallels and understanding the transformative nature of cloud technology. Whether you're an IT professional seeking to expand your expertise or a newcomer curious about cloud computing, having a solid grasp of these pre-requisite concepts will ensure a more enriching learning experience.

Software/hardware covered in the book	Operating system requirements
AWS Services	A web browser (Chrome, Firefox, or Edge) and an operating system (Windows, macOS, or Linux)
GCP, Google Cloud Services	A web browser (Chrome, Firefox, or Edge) and an operating system (Windows, macOS, or Linux)
Microsoft Azure Services	A web browser (Chrome, Firefox, or Edge) and an operating system (Windows, macOS, or Linux)

Access to Oracle Cloud Infrastructure, AWS, Microsoft Azure, and Google Cloud Platform is recommended but not necessary.

Conventions used

There are a number of text conventions used throughout this book.

`Code in text`: Indicates code words in text, database table names, folder names, filenames, file extensions, pathnames, dummy URLs, user input, and Twitter handles. Here is an example: "Replace `REGION` with the desired location for your bucket (e.g., `us-central1`) and replace `YOUR_BUCKET_NAME` with a globally unique name for your bucket."

Bold: Indicates a new term, an important word, or words that you see onscreen. For instance, words in menus or dialog boxes appear in **bold**. Here is an example: "In the AWS Management Console, navigate to the **Security, Identity & Compliance** section."

> **Tips or important notes**
> Appear like this.

Get in touch

Feedback from our readers is always welcome.

General feedback: If you have questions about any aspect of this book, email us at `customercare@packtpub.com` and mention the book title in the subject of your message.

Errata: Although we have taken every care to ensure the accuracy of our content, mistakes do happen. If you have found a mistake in this book, we would be grateful if you would report this to us. Please visit `www.packtpub.com/support/errata` and fill in the form.

Piracy: If you come across any illegal copies of our works in any form on the internet, we would be grateful if you would provide us with the location address or website name. Please contact us at `copyright@packt.com` with a link to the material.

If you are interested in becoming an author: If there is a topic that you have expertise in and you are interested in either writing or contributing to a book, please visit `authors.packtpub.com`.

Share Your Thoughts

Once you've read *The Cloud Computing Journey*, we'd love to hear your thoughts! Scan the QR code below to go straight to the Amazon review page for this book and share your feedback.

https://packt.link/r/1-805-12228-2

Your review is important to us and the tech community and will help us make sure we're delivering excellent quality content.

Download a free PDF copy of this book

Thanks for purchasing this book!

Do you like to read on the go but are unable to carry your print books everywhere? Is your eBook purchase not compatible with the device of your choice?

Don't worry, now with every Packt book you get a DRM-free PDF version of that book at no cost.

Read anywhere, any place, on any device. Search, copy, and paste code from your favorite technical books directly into your application.

The perks don't stop there, you can get exclusive access to discounts, newsletters, and great free content in your inbox daily

Follow these simple steps to get the benefits:

1. Scan the QR code or visit the link below

https://packt.link/free-ebook/9781805122289

2. Submit your proof of purchase

3. That's it! We'll send your free PDF and other benefits to your email directly

Part 1:
Fundamentals and
Components of the Cloud

In this part, we will discuss the history, present state, understanding, and future of cloud computing architecture. We will then explore the foundation of a cloud infrastructure, which includes physical data centers, networking, and storage systems. Additionally, this part discusses the importance of load balancers, firewalls, and security mechanisms in ensuring the integrity and protection of the cloud infrastructure.

This part has the following chapters:

- *Chapter 1, Fundamentals of Cloud Architecture*
- *Chapter 2, Components of a Cloud Infrastructure*

1

Fundamentals
of Cloud Architecture

In this chapter, we will embark on a comprehensive journey through the history, present state, understanding, and future of cloud computing architecture. We will delve into the origins of cloud computing, tracing its roots from time-sharing to the commercialization of services.

We will then explore the pervasive influence of cloud computing today, discussing its models, benefits, challenges, and real-world implementations. Understanding cloud architecture will become the focal point as we unravel the components, deployment models, and key concepts such as virtualization and load balancing. Finally, we will turn our attention to the future, exploring emerging trends such as edge computing, serverless computing, and quantum computing, while contemplating the challenges and opportunities that lie ahead. By embracing this comprehensive view, you will gain valuable insights into the transformative power and potential implications of cloud computing architecture.

In this chapter, we will cover the following topics:

- The history of cloud computing
- Cloud computing today
- Understanding cloud architecture
- The future of cloud architecture

The end goal of this chapter is to provide you with a comprehensive grasp of the essential elements, principles, and technologies that underpin cloud architecture. By exploring topics such as virtualization, containerization, compute resources, storage types, and networking, you will gain insights into the fundamental building blocks of cloud infrastructure. You will explore the history, current state, and future trends of cloud computing, and gain insights into the evolution of this technology and its potential impact on businesses and individuals. This chapter aims to equip you with the knowledge and insights necessary to make informed decisions about designing, implementing, and managing cloud-based solutions. Ultimately, the goal is to empower you with the foundational understanding needed to leverage cloud technologies effectively and harness the benefits of scalability, flexibility, and cost-efficiency that the cloud offers.

Technical requirements

To fully engage with the content in this chapter on cloud computing architecture, you should have a basic understanding of computer systems, networking concepts, and information technology.

Additionally, the following technical requirements are recommended:

- **Internet access**: You should have a reliable internet connection to access online resources, references, and examples related to cloud computing.

- **A computing device**: A desktop computer, laptop, tablet, or smartphone with a modern web browser is necessary to read this chapter's content and access any online materials.

- **A web browser**: The latest version of a modern web browser such as Google Chrome, Mozilla Firefox, Microsoft Edge, or Safari is recommended. This ensures compatibility and optimal viewing experience of web-based resources and interactive content.

- **Familiarity with cloud services**: Some familiarity with cloud services and their basic functionalities will enhance your understanding of this chapter. This includes knowledge of cloud computing models such as **Infrastructure-as-a-Service (IaaS)**, **Platform-as-a-Service (PaaS)**, and **Software-as-a-Service (SaaS)**.

The history of cloud computing

Cloud computing has a rich history that has evolved over several decades. The concept of cloud computing dates back to the 1960s when computer scientists at MIT and Dartmouth College proposed the idea of a "utility computing" system that would allow users to access computing resources on demand.

In the 1970s, IBM introduced virtualization technology, which allowed multiple operating systems to run on a single mainframe computer. This technology enabled companies to consolidate their IT resources and reduce costs.

In the 1990s, the development of the World Wide Web and the rise of e-commerce led to the creation of web-based applications and services. This led to the development of early cloud computing platforms such as Salesforce, which provided **customer relationship management** (**CRM**) services over the internet.

In 2002, Amazon launched its web services division, offering cloud-based infrastructure services such as storage and computing power. This was followed by the launch of **Amazon Elastic Compute Cloud** (**EC2**) in 2006, which allowed users to rent computing capacity on demand.

In 2008, Google launched its cloud computing platform, Google App Engine, which allowed developers to build and run web applications on Google's infrastructure.

Microsoft followed suit in 2010 with the launch of Windows Azure, which provided cloud-based services for building and deploying applications.

The growth of cloud computing has been fueled by advances in virtualization technology, which allows computing resources to be shared and used more efficiently. The development of cloud-based services and infrastructure has also made it easier for businesses to scale their IT resources up or down based on demand.

Today, cloud computing has become an integral part of many businesses, offering a range of benefits such as cost savings, scalability, flexibility, and improved collaboration. Cloud computing has also enabled the development of new technologies such as serverless computing, which allows developers to build and run applications without managing servers or infrastructure.

The main idea behind cloud computing was to provide a flexible and cost-effective way for users to access computing resources on demand. In the early days of computing, businesses and organizations had to invest in their IT infrastructure, including hardware, software, and networking equipment. This was expensive and often required a large upfront investment, which made it difficult for small and medium-sized businesses to compete with larger organizations.

Cloud computing was envisioned as a way to address this challenge by providing a shared pool of computing resources that could be accessed over the internet. This allowed businesses to pay only for the resources they needed, and to scale up or down as needed to meet changing demand.

In addition to cost savings, cloud computing was also seen as a way to improve the flexibility and agility of IT operations. By providing access to a shared pool of resources, cloud computing could enable businesses to quickly deploy new applications, scale up or down as needed, and respond to changing business needs more quickly than traditional IT infrastructure.

The thought behind cloud computing was to provide a more efficient, flexible, and cost-effective way for businesses to access the computing resources they need to operate and compete in today's fast-paced digital economy.

Cloud computing today

This section provides an up-to-date snapshot of the current state of cloud computing and its impact on businesses and individuals. It explores the widespread adoption of cloud computing across various industries and the benefits it offers, such as scalability, cost-efficiency, and enhanced flexibility. The section also delves into the different types of cloud services available today, including IaaS, PaaS, and SaaS, highlighting their respective features and use cases.

In recent years, cloud computing has transformed the way businesses and individuals access and use technology. It has revolutionized the way we store, process, and share data, enabling greater flexibility, scalability, and cost-efficiency than ever before. With the cloud computing market projected to reach $1 trillion by 2024, it is clear that cloud computing has become an essential part of the modern technology landscape. But what exactly is cloud computing, and how does it work? In this book, we will explore the fundamental concepts of cloud computing, from its history and evolution to its various types and deployment models. We will delve into the benefits and challenges of cloud computing and examine real-world examples of how organizations are leveraging this technology to drive innovation, growth, and success. Whether you are a seasoned IT professional or simply curious about the cloud, this book will provide you with the insights and knowledge you need to navigate this exciting and rapidly changing field.

Cloud computing has become a pervasive technology that has transformed the way businesses and individuals access and use computing resources. At its core, cloud computing is about delivering computing resources over the internet, rather than owning and managing physical infrastructure. This enables greater flexibility and scalability as users can easily scale up or down their resource usage based on their needs. It also offers cost-efficiency as users only pay for what they use and can avoid upfront capital expenses. Additionally, cloud computing offers greater resilience and reliability, as cloud providers typically offer redundancy and failover capabilities to ensure that services remain available even in the event of hardware failure or other issues.

Cloud computing is a paradigm that enables the provisioning of computing resources, encompassing servers, storage, applications, and services through the internet. Instead of possessing and overseeing physical infrastructure, individuals and businesses have the option to lease these resources from cloud providers, paying only for what they consume. This approach presents numerous benefits compared to conventional on-site infrastructure, including enhanced adaptability, scalability, cost-effectiveness, and dependability.

There are several different types of cloud computing services, each offering varying levels of abstraction and control. At the lowest level of abstraction is IaaS, which provides users with access to virtualized computing resources, such as VMs, storage, and networking, that they can use to build and deploy their applications. At a higher level of abstraction is PaaS, which provides a platform on top of which users can build and deploy applications, without having to worry about the underlying infrastructure. Finally, at the highest level of abstraction is SaaS, which provides complete applications that are accessed over the internet, without the need for any installation or maintenance on the user's part.

While cloud computing offers many benefits, it also comes with several challenges that must be addressed. One of the primary challenges is security, as cloud providers must ensure that users' data is protected from unauthorized access or disclosure. Another challenge is vendor lock-in, as users may find it difficult to switch between cloud providers due to differences in technologies and architectures. Finally, there is the challenge of managing cloud costs, as users must carefully monitor and optimize their resource usage to avoid unexpected expenses.

Despite these challenges, cloud computing has become an essential part of the modern technology landscape, enabling businesses and individuals to access and use technology more efficiently and effectively than ever before.

The following figure depicts the general idea behind cloud computing:

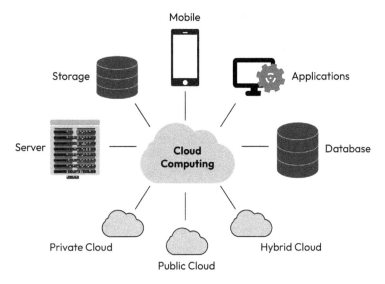

Figure 1.1 – The versatility and flexibility of cloud computing

This figure provides a concise overview of cloud computing, featuring key components such as databases, applications, compute, mobile devices, servers, and storage. It also highlights different cloud deployment models: public, private, and hybrid clouds. This figure visually represents these components and models, showcasing the interconnected nature of cloud computing.

Cloud computing has become an essential part of the modern technology landscape, enabling businesses and individuals to access and use technology more efficiently and effectively than ever before. With cloud computing, organizations can access technology resources as needed, without having to invest in and manage on-premises infrastructure. This allows companies to focus on their core business, while the cloud service provider manages the underlying technology. There are three main types of cloud computing: public cloud, private cloud, and hybrid cloud. The following figure depicts the basic design of cloud technology:

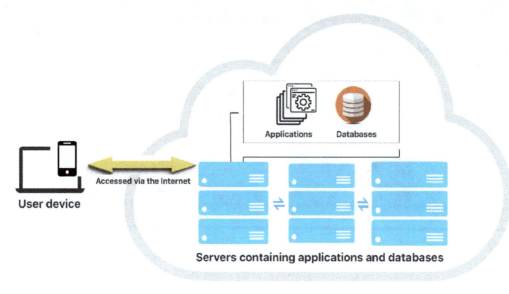

Figure 1.2 – Basic cloud design

The preceding figure depicts how basic cloud components reside within the cloud.

In this section, you learned about the origins and evolution of cloud computing, from time-sharing to the commercialization of services. You gained insights into key milestones, such as the development of virtualization technologies and the rise of utility computing.

Next, you explored the current state of cloud computing, including its models (IaaS, PaaS, and SaaS).

The next section dives into the foundational aspects of cloud architecture and provides you with a comprehensive understanding of its key components and design principles. It explores the fundamental building blocks of cloud architecture, including virtualization, resource pooling, and on-demand self-service.

Understanding cloud architecture

To comprehend the inner workings of cloud computing, it is crucial to understand its underlying architecture. This section provides a comprehensive overview of cloud architecture, elucidating the key components and their interconnections. It explains the concepts of virtualization, distributed computing, and load balancing, which form the building blocks of cloud infrastructure.

Cloud architecture is a term that's used to describe the design and organization of a cloud computing system. A cloud computing system typically consists of various components, including computing resources, storage, network infrastructure, security measures, and software applications. Cloud architecture refers to the way these components are organized and integrated to provide a seamless and efficient cloud computing environment. The following figure depicts a basic cloud architecture design. It covers the end user connection, backend/database, memory cache, middleware, and frontend in Google Cloud:

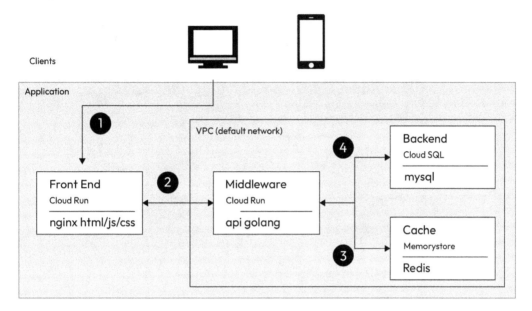

Figure 1.3 – A basic cloud architecture

Cloud architecture involves making critical decisions regarding the cloud deployment model, cloud service model, and cloud providers, among others. These decisions will affect the performance, scalability, security, and cost-effectiveness of the cloud computing system. A well-designed cloud architecture should enable an organization to leverage the benefits of cloud computing, such as cost savings, scalability, and flexibility, while minimizing the potential risks and drawbacks.

Cloud architecture is an essential aspect of any cloud computing project, and it requires a deep understanding of cloud computing technologies, business requirements, and architecture principles. A successful cloud architect must be able to design and implement cloud solutions that meet the specific needs of their organization, whether it is a small business, a large enterprise, or a government agency.

Cloud architecture can also be described as a set of principles, guidelines, and best practices that are used to design and manage cloud computing systems. It involves planning, designing, implementing, and managing cloud-based solutions that meet specific business needs and requirements.

The following figure showcases a visual representation of cloud computing, highlighting the different deployment models and service models:

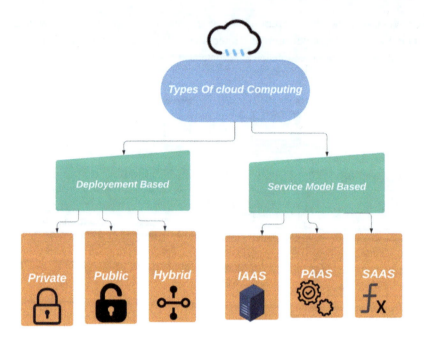

Figure 1.4 – A visual representation of cloud computing

At a high level, cloud architecture involves several key components, including the following:

- **Cloud service models**: Cloud computing provides three distinct service models: IaaS, PaaS, and SaaS. Each model offers users different levels of control, flexibility, and customization. For instance, IaaS examples include **Amazon Web Services (AWS)** EC2 and Microsoft Azure Virtual Machines, which grant users access to virtual servers and infrastructure resources. PaaS examples encompass Google Cloud Platform's App Engine and Heroku, which provide managed platforms for application development and deployment. Lastly, SaaS examples encompass Salesforce, a cloud-based CRM platform, and Google Workspace, a suite of productivity and collaboration tools. These examples demonstrate how IaaS empowers users to provision and oversee virtual infrastructure, PaaS abstracts the underlying platform for application development, and SaaS grants access to fully functional software over the internet. By utilizing these distinct service models, organizations can leverage cloud-based resources and software without the need to manage infrastructure or install software locally.

- **Cloud deployment models**: Cloud computing deployment models encompass public cloud, private cloud, hybrid cloud, and multi-cloud, each presenting unique advantages and challenges. Examples of these deployment models include well-known providers such as AWS, Microsoft Azure, and Google Cloud Platform. In a public cloud, computing resources are shared among multiple organizations and accessible over the internet. Private cloud, on the other hand, involves dedicated cloud infrastructure that can be deployed on-premises or hosted by a single organization, offering greater control and privacy. Hybrid cloud combines both public and private cloud environments, enabling organizations to leverage scalability and flexibility. Multi-cloud refers to utilizing multiple cloud service providers concurrently, allowing for workload distribution, redundancy, cost optimization, and access to specialized services. These deployment models grant varying levels of control, flexibility, and scalability, enabling organizations to tailor their cloud strategies to their specific needs and leverage the full benefits of cloud computing.

- **Cloud components**: Cloud computing involves several components, such as VMs, containers, storage, networking, security, databases, and middleware. A cloud architect must have a clear understanding of each component's capabilities and limitations to design and implement efficient and secure cloud solutions. Cloud computing encompasses various components that contribute to its functionality and infrastructure. Examples of these components include VMs, which allow you to run multiple operating systems on a single physical server, enabling efficient resource utilization. Containers, such as Docker and Kubernetes, offer lightweight, isolated environments for deploying and managing applications across different cloud environments. Storage services, such as Amazon S3 and Google Cloud Storage, provide scalable and reliable storage for data and files. Networking services, such as **Amazon Virtual Private Cloud** (**VPC**) and Azure Virtual Network, enable the creation of virtual networks to connect resources securely. Security services such as encryption, access control, and firewalls help protect data and applications. Cloud databases, such as Amazon RDS and Microsoft Azure SQL Database, provide scalable and managed database solutions. Middleware tools facilitate communication and integration between different software components and services in the cloud. These components collectively form the infrastructure and services that power cloud computing, offering organizations the flexibility, scalability, and convenience of cloud-based solutions.

- **Cloud providers**: Many cloud providers offer various cloud services and tools to build and deploy cloud solutions such as AWS, Microsoft Azure, and **Google Cloud Platform** (**GCP**). A cloud architect must have a deep understanding of these providers and their services to choose the right provider and services for their project. There are several prominent cloud providers in the market, each offering a wide range of services. AWS is a leading cloud provider, offering services such as Amazon EC2 for virtual servers, Amazon S3 for scalable storage, and Amazon RDS for managed databases. Microsoft Azure provides services such as Azure Virtual Machines, Azure Blob Storage, and Azure SQL Database. GCP offers services such as Google Compute Engine, Google Cloud Storage, and Google Cloud Spanner for distributed databases. Other notable cloud providers include IBM Cloud, with services such as IBM Cloud Virtual Servers and IBM Cloud Object Storage, and Oracle Cloud, offering services such as Oracle Compute and Oracle Database Cloud. These cloud providers offer a comprehensive suite of services, including compute, storage, databases, **machine learning** (**ML**), networking, and security, enabling organizations to build, deploy, and scale applications and infrastructure in the cloud. *Figure 1.5* depicts the basic cloud architecture in AWS with key services such as VPC, EC2 (Compute), DynamoDB, and others:

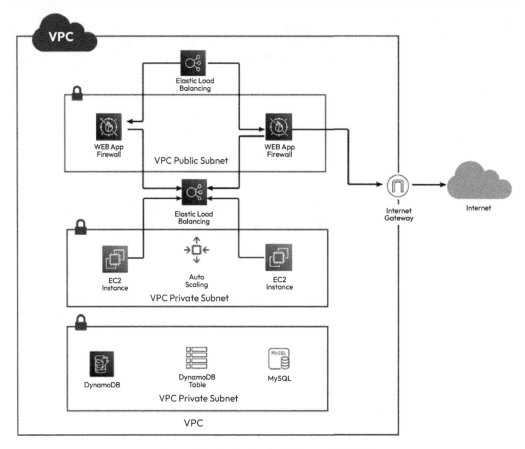

Figure 1.5 – Basic cloud architecture in AWS

- **Cloud security**: Cloud security is a critical component of cloud architecture. A cloud architect must design and implement security measures to protect the cloud infrastructure, data, and applications from unauthorized access, data breaches, and other security threats. Cloud security is a critical aspect of cloud computing, and several providers offer robust security services and solutions. One prominent cloud security provider is Cloudflare, which offers a range of security services such as DDoS protection, **web application firewalls** (**WAFs**), and **content delivery networks** (**CDNs**) to protect against malicious attacks. Another notable provider is Palo Alto Networks, which offers cloud security solutions such as Prisma Cloud, providing visibility, compliance, and threat protection across multi-cloud environments. Microsoft Azure also provides a comprehensive set of security services, including Azure Security Center, Azure Active Directory, and Azure Sentinel, offering identity management, threat detection, and security monitoring capabilities. AWS offers services such as AWS **Identity and Access Management** (**IAM**), AWS WAF, and AWS GuardDuty to help secure cloud environments. These cloud security providers and services play a crucial role in safeguarding data, applications, and infrastructure in the cloud, ensuring confidentiality, integrity, and availability of resources.

Overall, cloud architecture involves designing and managing cloud solutions that are scalable, reliable, secure, and cost-effective. A successful cloud architect must have a strong understanding of cloud technologies, architecture principles, and business needs to design and implement efficient and effective cloud solutions. In the upcoming section, we'll explore the significant advantages and benefits that cloud architecture offers to organizations and individuals. Cloud computing has revolutionized the way we store, access, and process data, providing numerous advantages over traditional on-premises infrastructure.

The benefits of cloud architecture

Cloud architecture provides a wide range of benefits that make it a compelling choice for organizations of all sizes. Firstly, it offers scalability, allowing businesses to easily adjust their resource allocation based on demand, ensuring optimal utilization and cost efficiency. Secondly, cloud architecture promotes cost savings by eliminating the need for upfront investments in hardware and infrastructure, while also reducing maintenance and upgrade expenses. Thirdly, cloud services provide high reliability and availability, minimizing downtime and ensuring seamless operations. Additionally, cloud providers prioritize security measures, protecting data and infrastructure with advanced technologies and stringent protocols. Lastly, cloud architecture enables collaboration and remote access, facilitating seamless teamwork and enhancing productivity. These benefits collectively empower organizations to leverage the advantages of cloud computing and drive their digital transformation initiatives:

- **Scalability**: Cloud architecture provides scalability, allowing organizations to rapidly scale up or down their computing resources to meet changing business needs. This means that they can easily add more computing power, storage capacity, or network bandwidth as their workload increases.

- **Cost-effective**: Cloud architecture allows organizations to reduce their upfront infrastructure costs as they don't have to invest in expensive hardware and software. Instead, they pay for what they use on a subscription or pay-as-you-go basis, allowing them to avoid over-provisioning and reduce their overall IT costs.

- **Flexibility**: Cloud architecture enables organizations to access their data and applications from anywhere, at any time, and on any device, providing greater flexibility and mobility for their employees.

- **Disaster recovery**: Cloud architecture provides built-in disaster recovery and business continuity capabilities, making it easier for organizations to recover their data and systems in the event of a disaster or outage.

- **Security**: Cloud architecture offers advanced security features such as encryption, authentication, and access control, helping organizations to protect their data and applications from cyber threats and unauthorized access.

- **Collaboration**: Cloud architecture provides easy collaboration tools and integration with other cloud-based services, enabling teams to work together more efficiently and productively.

The following figure presents a comprehensive overview of the benefits of cloud computing:

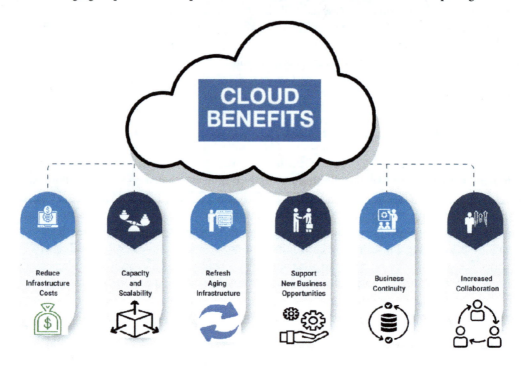

Figure 1.6 – Cloud benefits

The preceding figure depicts the key benefits of cloud computing, highlighting various aspects such as cost reduction, scalability, hardware refresh, new business opportunities, business continuity, and increased collaboration.

Overall, cloud architecture offers numerous benefits that can help organizations improve their productivity, reduce costs, and provide better services to their customers. By leveraging cloud architecture, organizations can focus on their core business objectives and leave the IT infrastructure management to cloud service providers.

Cloud services provide a range of collaboration tools that enable teams to work together more efficiently and productively. Some of the key collaboration features provided by cloud services are as follows:

- **Real-time collaboration**: Cloud services provide real-time collaboration features such as co-authoring, commenting, and chat, allowing teams to work on the same document or project simultaneously and communicate with each other in real time

- **Shared storage**: Cloud services provide shared storage, making it easier for teams to access and share files and documents, regardless of their location or device

- **Version control**: Cloud services offer version control features that allow teams to track changes made to documents and restore previous versions if necessary

- **Integration with other tools**: Cloud services integrate with a wide range of other collaboration tools such as project management tools, instant messaging, and video conferencing, providing a seamless collaboration experience

- **Access control**: Cloud services provide access control features that enable teams to control who has access to their files and documents, ensuring that sensitive data is protected

- **Mobile access**: Cloud services are accessible from anywhere, on any device, making it easy for teams to collaborate even when they are not in the same location

Cloud-based collaboration tools provided by cloud architecture can help organizations improve their productivity, streamline their workflows, and foster better collaboration among their teams. In today's fast-paced business environment, the increasing prevalence of remote work and distributed teams has elevated the significance of cloud-based collaboration. By embracing cloud services, organizations can effectively adapt to these changes and gain a competitive edge.

Integration with other tools in cloud architecture allows cloud services to seamlessly integrate with other collaboration and productivity tools used by an organization. This integration helps create a more efficient and streamlined workflow by allowing users to access all their tools and data from a single location.

Some examples of tools that can be integrated with cloud services include project management software, communication and collaboration tools, CRM systems, and email clients. Here are some benefits of integrating cloud services with other tools:

- **Improved productivity**: Integration with other tools enables users to access all their data and tools in one place, reducing the need to switch between different applications and improving productivity

- **Better collaboration**: Integration with collaboration tools such as instant messaging and video conferencing can improve communication and collaboration among team members.

- **Automation**: Integration with other tools can enable automation of repetitive tasks, such as data entry and reporting, saving time and reducing the risk of errors

- **Data consistency**: Integration with other tools can help ensure data consistency across different systems, reducing the risk of errors and improving data quality

- **Real-time updates**: Integration with other tools can enable real-time updates, ensuring that all team members have access to the latest data and information

Cloud computing systems are designed to seamlessly connect and collaborate with a wide range of existing tools and technologies. This integration enables organizations to leverage their existing infrastructure, applications, and data seamlessly within the cloud environment. By integrating with other tools, cloud architecture allows for smooth data transfer, streamlined workflows, and improved interoperability between different systems. This integration capability enhances productivity, efficiency, and the overall effectiveness of cloud-based solutions by providing a unified and cohesive ecosystem for organizations to leverage their existing tools and resources alongside cloud services. Integration with other tools is an important aspect of cloud architecture because it helps organizations create a more efficient and streamlined workflow, improving productivity, collaboration, and data quality. By integrating cloud services with other tools, organizations can create a more cohesive and effective technology ecosystem that supports their business objectives.

The following section provides a concise overview of the essential guidelines for designing and implementing effective cloud architectures. It emphasizes key practices such as scalability, high availability, performance optimization, security implementation, cost optimization, automation, and monitoring.

Cloud architecture best practices

Cloud architecture best practices are a set of guidelines and principles that organizations should follow to ensure the effective and efficient deployment of their cloud-based applications and services. These practices are designed to enhance the effectiveness, efficiency, scalability, security, and cost optimization of cloud architectures. By following these best practices, organizations can make informed decisions and implement cloud solutions that align with their business objectives. Here are some best practices that organizations should consider:

- **Design for scalability and flexibility**: Cloud architecture should be designed with scalability and flexibility in mind, allowing organizations to quickly and easily adjust their computing resources to meet changing business needs. By architecting cloud solutions with scalability and flexibility in mind, organizations can ensure their applications and services can efficiently handle varying workloads and accommodate future growth. Some examples of best practices for designing scalability and flexibility include utilizing auto-scaling, microservices architecture, containerization, serverless computing, distributed caching, and Elastic storage. We will learn about these in detail later in this book.

- **Emphasize security**: Cloud architecture should be designed with a strong focus on security, including encryption, authentication, and access control measures, to protect sensitive data and applications from cyber threats and unauthorized access. Emphasizing security is a critical component of cloud deployment best practices. Organizations must prioritize the protection of data and infrastructure to maintain user trust and safeguard sensitive information. Key security practices include implementing strong access controls, encrypting data at rest and in transit, regularly applying security patches and updates, implementing network security measures, conducting security audits and assessments, monitoring and logging, implementing data backup and disaster recovery strategies, and conducting employee training and awareness programs. By adhering to these practices, organizations can bolster the security of their cloud deployments, ensuring the confidentiality, integrity, and availability of data while mitigating the risks of unauthorized access and potential security breaches.

- **Leverage automation**: Automation tools should be used to streamline cloud deployment and management processes, reducing manual errors and increasing efficiency. Automation streamlines and simplifies various aspects of cloud management, enabling organizations to achieve greater efficiency, accuracy, and agility. Examples of leveraging automation include utilizing **Infrastructure as Code** (**IaC**) tools such as Terraform or AWS CloudFormation for consistent and automated provisioning of resources, employing **continuous integration and continuous deployment** (**CI/CD**) pipelines to automate application deployment and updates, implementing auto-scaling and load balancing mechanisms to dynamically adjust resource allocation based on demand, and utilizing automated monitoring and alerting systems to proactively detect and respond to performance issues. By harnessing the power of automation, organizations can reduce manual effort, minimize human error, and ensure rapid and consistent cloud deployment and management processes.

- **Use cloud-native services**: Organizations should leverage cloud-native services such as serverless computing, databases, and messaging services to reduce the need for infrastructure management and improve performance. Examples of leveraging cloud-native services include utilizing serverless computing platforms such as AWS Lambda or Google Cloud Functions to execute code without managing servers, adopting managed database services such as Amazon RDS or Azure Cosmos DB for scalable and fully managed databases, utilizing cloud-based message queues or event streaming platforms for reliable and scalable event-driven architectures, and leveraging cloud-based **artificial intelligence** (**AI**) and ML services for advanced data analytics and intelligent decision-making. By leveraging these cloud-native services, organizations can take full advantage of the cloud's capabilities, reduce operational overhead, improve scalability, and accelerate application development and deployment.

- **Optimize costs**: Cloud resources should be optimized to reduce costs, including using reserved instances and implementing auto-scaling policies to reduce waste. Examples of optimizing costs include using cloud resource tagging and monitoring to identify and manage underutilized or idle resources, leveraging reserved instances or savings plans to benefit from discounted pricing for long-term commitments, implementing auto-scaling to dynamically adjust resource allocation based on demand, adopting serverless computing to pay only for actual usage, optimizing storage costs by utilizing tiered storage options or data life cycle management, and leveraging cloud cost management tools and services to analyze usage patterns and identify cost-saving opportunities. By implementing these cost optimization practices, organizations can maximize their return on investment, reduce unnecessary expenditures, and ensure efficient utilization of cloud resources.

- **Implement a multi-layered security approach**: Protect your cloud environment with multiple layers of security, such as firewalls, **intrusion detection and prevention systems** (**IDPSs**), and access controls. Ensure that you regularly monitor and update security measures. Examples of implementing a multi-layered security approach include utilizing network security measures such as firewalls, implementing access controls and IAM policies to manage user permissions, implementing encryption mechanisms to protect data at rest and in transit, deploying IDPSs to detect and prevent malicious activities, conducting regular security assessments and penetration testing to identify vulnerabilities, implementing **security information and event management (SIEM)** solutions to monitor and analyze security events, and implementing data backup and disaster recovery mechanisms to ensure business continuity. By adopting a multi-layered security approach, organizations can significantly enhance the overall security posture of their cloud deployments and effectively mitigate various security risks.

- **Use automation**: Automate as many processes as possible, such as deployment, monitoring, and scaling. This reduces the chance of human error and improves efficiency. Automation enables organizations to streamline and expedite various tasks and processes, improving efficiency and reducing manual effort. Examples of using automation include leveraging IaC tools such as Terraform or Ansible to provision and manage cloud resources, implementing CI/CD pipelines to automate application deployment and updates, utilizing configuration management tools such as Puppet or Chef to ensure consistent system configurations, and employing automated monitoring and alerting systems to proactively detect and respond to performance issues. By leveraging automation, organizations can achieve faster deployment cycles, reduce the risk of human errors, and optimize resource utilization, ultimately enhancing the overall effectiveness and efficiency of their cloud deployments.

- **Plan for disaster recovery**: Disaster recovery and business continuity plans should be developed and tested to ensure that data and systems can be quickly recovered in the event of a disaster or outage. Organizations should have measures in place to ensure business continuity and minimize downtime in the event of unexpected disruptions or disasters. Examples of planning for disaster recovery include regularly backing up data and storing backups in offsite locations, implementing replication and failover mechanisms to ensure redundancy and high availability, conducting periodic disaster recovery drills to test the effectiveness of recovery procedures, utilizing cloud-based disaster recovery services or solutions, and documenting and maintaining comprehensive disaster recovery plans. By proactively planning for disaster recovery, organizations can minimize the impact of potential disruptions, protect critical data and systems, and quickly restore operations, ensuring uninterrupted service delivery and minimizing financial and reputational risks.

- **Use a DevOps approach**: Embrace a DevOps approach to cloud architecture. This means developing and deploying applications collaboratively and iteratively, with a focus on continuous improvement. Examples of using a DevOps approach include implementing CI/CD pipelines to automate the software development and release cycles, using configuration management tools to manage infrastructure as code, adopting containerization technologies such as Docker to ensure consistent deployment environments, employing monitoring and logging tools for real-time visibility into system performance, and promoting a culture of collaboration and communication between development and operations teams. By embracing a DevOps approach, organizations can achieve faster time to market, higher quality software releases, improved scalability, and enhanced overall efficiency in their cloud deployments.

- **Follow compliance regulations**: Cloud architecture should adhere to relevant compliance regulations, including data privacy laws and industry-specific regulations. Organizations must adhere to relevant industry-specific regulations and standards to ensure the security, privacy, and integrity of data and to avoid legal and financial penalties. Examples of following compliance regulations include implementing appropriate access controls and encryption measures to protect sensitive data, conducting regular audits and assessments to ensure compliance with regulations such as GDPR or HIPAA, adopting secure data handling practices and data retention policies, and maintaining clear documentation of compliance efforts. By adhering to compliance regulations, organizations can demonstrate their commitment to data protection and privacy, build trust with customers, and mitigate legal and reputational risks associated with non-compliance.

- **Monitor and analyze performance**: Cloud architecture should be monitored and analyzed regularly to identify performance issues and improve service delivery. Organizations must continuously monitor their cloud infrastructure, applications, and services to ensure optimal performance, identify bottlenecks, and proactively address any issues. Examples of monitoring and analyzing performance include implementing real-time monitoring tools to track resource utilization, response times, and availability, setting up alerts and notifications for abnormal behavior or performance degradation, conducting performance testing to simulate high loads and identify performance bottlenecks, analyzing logs and metrics to gain insights into system behavior, and leveraging analytics tools to identify trends and patterns for capacity planning and optimization. By actively monitoring and analyzing performance, organizations can optimize resource allocation, enhance the user experience, and ensure the efficient operation of their cloud deployments.

These best practices can help organizations effectively and efficiently leverage cloud architecture to improve their agility, scalability, security, and performance while reducing costs and improving customer satisfaction.

In this section, we explored a set of guidelines and principles to ensure effective and efficient cloud deployment. These best practices include designing for scalability and flexibility, emphasizing security, leveraging automation, using cloud-native services, optimizing costs, implementing a multi-layered security approach, planning for disaster recovery, adopting a DevOps approach, following compliance regulations, and monitoring and analyzing performance. By adhering to these best practices, organizations can maximize the benefits of cloud architecture, enhance security, streamline operations, optimize resource utilization, ensure business continuity, and achieve better overall performance and efficiency in their cloud deployments.

The next section delves into the anticipated advancements and emerging trends in the realm of cloud computing. It explores how cloud architecture is evolving to meet the evolving needs of organizations and the challenges of the digital era. This section discusses key areas of development such as edge computing, serverless computing, and hybrid and multi-cloud architecture.

The future of cloud architecture

This section explores the evolving landscape of cloud computing and provides insights into the anticipated developments and trends. It discusses the emergence of advanced technologies such as edge computing, serverless computing, and containers, which offer increased agility and efficiency in deploying applications. This section also delves into the growing importance of hybrid and multi-cloud environments, enabling organizations to leverage the strengths of different cloud platforms. Additionally, it highlights the significance of AI and ML in optimizing cloud operations, enhancing security, and enabling intelligent automation. This section concludes by emphasizing the continued evolution of cloud architecture, driven by technological advancements and the ever-changing needs of businesses, and highlights the importance of staying updated with the latest trends and innovations in the field.

How we see the future of cloud architecture is something the whole world has been curious about. The future of cloud architecture is expected to be shaped by several emerging trends and technologies that are likely to have a significant impact on the way cloud-based systems and applications are designed, deployed, and managed.

Here are some of the key trends and technologies that are likely to shape the future of cloud architecture:

- **Multi-cloud and hybrid cloud**: As more organizations adopt cloud computing, they are likely to seek out solutions that combine the benefits of multiple cloud providers, such as public and private clouds, to create hybrid cloud environments that offer greater flexibility, scalability, and cost-effectiveness.

- **Edge computing**: As the amount of data generated by connected devices continues to grow, there is increasing demand for edge computing solutions that can process and analyze data closer to the source, reducing latency and improving performance.

- **Serverless computing**: Serverless computing provides a solution for deploying and operating applications without the burden of managing the underlying infrastructure, streamlining the development and deployment of cloud-based applications in a swift and cost-efficient manner.

- **AI and ML**: The role of AI and ML in cloud computing is set to become increasingly significant. Organizations are actively leveraging these technologies to unlock valuable insights from vast amounts of data and automate intricate tasks. The integration of AI and ML in cloud computing allows businesses to harness the power of advanced analytics and pattern recognition to make data-driven decisions, optimize processes, and enhance operational efficiency. By utilizing AI and ML algorithms within the cloud, organizations can process and analyze large datasets at scale, identify patterns, detect anomalies, and drive predictive capabilities. This convergence of AI, ML, and cloud computing empowers organizations to unlock new opportunities, gain a competitive edge, and drive innovation across various industries and sectors.

- **Containerization and microservices**: Containerization and microservices architectures are gaining popularity as a way to create highly scalable and flexible cloud-based applications that can be easily deployed and managed.
- **Quantum computing**: Although still in its early stages, quantum computing has the potential to revolutionize cloud computing by providing vastly improved processing power and enabling new applications and services.

The future of cloud architecture is likely to be shaped by these and other emerging trends and technologies as organizations seek to leverage the power of cloud computing to innovate, grow, and compete in an increasingly digital and interconnected world.

This seems like a mouthful, but we shall be discussing all these in detail throughout this book.

Summary

Overall, this chapter provided a comprehensive overview of cloud architecture and the key components that are essential for building a successful cloud environment. It emphasized the importance of choosing the right components and designing for scalability and adaptability and provides practical advice on how to achieve these goals. As businesses increasingly rely on cloud technology, understanding cloud architecture is essential for staying competitive and delivering value to customers.

In this chapter, we explored the fascinating journey of cloud computing, covering its history, present state, and future prospects. We began by delving into the origins of cloud computing, tracing its development and evolution over time. Then, we examined the current landscape of cloud computing, highlighting its widespread adoption and the myriad benefits it brings to organizations of all sizes. We explored the fundamental concepts and principles of cloud architecture, providing a deeper understanding of its key components and design considerations. Lastly, we peered into the future of cloud architecture, discussing emerging trends and technologies that are poised to shape the future of cloud computing. By delving into the historical context, current applications, and future direction of cloud computing, this chapter has equipped you with valuable insights to navigate the ever-evolving world of cloud architecture. After reading this chapter, you will have acquired several new skills and pieces of knowledge related to cloud computing. You should now have a historical understanding of the development and evolution of cloud computing, enabling you to appreciate the context and foundations of the technology. You have gained insights into the current state of cloud computing, including its widespread adoption and the benefits it offers to organizations. You also have a solid understanding of cloud architecture, including its components, design principles, and best practices. This means you are now well-equipped with knowledge about the future of cloud architecture, including emerging trends and technologies that are likely to shape the cloud landscape. Overall, you have developed a comprehensive understanding of cloud computing, allowing you to make informed decisions, architect effective cloud solutions, and stay updated with the evolving nature of cloud technology.

In the upcoming chapter, you will explore the key elements that make up a robust and reliable cloud environment. We will delve into the essential components necessary for building and maintaining a successful cloud infrastructure. You can expect to learn about physical data centers and their importance in providing a foundation for cloud services. You will also gain insights into virtualization and hypervisors, which enable efficient resource allocation and management in a virtualized environment. You will gain a comprehensive understanding of the components necessary for a robust and scalable cloud infrastructure, enabling you to design, deploy, and manage your cloud environments effectively.

2

Components of a Cloud Infrastructure

In this chapter, we will delve into the various essential elements that make up a cloud infrastructure, providing you with a comprehensive understanding of its key components. This chapter begins by exploring the foundation of a cloud infrastructure, which includes physical data centers, networking, and storage systems. It discusses the importance of server virtualization and hypervisors in enabling the efficient utilization of computing resources. This chapter then delves into the concept of virtual networks and their role in facilitating communication between different components of the cloud infrastructure. It also explores storage technologies such as block, file, and object storage, highlighting their unique characteristics and use cases. Additionally, this chapter discusses the importance of load balancers, firewalls, and security mechanisms in ensuring the integrity and protection of the cloud infrastructure. By providing an overview of these crucial components, this chapter will equip you with the knowledge of how to to design, deploy, and manage a robust and scalable cloud infrastructure.

Overall, this chapter will provide you with a comprehensive understanding of the components that constitute a cloud infrastructure. By grasping the intricacies of these elements, you will gain the knowledge required to design, deploy, and manage a robust and scalable cloud infrastructure that meets the needs of modern businesses.

In this chapter, we will cover the following topics:

- Essential cloud infrastructure components
- Overview of virtualization and containerization

By reading this chapter, you will gain in-depth knowledge of the foundational components, their characteristics, and their significance in enabling cloud-based services. Throughout this chapter, you will explore various topics, including compute resources, storage options, network architecture, and virtualization. By understanding these components, you will be equipped with the necessary knowledge to design, deploy, and manage cloud environments effectively.

Technical requirements

To fully engage with the content in this chapter on cloud computing architecture, you should have a basic understanding of computer systems, networking concepts, and information technology.

Additionally, the following are required:

- **Internet access**: You should have a reliable internet connection to access online resources, references, and examples related to cloud computing.

- **A computing device**: A desktop computer, laptop, tablet, or smartphone with a modern web browser is necessary to read this chapter's content and access any online materials.

- **A web browser**: The latest version of a modern web browser such as Google Chrome, Mozilla Firefox, Microsoft Edge, or Safari is recommended. This ensures compatibility and an optimal viewing experience for web-based resources and interactive content.

- **Familiarity with cloud services**: Some familiarity with cloud services and their basic functionalities will enhance your understanding of this chapter. This includes knowledge of cloud computing models such as IaaS, PaaS, and SaaS, as well as virtualization.

Essential cloud infrastructure components

In this section, we will learn about the key elements that form the foundation of cloud infrastructure. We will cover physical data centers, server virtualization and hypervisors, networking components, storage systems (including block, file, and object storage), and security mechanisms. This section explores the significance of each component, highlighting their roles in supporting cloud services and applications. By understanding these essential components, you will gain insights into the design, deployment, and management of a scalable and secure cloud infrastructure that meets the needs of modern businesses.

Understanding the essential components of cloud infrastructure is crucial for architects, IT professionals, and decision-makers involved in designing, implementing, and managing cloud environments.

Cloud infrastructure encompasses several essential components that work together to support the delivery of cloud services. These components include physical data centers, virtualization and hypervisors for efficient resource utilization, networking elements such as switches and routers to establish connectivity, various storage options such as block storage and object storage, robust security measures to protect data and systems, management and orchestration tools for streamlined operations, monitoring and analytics solutions for performance tracking, disaster recovery mechanisms for business continuity, compliance and governance frameworks to ensure adherence to regulations, and scalable compute resources. Together, these components form the foundation of a cloud infrastructure, enabling organizations to leverage the benefits of scalability, flexibility, and cost-efficiency offered by cloud computing. In the basic architecture of cloud infrastructure, the essential components are interconnected and interdependent, forming a cohesive system. Compute resources, such as

virtual machines (**VMs**) or containers, rely on storage systems to access and store data. Networking components facilitate communication and connectivity between compute resources and storage systems, enabling the transfer of data. Virtualization technologies provide the foundation for creating and managing compute resources, ensuring the efficient utilization of physical resources. Management and orchestration tools oversee the provisioning, monitoring, and management of compute resources, storage systems, and networking components. Each component relies on the others to function effectively, creating a seamless environment for delivering scalable and flexible computing and storage resources. The interdependencies between these components ensure the smooth operation of the cloud infrastructure, enabling organizations to leverage the benefits of cloud computing. The following figure shows a typical AWS web app reference architecture and depicts some of the key components in the AWS cloud, which include S3 storage buckets, EC2 for compute, load balancing, and Availability Zones, and how they work in tandem with each other:

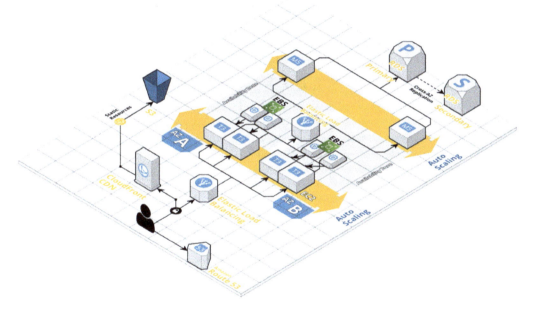

Figure 2.1 – AWS web app reference architecture

The web architectural diagram in an AWS environment depicts the dependencies and interactions among various cloud components. These components include load balancers, compute instances, databases, storage services, and networking components. This diagram illustrates how these components work together to deliver a scalable and secure web application or service, with features such as auto-scaling, content delivery networks, and centralized access management. It provides a visual representation of the relationships and dependencies within the cloud infrastructure. In the upcoming section, we will cover the key components of cloud infrastructure, including physical data centers, virtualization and hypervisors, networking, storage, security, management and orchestration, monitoring, backup and recovery, and compliance. We will explore the role and characteristics of each component and discuss their interdependencies in creating a robust cloud environment. By understanding these components, you will gain insights into designing and managing an efficient and secure cloud infrastructure that meets your organization's needs.

We'll look at these key components in detail in the following sections.

Physical data centers

Data centers form the foundation of cloud infrastructure as they house the necessary hardware, including servers, storage systems, and networking equipment. They provide the physical space, power, and cooling required to support the operation of cloud services.

Physical data centers serve as the foundation of cloud infrastructure, playing a crucial role in hosting and managing the hardware components required for cloud services. These data centers are purpose-built facilities designed to house servers, storage systems, networking equipment, and other critical infrastructure. They provide the physical space, power supply, cooling systems, and security measures necessary to ensure the reliable operation of cloud services.

One of the primary functions of physical data centers is to house the servers that host VMs and other computing resources. These servers are responsible for processing and executing the applications and services that run in the cloud. Data centers typically contain racks of servers, each with multiple processing units and large amounts of memory and storage capacity. The servers are interconnected to form a robust and scalable computing environment.

Data centers are also designed to provide high-speed and reliable connectivity. They incorporate networking infrastructure, including switches, routers, and fiber optic cables, to facilitate the communication and data transfer between servers and other components. Network redundancy is often implemented to ensure uninterrupted connectivity and prevent single points of failure.

Thus, physical data centers are the backbone of cloud infrastructure, providing the necessary physical space, power, cooling, security, and networking infrastructure to host and manage the hardware components that support cloud services. They serve as the central hub for processing, storing, and delivering data, enabling organizations to leverage the benefits of cloud computing. The design, maintenance, and management of physical data centers are critical to ensuring the availability, scalability, and reliability of cloud services.

Virtualization and hypervisors

Virtualization allows multiple VMs to run on a single physical server, enabling efficient resource utilization. Hypervisors, such as VMware ESXi and KVM, manage the creation, allocation, and management of these VMs.

Virtualization and hypervisors are essential components of cloud infrastructure that enable the efficient allocation and management of computing resources. Virtualization technology allows multiple VMs to run on a single physical server, effectively maximizing the utilization of hardware resources and providing flexibility and scalability in cloud environments. At the core of virtualization is the hypervisor, also known as the **virtual machine monitor (VMM)**. The hypervisor is responsible for creating and managing the virtualization layer, which abstracts the underlying physical hardware and allows for the creation and operation of multiple VMs. It acts as a bridge between the physical infrastructure and the virtualized environment, providing a layer of isolation and resource allocation.

There are two types of hypervisors – Type 1 and Type 2:

- **Type 1 hypervisors**, also known as bare-metal hypervisors, run directly on the host hardware without the need for an underlying operating system. They provide direct access to the hardware resources, offering high performance and efficiency. Examples of Type 1 hypervisors are VMware ESXi, Microsoft Hyper-V, and KVM.

- **Type 2 hypervisors**, on the other hand, run on top of an existing operating system. They are typically used for desktop virtualization or testing and development environments. Type 2 hypervisors introduce an additional layer of software between the VMs and the hardware, resulting in slightly lower performance compared to Type 1 hypervisors. Examples of Type 2 hypervisors are Oracle VirtualBox and VMware Workstation.

Virtualization allows for the creation of VMs that emulate the behavior of physical servers. Each VM operates as an independent entity with its own operating system, applications, and resources. The hypervisor manages the allocation of CPU, memory, storage, and network resources to each VM, ensuring fair and efficient utilization.

The benefits of virtualization in cloud infrastructure are numerous. First and foremost, it enables server consolidation, allowing multiple VMs to run on a single physical server. This leads to improved hardware utilization, reduced costs, and energy savings. Virtualization also offers flexibility and agility by allowing the easy creation, duplication, and movement of VMs across different physical servers. This flexibility enables workload balancing, resource optimization, and efficient scaling of resources based on demand.

Moreover, virtualization enhances the availability and reliability of cloud services. In the event of hardware failure or maintenance, VMs can be migrated or restarted on alternate hardware without impacting the overall service. This feature, known as live migration, ensures high availability and minimizes downtime.

Security is another aspect that virtualization addresses. By isolating VMs from each other and the underlying physical infrastructure, potential security risks are contained within each VM. This isolation enhances security and reduces the risk of unauthorized access or data breaches.

Virtualization and hypervisors are fundamental components of cloud infrastructure that enable efficient resource utilization, flexibility, scalability, and reliability. By abstracting the underlying physical hardware, virtualization technology provides the foundation for creating and managing multiple VMs in a cloud environment. This technology has revolutionized the way computing resources are provisioned and managed, enabling organizations to leverage the benefits of cloud computing and optimize their IT infrastructure.

Networking

Networking components include switches, routers, load balancers, and firewalls. They establish and maintain connections between different cloud components, enabling communication and data transfer. **Software-defined networking** (**SDN**) technologies provide programmable and flexible networking capabilities to adapt to changing requirements. Networking is a critical component of cloud infrastructure that enables communication and connectivity between various components, services, and users within a cloud environment. It plays a crucial role in ensuring the performance, reliability, and security of cloud-based applications and services.

In a cloud infrastructure, networking encompasses a wide range of technologies and protocols that facilitate the transfer of data between different entities. These entities include physical servers, VMs, storage systems, load balancers, firewalls, routers, switches, and client devices. At the heart of cloud networking is the network infrastructure, which consists of physical networking devices such as routers, switches, and cables. These devices form the backbone of the cloud environment, providing the necessary connectivity and routing capabilities for data transmission. To ensure efficient and secure communication within the cloud infrastructure, networking protocols are used. Protocols such as **Transmission Control Protocol/Internet Protocol** (**TCP/IP**) and **User Datagram Protocol** (**UDP**) facilitate the exchange of data packets between different devices and enable reliable and efficient data transfer. In addition to the underlying network infrastructure and protocols, cloud networking also involves various networking services and technologies:

- **Virtual private networks** (**VPNs**): VPNs establish secure and encrypted connections over public networks, enabling users to access cloud resources securely from remote locations. VPNs provide a secure tunnel for data transmission, protecting sensitive information from unauthorized access.

- **Load balancing**: Load balancing distributes incoming network traffic across multiple servers to ensure optimal resource utilization and performance. It helps distribute workloads evenly and prevents any single server from being overloaded, thereby improving application availability and responsiveness.

- **Firewalls**: Firewalls act as a security barrier between the internal network and the external network, filtering incoming and outgoing traffic based on predefined security rules. They play a crucial role in protecting cloud resources from unauthorized access, malware, and other security threats.

- **Virtual LANs (VLANs)**: VLANs enable the segmentation of a physical network into multiple virtual networks, providing enhanced security, flexibility, and isolation. VLANs help to logically separate different departments, applications, or user groups within the cloud infrastructure, improving network performance and security.

- **SDN**: SDN is a network architecture that separates the network control plane from the data plane. It allows for centralized network management and control, enabling dynamic configuration and orchestration of network resources. SDN simplifies network management, enhances scalability, and facilitates the implementation of network policies.

We will learn about these network components in detail in the chapters to follow.

Networking in cloud infrastructure is crucial for ensuring the high availability, scalability, and performance of cloud-based services. It enables seamless communication between different components, facilitates data transfer, and supports the delivery of applications and services to end users. By implementing robust networking solutions and best practices, organizations can optimize their cloud infrastructure and provide a reliable and secure environment for their cloud-based operations. Networking is an essential component of cloud infrastructure, providing the necessary connectivity, communication, and security for cloud-based applications and services. It encompasses a range of technologies, protocols, and services that enable efficient data transfer, load balancing, security enforcement, and network management. By leveraging networking technologies and best practices, organizations can ensure the optimal performance, reliability, and security of their cloud infrastructure, enabling them to deliver seamless and scalable cloud services to their users. Establishing a reliable and secure networking setup is essential for connecting the cloud environment to the on-premises infrastructure. This involves using technologies such as VPNs or Direct Connect to ensure encrypted and private communication between the two environments. Setting up a **virtual private cloud** (**VPC**) allows organizations to create a logical network within the cloud, mimicking the on-premises network structure. Proper IP addressing, routing, and network security measures are crucial for connectivity and protection. Implementing hybrid DNS enables consistent name resolution. The following figure depicts the basic networking between an on-premises environment and the cloud:

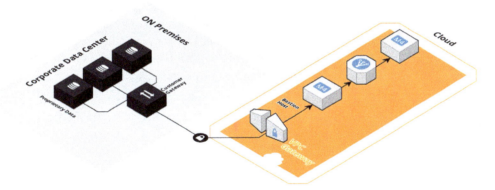

Figure 2.2 – Basic on-premises and cloud network connectivity

Storage

Cloud storage encompasses different types, such as block storage, file storage, and object storage. Block storage provides raw storage blocks, similar to traditional hard drives. File storage offers a hierarchical filesystem, while object storage provides scalable and durable storage for unstructured data. **Storage area networks** (**SANs**) and **network-attached storage** (**NAS**) are commonly used in cloud environments. Storage is a fundamental component of cloud infrastructure that plays a crucial role in storing and managing vast amounts of data for cloud-based applications and services. It encompasses various technologies and systems that enable reliable, scalable, and accessible storage solutions within the cloud environment.

In cloud infrastructure, storage serves as a repository for different types of data, including application files, databases, user files, and system backups. It provides the necessary capacity and performance for data storage, retrieval, and management.

There are different types of storage options available in cloud infrastructure, each suited for specific use cases and requirements:

- **Object storage**: Object storage is a scalable and highly available storage system that stores data as objects. Objects are typically accessed via a unique identifier, such as a URL or an API call. This storage model is ideal for storing unstructured data, such as images, videos, documents, and log files. Object storage systems provide durability, scalability, and easy accessibility, making them well suited for cloud-based applications that require massive storage capacity and high levels of data availability.

- **Block storage**: Block storage provides storage volumes that can be mounted to VMs or physical servers. It offers a traditional block-level storage interface, allowing for random read and write operations. Block storage is commonly used for databases, filesystems, and applications that require low-latency and high-performance storage. It offers features such as snapshots and replication for data protection and redundancy.

- **File storage**: File storage provides a shared filesystem accessible by multiple users or systems. It allows for the hierarchical organization of data into directories and files, similar to a traditional filesystem. File storage is suitable for applications that require shared access to data, such as content management systems, file-sharing platforms, and collaborative tools.

- **Archive storage**: Archive storage is designed for long-term data retention at a lower cost. It is used for storing infrequently accessed data that needs to be retained for compliance or regulatory purposes. Archive storage offers high durability and low-cost storage options for data that is rarely accessed but needs to be preserved.

We will learn about these components in detail in the chapters to follow.

Cloud storage systems incorporate various technologies and features to ensure data reliability, availability, and durability:

- **Redundancy and replication**: Data is often replicated across multiple storage devices or data centers to provide redundancy and ensure high availability. Replication helps to protect against hardware failures and ensures data accessibility in case of failures or disasters.

- **Data encryption**: Cloud storage systems often provide encryption mechanisms to secure data at rest and during transit. Encryption safeguards sensitive data from unauthorized access and ensures data confidentiality and integrity.

- **Data backup and recovery**: Cloud storage services usually offer backup and recovery capabilities, allowing organizations to create backups of their data and restore it in case of accidental deletion, data corruption, or system failures.

- **Scalability**: Cloud storage solutions are designed to scale dynamically to accommodate growing data storage requirements. They can scale up or down based on demand, allowing organizations to efficiently manage their storage needs without upfront investment in hardware.

- **Data life cycle management**: Cloud storage systems provide features for managing the life cycle of data, including automated data tiering, data retention policies, and data expiration. These features help optimize storage costs and ensure compliance with data retention regulations.

We will learn about these components in detail in the chapters to follow.

Effective storage management is crucial for efficient data storage and retrieval in cloud environments. By leveraging the appropriate storage options and implementing best practices, organizations can ensure the scalability, availability, and durability of their data in the cloud.

Storage is a vital component of cloud infrastructure, providing the necessary capacity and performance for storing and managing data in cloud-based applications and services. It encompasses different storage options, including object storage, block storage, file storage, and archive storage, each suited for specific use cases and requirements. Cloud storage systems incorporate features such as redundancy, encryption, backup and recovery, scalability, and data life cycle management. The following figure depicts the two most common storage options in the AWS cloud – EBS and S3 buckets. Note how the S3 bucket is being accessed from a public instance while EBS is being accessed locally:

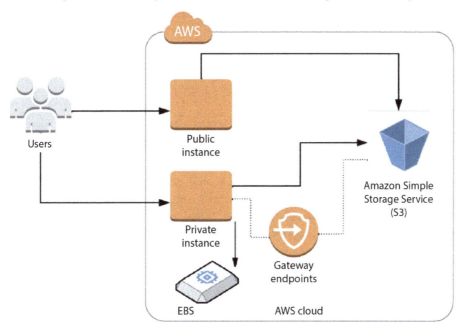

Figure 2.3 – AWS cloud storage – EBS and S3 buckets

Security

Security components ensure the protection and integrity of cloud infrastructure and data. This includes encryption mechanisms, firewalls, access control, authentication, and intrusion detection systems. Security measures are crucial to safeguard against unauthorized access, data breaches, and other security threats. Security is of paramount importance in cloud infrastructure as it involves safeguarding data, applications, and resources from unauthorized access, breaches, and vulnerabilities. Cloud providers and organizations must implement robust security measures to protect sensitive information, maintain data integrity, and ensure the confidentiality and availability of resources.

In cloud infrastructure, security encompasses various aspects, including the following:

- **Authentication and access control**: Authentication mechanisms are used to verify the identity of users and ensure that only authorized individuals can access the cloud resources. Access control mechanisms define and enforce the permissions and privileges granted to users, ensuring that they can access only the necessary resources based on their roles and responsibilities. Strong authentication methods, such as multi-factor authentication, enhance the security of cloud environments.

- **Data encryption**: Data encryption is essential for protecting sensitive information stored in the cloud. It involves transforming data into an unreadable format using cryptographic algorithms. Encryption ensures that even if unauthorized individuals gain access to the data, they cannot decipher it without the encryption keys. Encryption is applied to data both in transit and at rest, providing end-to-end security.

- **Network security**: Network security focuses on securing the communication channels and network infrastructure within the cloud environment. It involves implementing firewalls, intrusion detection and prevention systems, and VPNs to protect against unauthorized access, network attacks, and data interception. Network segmentation and isolation techniques are employed to isolate different components and protect critical resources.

- **Vulnerability management**: Vulnerability management includes identifying and mitigating security vulnerabilities in the cloud infrastructure. Regular vulnerability assessments and penetration testing help identify weaknesses and potential entry points for attackers. Patch management ensures that software and systems are kept up to date with the latest security patches to address known vulnerabilities.

- **Security monitoring and logging**: Cloud environments require continuous monitoring to detect and respond to security incidents promptly. Security monitoring involves analyzing network traffic, system logs, and events to identify suspicious activities and potential security breaches. Logging and audit trails record and store relevant security events, enabling forensic analysis and compliance auditing.

- **Incident response and disaster recovery**: Incident response plans outline the steps to be taken in the event of a security incident or breach. This includes containment, eradication, and recovery procedures to minimize the impact and restore normal operations. Disaster recovery plans ensure that critical data and systems can be restored in case of data loss or system failures, providing business continuity.

- **Compliance and regulatory requirements**: Cloud infrastructure must comply with industry-specific regulations and data protection laws. Organizations need to ensure that their cloud environment meets the necessary compliance requirements, such as HIPAA, GDPR, or PCI DSS. This includes implementing appropriate security controls, data privacy measures, and audit mechanisms to demonstrate compliance.

We will learn about these components in detail in the chapters to follow.

Cloud providers often offer a shared responsibility model, where they are responsible for securing the underlying infrastructure, while customers are responsible for securing their applications, data, and user access. Organizations should carefully evaluate the security capabilities and certifications of cloud providers to ensure they meet their specific security requirements.

Security is a critical component of cloud infrastructure that requires robust measures to protect data, applications, and resources from unauthorized access, breaches, and vulnerabilities. Authentication and access control, data encryption, network security, vulnerability management, security monitoring, incident response, and compliance are key aspects of cloud security. By implementing comprehensive security measures and following best practices, organizations can mitigate security risks and ensure the confidentiality, integrity, and availability of their cloud-based resources.

Management and orchestration

Cloud management platforms enable centralized management and control of the cloud infrastructure. These platforms facilitate tasks such as provisioning and monitoring resources, managing user access, and implementing automation and orchestration for efficient resource allocation and deployment. Management and orchestration are crucial components of cloud infrastructure that enable efficient administration, monitoring, and control of cloud resources and services. They provide the tools and frameworks necessary for organizations to effectively manage their cloud environments, streamline operations, and optimize resource utilization.

Some of the key aspects of management and orchestration are as follows:

- **Provisioning and resource allocation**: Management and orchestration systems facilitate the provisioning of resources in the cloud. They automate the process of allocating VMs, storage, and networking resources, ensuring that applications have the necessary resources to operate efficiently. Through resource allocation policies and intelligent algorithms, these systems optimize resource utilization and minimize waste.

- **Monitoring and performance management**: Cloud management platforms enable the real-time monitoring and performance management of cloud resources. They collect and analyze data on resource usage, application performance, and system health. Monitoring tools provide insights into resource utilization, network traffic, and application performance, helping organizations identify bottlenecks, optimize resource allocation, and ensure **service-level agreements (SLAs)** are met.

- **Automation and orchestration**: Management systems automate routine operational tasks and workflows, reducing manual effort and improving efficiency. They enable the automation of resource provisioning, scaling, and deployment processes, allowing organizations to quickly respond to changing demands. Orchestration frameworks provide the means to define and manage complex workflows, coordinating the deployment and configuration of multi-tier applications and services.

- **Configuration and change management**: Cloud management platforms facilitate centralized configuration and change management. They enable administrators to define and enforce configuration standards, deploy software updates, and track changes across the cloud infrastructure. Configuration management tools help ensure consistency, security, and compliance by managing configurations and enforcing policies across a large number of cloud resources.

- **Service catalogs and self-service portals**: Cloud management systems often provide service catalogs and self-service portals, allowing users to request and provision resources on demand. These catalogs contain predefined service offerings, such as VMs, storage volumes, or database instances, with standardized configurations and pricing. Self-service portals empower users to provision resources without IT intervention, reducing administrative overhead and improving agility.

- **Cost management and billing**: Management systems include cost management and billing features to track and allocate cloud costs. They provide visibility into resource usage and associated costs, enabling organizations to optimize spending, allocate costs to specific projects or departments, and enforce budgetary controls. Cost management tools offer insights into usage patterns, identify cost-saving opportunities, and facilitate chargeback or showback models.

- **Governance and compliance**: Management and orchestration systems support governance and compliance requirements in the cloud. They enforce policies for access control, security, data protection, and regulatory compliance. These systems provide audit trails, log management, and reporting capabilities to demonstrate compliance with industry regulations and internal policies.

We will learn about these components in detail in the chapters to follow.

Effective management and orchestration of cloud infrastructure is vital for organizations to achieve operational efficiency, optimize resource utilization, and ensure a seamless user experience. By leveraging provisioning, monitoring, automation, configuration management, self-service portals, cost management, and governance capabilities, organizations can effectively manage their cloud resources and services, enabling them to focus on delivering value and innovation to their customers.

Monitoring and analytics

Monitoring tools track the performance, availability, and health of the cloud infrastructure and applications. They provide real-time insights, enabling the proactive identification and resolution of issues. Analytics tools leverage collected data to optimize resource usage, detect trends, and make data-driven decisions. Monitoring and analytics are critical components of cloud infrastructure that enable organizations to gain insights, ensure optimal performance, and make informed decisions regarding their cloud resources and services. These components provide comprehensive visibility into the health, availability, and performance of the cloud environment, enabling organizations to proactively monitor and manage their infrastructure.

Some of the key aspects of monitoring and analytics are as follows:

- **Real-time monitoring**: Monitoring tools collect and analyze data in real time, providing organizations with continuous visibility into the performance and availability of their cloud resources. They monitor key metrics such as CPU utilization, memory usage, network traffic, and storage performance. Real-time monitoring enables organizations to detect and respond to issues promptly, ensuring high availability and minimizing service disruptions.

- **Alerting and incident management**: Monitoring systems generate alerts and notifications when predefined thresholds or anomalies are detected. These alerts can be configured to trigger notifications to administrators or operations teams, allowing them to take immediate action and resolve issues proactively. Incident management processes are put in place to ensure that alerts are properly handled, documented, and escalated if necessary, reducing downtime and minimizing the impact on users.

- **Performance optimization**: Monitoring tools provide insights into resource utilization and performance bottlenecks, enabling organizations to optimize their cloud infrastructure. By analyzing performance data, organizations can identify areas for improvement, such as scaling resources, optimizing configurations, or adjusting workload distribution. Performance optimization helps ensure that applications and services run efficiently, delivering a high-quality user experience.

- **Capacity planning**: Monitoring and analytics enable organizations to plan for future resource requirements effectively. By analyzing historical usage data and trends, organizations can forecast capacity needs, anticipate demand fluctuations, and scale resources accordingly. Capacity planning helps organizations optimize resource allocation, avoid overprovisioning or underprovisioning, and control costs.

- **Cost optimization**: Monitoring and analytics play a crucial role in optimizing cloud costs. These tools provide insights into resource utilization, cost breakdowns, and trends, helping organizations identify cost-saving opportunities. By analyzing usage patterns and optimizing resource allocation, organizations can ensure that resources are efficiently utilized, resulting in cost savings and improved **return on investment (ROI)**.

- **Security monitoring**: Monitoring systems also play a vital role in ensuring the security of cloud infrastructure. They provide visibility into security events, anomalies, and potential threats. Security monitoring tools analyze logs, network traffic, and user behavior to detect and respond to security incidents promptly. These tools enhance the organization's ability to identify and mitigate security risks, safeguarding sensitive data and protecting against unauthorized access.

- **Analytics and reporting**: Monitoring and analytics tools provide advanced analytics capabilities, enabling organizations to derive valuable insights from their monitoring data. These tools use machine learning and data analytics techniques to identify patterns, correlations, and anomalies in performance data. Organizations can leverage these insights to make data-driven decisions, optimize resource utilization, and improve overall system performance. Reporting features provide customized dashboards and reports, enabling stakeholders to access relevant information and track **key performance indicators (KPIs)**.

We will learn about these components in detail in the chapters to follow.

Monitoring and analytics are essential components of cloud infrastructure, enabling organizations to ensure high availability, optimize performance, control costs, enhance security, and make informed decisions. By leveraging real-time monitoring, alerting, performance optimization, capacity planning, cost optimization, security monitoring, and analytics capabilities, organizations can effectively manage their cloud resources, improve operational efficiency, and deliver a seamless and reliable user experience.

Disaster recovery and backup

Disaster recovery mechanisms ensure business continuity by replicating data and applications to alternate locations. Backup strategies involve regularly creating copies of data to protect against data loss or corruption. Disaster recovery and backup are crucial components of cloud infrastructure that help organizations protect their data and ensure business continuity in the event of unexpected incidents or disasters. These components provide mechanisms for data replication, backup, and recovery to minimize the impact of downtime and data loss.

Some of the key aspects of disaster recovery and backup are as follows:

- **Data replication**: Cloud infrastructure offers the capability to replicate data across multiple geographic locations or data centers. This ensures that data is redundantly stored, reducing the risk of data loss in the event of a localized failure or disaster. By replicating data in real time or near real time, organizations can maintain consistent copies of their data that can be quickly accessed and restored.

- **Backup and restore**: Cloud infrastructure provides built-in backup and restore mechanisms that allow organizations to create copies of their data and applications at specific points in time. These backups can be stored in the same cloud environment or separate off-site locations for added redundancy. In the event of data corruption, accidental deletion, or system failures, organizations can restore their data from these backups, minimizing the impact on operations and ensuring data integrity.

- **Disaster recovery planning**: Cloud infrastructure enables organizations to develop comprehensive disaster recovery plans to mitigate the impact of potential disasters or disruptions. These plans outline the steps, processes, and resources required to recover critical systems and data. By leveraging cloud services, organizations can replicate their entire infrastructure, including VMs, applications, and data, to a separate geographic region or data center. This ensures that the organization can quickly recover and resume operations in the event of a disaster.

- **Failover and high availability**: Cloud infrastructure provides failover capabilities that automatically redirect traffic and workloads to alternative resources in the event of a failure or disruption. By leveraging load-balancing and failover mechanisms, organizations can ensure continuous availability of their applications and services. This reduces downtime and minimizes the impact on users, ensuring seamless access to critical systems.

- **Testing and validation**: Disaster recovery and backup components allow organizations to regularly test and validate their recovery processes. By conducting periodic disaster recovery drills, organizations can ensure that their backup and recovery mechanisms are functioning as expected. Testing also helps identify any gaps or vulnerabilities in the recovery process, allowing organizations to refine their disaster recovery strategies.

- **Data protection and compliance**: Disaster recovery and backup mechanisms play a crucial role in data protection and compliance. By regularly backing up data and ensuring its availability, organizations can meet regulatory requirements and maintain the integrity of sensitive information. Cloud infrastructure offers features such as encryption, access controls, and audit trails to enhance data protection and compliance with industry standards.

- **Cost-efficiency**: Cloud-based disaster recovery and backup solutions offer cost efficiencies compared to traditional on-premises solutions. Organizations can leverage the scalability and pay-as-you-go model of cloud services, enabling them to optimize costs based on their specific needs. Additionally, cloud providers often offer built-in backup and recovery capabilities as part of their service offerings, eliminating the need for separate infrastructure and reducing maintenance costs.

- **Rapid recovery**: Cloud infrastructure enables organizations to recover from disasters or disruptions more quickly compared to traditional on-premises solutions. By leveraging the scalable and elastic nature of the cloud, organizations can rapidly provision resources, restore data, and resume operations. This helps minimize downtime, reduce the impact on business operations, and maintain customer satisfaction.

Disaster recovery and backup are vital components of cloud infrastructure that help organizations safeguard their data, ensure business continuity, and mitigate the impact of unforeseen events. By leveraging data replication, backup mechanisms, failover capabilities, and comprehensive disaster recovery planning, organizations can protect their critical systems and data, maintain high availability, and recover rapidly in the face of disruptions. Cloud-based disaster recovery and backup solutions offer scalability, cost efficiency, and flexibility, making them an essential aspect of modern cloud infrastructure.

Compliance and governance

Cloud infrastructure components adhere to industry-specific compliance requirements and governance policies. This ensures the security, privacy, and regulatory compliance of data and services hosted in the cloud. Compliance and governance are critical components of cloud infrastructure that ensure organizations adhere to legal and regulatory requirements, industry standards, and internal policies. These components provide frameworks and mechanisms to monitor, enforce, and report on compliance-related activities within the cloud environment.

Some of the key aspects of compliance and governance are as follows:

- **Regulatory compliance**: Cloud infrastructure enables organizations to meet regulatory requirements specific to their industry or geographical location. It provides tools and features to ensure data privacy, protection, and secure handling as per regulations such as the **General Data Protection Regulation (GDPR)**, the **Health Insurance Portability and Accountability Act (HIPAA)**, the **Payment Card Industry Data Security Standard (PIC-DSS)**, and others. Compliance controls, such as data encryption, access controls, and audit trails, are implemented to protect sensitive data and meet regulatory obligations.

- **Data privacy and protection**: Cloud infrastructure offers robust data privacy and protection mechanisms to safeguard sensitive information. Encryption techniques are employed to secure data both at rest and in transit, ensuring that data remains confidential and protected from unauthorized access. Additionally, access controls and identity management solutions are implemented to ensure that only authorized individuals can access and manage data within the cloud environment.

- **Security assessments and audits**: Compliance and governance in cloud infrastructure involve conducting security assessments and audits to evaluate the effectiveness of security controls, policies, and procedures. These assessments help identify potential vulnerabilities, risks, and non-compliance issues. Regular audits ensure that the cloud environment adheres to established security standards and best practices.

- **Risk management**: Compliance and governance frameworks within cloud infrastructure enable organizations to identify and manage risks effectively. Risk assessments are conducted to identify potential threats and vulnerabilities to data and systems. Risk mitigation strategies, such as implementing security controls, disaster recovery plans, and incident response procedures, are developed and implemented to reduce the likelihood and impact of risks.

- **Policy management**: Cloud infrastructure facilitates policy management, allowing organizations to define and enforce policies related to data handling, access controls, user permissions, and other security measures. Policies can be centrally managed and enforced across the cloud environment, ensuring consistency and adherence to security and compliance requirements.

- **Auditing and reporting**: Cloud infrastructure provides tools for auditing and generating compliance reports. These reports capture activities, events, and security-related information within the cloud environment, enabling organizations to demonstrate compliance with regulatory requirements. Auditing and reporting mechanisms also aid in identifying potential security incidents, unauthorized access attempts, and other compliance violations.

- **Legal and contractual compliance**: Cloud infrastructure helps organizations adhere to legal and contractual obligations. It provides mechanisms to manage SLAs, confidentiality agreements, and data-processing agreements. Compliance with contractual obligations ensures that data is handled, stored, and processed as per the agreed-upon terms and conditions.

- **Incident response and forensics**: Compliance and governance within cloud infrastructure encompass incident response and forensic capabilities. Organizations establish procedures and protocols to detect, respond to, and investigate security incidents and breaches. Incident response plans outline the steps to be taken in the event of an incident, including containment, mitigation, and recovery. Forensic capabilities enable organizations to investigate security incidents, gather evidence, and support legal or regulatory requirements.

- **Continuous monitoring and compliance**: Cloud infrastructure supports continuous monitoring and compliance efforts. It includes tools and solutions for the real-time monitoring of system activities, log analysis, and intrusion detection. Continuous monitoring ensures that security controls and compliance measures are consistently applied and that any deviations or anomalies are detected and addressed promptly.

Compliance and governance are vital components of cloud infrastructure that enable organizations to meet legal, regulatory, and industry requirements. By implementing robust security controls, conducting risk assessments, enforcing policies, and conducting regular audits, organizations can ensure data privacy, protection, and integrity within the cloud environment. Compliance and governance frameworks provide the necessary mechanisms to monitor, enforce, and report on compliance-related activities, helping organizations maintain trust, mitigate risks, and adhere to the highest standards of security and compliance.

By integrating these essential components, cloud infrastructure enables organizations to leverage the benefits of scalability, agility, and cost-efficiency offered by cloud computing. It forms the backbone of cloud services, empowering businesses to deliver robust and reliable applications while meeting their specific requirements and objectives.

The following section, *Overview of virtualization and containerization*, introduces two key concepts in cloud computing: **virtualization** and **containerization**. We will cover various aspects of virtualization and containerization in cloud computing, explore different types of virtualizations, such as hardware virtualization and software virtualization, and examine their benefits and use cases in cloud environments.

Overview of virtualization and containerization

This section aims to provide a comprehensive overview of virtualization and containerization in cloud computing, equipping you with a solid understanding of these fundamental concepts and their significance in modern cloud architectures. We will start by discussing the concept of virtualization and its role in creating virtual instances of operating systems and servers. Next, we will delve into containerization, which involves encapsulating applications and their dependencies into self-contained units called containers. We will explore containerization technologies such as Docker and Kubernetes, and understand how they provide lightweight, portable, and isolated execution environments for applications. Furthermore, we will examine the advantages and challenges associated with virtualization and containerization in cloud computing. We will discuss topics such as resource optimization, scalability, security, and application deployment efficiency. We will also explore real-world use cases where virtualization and containerization have transformed the way organizations develop, deploy, and manage their applications in the cloud.

Cloud computing has emerged as a transformative technology that revolutionizes the way organizations store, access, and manage their data and applications. Among the many innovations that drive the efficiency and flexibility of cloud computing, virtualization and containerization stand out as fundamental pillars. These technologies enable organizations to optimize resource utilization, enhance scalability, and streamline application deployment in the cloud. We will delve into the details of virtualization and containerization in the context of cloud computing, exploring their key concepts, benefits, and use cases.

The following sections explain the key aspects of virtualization and containerization in cloud computing.

Virtualization in cloud computing

Virtualization is a foundational concept in cloud computing that involves creating virtual instances of operating systems, servers, or other resources. It allows for the abstraction of underlying physical infrastructure, enabling multiple VMs to run concurrently on a single physical server. The hypervisor, also known as a VMM, plays a crucial role in managing and allocating resources to each VM. Through virtualization, organizations can achieve better utilization of hardware resources, consolidate servers, and dynamically allocate resources based on workload demands.

It involves creating virtual instances or VMs that abstract the underlying physical infrastructure, allowing multiple VMs to run concurrently on a single physical server. The core concept of virtualization lies in the hypervisor, also known as a VMM, which acts as a software layer between the physical hardware and the VMs. The hypervisor allocates and manages the physical resources such as CPU, memory, storage, and network bandwidth among the VMs. There are two types of hypervisors: Type 1, or bare-metal, hypervisors, which run directly on the hardware, and Type 2, or hosted, hypervisors, which run on top of an operating system. This ensures that each VM has its fair share of resources and operates independently of other VMs. This isolation prevents any application or system failures in one VM from affecting others. Examples of Type 1 hypervisors include VMware ESXi and Microsoft Hyper-V. On the other hand, Type 2 hypervisors are easier to install and manage but may introduce a slight overhead due to the additional layer. Examples of Type 2 hypervisors include Oracle VirtualBox and VMware Workstation.

With virtualization, organizations can consolidate their servers by running multiple VMs on a single physical server. This consolidation leads to improved resource utilization, reduced hardware costs, and lower energy consumption. By dynamically allocating resources based on workload demands, virtualization enables efficient scalability, allowing organizations to allocate more resources to VMs as needed, or migrate VMs across physical servers to balance the workload.

Virtualization also offers benefits in terms of isolation and security. Each VM operates in an isolated environment, ensuring that any issues or changes in one VM do not affect others. This isolation provides enhanced security by minimizing the impact of potential vulnerabilities or malicious activities. It also allows for easier management of different operating systems and software environments within separate VMs.

Furthermore, virtualization facilitates workload portability and flexibility. VMs can be easily migrated between physical servers without disruption, enabling maintenance, load balancing, and high availability. This flexibility allows organizations to adapt their infrastructure to changing demands and optimize resource allocation based on application requirements.

Virtualization is a crucial component of **infrastructure-as-a-service** (**IaaS**) cloud offerings. Cloud service providers leverage virtualization to provide customers with virtualized resources, such as virtual servers, storage, and networking, on demand. Users can provision, manage, and scale VMs and resources through the cloud provider's management interface or APIs, without having to worry about the underlying physical infrastructure. The following figure depicts the difference between Type 1 and Type 2 hypervisors. On the left-hand side, there is a Type 1 hypervisor, also known as a bare-metal hypervisor. It is installed directly on the underlying physical hardware and controls the hardware resources. VMs run directly on top of the hypervisor, allowing for efficient and direct access to the hardware. On the right-hand side, there is a Type 2 hypervisor, also known as a hosted hypervisor. It is installed on top of an existing operating system. VMs are then created and run within the hosted hypervisor, which acts as an intermediary layer between the VMs and the underlying hardware:

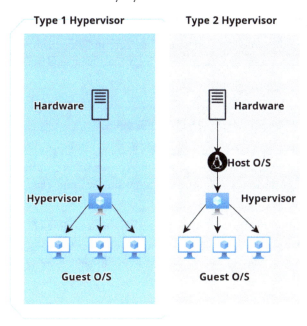

Figure 2.4 – Type 1 and Type 2 hypervisors

The preceding figure showcases the different approaches to virtualization and the placement of the hypervisor within the architecture. It provides a visual representation of how the hypervisor interacts with the hardware and facilitates the creation and management of VMs in both Type 1 and Type 2 hypervisor scenarios.

Now that we have a good idea of hypervisors, we can dig deep into hardware and software virtualization.

Hardware virtualization

Hardware virtualization, also known as server virtualization, abstracts the physical server's hardware, enabling the creation of multiple VMs. Each VM operates independently, running its own operating system and applications. This approach allows for efficient resource sharing and isolation, leading to improved scalability, flexibility, and cost-effectiveness. Additionally, virtualization facilitates the migration of VMs across physical servers, enabling workload balancing and enhancing high availability.

Software virtualization

Software virtualization, on the other hand, focuses on virtualizing specific software components rather than entire machines. This approach allows for the creation of virtualized environments for applications, databases, or other software components. By encapsulating the software within a virtual environment, organizations can achieve portability, ease of management, and isolation of dependencies.

Advantages of virtualization

Virtualization provides several advantages in cloud computing:

- **Resource optimization**: By consolidating multiple VMs onto a single physical server, virtualization enables better utilization of hardware resources. This consolidation reduces the need for physical servers, resulting in cost savings, reduced power consumption, and a smaller physical footprint in data centers.

- **Scalability**: Virtualization allows for the easy and dynamic scaling of resources. With VMs, organizations can quickly allocate additional CPU, memory, or storage capacity to meet changing demands. This elasticity helps optimize resource allocation and ensures that applications can scale up or down as needed without disruption.

- **Disaster recovery**: Virtualization simplifies disaster recovery strategies by allowing for the creation of VM snapshots or replica VMs. These snapshots serve as point-in-time backups that can be restored in case of system failures or disasters. By leveraging virtualization, organizations can recover their systems more efficiently and minimize downtime.

- **Testing and development**: Virtualization provides an ideal environment for testing and development purposes. Developers can create multiple VMs with different operating systems or software configurations, enabling them to test new applications or conduct experiments without impacting the production environment.

- **Application compatibility**: Virtualization facilitates running applications in different operating systems and software environments on the same physical hardware. This feature is particularly useful for legacy applications that require specific hardware or software configurations. By virtualizing these applications, organizations can extend their lifespan and avoid the need for costly hardware upgrades or system migrations.

- **Enhanced security**: Virtualization enhances security by isolating applications and operating systems within their virtual environments. Any vulnerabilities or breaches in one VM are contained and do not affect others. Additionally, VMs can be configured with security features such as firewalls, access controls, and intrusion detection systems, further strengthening the overall security posture.

Virtualization is a fundamental technology in cloud computing as it enables the efficient utilization of resources, simplifies management, and provides flexibility and scalability. Cloud service providers leverage virtualization to offer IaaS, where users can deploy and manage VMs in the cloud. Virtualization is a critical enabler for achieving the benefits of cloud computing, such as cost optimization, rapid deployment, and scalability, while maintaining high levels of performance and security.

Containerization in cloud computing

Containerization, a more recent innovation in cloud computing, builds upon the principles of virtualization but takes a different approach. It involves packaging software applications and their dependencies into self-contained units called containers. Each container provides an isolated runtime environment that includes the necessary libraries, binaries, and configuration files. Containers are lightweight and portable, allowing for seamless execution across different operating systems and cloud platforms. At the core of containerization is the container engine or runtime, such as Docker. The container engine creates and manages containers, which are instances of pre-configured images. These images contain the application code, runtime environment, libraries, and dependencies required for the application to run. Containers are isolated from each other and share the host operating system kernel, enabling efficient resource utilization and faster startup times compared to traditional VMs.

Docker is one of the most popular containerization technologies that has gained widespread adoption in the cloud computing landscape. It simplifies the process of creating, deploying, and managing containers. Docker containers offer advantages such as faster application startup, improved resource utilization, and easy scaling. The following figure depicts the composition and core components of a container.

At the center of the figure is the container itself, which encapsulates all the necessary components. Surrounding the container, several elements are depicted:

- **Environment**: This component represents the underlying infrastructure and resources required to support the container. It includes the host operating system, networking, and other system-level dependencies.

- **Code**: This component represents the application code that is packaged within the container. It includes all the necessary files, scripts, and binaries required to run the application.

- **Runtime**: The runtime component refers to the container engine responsible for managing and executing the container. It provides an isolated runtime environment for the application code to run securely and independently.

- **Libraries**: Libraries are collections of code modules that provide specific functionality to the application. They are included within the container to ensure that all required dependencies are available for the application to execute properly.

- **Config**: The configuration component represents the settings and parameters that define how the container and application should behave. It includes environment variables, network configurations, security settings, and other configuration files:

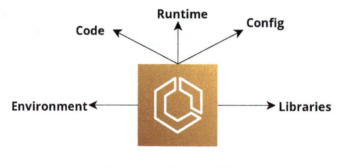

Container Composition

Figure 2.5 – Container composition

The preceding figure showcases the relationship and interdependence of these components within a container. It emphasizes that the container combines the application code, required dependencies, runtime, and configuration into a single, portable unit that can be easily deployed and executed across different environments.

Furthermore, container orchestration platforms such as Kubernetes provide advanced capabilities for managing large-scale container deployments, automating scaling, load balancing, and application health monitoring.

Here are some key concepts and details about containerization in cloud computing:

- **Container images**: A container image is a lightweight, standalone, and executable package that contains everything needed to run an application, including the application code, runtime environment, libraries, and dependencies. Container images are typically created from a base image, such as an operating system image, and layered with additional components specific to the application. These images can be easily distributed and shared, allowing for seamless deployment across different environments.

- **Container orchestration**: Container orchestration platforms, such as Kubernetes, provide management and automation capabilities for deploying, scaling, and managing containers at scale. These platforms enable efficient resource allocation, load balancing, and high availability of containerized applications. They also offer features such as automatic scaling, self-healing, and rolling updates, making it easier to manage and maintain containerized applications in a cloud environment.

- **Portability**: Containerization provides application portability, allowing containers to run consistently across different environments, including public clouds, private clouds, and on-premises infrastructure. Containers abstract the underlying infrastructure, making it easier to migrate applications between different cloud providers or on-premises data centers without significant modifications. This portability enables flexibility and vendor-agnostic deployment options.

- **Resource efficiency**: Containers are lightweight and share the host operating system kernel, which reduces resource overhead compared to traditional VMs. They have faster startup times and lower memory footprint, allowing for higher density and more efficient resource utilization on the underlying infrastructure. This efficiency is particularly beneficial in cloud environments where optimizing resource usage is crucial for cost-effectiveness.

- **Scalability and elasticity**: Containerization enables the easy scaling of applications. By leveraging container orchestration platforms, organizations can dynamically scale the number of containers based on workload demands. Containers can be quickly spun up or down, ensuring that applications can handle varying traffic levels and maintain optimal performance. This scalability and elasticity are key factors in cloud computing environments where applications need to respond to changing demands.

- **Application isolation and security**: Containers provide isolation between applications and their dependencies, preventing conflicts and ensuring that each application runs in its own secure environment. The lightweight and isolated nature of containers helps reduce the attack surface and improve application security. Additionally, containerization allows for the implementation of security measures such as fine-grained access controls, network policies, and secure container registries.

Containerization has revolutionized cloud computing by enabling faster application deployment, scalability, portability, and resource efficiency. It has become the foundation of modern application development and deployment strategies, facilitating the adoption of microservices architecture and enabling organizations to build and run cloud-native applications. With its benefits in terms of agility, efficiency, and scalability, containerization has become an essential technology for cloud-native and cloud-enabled environments.

Benefits and use cases of virtualization and containerization

Virtualization and containerization offer a multitude of benefits in cloud computing. Firstly, they enhance resource utilization by enabling the consolidation of VMs or containers onto a smaller number of physical servers. This leads to reduced hardware costs, optimized power consumption, and improved scalability. Organizations can dynamically allocate resources based on workload demands, scaling up or down as needed without disrupting other services.

Secondly, virtualization and containerization facilitate efficient application deployment and management. With VMs or containers, organizations can package applications and their dependencies into standardized units that are easily deployable and reproducible. This simplifies the process of application deployment, reduces conflicts between different software components, and streamlines the management of complex application environments.

Moreover, virtualization and containerization contribute to enhanced security and isolation. Each VM or container operates in an isolated environment, preventing one application from interfering with others. This isolation enhances security by limiting the impact of potential vulnerabilities or malicious activities.

In terms of use cases, virtualization and containerization have transformed various aspects of cloud computing. They enable organizations to build scalable and resilient infrastructure, deliver cloud-based services efficiently, and support the rapid deployment of applications. Cloud service providers leverage virtualization and containerization to deliver IaaS, **Platform-as-a-Service (PaaS)**, and **Software-as-a-Service (SaaS)** offerings.

Virtualization and containerization have become integral components of cloud computing, revolutionizing resource management and application deployment. Through virtualization, organizations can optimize hardware utilization, achieve workload flexibility, and enhance resource allocation. Containerization, on the other hand, provides lightweight, portable, and scalable environments for applications, enabling efficient deployment and management. The benefits of virtualization and containerization include improved resource utilization, enhanced scalability, simplified application deployment, and enhanced security. As cloud computing continues to evolve, these technologies will play a vital role in shaping the future of resource management and application delivery in the cloud.

We'll delve into more details, analysis, and use cases for containerization in cloud computing in the following subsections.

Microservices architecture

Containerization is closely aligned with the microservices architecture, where applications are broken down into smaller, loosely coupled services. Each service can be encapsulated within a container, enabling independent development, deployment, and scalability. Containerization allows organizations to efficiently manage and orchestrate these microservices, enabling rapid development, deployment, and scaling of individual components without impacting the entire application.

DevOps and CI/CD

Containerization plays a vital role in DevOps practices, enabling the seamless integration and deployment of applications. By packaging applications and their dependencies into containers, developers and operations teams can work together more effectively. Containers provide consistent environments across development, testing, and production, reducing issues caused by differences in environments. **Continuous integration/continuous deployment (CI/CD)** pipelines can be established, automating the process of building, testing, and deploying containers, thereby accelerating the software delivery life cycle.

Hybrid and multi-cloud deployments

Containerization simplifies the deployment of applications in hybrid and multi-cloud environments. Containers abstract the underlying infrastructure, enabling applications to be deployed consistently across different cloud providers or on-premises infrastructure. Organizations can leverage container orchestration platforms such as Kubernetes to manage and deploy containers seamlessly across multiple environments, ensuring flexibility, workload portability, and optimal resource utilization.

Scalable and elastic applications

Containerization allows applications to scale dynamically based on workload demands. With container orchestration platforms such as Kubernetes, organizations can automatically scale the number of containers up or down to handle varying traffic levels. Containers are lightweight and can be rapidly provisioned, enabling fast and efficient scaling, and ensuring that applications can handle increased user demands while maintaining optimal performance.

Fault tolerance and high availability

Container orchestration platforms provide built-in capabilities for fault tolerance and high availability. Containers can be replicated across multiple nodes or availability zones, ensuring that applications can withstand failures and continue running without interruption. Orchestration platforms such as Kubernetes monitor the health of containers and automatically restart or relocate them in case of failures, enhancing the overall reliability and availability of containerized applications.

Testing and QA environments

Containerization facilitates the creation of isolated testing and QA environments. Developers can package the application and its dependencies into containers, ensuring consistent environments for testing purposes. Containers can be easily spun up and torn down, providing on-demand and disposable testing environments. This enables organizations to conduct efficient testing, identify issues early in the development cycle, and accelerate the release of high-quality software.

Resource efficiency and cost savings

Containerization offers resource efficiency and cost savings compared to traditional VM-based deployments. Containers have a smaller footprint, faster startup times, and lower memory overhead. Multiple containers can run on a single host, maximizing resource utilization. This efficiency leads to cost savings by reducing infrastructure requirements and optimizing cloud spend.

Legacy application modernization

Containerization allows organizations to modernize legacy applications by encapsulating them within containers. By doing so, legacy applications can take advantage of the benefits of containerization, such as scalability, portability, and improved resource utilization. Containerization provides a pathway for migrating monolithic applications to a more modular and scalable architecture, paving the way for future enhancements and modernization efforts.

Containerization in cloud computing offers numerous advantages, including enabling microservices architecture, streamlining DevOps practices, supporting hybrid and multi-cloud deployments, facilitating scalable and elastic applications, providing fault tolerance and high availability, enhancing testing and QA environments, optimizing resource utilization and cost savings, and enabling legacy application modernization. These benefits make containerization a key technology for modern cloud-native and cloud-enabled applications, driving agility, efficiency, and scalability in the cloud computing landscape.

Understanding the difference between virtualization and containerization

Virtualization and containerization are two distinct technologies that are used in cloud computing, each with its characteristics and use cases. Here's a comparison of the key differences between virtualization and containerization.

- **Architecture and abstraction level**:

  - **Virtualization**: Virtualization operates at the infrastructure level. It creates a virtual layer between the physical hardware and the operating system, allowing multiple VMs to run on a single physical server. Each VM runs its own operating system and applications, simulating a complete computing environment.

  - **Containerization**: Containerization operates at the application level. It encapsulates applications and their dependencies into isolated containers. Containers share the same operating system kernel, but each container appears as a separate and isolated instance, running its own processes and resources.

- **Resource utilization**:

  - **Virtualization**: VMs require a dedicated amount of system resources, including memory, storage, and processing power. Each VM runs a full-fledged operating system, which can result in higher resource consumption and slower startup times.

  - **Containerization**: Containers are lightweight and share the host system's operating system kernel. They consume fewer resources, as they do not require a separate operating system instance. Containers have faster startup times and can be provisioned and scaled more quickly.

- **Isolation and security**:

  - **Virtualization**: VMs provide stronger isolation between instances as they operate with separate operating system instances. This isolation offers better security and prevents applications in one VM from affecting others.

  - **Containerization**: Containers provide a level of isolation, but they share the same operating system kernel. While this shared kernel may introduce a potential security risk, containerization technologies employ various security mechanisms, such as namespaces and control groups, to enforce isolation between containers.

- **Application portability**:

  - **Virtualization**: VMs are highly portable, allowing applications to run on different physical servers or hypervisors with minimal modification. However, there may be dependencies on specific hardware or hypervisor configurations.

  - **Containerization**: Containers are designed for portability. Applications packaged in containers can run consistently across different environments, including different operating systems and cloud platforms, so long as the host system supports the containerization runtime (for example, Docker or Kubernetes).

- **Performance**:

  - **Virtualization**: VMs have a slight performance overhead due to the emulation of hardware and the presence of a complete operating system instance

  - **Containerization**: Containers have lower overhead as they share the host system's operating system kernel, resulting in faster performance and better utilization of system resources

- **Use cases**:

  - **Virtualization**: Virtualization is well suited for running multiple applications with different operating system requirements on a single physical server. It is commonly used for server consolidation, running legacy applications, and managing complex network topologies.

  - **Containerization**: Containerization excels in deploying and scaling cloud-native applications, microservices architecture, and DevOps practices. It enables efficient resource utilization, fast application deployment, and portability across different environments.

The following figure depicts the architectural difference between virtualization and containerization:

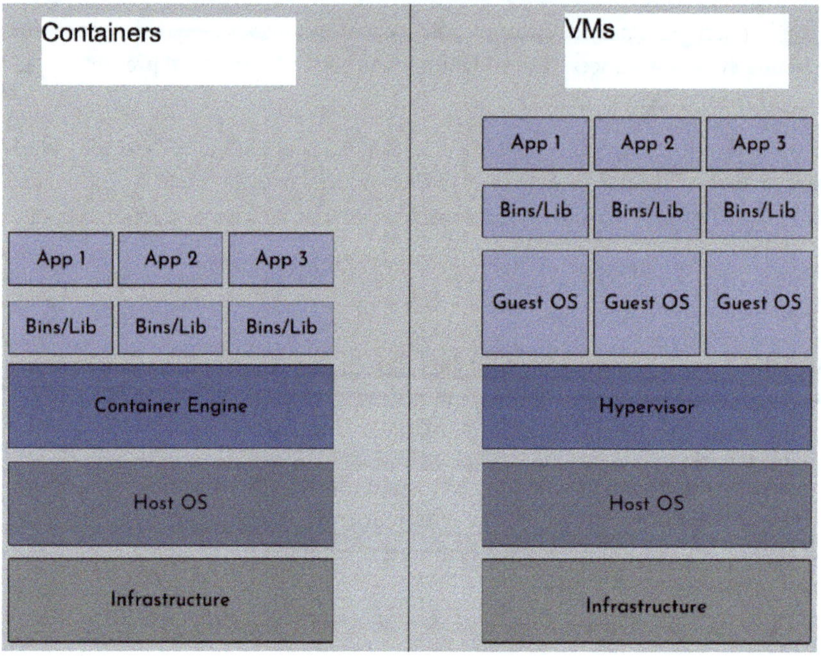

Figure 2.6 – VMs versus containers

VMs and containers have distinct differences. VMs operate on a hypervisor layer, utilizing separate guest operating systems, resulting in higher resource overhead. In contrast, containers share the host operating system, making them lightweight with reduced resource utilization. VMs offer strong isolation, while containers provide process-level isolation. VMs have higher performance overhead, while containers perform better due to direct resource usage. VMs are highly portable but face compatibility challenges, whereas containers excel in portability. VMs scale by adding or removing instances, while containers enable rapid scaling. VMs require separate management tools, while containers can be managed with container orchestration platforms. Understanding these differences aids in selecting the appropriate technology based on specific needs and considerations.

Virtualization and containerization offer different approaches to resource isolation, application deployment, and management in cloud computing. Virtualization operates at the infrastructure level, providing full operating system instances for each VM, while containerization operates at the application level, encapsulating applications and sharing the host operating system. Both technologies have their advantages and use cases, and the choice depends on factors such as workload requirements, resource utilization, portability needs, and security considerations.

Summary

Overall, this chapter provided a comprehensive overview of cloud architecture and the key components that are essential for building a successful cloud environment.

In this chapter, we explored two crucial topics in cloud computing: essential cloud infrastructure components and an overview of virtualization and containerization.

We began by discussing the essential components of cloud infrastructure, which are the building blocks that enable the functioning of cloud services. These components include physical data centers, virtualization and hypervisors, networking, storage, security, management and orchestration, monitoring and analytics, disaster recovery and backup, and compliance and governance. Each component plays a vital role in supporting the operations and capabilities of cloud environments.

Next, we delved into the concept of virtualization, which involves creating virtual instances of hardware, storage, and network resources. We explored how virtualization enables the efficient utilization of physical infrastructure, enhances flexibility, and allows for workload isolation.

Moving on, we explored containerization, a technology that enables the creation and management of lightweight, isolated containers for deploying applications. We discussed the key features of containerization, including resource efficiency, fast startup times, and portability across different environments. We also introduced containerization platforms such as Docker and Kubernetes, which facilitate the management and orchestration of containers at scale.

The topics we covered in this chapter are of paramount importance in the world of cloud computing. Understanding the essential components of cloud infrastructure equips organizations with the knowledge to design and deploy robust and reliable cloud environments. By harnessing the power of virtualization, businesses can maximize resource utilization, achieve cost savings, and rapidly scale their infrastructure to meet changing demands. Containerization, on the other hand, offers a lightweight and portable approach to application deployment, enabling faster development cycles and improved application consistency.

Overall, you gained a comprehensive understanding of the essential components of cloud infrastructure and the concepts of virtualization and containerization. You learned how these technologies contribute to the efficient delivery of cloud services, resource optimization, application deployment, and scalability. By grasping the significance of these topics, you are better equipped to make informed decisions regarding cloud infrastructure design, deployment, and management in their respective organizations.

In the upcoming chapter, *Chapter 3, Compute*, you will dive into the fundamental aspects of compute resources and storage in the context of cloud computing. This chapter will provide a comprehensive overview of the various technologies, concepts, and best practices associated with compute and storage in the cloud. You can expect to gain a deep understanding of VMs, containerization, and serverless computing, along with their respective benefits and use cases. This chapter will also explore different types of cloud storage, such as block storage, file storage, and object storage, discussing their definitions, characteristics, and practical applications. By the end of this chapter, you will have a solid grasp of the compute and storage capabilities offered by cloud computing, enabling you to make informed decisions and leverage these technologies effectively in your cloud-based solutions.

Part 2: Compute, Storage, and Networking

This part provides a comprehensive exploration of the essential components and concepts related to compute and storage in cloud computing. It introduces you to the fundamental role of storage solutions in cloud computing. It covers a range of cloud storage types, including object storage, file storage, block storage, and hybrid storage, discussing their unique characteristics and use cases. The part also covers various networking types, including a **Virtual Private Cloud** (**VPC**), subnetting, load balancing, **Content Delivery Networks** (**CDNs**), and **Virtual Private Networks** (**VPNs**), providing insights into their functionalities and benefits.

This part has the following chapters:

- *Chapter 3, Compute*
- *Chapter 4, Storage*
- *Chapter 5, Networking*

3

Compute

This chapter provides a comprehensive exploration of the essential components and concepts related to compute and storage in cloud computing. The chapter delves into the various compute options available in cloud computing. It covers the concept of **virtual machines** (**VMs**), which allow users to create and run multiple instances of operating systems on a single physical server. The advantages of VMs, such as resource isolation and scalability, are discussed in detail. Additionally, the chapter explores the concept of serverless computing, where users can run their applications without the requirement to manage the underlying infrastructure. This serverless model offers benefits such as automatic scaling, cost efficiency, and reduced operational overhead. The chapter then delves into the concept of virtual networks and their role in facilitating communication between different components of the cloud infrastructure. It also explores storage technologies such as block, file, and object storage, highlighting their unique characteristics and use cases.

The chapter examines different storage options in the cloud. It covers traditional storage approaches such as block storage, which provides raw storage volumes that can be attached to VMs, and file storage, which allows for the creation and management of shared filesystems. The chapter also explores object storage, a highly scalable and durable storage option that is ideal for storing unstructured data such as images, videos, and documents. The benefits of each storage option, including scalability, durability, and cost effectiveness, are discussed in detail.

Throughout the chapter, real-world use cases and examples are provided to illustrate the practical applications of compute and storage in cloud infrastructure. These examples range from running high-performance computing workloads to managing large-scale data analytics projects.

In this chapter, we will cover the following topics:

- Introduction to compute and storage in cloud computing
- Cloud storage types
- Considerations and cost optimization strategies for compute and storage

By the end of the chapter, you will have gained a comprehensive understanding of the compute and storage components of cloud infrastructure. You will be familiar with different compute options such as VMs and serverless computing, as well as various storage options such as block storage, file storage, and object storage. Additionally, you will have a clear understanding of the benefits and considerations associated with each compute and storage option, enabling you to make informed decisions when designing and implementing cloud-based solutions.

Technical requirements

To fully engage with the content of this chapter on cloud computing architecture, you should have a basic understanding of computer systems, networking concepts, and information technology.

Additionally, the following technical requirements are recommended:

- **Internet access**: You should have a reliable internet connection to access online resources, references, and examples related to cloud computing.

- **Computing device**: A desktop computer, laptop, tablet, or smartphone with a modern web browser is necessary to read the chapter content and access any online materials.

- **Web browser**: The latest version of a web browser such as Google Chrome, Mozilla Firefox, Microsoft Edge, or Safari is recommended. This ensures compatibility and an optimal viewing experience of web-based resources and interactive content.

- **Familiarity with cloud services**: Some familiarity with cloud services and their basic functionalities will enhance the understanding of the chapter. This includes knowledge of basic storage, O/S, VMs, and servers.

Introduction to compute and storage in cloud computing

This section serves as a comprehensive introduction to the fundamental concepts and importance of compute and storage in the context of cloud infrastructure. In this section, you will gain a deep understanding of the crucial roles that compute and storage play in enabling and supporting cloud-based services and applications.

Throughout the section, real-world examples and industry case studies are incorporated to illustrate how organizations leverage compute and storage in the cloud. You will gain insights into how compute and storage resources are utilized in various domains such as e-commerce, media streaming, data analytics, and more. These examples bring the concepts to life and demonstrate the practical applications and benefits of compute and storage in cloud computing.

Furthermore, the section explores considerations such as cost optimization, performance tuning, security, and data management in the context of compute and storage. You will understand the importance of selecting the right compute and storage resources to meet specific application requirements and business objectives. By the end of the section, you will have a solid foundation in compute and storage concepts in cloud computing. You will appreciate the integral role these components play in building robust and scalable cloud infrastructures. Armed with this knowledge, you can make informed decisions about compute and storage options, effectively design and manage cloud-based solutions, and leverage the full potential of compute and storage resources in your cloud environments.

Compute resources form a fundamental aspect of cloud computing, serving as the backbone for executing applications and services in the cloud environment. In this topic, we will explore compute models that enable organizations to leverage the scalability, flexibility, and efficiency of the cloud.

In the following sections, we will look at the widely known compute resources.

Virtual machines (VMs)

We discussed VMs briefly in the previous chapter, so let's talk about them in some more detail in this section. VMs are software emulations of physical computers that enable multiple operating systems and applications to run simultaneously on a single physical server. VMs provide a layer of abstraction between the hardware and the operating system, allowing for better resource utilization and flexibility in the cloud computing environment.

Key characteristics of VMs include the following:

- **Isolation**: VMs provide strong isolation between different instances running on the same physical server. Each VM operates independently and is isolated from other VMs, ensuring that a failure or issue in one VM does not affect others.

- **Virtualization**: VMs leverage virtualization technology to emulate the hardware components of a physical computer, including CPU, memory, storage, and network interfaces. This abstraction allows for the efficient sharing of physical resources among multiple VMs.

- **Compatibility**: VMs can run different operating systems and applications, making them versatile for organizations with diverse software requirements. This compatibility enables the consolidation of various workloads onto a single physical server, reducing hardware costs and simplifying management.

- **Resource allocation**: VMs allow for granular control over resource allocation. System administrators can allocate specific amounts of CPU, memory, and storage to each VM based on its workload requirements. This flexibility ensures that resources are efficiently utilized and scaled according to the demands of the applications.

- **Mobility**: VMs offer the capability to migrate or move instances from one physical server to another without interrupting their operation. This mobility feature allows for load balancing, hardware maintenance, and disaster recovery scenarios.

- **Snapshots and cloning**: VMs support the creation of snapshots, which capture the state of a VM at a specific point in time. These snapshots can be used for backups, testing, and reverting to a previous configuration if needed. VM cloning allows for the rapid provisioning of multiple instances with the same configuration, simplifying deployment processes.

VMs play a crucial role in cloud computing by enabling organizations to achieve better hardware utilization, flexibility, and scalability. They offer the ability to run multiple operating systems and applications on a single physical server, providing efficient resource allocation and isolation. With their compatibility and mobility features, VMs facilitate workload consolidation, system maintenance, and disaster recovery strategies. Let's see how it is typically placed in a cloud environment. The following figure depicts the typical layout of a VM in a cloud environment. In the figure, T3 is the EC2 instance, a VM in the **Amazon Web Services (AWS)** cloud environment:

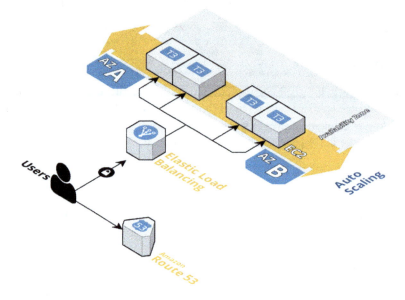

Figure 3.1 – VM layout in an AWS environment

Using VMs in cloud computing offers several benefits that contribute to the efficiency, flexibility, and scalability of the infrastructure. Some key benefits of using VMs include the following:

- **Resource optimization**: VMs allow for better utilization of physical server resources by enabling multiple VMs to run concurrently on a single server. This consolidation leads to improved hardware efficiency, reduced power consumption, and cost savings.

- **Flexibility and compatibility**: VMs provide the flexibility to run different operating systems and applications on the same physical infrastructure. This compatibility allows organizations to deploy and manage diverse software environments, accommodating a wide range of application requirements.

- **Isolation and security**: VMs offer strong isolation between different instances running on the same physical server. Each VM operates independently, providing enhanced security by preventing one VM from accessing or interfering with the resources of another. This isolation helps in containing security breaches and minimizing the impact of vulnerabilities.

- **Scalability and elasticity**: VMs enable easy scalability by allowing organizations to quickly provision new instances as the demand for computing resources increases. Scaling can be achieved by adding more VMs or adjusting the resources allocated to existing VMs, providing the flexibility to meet changing workload requirements.

- **Disaster recovery and high availability**: VMs facilitate efficient disaster recovery strategies. VM snapshots and backups can be taken to capture the state of a VM at a specific point in time, allowing for quick restoration in the event of system failures or data loss. Additionally, VM mobility enables seamless migration of instances between physical servers, supporting high availability configurations.

- **Testing and development**: VMs are valuable for testing and development environments. They allow developers to create isolated sandboxes, replicate production environments, and quickly provision new instances for testing purposes. VMs provide a cost-effective and efficient way to experiment with different configurations and software versions.

- **Simplified management**: VMs offer centralized management and administration of computing resources. System administrators can leverage management tools to provision, monitor, and control VM instances from a single interface, streamlining management tasks and reducing operational complexity.

The use of VMs in cloud computing provides organizations with increased flexibility, resource optimization, security, scalability, and simplified management. These benefits contribute to the overall efficiency and effectiveness of cloud infrastructure, enabling organizations to meet their computing needs in a more agile and cost-effective manner.

Let's understand how we can deploy a VM on a cloud platform. To deploy a VM in a cloud environment such as Azure, you can follow these general steps (I'll provide an example using the Azure cloud platform):

1. Sign in to the Azure portal: Go to the Azure portal (`https://portal.azure.com/`) and sign in with your Azure account.

2. Create a resource group: A resource group is a logical container for resources. It helps you manage and organize resources in your Azure subscription. Create a new resource group or use an existing one if you have already created it.

    An example in the Azure CLI is as follows:

    ```
    az group create -name MyResourceGroup -location eastus
    ```

3. Choose the VM image: Select the operating system and VM image you want to use. Azure provides a variety of images, including Windows Server, Ubuntu, CentOS, and so on.

    An example in Azure CLI is as follows:

    ```
    az vm image list --output table
    ```

4. Create the VM: Choose a name for your VM, determine the size (hardware configuration), and specify the login credentials (username and password or SSH key) for accessing the VM.

An example in Azure CLI is as follows:

```
az vm create --resource-group MyResourceGroup --name
MyVirtualMachine --image UbuntuLTS --size Standard_B2s --admin-
username azureuser --admin-password MyPassword1234
```

5. Configure network settings: Specify the network settings such as virtual network, subnet, public IP (if needed), and network security group rules (firewall settings).

An example in Azure CLI (creating a new virtual network and subnet) is as follows:

```
az network vnet create --resource-group MyResourceGroup --name
MyVnet --address-prefix 192.168.0.0/16 --subnet-name MySubnet
--subnet-prefix 192.168.1.0/24
```

6. Assign a public IP (optional): If you want your VM to have a public IP address to access it over the internet, you can allocate a public IP and associate it with your VM.

An example in Azure CLI is as follows:

```
az network public-ip create --resource-group MyResourceGroup
--name MyPublicIP --sku Standard

az network nic ip-config update --resource-group MyResourceGroup
--nic-name MyVirtualMachineVMNic --name ipconfig1 --public-ip
MyPublicIP
```

7. Open ports (optional): If you need specific ports to be accessible from the internet, configure **network security group** (**NSG**) rules to allow incoming traffic.

An example in Azure CLI (allowing SSH traffic on port 22) is as follows:

```
az network nsg rule create --resource-group MyResourceGroup
--nsg-name MyNetworkSecurityGroup --name AllowSSH --protocol
Tcp --direction Inbound --priority 1000 --source-address-prefix
'*' --source-port-range '*' --destination-address-prefix '*'
--destination-port-range 22 --access Allow
```

8. Connect to the VM: Once the VM is deployed, you can connect to it using **remote desktop** (**RDP**) for Windows VMs or SSH for Linux VMs. Use the public IP address or the **fully qualified domain name** (**FQDN**) to connect.

That's it! You now have a VM running in the Azure cloud environment. Remember to manage your resources efficiently and stop or deallocate the VM when not in use to avoid unnecessary costs.

Deploying a VM in the AWS environment involves similar steps as in Azure. The following steps highlight the process to deploy a VM in AWS, along with corresponding AWS CLI examples:

1. Sign in to the AWS console: Go to the AWS Management Console (https://aws.amazon.com/console/) and sign in with your AWS account.

2. Choose a region: Select the AWS region where you want to deploy your VM. Each region has its own availability zones, which are distinct data centers within the region.

3. Create a **virtual private cloud** (**VPC**): A VPC is a virtual network that allows you to isolate and control networking resources for your AWS resources. Create a new VPC or use an existing one.

   An example in AWS CLI is as follows:

   ```
   aws ec2 create-vpc -cidr-block 10.0.0.0/16
   ```

4. Create a subnet within the VPC: Create a subnet where your VM will reside. Each subnet is associated with a specific availability zone.

   An example in AWS CLI is as follows:

   ```
   aws ec2 create-subnet --vpc-id <VPC-ID> --cidr-block 10.0.1.0/24
   --availability-zone us-east-1a
   ```

5. Choose the VM image: Select the **Amazon Machine Image** (**AMI**) that corresponds to the operating system and software you want to run on the VM.

   An example in AWS CLI (listing available AMIs) is as follows:

   ```
   aws ec2 describe-images --owners amazon --query
   "Images[?Architecture=='x86_64' && VirtualizationType=='hvm' &&
   RootDeviceType=='ebs']"
   ```

6. Create the VM: Specify the instance type (hardware configuration), IAM role (if required for specific permissions), security groups (firewall settings), and other details.

   An example in AWS CLI is as follows:

   ```
   aws ec2 run-instances --image-id <AMI-ID> --count 1 --instance-
   type t2.micro --key-name MyKeyPair --security-group-ids
   <Security-Group-ID> --subnet-id <Subnet-ID> --associate-public-
   ip-address
   ```

7. Allocate a public IP (optional): By default, an EC2 instance in a public subnet will get a public IP. However, for instances in private subnets, you may need to assign an **Elastic IP** (**EIP**) and associate it with your instance.

   An example in AWS CLI is as follows:

   ```
   aws ec2 allocate-address
   aws ec2 associate-address --instance-id <Instance-ID>
   --public-ip <EIP>
   ```

8. Open ports (optional): Configure security group rules to allow incoming traffic to specific ports, similar to NSG rules in Azure.

   An example in AWS CLI (allowing SSH traffic on port 22) is as follows:

   ```
   aws ec2 authorize-security-group-ingress --group-id <Security-
   Group-ID> --protocol tcp --port 22 --cidr 0.0.0.0/0
   ```

9. Connect to the VM: Once the VM is deployed, connect to it using SSH for Linux instances or RDP for Windows instances. Use the public IP or EIP associated with the instance.

That's it! Now you have a VM running in the AWS environment. Again, remember to manage your resources efficiently, and stop or terminate instances when not in use to control costs.

VMs are widely used in various use cases within cloud computing, providing solutions for legacy application migration and workload isolation. Let's delve into these use cases and understand their significance:

- Legacy application migration: Many organizations have legacy applications that were designed to run on specific hardware or operating systems. Virtualization technology enables these legacy applications to be migrated to VMs, eliminating the need for dedicated hardware. By encapsulating the entire application environment within a VM, organizations can run their legacy applications on modern infrastructure, benefiting from improved scalability, resource utilization, and easier management. This approach also ensures that the legacy applications remain functional without the need for extensive modifications.

- Workload isolation: In cloud computing environments, workload isolation is crucial to ensure the stability and security of applications. VMs offer strong isolation between different workloads running on the same physical infrastructure. Each VM operates as an independent entity with its own dedicated resources, operating system, and application stack. Workload isolation helps prevent resource conflicts, performance degradation, and security breaches. It allows organizations to securely host multiple applications or services on a single physical server while ensuring that failures or issues in one VM do not affect others.

- Test and development environments: VMs are commonly used for creating isolated test and development environments. Developers can provision VMs quickly, replicate production environments, and experiment with different configurations or software versions. VM snapshots and clones allow developers to roll back to a known state, making it easier to test and debug applications without impacting the production environment. By using VMs for testing and development, organizations can ensure better software quality, accelerate application development cycles, and minimize the risk of conflicts between development and production environments.

- Scalability and elasticity: VMs provide scalability and elasticity to accommodate changing workload demands. With VMs, organizations can easily provision or deprovision instances based on workload requirements. This flexibility enables them to scale resources up or down quickly, ensuring optimal performance and cost efficiency. By leveraging VMs, organizations can dynamically allocate computing resources, respond to spikes in demand, and meet fluctuating workload needs without disrupting existing services.

- Hybrid cloud deployment: VMs are instrumental in hybrid cloud deployments, where organizations use a combination of on-premises infrastructure and public cloud services. VMs enable workload portability between private and public clouds, allowing seamless migration of applications and data. This flexibility allows organizations to leverage the benefits of both environments, such as maintaining sensitive data on-premises while utilizing public cloud scalability for certain workloads. VMs provide a common abstraction layer, facilitating the integration and management of hybrid cloud deployments.

VMs offer versatile solutions for legacy application migration, workload isolation, test and development environments, scalability, and hybrid cloud deployments. By leveraging VM technology, organizations can optimize resource utilization, enhance application portability, improve security, and achieve greater flexibility in managing their computing workloads within the cloud environment.

In the world of virtualization, two popular VM technologies stand out: VMware and Hyper-V. Let's delve into an overview of these technologies and understand their key features and capabilities.

VMware

VMware is a leading virtualization software provider that offers a range of products catering to different virtualization needs. One of its flagship products is VMware vSphere, which provides a comprehensive virtualization platform for creating and managing VMs.

Key features:

- High performance: VMware offers advanced features such as memory overcommitment, live migration (vMotion), and **distributed resource scheduling** (**DRS**) that enhance VM performance and resource utilization

- Robust management tools: VMware provides a suite of management tools such as vCenter Server, which enables centralized VM management, monitoring, and resource allocation

- High availability: VMware offers features such as fault tolerance and automatic VM restart, ensuring continuous availability of critical applications

- Scalability: With VMware, organizations can scale their virtual infrastructure horizontally and vertically, adding more VMs or expanding resources as needed

- Ecosystem and compatibility: VMware has a broad ecosystem of third-party vendors and supports a wide range of operating systems, making it compatible with diverse application environments

Hyper-V

Hyper-V is a hypervisor-based virtualization technology developed by Microsoft. It is an integral component of Windows Server operating systems and provides a robust platform for creating and managing VMs.

Key features:

- Integration with the Microsoft ecosystem: Hyper-V seamlessly integrates with other Microsoft technologies, such as Active Directory, System Center Suite, and Windows PowerShell, providing a cohesive virtualization solution within the Microsoft ecosystem.

- Live migration and high availability: Hyper-V supports live migration, allowing VMs to be moved between physical hosts with minimal downtime. It also provides features such as failover clustering for the high availability of VMs.

- Extensive management tools: Hyper-V offers various management tools such as Hyper-V Manager, Windows Admin Center, and PowerShell, enabling efficient VM management, monitoring, and automation.

- Secure virtualization: Hyper-V incorporates security features such as shielded VMs and BitLocker encryption to protect VMs and their data from unauthorized access.

- Scalability: Hyper-V supports scaling VM deployments through features such as dynamic memory allocation and **virtual machine queues** (**VMQs**), enabling efficient utilization of resources.

Both VMware and Hyper-V are mature and widely adopted VM technologies, each with its own strengths and capabilities. Organizations often choose between them based on factors such as specific requirements, existing infrastructure, ecosystem compatibility, and budget considerations. It's important for organizations to assess their needs and evaluate these technologies to determine which one aligns best with their virtualization goals and objectives.

Here's an example of how to set up Hyper-V on a Windows machine:

1. Check system requirements: First, ensure that your computer meets the system requirements for Hyper-V. You need a 64-bit Windows operating system with **Second Level Address Translation** (**SLAT**) and **Data Execution Prevention** (**DEP**) features enabled in the BIOS.

2. Enable the Hyper-V feature: Hyper-V is a Windows feature that needs to be enabled. Open **Control Panel** and go to **Programs** > **Programs and Features** > **Turn Windows features on or off**. Check the **Hyper-V** box and click **OK**. Windows will install the necessary components and prompt you to restart your computer.

3. Configure Hyper-V settings (optional): Once Hyper-V is installed, you can configure its settings. To do this, use the **Hyper-V Manager** application. You can access it through the **Start** menu or by searching for `Hyper-V Manager` in the search bar.

4. Create a VM: With Hyper-V installed, you can now create VMs. In Hyper-V Manager, right-click on the server name and select **New** > **Virtual Machine**. The Virtual Machine Wizard will guide you through creating the VM, where you'll specify settings such as the VM name, memory, network, and storage.

5. Install an operating system on the VM: After creating the VM, you need to install an operating system on it. In Hyper-V Manager, right-click on the VM you just created and select **Connect**. This will open a console where you can start the VM and install the OS from an ISO file or installation media.

6. Manage VMs: You can manage your VMs through Hyper-V Manager. This includes starting, stopping, pausing, and deleting VMs, as well as adjusting their settings.

7. Enable nested virtualization (optional): If you need to run VMs within a VM (nested virtualization), you can enable this feature in Hyper-V. This is useful for scenarios such as running Docker within a VM.

Remember that Hyper-V is a powerful tool that allows you to create and manage virtualized environments on Windows machines, enabling you to run multiple operating systems and applications in isolated environments for testing, development, or production purposes.

The previous section covered VMware, Hyper-V, and VMs, and you learned about leading virtualization platforms that enable the creation and management of multiple virtual environments on a single physical host. VMs were introduced as self-contained instances of an operating system, offering benefits such as resource optimization, cost savings, and simplified testing and development. The section highlighted the versatility of VMs in various use cases, including software testing, application development, and server consolidation. You also understood the significance of choosing the appropriate virtualization solution based on specific needs and project requirements.

Containers

Containerization technology, exemplified by popular tools such as Docker and Kubernetes, has revolutionized the way applications are developed, deployed, and managed in the cloud computing landscape. Containers provide lightweight and isolated runtime environments for applications, encapsulating the application and its dependencies. Containerization technology, such as Docker, enables developers to package applications with their libraries, frameworks, and configurations, ensuring consistent execution across different environments. Containers offer advantages such as portability, scalability, and faster application deployment. Container orchestration platforms such as Kubernetes provide automated management, scaling, and networking capabilities for containerized applications. Containers are particularly suitable for microservices architecture, where applications are divided into smaller, loosely coupled components. They facilitate agile development, **continuous integration/continuous deployment (CI/CD)**, and efficient resource utilization.

Containers offer several advantages in terms of portability and resource efficiency, making them a preferred choice for application deployment in cloud computing environments. Let's explore these advantages in detail:

- Consistent environment: Containers encapsulate an application and its dependencies into a single package, ensuring consistency across different environments. Applications developed in containers can be easily deployed and run on various platforms, including local development machines, VMs, and cloud infrastructure.

- Elimination of dependency issues: Containers include all the necessary libraries and dependencies within their image, removing the need to worry about compatibility issues with the underlying host system. This makes it easier to move applications across different environments without concerns about compatibility or dependency conflicts.

- Easy replication: Containers can be easily replicated and distributed across different systems, enabling seamless migration between development, testing, and production environments. This portability allows for efficient scaling and deployment of applications, promoting agile development and deployment practices.

- Lightweight: Containers are lightweight compared to VMs, as they share the host system's kernel and utilize its resources efficiently. Each container operates in its isolated environment, consuming only the necessary resources for the application to run, resulting in reduced overhead and improved resource utilization.

- Rapid startup and scaling: Containers have faster startup times compared to VMs since they don't require booting an entire operating system. Containers can be quickly spun up or down based on demand, enabling rapid scaling of applications to handle varying workloads efficiently.

- Efficient resource allocation: Container orchestration platforms, such as Kubernetes, optimize resource allocation by dynamically assigning containers to hosts based on resource availability and application requirements. This ensures efficient utilization of computing resources, minimized wasted capacity, and reduced costs.

Let's understand how we can create a container in a cloud environment such as **Google Cloud Platform** (**GCP**). Creating a container in Google Cloud typically involves using **Google Kubernetes Engine** (**GKE**), a managed Kubernetes service provided by GCP. Kubernetes is an open source container orchestration platform that allows you to deploy, manage, and scale containerized applications. Here are the steps to create a container in Google Cloud using GKE:

1. Set up a Google Cloud project: If you don't have a Google Cloud account, create one and set up a new project within the Google Cloud console.

2. Enable GKE: Within your Google Cloud project, navigate to the GKE section in the Cloud console and enable the Kubernetes Engine API.

3. Install and set up Google Cloud SDK (gcloud): Install the Google Cloud SDK on your local machine. This SDK allows you to interact with your Google Cloud resources from the command line.

4. Authenticate with Google Cloud: After installing the SDK, use the `gcloud auth login` command to authenticate yourself with your Google Cloud account.

5. Create a Kubernetes cluster: Use the `gcloud container clusters create` command to create a Kubernetes cluster in GKE. You can specify various options such as the number of nodes, the machine types, and the GCP zone where the cluster will be located.

6. Configure kubectl: Install the Kubernetes `kubectl` command-line tool and configure it to use the newly created GKE cluster. You can use the `gcloud container clusters get-credentials` command to set up `kubectl`.

7. Create a Docker container: Before deploying your application to the Kubernetes cluster, you need to have your application containerized using Docker. Create a `Dockerfile` for your application, and then build a Docker image using the `docker build` command.

8. Push the Docker image to a container registry: Store the Docker image in a container registry, such as **Google Container Registry (GCR)** or Docker Hub. In the case of GCR, use the `gcloud docker -- push` command to push your Docker image to GCR.

9. Create Kubernetes deployment: Create a Kubernetes deployment YAML file that describes how your container should be deployed. This file specifies the container image to use, the number of replicas, networking, and other settings.

10. Apply the Kubernetes deployment: Use the `kubectl apply` command to deploy your application to the Kubernetes cluster. This command will create the specified number of replicas of your container.

11. Expose the deployment (optional): If you want to make your application accessible from outside the cluster, you can expose it using a Kubernetes Service. This will create a stable endpoint (**LoadBalancer**, **NodePort**, or **ClusterIP**) that can be accessed externally.

That's it! Now your containerized application is running on GKE. You can scale, update, and manage the application easily through the Kubernetes API or the GKE web console.

By leveraging the advantages of portability and resource efficiency, containers enable organizations to streamline application development, deployment, and management processes. They promote a modular and scalable approach to building applications, allowing teams to focus on innovation and accelerate software delivery. Additionally, the use of containers contributes to cost savings by maximizing resource utilization and facilitating efficient infrastructure management.

Let's delve into an introduction to containerization and explore these technologies in more detail.

Docker

Docker is a freely available containerization platform enabling developers to bundle applications and their dependencies into self-contained and portable containers. These containers create lightweight and isolated environments, encompassing all the essential components required for seamless application execution.

Key features:

- Containerization: Docker utilizes containerization technology to create consistent and reproducible environments for applications, ensuring that they run consistently across different infrastructure platforms.

- Image-based deployment: Docker uses images as the building blocks for containers. Images are lightweight, standalone, executable packages that contain the application along with all its dependencies and configuration settings.

- Scalability and portability: Docker enables easy scaling of applications by allowing containers to be replicated and distributed across multiple hosts. The portable nature of Docker containers allows applications to run seamlessly across different environments, such as development, testing, and production.

- Version control: Docker enables versioning of container images, making it easier to track changes, roll back to previous versions, and collaborate on application deployments.

- Docker Hub and Docker Registry: Docker Hub is a public repository of container images, while Docker Registry provides a private repository for organizations to store and share their container images.

Kubernetes

Kubernetes (K8s) is an open source container orchestration platform that automates the deployment, scaling, and management of containerized applications. It provides a robust framework for managing clusters of containers.

Key features:

- Automated deployment and scaling: Kubernetes automates the deployment process, allowing for easy scaling of applications by dynamically provisioning and managing containers based on resource demand

- Service discovery and load balancing: Kubernetes offers built-in service discovery and load balancing capabilities, ensuring that traffic is efficiently routed to containers within a cluster

- Self-healing and fault tolerance: Kubernetes monitors the health of containers and automatically restarts or replaces failed containers to maintain application availability

- Configurable deployments: Kubernetes allows fine-grained control over application deployments, including rollout strategies, scaling policies, and resource allocation

- Declarative configuration: Kubernetes uses declarative YAML or JSON files to define the desired state of the infrastructure, enabling easy replication and management of application deployments

Docker and Kubernetes are highly complementary technologies. Docker provides the containerization foundation, while Kubernetes orchestrates and manages the life cycle of containers. Together, they offer a powerful solution for building, deploying, and scaling applications in cloud environments. Their popularity stems from their ability to simplify the development process, enhance application portability, and streamline infrastructure management.

Container orchestration using Kubernetes and Docker Swarm

Container orchestration and management platforms, such as Kubernetes and Docker Swarm, play a crucial role in managing and scaling containerized applications in cloud computing environments. Let's delve into the details of these platforms.

Kubernetes:

- Scalability and load balancing: Kubernetes provides robust scaling capabilities, allowing applications to scale up or down based on demand. It automatically distributes containerized workloads across multiple nodes, balancing the load to ensure optimal performance and resource utilization.

- Service discovery and load balancing: Kubernetes offers built-in service discovery mechanisms that enable containers to communicate with each other seamlessly. It also provides load balancing for distributing traffic across containers, ensuring high availability and efficient utilization of resources.

- Self-healing and fault tolerance: Kubernetes monitors the health of containers and automatically restarts or replaces failed containers. It ensures the desired state of applications, automatically healing and recovering from failures without manual intervention, thereby enhancing application resilience.

- Container networking and storage: Kubernetes facilitates networking between containers and exposes services within the cluster or to external users. It also supports various storage options, allowing applications to securely store and access data.

Docker Swarm:

- Simplicity and ease of use: Docker Swarm is a native clustering and orchestration solution provided by Docker. It offers a user-friendly interface, making it relatively easy to set up and manage containerized applications. Docker Swarm leverages the existing Docker ecosystem, allowing users to seamlessly transition from running single containers to managing clustered environments.

- High availability and load balancing: Docker Swarm ensures high availability of applications by distributing containers across multiple nodes in a swarm cluster. It provides load balancing mechanisms to evenly distribute traffic, optimizing resource usage and enhancing application performance.

- Self-healing and rolling updates: Docker Swarm automatically detects and replaces failed containers to maintain the desired state of services. It also supports rolling updates, allowing seamless updates of applications without downtime, ensuring continuous availability, and minimizing service disruptions.

- Integration with Docker tools: Docker Swarm seamlessly integrates with other Docker tools, such as Docker Compose, to simplify the deployment and management of multi-container applications. It provides a cohesive ecosystem for building, packaging, and deploying containerized applications.

Both Kubernetes and Docker Swarm offer powerful features for managing containerized applications at scale. They provide robust orchestration capabilities, ensuring efficient resource utilization, high availability, and fault tolerance. These platforms simplify the management of containerized environments, enabling organizations to deploy and scale applications with ease while maintaining operational efficiency and reliability.

Containers have gained popularity in the realm of cloud computing due to their versatility and numerous use cases. Let's explore some of the prominent use cases for containers.

Use cases for containers

This section delves into the diverse and valuable applications of containers across different industries and environments. By examining real-world scenarios, this section highlights the benefits of using containers for efficient software deployment, microservices architecture, scaling applications, and simplifying the management of complex systems. Whether in cloud-native development, DevOps practices, or hybrid infrastructure setups, containers prove to be a versatile and essential technology:

- Microservices architecture: Containers are well-suited for implementing microservices architecture where applications are decomposed into smaller, independent services. Each microservice runs in its own container, enabling scalability, flexibility, and ease of deployment. Containers allow developers to build, test, and deploy microservices independently, promoting agility and modular development practices.

- Application deployment and isolation: Containers provide an efficient way to package applications and their dependencies into portable units. With containers, developers can encapsulate an application, including its libraries, dependencies, and runtime environment, ensuring consistency across different environments. Containers simplify the deployment process, allowing applications to run reliably and consistently across various platforms, from development to production.

- Hybrid and multi-cloud deployments: Containers enable seamless application deployment and portability across different cloud providers and environments. Organizations can leverage containers to build hybrid and multi-cloud architectures, distributing workloads across multiple clouds or on-premises infrastructure. Containers abstract the underlying infrastructure, making it easier to migrate applications between different environments without significant modifications.

- DevOps and CI/CD: Containers align well with DevOps practices, enabling faster and more efficient software development and deployment. By using containers, development and operations teams can work in parallel, with developers focusing on building and packaging applications while operations teams handle container orchestration and deployment. Containers facilitate continuous integration, enabling automated build and testing processes, and continuous deployment, allowing rapid and frequent software releases.

- Scalable web applications: Containers are an ideal choice for deploying scalable web applications. Container orchestration platforms such as Kubernetes provide automatic scaling capabilities, allowing applications to handle varying levels of traffic. Containers can quickly scale up or down based on demand, ensuring efficient resource utilization and providing a seamless user experience.

- Testing and QA environments: Containers simplify the creation of isolated testing and **quality assurance** (**QA**) environments. Each container can represent a specific testing scenario, allowing developers and QA teams to run tests in isolated environments without interference. Containers provide a consistent and reproducible testing environment, improving the accuracy and efficiency of the testing process.

These are just a few examples of how containers can be used in various scenarios within cloud computing. Containers offer flexibility, scalability, and portability, making them a valuable tool for modern application development, deployment, and management. With their lightweight nature and efficient resource utilization, containers have revolutionized the way applications are built, deployed, and scaled in cloud environments.

Serverless computing

Serverless computing, also known as **function as a service** (**FaaS**), is a cloud computing model where developers focus on writing and deploying functions without the need to manage the underlying infrastructure. In serverless computing, functions are executed in response to specific events or triggers, and the cloud provider dynamically allocates resources to handle the workload. This model eliminates the need for provisioning and managing servers, allowing developers to focus on writing code. Serverless computing offers benefits such as automatic scaling, reduced operational overhead, and pay-per-use pricing. AWS Lambda and Azure Functions are popular serverless platforms that enable organizations to build event-driven applications, backend services, and APIs without worrying about infrastructure management.

Here are some key aspects and details to understand about serverless computing:

- Event-driven architecture: Serverless computing follows an event-driven architecture where functions are triggered by specific events or requests. These events can include HTTP requests, database updates, file uploads, or scheduled tasks. When an event occurs, the associated function is executed and the required resources are automatically provisioned and managed by the cloud provider.

- Pay-per-use model: Serverless platforms typically charge users based on the actual usage of their functions, rather than charging for idle resources. This pay-per-use model offers cost savings, as organizations only pay for the actual execution time as well as the resources consumed by their functions. It also allows for automatic scaling, where additional instances of the function are created as the demand increases.

- Function scalability: Serverless platforms are designed to handle scalable workloads. Functions automatically scale up or down based on the incoming workload, ensuring optimal performance and resource utilization. The cloud provider manages the infrastructure scaling behind the scenes, allowing developers to focus on writing the code.

- Stateless execution: Serverless functions are stateless, meaning they don't maintain any persistent state or context between invocations. Each function execution is independent and isolated, making it easier to scale and distribute requests. If state needs to be maintained, it can be stored in external databases or services, such as object storage or a **database as a service** (**DBaaS**).

- Vendor-specific implementations: Different cloud providers offer their own serverless computing platforms, such as AWS Lambda, Azure Functions, and Google Cloud Functions. While the underlying principles remain the same, there may be variations in programming languages, runtime environments, and additional services provided by each vendor.

- Use cases: Serverless computing is well-suited for event-driven, lightweight, and scalable applications. It is commonly used for tasks such as data processing, real-time file processing, microservices architectures, chatbots, API integrations, and IoT data processing. The serverless model allows developers to focus on writing the business logic without worrying about server management and infrastructure maintenance.

- Development and deployment: Developers typically write serverless functions using supported programming languages such as JavaScript, Python, or Java. The functions are packaged into deployment artifacts and uploaded to the serverless platform. The cloud provider handles the deployment, scaling, and execution of the functions, ensuring high availability and fault tolerance.

Serverless computing offers several advantages, including reduced operational overhead, automatic scalability, cost optimization, and faster time-to-market. By abstracting away infrastructure management, serverless computing enables developers to focus on building application logic, increases development agility, and allows organizations to optimize resource usage and costs.

Serverless computing, or FaaS, offers numerous benefits that can greatly enhance application development and deployment. Here are the key benefits of serverless computing:

- Reduced operational overhead: With serverless computing, developers no longer need to manage or provision servers, operating systems, or infrastructure components. The cloud provider takes care of these tasks, allowing developers to focus solely on writing the application logic. This reduction in operational overhead translates to less time spent on infrastructure management and maintenance, enabling teams to be more productive and efficient.

- Cost optimization: Serverless computing follows a pay-per-use model, where users are billed based on the actual execution time and resources consumed by their functions. This means organizations only pay for the exact amount of resources needed to handle their workload, eliminating the cost of idle resources. Additionally, serverless platforms automatically scale functions based on demand, ensuring optimal resource utilization and cost efficiency.

- Auto-scaling: Serverless platforms have built-in auto-scaling capabilities, allowing functions to scale up or down based on the incoming workload. As the number of requests increases, additional instances of the function are automatically provisioned to handle the load. Conversely, when the workload decreases, the platform scales down the resources to avoid unnecessary costs. This auto-scaling feature ensures that applications can handle sudden spikes in traffic without any manual intervention.

- Improved developer productivity: Serverless computing allows developers to focus solely on writing the business logic of their applications without worrying about infrastructure management. This improves developer productivity as they can dedicate more time to coding and building features, rather than dealing with server setup, configuration, and maintenance tasks. It also promotes faster development cycles and shorter time-to-market for applications.

- High availability and fault tolerance: Serverless platforms inherently provide high availability and fault tolerance. Functions are automatically distributed across multiple availability zones, ensuring that they can withstand failures in specific data centers or regions. If a function instance fails, the platform automatically spins up a new instance to handle subsequent requests. This built-in resilience ensures that applications remain highly available, reducing the risk of downtime and data loss.

- Scalability and elasticity: Serverless platforms excel at handling variable workloads and sudden spikes in traffic. Functions can scale almost instantly to accommodate increased demand and then scale back down when the load decreases. This scalability and elasticity enable organizations to handle unpredictable or bursty workloads without over-provisioning resources, leading to improved performance and user experience.

- Seamless integration with other services: Serverless computing integrates well with other cloud services and components. It enables developers to easily connect functions with storage services, databases, messaging systems, event streams, and other cloud resources. This seamless integration allows for the creation of powerful and complex applications that leverage the full capabilities of the cloud ecosystem.

Serverless computing offers several significant benefits, including reduced operational overhead, cost optimization, auto-scaling, improved developer productivity, high availability, fault tolerance, scalability, and seamless integration. These advantages make serverless computing an attractive option for organizations looking to streamline their application development processes, optimize resource utilization, and achieve greater efficiency in the cloud environment.

FaaS platforms, such as AWS Lambda and Azure Functions, are at the forefront of serverless computing, offering developers a powerful and scalable environment to deploy and run their code. Here are some details on FaaS platforms.

AWS Lambda

AWS Lambda is a leading FaaS platform provided by AWS. It allows developers to run their code in response to events without having to manage or provision servers. Lambda supports multiple programming languages including Python, Java, Node.js, C#, and Go. It offers seamless integration with other AWS services, enabling developers to build complex and event-driven applications. Lambda functions are triggered by events such as API calls, file uploads, database changes, and messaging system events. Here's an example of creating an AWS Lambda function using the AWS Management Console:

1. Sign in to the AWS Management Console:

   Go to the AWS Management Console (`https://aws.amazon.com/console/`) and sign in with your AWS account.

2. Create a Lambda function:

    I.   Click on **Services** at the top of the page, then select **Lambda** from the **Compute** section.

    II.   Click on the **Create function** button.

    III. Choose the **Author from scratch** option.

    IV. Fill in the required details:

- Function name: Give your Lambda function a name (e.g., `MyLambdaFunction`).

- Runtime: Choose the runtime environment for your function (e.g., Node.js, Python, Java, etc.).

- In the **Permissions** section, you can choose an existing execution role or create a new one. Execution roles define the permissions that the Lambda function has when interacting with other AWS services.

    V.   Click on the **Create function** button to create your Lambda function.

3. Write the Lambda function code:

In the function editor, you can write the code for your Lambda function based on the selected runtime.

Here is an example (Node.js):

```javascript
exports.handler = async (event, context) => {
  console.log("Lambda function executed!");
  return {
    statusCode: 200,
    body: JSON.stringify({ message: "Hello from AWS Lambda!" }),
  };
};
```

4. Test the Lambda function:

You can test your Lambda function using the **Test** button in the AWS Lambda console. You can create sample test events or use test data to check the function's behavior.

5. Configure a trigger (optional):

Lambda functions can be triggered by various events, such as HTTP requests, file uploads, database changes, and so on. You can set up triggers in the **Add trigger** section of the Lambda function configuration.

For example, to create an HTTP trigger, you can use API Gateway as the trigger.

6. Deploy the Lambda function:

    Once your Lambda function is working as expected, click on the **Deploy** button to deploy the latest changes.

7. Test the Lambda function in action:

    If you have set up a trigger, test your Lambda function by invoking the trigger event. For example, if it's an HTTP trigger, use the provided URL to make an HTTP request.

That's it! You have successfully created an AWS Lambda function and tested it with a trigger (if applicable). Your Lambda function is now ready to be used and will execute whenever the defined trigger conditions are met. The following figure depicts the use of Lambda functions in an AWS environment. It shows how the function interacts with DynamoDB and S3 storage bucket:

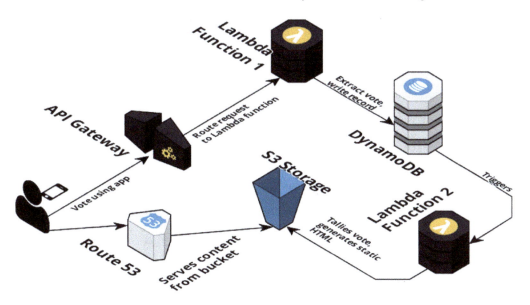

Figure 3.2 – Lambda function in an AWS environment

Azure Functions

Azure Functions is Microsoft's FaaS offering within the Azure cloud platform. It provides a serverless environment for developers to build and deploy event-driven applications. Azure Functions supports various programming languages, including C#, JavaScript, Python, PowerShell, and TypeScript. It integrates well with other Azure services and can be triggered by events from sources such as HTTP requests, timers, message queues, and data changes. Azure Functions offers flexibility and scalability to handle workloads of varying sizes and complexity.

Here's an example of creating an Azure Function using the Azure web portal:

1. Sign in to the Azure portal:

   Go to the Azure web portal (`https://portal.azure.com/`) and sign in with your Azure account.

2. Create a function app:

   A function app is a container for your functions. It provides the runtime environment for your functions to run. Complete the following steps:

   I.   Click on **Create a resource** in the Azure portal.

   II.   Search for `Function App` and click on **Function App** from the search results.

   III. Click **Create** to start the function app creation process.

   IV.   Fill in the required details:

   - App name: Choose a unique name for your function app (e.g., `MyFunctionApp`).

   - Subscription: Select the desired Azure subscription.

   - Resource group: Create a new one or use an existing resource group to organize your resources.

   - OS: Choose Windows or Linux, depending on your requirements.

   - Hosting plan: Choose the appropriate hosting plan (**consumption plan** for serverless execution or **app service plan** for dedicated resources).

   - Region: Select the region where you want to deploy your function app.

   V.   Click **Review + create**, then **Create** to create the function app.

3. Create a function:

   After the function app is deployed, you can create a new function inside it:

   I.   Go to your function app in the Azure portal.

   II.   Click on **Functions** in the left menu.

   III. Click on **+ Add** to create a new function.

   IV.   Choose a development environment:

   - Select **In-portal** for a browser-based code editor or **VS Code** if you prefer to develop locally.

   V.   Choose a template:

   - For this example, select a template based on the language you prefer (e.g., JavaScript, C#, or Python).

VI.   Configure the function:

- Give your function a name.

- Choose the **Authorization level** (anonymous, function, or admin) to define how your function can be accessed.

- Click **Create** to create the function.

4.   Write and test your function:

Now, you can write the code for your function. The code will be specific to the chosen template and language. For example, if you selected the JavaScript template, you'll be writing Node.js code. Complete the following steps:

I.   Edit the function code according to your requirements.

II.   Click **Save** when you're done.

To test your function, you can use the **Test** tab in the function editor. You can provide sample input and see the output of your function.

5.   Trigger and deploy your function:

Azure Functions can be triggered by various events, such as HTTP requests, timers, or messages from Azure services. You can configure the trigger type for your function under the **Integrate** tab. Once your function is working as expected, click **Deploy** to deploy the latest changes to the live environment.

That's it! You have successfully set up an Azure Function and deployed it to the Azure cloud. Your function is now ready to execute whenever its trigger conditions are met.

Figure 3.4 depicts how Azure Blob Storage is deployed in an Azure cloud infrastructure. Please note how the storage is being accessed from the Azure Front Door service:

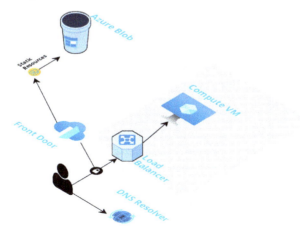

Figure 3.3 – Azure Blob Storage bucket in Azure Cloud

Event-driven architecture

FaaS platforms such as AWS Lambda and Azure Functions are designed for event-driven architectures. In this model, code is executed in response to specific events or triggers. Events can originate from various sources, such as API requests, file uploads, database updates, message queues, and IoT devices. FaaS platforms automatically manage the scaling, execution, and availability of functions, allowing developers to focus solely on writing the code that handles the events. This event-driven architecture enables developers to build highly scalable and responsive applications that respond in real time to user actions or system events.

- Pay-per-use pricing model: FaaS platforms follow a pay-per-use pricing model, which means developers are only charged for the actual execution time as well as resources consumed by their functions. This granular billing model offers cost efficiency, as organizations pay only for the processing time required for their code to run. It eliminates the need for provisioning and managing idle resources, resulting in significant cost savings, especially for applications with sporadic or unpredictable workloads.

- Developer productivity and deployment flexibility: FaaS platforms provide developers with the flexibility to deploy their functions independently, without the need to manage the underlying infrastructure. This allows for faster development cycles and shorter time-to-market. Developers can focus on writing modular and reusable functions, which can be easily composed and orchestrated to build complex applications. FaaS platforms also offer deployment automation and versioning capabilities, making it effortless to roll out updates or rollbacks.

- Scalability and fault tolerance: FaaS platforms excel at automatic scaling, allowing applications to handle varying workloads efficiently. As the incoming traffic increases, the platform automatically provisions additional function instances to cope with the demand. This horizontal scaling ensures optimal performance and responsiveness. FaaS platforms also provide built-in fault tolerance by distributing function instances across multiple availability zones or regions. If a function instance fails, the platform automatically replaces it with a new instance, ensuring high availability and reliability.

- Ecosystem and integration: FaaS platforms such as AWS Lambda and Azure Functions offer rich ecosystems of services, tools, and integrations. They provide pre-built connectors and libraries to interact with various cloud services, databases, storage systems, messaging queues, and more. This seamless integration enables developers to leverage the full capabilities of the cloud ecosystem and easily build applications that interact with other services or data sources.

FaaS platforms such as AWS Lambda and Azure Functions have revolutionized the way developers build and deploy applications by abstracting away the complexities of infrastructure management. With their event-driven architecture, pay-per-use pricing, scalability, and ease of integration, FaaS platforms empower developers to focus on writing application logic and delivering value to end users. They provide a highly efficient and cost-effective approach to building scalable and responsive applications in the cloud environment.

Serverless computing has gained popularity due to its ability to handle specific use cases effectively. Here are some details on the use cases for serverless computing:

- Event-driven applications: Serverless computing is particularly well-suited for event-driven applications. These applications are triggered by specific events, such as HTTP requests, database updates, file uploads, or messages from queues. With serverless platforms such as AWS Lambda and Azure Functions, developers can write functions that respond to these events in real time. Serverless functions are event-driven and automatically scale to handle incoming requests, ensuring efficient resource utilization. Event-driven applications include real-time data processing, webhooks, chatbots, and IoT applications.

- Backend services and APIs: Serverless computing is an excellent choice for building backend services and APIs. With serverless platforms, developers can deploy individual functions that handle specific tasks, such as data validation, database operations, authentication, or file processing. These functions can be orchestrated to build a complete backend service or API, allowing developers to focus on the business logic rather than managing infrastructure. Serverless backend services are highly scalable, as they automatically scale based on the incoming traffic. They also benefit from reduced operational overhead, as serverless platforms handle infrastructure provisioning and management.

- Batch processing and data pipelines: Serverless computing is well-suited for batch processing and data pipeline scenarios. Organizations often have tasks that require periodic execution, such as data processing, file transformations, or data analytics. Serverless platforms can be used to run functions that handle these tasks on a schedule or based on predefined triggers. By leveraging the auto-scaling capabilities of serverless computing, organizations can efficiently process large volumes of data without the need to manage and provision dedicated infrastructure.

- Microservices architecture: Serverless computing aligns well with microservices architecture, which focuses on breaking down monolithic applications into smaller, decoupled services. Each microservice can be implemented as a serverless function, providing independent scalability, fault tolerance, and flexibility. Serverless microservices can be developed, deployed, and scaled individually, allowing organizations to iterate and evolve specific components without impacting the entire application. This approach enables organizations to build highly modular, scalable, and maintainable applications.

- Prototyping and rapid development: Serverless computing provides a quick and efficient way to prototype and develop applications. With serverless platforms, developers can rapidly write and deploy functions without the need to set up and manage infrastructure. This enables faster experimentation and iteration, as developers can quickly test ideas and validate concepts. Serverless computing also facilitates rapid development by abstracting away the complexities of infrastructure, allowing developers to focus on writing application logic and delivering value to users.

Serverless computing offers a flexible and scalable approach to handling specific use cases in the cloud environment. By leveraging event-driven architectures, developers can build real-time applications, backend services, and data processing pipelines efficiently. Additionally, serverless computing complements microservices architecture and accelerates prototyping and rapid development. With its ability to automatically scale, reduced operational overhead, and pay-per-use pricing model, serverless computing has become an attractive option for organizations seeking agility and cost optimization in their cloud applications.

Summary

This chapter covered various essential topics that provide a comprehensive understanding of the primary key component, compute. It began with an introduction to compute in cloud computing, explaining its significance and the role it plays in enabling cloud-based services and applications.

The chapter further delved into considerations and cost optimization strategies for compute. It covered important factors to consider when selecting compute resources, including workload requirement analysis, cost optimization strategies, evaluating cloud provider offerings and SLAs, life cycle policies, and rightsizing compute resources. These topics provided you with insights into making informed decisions about resource allocation, optimizing costs, and maximizing resource utilization in cloud environments.

Throughout the chapter, you gained knowledge about the fundamental concepts of compute in cloud computing, explored different compute types and their use cases, and learned about important considerations and strategies for cost optimization. You also understood the significance of workload analysis, selecting the right compute type, and efficiently managing compute resources. By the end of the chapter, you have developed a strong foundation in compute concepts, enabling you to make informed decisions when designing and managing cloud architectures.

The next chapter, *Storage: Cloud Perspective*, explores the crucial aspect of storage in cloud computing. It delves into the fundamentals of cloud storage, including the technologies, architectures, and considerations involved in establishing and managing storage in the cloud.

4

Storage

This chapter provides a comprehensive exploration of the essential components and concepts related to storage in cloud services and introduces you to the fundamental role of storage solutions in cloud computing. It covers a range of cloud storage types, including object storage, file storage, block storage, and hybrid storage, all while discussing their unique characteristics and use cases. This chapter also emphasizes essential considerations for selecting and managing cloud storage, such as security measures, performance factors, data transfer and migration strategies, data durability, availability, and scalability. Furthermore, it provides practical insights into cost optimization strategies for cloud storage, including data life cycle management, storage tiers, data deduplication, compression techniques, and cost monitoring and analysis. By the end of this chapter, you will have gained a comprehensive understanding of cloud storage and be well-equipped to make informed decisions on storage solutions, ensuring cost-effectiveness and data integrity in cloud computing environments.

This chapter examines different storage options in the cloud. It covers traditional storage approaches such as block storage, which provides raw storage volumes that can be attached to VMs, and file storage, which allows for the creation and management of shared filesystems. This chapter also explores object storage, a highly scalable and durable storage option that is ideal for storing unstructured data such as images, videos, and documents. The benefits of each storage option, including scalability, durability, and cost-effectiveness, will be discussed in detail.

Throughout this chapter, real-world use cases and examples will be provided to illustrate the practical applications of storage in cloud infrastructure.

In this chapter, we will cover the following topics:

- Cloud storage types
- Considerations and cost optimization strategies for storage

By the end of this chapter, you will have gained a comprehensive understanding of the storage components in cloud infrastructure. You will be familiar with different storage options such as block storage, file storage, and object storage. Additionally, you will have a clear understanding of the benefits and considerations associated with each storage option, enabling you to make informed decisions when designing and implementing cloud-based solutions.

Technical requirements

To fully engage with the content of this chapter on cloud computing architecture, you should have a basic understanding of computer systems, networking concepts, and information technology.

Additionally, the following technical requirements are recommended:

- **Internet access**: You should have a reliable internet connection to access online resources, references, and examples related to cloud computing.

- **A computing device**: A desktop computer, laptop, tablet, or smartphone with a modern web browser is necessary to read the chapter content and access any online materials.

- **A web browser**: The latest version of a modern web browser such as Google Chrome, Mozilla Firefox, Microsoft Edge, or Safari is recommended. This ensures compatibility and optimal viewing experience of web-based resources and interactive content.

- **Familiarity with cloud services**: Some familiarity with cloud services and their basic functionalities will enhance your understanding of this chapter. This includes knowledge of basic storage, operating systems, VMs, and servers.

Introduction to storage in cloud computing

This section serves as a comprehensive introduction to the fundamental concepts and importance of storage in the context of cloud infrastructure. In this section, you will gain a deep understanding of the crucial roles that storage plays in enabling and supporting cloud-based services and applications.

Throughout this section, real-world examples and industry case studies will be incorporated to illustrate how organizations leverage storage in the cloud. You will gain insights into how storage resources are utilized in various domains such as e-commerce, media streaming, data analytics, and more. These examples bring the concepts to life and demonstrate the practical applications and benefits of storage in cloud computing.

Furthermore, this section explores considerations such as cost optimization, performance tuning, security, and data management in the context of storage. You will understand the importance of selecting the right storage resources to meet specific application requirements and business objectives. By the end of this section, you will have a solid foundation in storage concepts in cloud computing. You will appreciate the integral role these components play in building robust and scalable cloud infrastructures. Armed with this knowledge, you will be able to make informed decisions about storage options, effectively design and manage cloud-based solutions, and leverage the full potential of storage resources in their cloud environments.

Storage resources form a fundamental aspect of cloud computing, serving as the backbone for executing applications and services in the cloud environment. In this section, we will explore storage models that enable organizations to leverage the scalability, flexibility, and efficiency of the cloud. Serverless computing offers a flexible and scalable approach to handle specific use cases in the cloud environment. By leveraging event-driven architectures, developers can build real-time applications, backend services, and data processing pipelines efficiently. Additionally, serverless computing complements microservices architecture and accelerates prototyping and rapid development. With its ability to automatically scale, reduced operational overhead, and pay-per-use pricing model, serverless computing has become an attractive option for organizations seeking agility and cost optimization in their cloud applications.

In this section, we will provide an overview of the different storage options available in cloud computing. We will discuss the various types of cloud storage services and their characteristics, enabling you to understand and choose the most suitable storage solution for their specific requirements. The section will cover topics such as object storage, block storage, file storage, and archival storage. You will learn about the key features, benefits, and use cases of each storage type. Additionally, this section will explore the concepts of data durability, availability, and scalability in cloud storage. By the end of this section, you will have a comprehensive understanding of the different storage options available in the cloud and be equipped to make informed decisions regarding your storage needs in a cloud computing environment.

Exploring storage options in cloud computing

In this section, you will delve into the world of cloud storage and explore the various types of storage services available in cloud computing. This section aims to provide a comprehensive understanding of the different storage options and their specific use cases. You will learn about popular storage types such as object storage, block storage, file storage, and archival storage. You will gain insights into the characteristics, benefits, and limitations of each storage type, enabling you to make informed decisions based on their specific storage requirements. Additionally, this section will cover essential concepts such as data durability, availability, and scalability in the context of cloud storage. By the end of this section, you will have a clear understanding of the different cloud storage types and their applications, empowering you to select the most appropriate storage solution for your needs in a cloud computing environment.

Storage is a critical component of cloud computing, enabling the persistent storage and retrieval of data in a scalable and reliable manner. In this section, we will delve into different storage options available in cloud computing and their use cases.

Block storage

Block storage is a type of cloud storage that breaks data into individual blocks, which are then stored independently. Each block is assigned a unique identifier and can be accessed and manipulated individually. Unlike other storage types, such as object storage or file storage, block storage does not have a hierarchical structure or metadata associated with each block.

One of the key characteristics of block storage is its low-level access to data. It provides direct access to storage blocks, allowing for efficient read and write operations at the block level. This level of access is particularly useful in scenarios that require random or frequent read/write operations, such as databases or VM disk storage.

Block storage offers several benefits. Firstly, it provides high performance and low latency, making it suitable for applications that require fast and consistent I/O operations. It allows for efficient storage allocation and utilization as blocks can be allocated and released independently without affecting the rest of the storage. Additionally, block storage supports features such as snapshots and cloning, enabling data protection, backup, and rapid provisioning of new storage volumes.

Block storage is commonly used in scenarios where data needs to be directly accessed by applications or operating systems. It serves as the underlying storage layer for various systems, including databases, VMs, and high-performance computing clusters. With block storage, applications can achieve precise control over data storage and achieve better performance optimization.

It's important to note that block storage is typically associated with higher management complexity compared to other storage types. As it requires manual partitioning and management of storage blocks, organizations may need to implement additional tools or techniques for effective administration and provisioning of block storage resources.

Overall, block storage provides a flexible and scalable storage solution suitable for demanding workloads that require fast and direct access to data. Its characteristics and features make it an essential component in cloud infrastructure for applications that require high performance, data integrity, and efficient storage management.

Block storage offers several advantages for performance-sensitive applications that require fast and consistent I/O operations. These advantages make it a preferred choice for organizations looking to optimize their storage infrastructure for high-performance workloads. Here are some key advantages of block storage:

- **Low latency**: Block storage provides direct access to storage blocks, resulting in low latency for read and write operations. This is crucial for applications that require real-time data processing or low response times, such as financial trading systems, real-time analytics, or high-performance databases.

- **High throughput**: Block storage is designed to handle high-volume data transfers efficiently. It can deliver high throughput, enabling applications to process large amounts of data quickly.

This is particularly beneficial for applications that deal with streaming data, video processing, scientific simulations, or data-intensive analytics.

- **Predictable performance**: With block storage, performance can be precisely controlled and optimized for specific applications. Administrators can allocate dedicated resources and adjust parameters to meet the performance requirements of individual applications. This predictability ensures consistent performance even during peak usage periods, ensuring smooth and reliable operations.

- **Scalability**: Block storage allows for easy scalability as storage needs grow. Organizations can add more storage blocks to accommodate increasing data volumes without disrupting existing operations. This scalability is essential for applications that experience rapid data growth or require on-demand scaling to handle variable workloads.

- **Data protection**: Block storage offers features such as snapshots and cloning, which enable efficient data protection and backup strategies. Snapshots allow for point-in-time copies of data, enabling quick recovery in case of data loss or corruption. Cloning allows for rapid provisioning of new storage volumes by creating copies of existing blocks, reducing downtime during resource scaling or testing scenarios.

- **Flexibility**: Block storage provides flexibility in terms of storage management and allocation. Administrators have granular control over storage resources, allowing them to allocate storage blocks based on specific application requirements. This flexibility enables efficient utilization of storage resources and cost optimization.

- **Compatibility**: Block storage is widely supported by various operating systems, hypervisors, and applications. This compatibility ensures seamless integration with existing infrastructure and minimizes the need for application modifications or complex data migration processes.

Overall, the advantages of block storage make it an ideal choice for performance-sensitive applications that require low latency, high throughput, scalability, data protection, and fine-grained control over storage resources. By leveraging the benefits of block storage, organizations can optimize the performance of their applications, enhance user experience, and achieve efficient storage management in cloud environments.

Block storage is widely used in various use cases, especially those that require high-performance storage and reliable data access. Here are some common use cases where block storage excels:

- **Databases**: Block storage is well-suited for database applications that demand fast and consistent I/O operations. Databases rely on random access to data, and block storage provides the necessary low-latency and high-throughput performance required for efficient database operations. Whether it's a **relational database management system** (**RDBMS**) or a NoSQL database, block storage ensures optimal performance for data-intensive applications such as transaction processing, data warehousing, and analytics.

- **High-performance computing** (**HPC**): HPC applications often deal with massive datasets and require high-performance storage to process large volumes of data quickly. Block storage provides the speed, scalability, and predictable performance needed for HPC workloads such as scientific simulations, computational fluid dynamics, weather modeling, and seismic data analysis. It allows researchers and scientists to process complex computations efficiently and make timely discoveries.

- **Content delivery**: **Content delivery networks** (**CDNs**) rely heavily on block storage to store and distribute static content globally. Block storage enables fast and reliable delivery of multimedia files, software updates, website assets, and other digital content. With the ability to handle high volumes of data and provide low-latency access, block storage ensures optimal content delivery performance, enhancing the end user experience.

- **Virtualized environments**: Virtualization technologies, such as hypervisors, rely on block storage to store VM images and virtual disks. Block storage provides the necessary performance and scalability to support multiple VMs running concurrently. It allows organizations to consolidate their infrastructure, optimize resource utilization, and provide flexible storage allocation to virtualized environments.

- **Backup and disaster recovery**: Block storage plays a crucial role in backup and disaster recovery strategies. By using block-level snapshots, organizations can take efficient and point-in-time backups of their data, ensuring data integrity and minimizing recovery time in case of data loss or system failures. Block storage's ability to handle high-throughput data transfer also makes it suitable for replicating and synchronizing data between geographically dispersed locations for disaster recovery purposes.

- **DevOps environments**: In DevOps practices, where CI/CD is key, block storage is essential for managing application life cycle processes. It provides the persistent storage needed for storing application code, build artifacts, and configuration files. Block storage ensures that the resources required for development, testing, and production environments remain consistent and accessible throughout the software development life cycle.

Block storage is well-suited for use cases that require high-performance storage, low latency, scalability, and data reliability. Whether it's powering databases, supporting HPC workloads, delivering content globally, facilitating virtualization, enabling backup and disaster recovery, or supporting DevOps practices, block storage provides the necessary infrastructure for efficient and reliable data management in various cloud computing scenarios.

File storage

File storage is a type of cloud storage that organizes and stores data in a hierarchical structure of files and folders. It provides a shared storage environment where multiple users and applications can access and manipulate files concurrently. Here are some key characteristics and details of file storage:

- **Structure**: File storage organizes data into a hierarchical structure with directories (folders) and files. This structure allows for easy organization, navigation, and management of data. Users can create, delete, modify, and share files within the filesystem.

- **Shared access**: One of the main advantages of file storage is its ability to provide shared access to files. Multiple users or applications can access and collaborate on the same files simultaneously. This makes file storage suitable for collaborative work environments, where teams need to access and share files across different locations and devices.

- **File-level operations**: File storage systems allow users to perform operations at the file level, such as reading, writing, appending, and modifying individual files. This level of granularity enables efficient file manipulation and flexibility in managing data.

- **Network File System (NFS) and Common Internet File System (CIFS)**: File storage often utilizes industry-standard protocols such as NFS and CIFS to enable seamless file sharing across different operating systems and platforms. NFS is commonly used in Unix-like environments, while CIFS (or **Server Message Block (SMB)**) is prevalent in Windows-based systems.

- **Scalability**: File storage systems are designed to scale horizontally, allowing for the addition of more storage capacity as data needs grow. This scalability is achieved by distributing the data across multiple storage nodes or servers, providing ample storage space for growing file repositories.

- **File-level snapshots**: File storage systems often offer snapshot capabilities, allowing users to create point-in-time copies of their files or directories. Snapshots provide data protection and recovery options, enabling users to roll back to previous versions of files or restore deleted files.

- **Compatibility**: File storage is compatible with a wide range of applications and workloads. It can accommodate various file formats, making it suitable for storing and accessing documents, media files, application files, logs, and other types of unstructured data.

- **Access control and permissions**: File storage systems include robust access control mechanisms, enabling administrators to set permissions and restrict access to files and directories. This ensures data security and privacy by defining who can read, write, or modify specific files.

- **Data consistency**: File storage systems ensure data consistency across multiple access points. When multiple users or applications modify the same file simultaneously, file-locking mechanisms prevent conflicts and maintain data integrity.

File storage is commonly used in scenarios that involve shared file access, collaboration, and the management of unstructured data. It is well-suited for use cases such as document management, content repositories, media storage and streaming, shared file servers, and file-based workflows in various industries. It offers shared access capabilities, allowing multiple users and applications to concurrently access and manipulate files within the storage system. Here are some key points to understand about file storage and its shared access capabilities:

- **Hierarchical structure**: File storage organizes data into a hierarchical structure, similar to a traditional filesystem. It consists of directories (folders) that can contain subdirectories and files. This hierarchical structure enables easy organization and navigation of data, providing a familiar filesystem interface.

- **Shared access**: One of the primary advantages of file storage is its ability to provide shared access to files. Multiple users or applications can access and collaborate on the same files simultaneously. This shared access enables teams to work together, share information, and collaborate on projects more effectively.

- **Concurrent read and write operations**: File storage allows concurrent read and write operations on files, meaning multiple users or applications can read from and write to the same file simultaneously. This capability is crucial for collaborative work environments, where real-time access to shared files is essential for productivity.

- **File locking**: To prevent conflicts when multiple users attempt to modify the same file simultaneously, file storage systems employ file-locking mechanisms. File locking ensures that only one user or application has exclusive write access to a file at any given time. Other users can still read the file but cannot modify it until the lock is released.

- **Access control**: File storage systems provide granular access control mechanisms to manage permissions for files and directories. Administrators can define user or group-based access permissions, specifying who can read, write, modify, or delete files. Access control ensures data security and restricts unauthorized access to sensitive files.

- **File versioning**: Many file storage systems offer file versioning capabilities. File versioning allows users to keep track of multiple versions of a file, enabling easy retrieval of previous versions if needed. This feature provides data protection, recovery, and the ability to revert to the previous state of a file.

- **Collaboration features**: File storage platforms often include collaboration features, such as file sharing, commenting, and real-time editing. These features enable teams to work together seamlessly, share feedback, and make changes collaboratively, enhancing productivity and streamlining workflows.

- **Compatibility**: File storage supports a wide range of file formats and is compatible with various operating systems and applications. This versatility makes it suitable for storing and accessing different types of files, including documents, images, videos, audio files, and more.

- **Scalability**: File storage systems can scale horizontally to accommodate growing storage needs. As data requirements increase, additional storage nodes or servers can be added to expand the capacity of the file storage infrastructure. This scalability ensures that organizations can handle expanding file repositories efficiently.

File storage with shared access capabilities is widely used in various industries and applications. It is particularly beneficial for collaborative projects, document management, content repositories, media storage and streaming, and file-based workflows. The ability to share and collaborate on files in real time enhances teamwork, simplifies data management, and improves overall productivity.

NFS and CIFS are two popular network protocols that are used for file sharing and accessing remote files over a network. Let's explore each of these protocols in detail.

NFS is a distributed filesystem protocol that allows clients to access files and directories on remote servers as if they were local. NFS is widely used in Unix-like systems and is supported by various operating systems, including Linux and Unix.

The following are the key features and characteristics of NFS:

- **Remote file access**: NFS enables clients to access files and directories stored on remote servers over a network. It provides a transparent mechanism for remote file mounting, allowing users to access remote files as if they were local.

- **Client-server architecture**: NFS follows a client-server model, where the server exports its filesystems, and clients mount them to access the files. The server provides the shared filesystem, and clients request file operations through the NFS protocol.

- **Transparent file access**: NFS provides transparent file access, meaning that users interact with remote files as if they were stored locally. They can perform standard file operations such as reading, writing, and modifying files without being aware of the underlying network communication.

- **Caching and performance**: NFS incorporates caching mechanisms to improve performance. Clients can cache frequently accessed files locally, reducing the need for repeated network requests. This caching helps enhance the performance of file access operations.

CIFS, also known as SMB, is a network protocol designed for sharing files, printers, and other resources between networked computers. CIFS is widely used in Windows-based environments and is the native file-sharing protocol for Microsoft Windows.

Here are the key features and characteristics of CIFS:

- **Windows compatibility**: CIFS is the native file-sharing protocol for Windows operating systems. It enables seamless file sharing and collaboration between Windows machines and provides support for features such as file and print sharing, access control, and user authentication.

- **Cross-platform support**: While CIFS originated in the Windows environment, it is also supported by other operating systems such as Linux, macOS, and Unix. This cross-platform compatibility allows different operating systems to access and share files using the CIFS protocol.

- **Authentication and authorization**: CIFS incorporates authentication and authorization mechanisms to ensure secure access to shared resources. It supports user-level security, enabling administrators to define access rights and permissions for individual users or groups.

- **File locking**: CIFS provides file-locking mechanisms to prevent conflicts when multiple users attempt to access or modify the same file concurrently. File locking ensures data integrity and prevents data corruption due to simultaneous modifications.

- **Distributed filesystems**: CIFS supports the creation and management of distributed filesystems, allowing multiple servers to share files and resources. This enables scalable and fault-tolerant file-sharing architectures.

Both NFS and CIFS have their strengths and are commonly used in different environments. NFS is popular in Unix-like systems and is known for its simplicity and performance in those environments. CIFS, on the other hand, is widely used in Windows-based environments, offering seamless integration with Windows operating systems and providing advanced features such as access control and user authentication.

In summary, NFS and CIFS are network protocols used for file sharing and remote file access. NFS is commonly used in Unix-like systems, while CIFS is widely used in Windows-based environments. Understanding these protocols is essential for setting up efficient file sharing and accessing files across networks, ensuring seamless collaboration and resource sharing.

File storage plays a crucial role in various use cases, offering reliable and scalable solutions for managing and sharing files across organizations. Let's explore some common use cases for file storage:

- **Content management systems (CMSs)**:

    CMSs are widely used for creating, organizing, and publishing digital content. File storage is integral to CMS platforms as they require efficient management and storage of media files such as images, videos, documents, and other assets. File storage systems provide a centralized repository for storing and accessing these files, allowing CMS users to manage and distribute content seamlessly.

- **Shared file repositories**:

    In collaborative environments, shared file repositories are essential for teams to access and collaborate on files. File storage solutions enable the creation of shared folders or directories where multiple users can upload, modify, and retrieve files. This facilitates real-time collaboration, version control, and easy file sharing among team members. Shared file repositories are commonly used in project management, document sharing, and team collaboration scenarios.

- **Document management systems (DMSs)**:

    DMSs are designed to organize, track, and store documents efficiently. File storage systems provide the underlying infrastructure for storing and managing documents in DMS platforms. These systems allow users to upload, categorize, search, and retrieve documents with ease, ensuring secure access and version control. Document workflows, approvals, and permissions can also be integrated into file storage solutions to streamline document management processes.

- **Media libraries and archives**:

- Media-intensive industries such as broadcasting, entertainment, and advertising rely on file storage for managing large media libraries and archives. These industries deal with vast amounts of audio, video, and image files that require long-term storage and easy retrieval. File storage systems provide scalable and cost-effective solutions for organizing and preserving media assets, ensuring quick access and efficient media management.

- **Backup and disaster recovery**:

    File storage plays a critical role in backup and disaster recovery strategies. Organizations need reliable and scalable storage solutions to protect their data and ensure business continuity. File storage systems allow organizations to create backups of critical files and applications, enabling quick recovery in the event of data loss or system failures. By replicating files across multiple storage locations, file storage solutions provide data redundancy and resilience.

- **File sharing and collaboration platforms**:

    File storage is the backbone of file-sharing and collaboration platforms, enabling users to share files with colleagues, clients, or external stakeholders. These platforms offer secure file sharing, version control, and collaboration features such as document commenting and real-time editing. File storage systems provide the necessary infrastructure to support these features, ensuring secure and efficient file sharing among users.

In summary, file storage has diverse use cases across various industries and organizational needs. Whether it's managing digital content, facilitating collaboration, preserving media assets, or ensuring data backup and recovery, file storage solutions provide the necessary infrastructure to store, manage, and share files effectively.

Understanding the use cases for file storage helps organizations select the appropriate storage solutions that align with their specific requirements and enhance their overall productivity and data management capabilities.

Object storage

Object storage is a storage architecture that organizes and manages data as discrete units called objects. Unlike traditional file or block storage, which organizes data into a hierarchical filesystem or fixed-sized blocks, object storage stores data as independent objects with unique identifiers. Each object consists of data, metadata, and a unique identifier, typically in the form of a **globally unique identifier (GUID)**.

Let's look at the characteristics of object storage :

- **Scalability**: Object storage is highly scalable, allowing organizations to store and manage vast amounts of data. It eliminates the limitations of traditional storage systems, as objects can be added or removed without affecting the overall system performance. This scalability makes it suitable for applications with massive data requirements, such as big data analytics, content delivery networks, and archival storage.

- **Metadata**: Objects in object storage are associated with metadata, which provide descriptive information about the object. Metadata can include attributes such as object name, creation date, file type, and user-defined metadata. This rich metadata allows for efficient searching, indexing, and categorization of objects, facilitating data organization and retrieval.

- **Durability and reliability**: Object storage systems employ data redundancy mechanisms to ensure high durability and reliability. Objects are typically stored across multiple physical devices or distributed storage nodes, ensuring that data remains intact even in the event of hardware failures. Redundancy techniques such as data replication or erasure coding are used to protect against data loss and ensure data integrity.

- **Data accessibility**: Object storage provides universal access to data through simple **application programming interfaces (APIs)** such as **Representational State Transfer (REST)** or **Simple Storage Service (S3)**. These APIs allow applications and users to access and manipulate objects over the network, making it easier to integrate object storage with various applications, cloud services, and platforms.

- **Cost-effectiveness**: Object storage offers cost advantages compared to traditional storage systems. It eliminates the need for expensive infrastructure upgrades and simplifies data management by leveraging commodity hardware and distributed storage architectures. Object storage systems are designed to optimize storage efficiency, reducing overall storage costs, and allowing organizations to scale their storage infrastructure economically.

Amazon S3, Google Cloud Storage, and Azure Blob Storage are three prominent cloud-based object storage services offered by leading cloud service providers. These services provide highly scalable, durable, and secure storage solutions for a wide range of applications and use cases:

Amazon S3 is a widely used object storage service offered by **Amazon Web Services (AWS)**. It allows users to store and retrieve any amount of data from anywhere on the web. Some of the key features and details of Amazon S3 are as follows:

- **Scalability**: Amazon S3 is designed to scale seamlessly, allowing users to store and retrieve virtually unlimited amounts of data. It can handle any volume of data, from a few gigabytes to multiple petabytes, without any upfront capacity planning.

- **Durability and availability**: Amazon S3 provides high durability by automatically replicating data across multiple Availability Zones within a region. It offers 99.999999999% (11 nines) durability, ensuring that data remains intact even in the event of hardware failures or natural disasters.

- **Security**: Amazon S3 offers robust security features to protect stored data. It supports access control mechanisms, including **Identity and Access Management (IAM)** policies, bucket policies, and **access control lists (ACLs)**. Additionally, it provides encryption options for data at rest and in transit. *Figure 4.1* depicts the use of an object storage AWS S3 bucket in an AWS cloud environment. Please note that the S3 bucket lies outside of the Availability Zone shown in this figure:

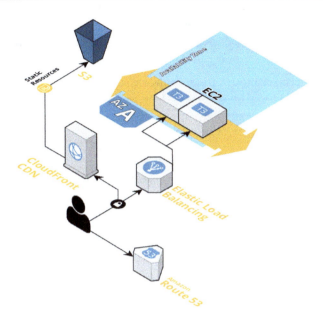

Figure 4.1 – An S3 object storage bucket in an AWS environment

Now, let's understand the steps involved in setting up an S3 bucket in a basic AWS cloud architecture.

Setting up an S3 storage bucket in AWS involves a few simple steps. Here's a step-by-step guide to creating an S3 bucket:

1. **Sign in to the AWS console**: Log in to your AWS account using your credentials at https://aws.amazon.com/console/.

2. **Open the S3 service**: Once logged in, go to the AWS Management Console and search for S3 in the **services** search bar or navigate to the **Storage** section and click on **S3**.

3. **Create a bucket**: Click on the **Create bucket** button to start the process of creating a new S3 bucket.

4. **Configure bucket settings**: You'll need to configure various settings for your bucket, including the following:

    A. **Bucket name**: Provide a globally unique name for your bucket. Bucket names must be unique across all existing bucket names in AWS.

    B. **Region**: Choose the AWS region where you want your bucket to be created. Consider choosing the region closest to your users to reduce latency.

    C. **Block all public access**: Choose whether you want to block all public access to your bucket or allow public access (read or write) to some extent.

5. **Set up bucket permissions**: You can set up bucket permissions to control access to your S3 bucket. This includes bucket policies and ACLs. By default, the bucket owner has full control over the bucket.

6. **Configure advanced settings**: You can configure additional options such as logging, tags, events, and versioning based on your requirements. These settings help you manage and track activities within your bucket effectively.

7. **Review and create**: After configuring all the necessary settings, review your choices and click on the **Create bucket** button to create the S3 bucket.

8. **Bucket created**: Once the bucket has been created successfully, you will see it listed in your S3 dashboard.

That's it! You've now set up an S3 bucket in AWS. From here, you can start uploading objects (files) to your bucket and manage them as needed. Remember to follow AWS best practices for securing and managing your S3 bucket to ensure the safety of your data.

Now, to create an S3 bucket using the AWS **Command-Line Interface** (**CLI**) in the AWS CloudShell utility, follow these steps:

1. **Access AWS CloudShell**: Go to the AWS Management Console and click on the **Services** menu. In the **Security, Identity, & Compliance** section, click on **CloudShell**.

2. **AWS CLI installation**: AWS CloudShell comes pre-installed with the AWS CLI. If you are using the CLI on your local machine, make sure you have it installed and configured with your AWS credentials. In CloudShell, this step is not required as it's already set up.

3. **Create an S3 bucket**: To create an S3 bucket, open the AWS CloudShell terminal and execute the following command:

```
aws s3api create-bucket --bucket YOUR_BUCKET_NAME --region YOUR_
REGION
```

4. Replace YOUR_BUCKET_NAME with the desired name for your bucket and YOUR_REGION with the AWS region where you want to create the bucket (for example, us-east-1).

5. **Set up bucket permissions (optional)**: By default, the bucket owner has full control over the newly created bucket. If you want to grant public read access to the bucket, you can add the following command:

```
aws s3api put-bucket-acl --bucket YOUR_BUCKET_NAME --acl public-
read
```

This will set the bucket ACL to allow public read access to objects in the bucket.

6. **Configure advanced settings (optional)**: You can configure additional settings for your bucket using various CLI commands, such as enabling versioning, logging, and adding tags. Here are some examples:

    - Enable versioning:

    ```
    aws s3api put-bucket-versioning --bucket YOUR_BUCKET_NAME
    --versioning-configuration Status=Enabled
    ```

    - Enable server access logging:

    ```
    aws s3api put-bucket-logging --bucket YOUR_BUCKET_NAME --bucket-
    logging-status file://logging-config.json
    ```

    - Add tags to the bucket:

    ```
    aws s3api put-bucket-tagging --bucket YOUR_BUCKET_NAME --tagging
    file://tagging-config.json
    ```

> **Note**
>
> For the preceding commands, you need to provide the corresponding JSON files (`logging-config.json` and `tagging-config.json`) with the appropriate configurations.

Remember to replace `YOUR_BUCKET_NAME` and `YOUR_REGION` with your desired values in each command.

Once the commands are executed successfully, your S3 bucket will be created with the specified settings. You can check your S3 dashboard in the AWS Management Console to verify the bucket creation and configurations.

Google Cloud Storage

Google Cloud Storage is the object storage service provided by Google Cloud Platform. It offers scalable and globally distributed storage for a variety of use cases. Here are the key features and details of Google Cloud Storage:

- **Multi-regional and regional buckets**: Google Cloud Storage provides the flexibility to choose between multi-regional and regional storage buckets. Multi-regional buckets offer high availability and low-latency access across multiple regions, while regional buckets focus on a specific region for cost optimization.

- **Data transfer and network performance**: Google Cloud Storage leverages Google's global network infrastructure to provide fast and efficient data transfer. It offers options such as **Transfer Service** for on-premises data migration and **Direct Peering** for optimized network performance.

- **Life cycle management**: Google Cloud Storage includes life cycle management capabilities that allow users to automatically transition data to different storage classes based on predefined rules. This feature helps optimize storage costs by moving data to more cost-effective storage tiers as it ages.

To set up Google Cloud Storage using the Cloud Shell utility in Google Cloud Platform, follow these steps:

1. **Access Google Cloud Shell**: Go to the Google Cloud Console at `https://console.cloud.google.com/` and click on the **Activate Cloud Shell** button in the top-right corner of the screen.

2. **Create a Google Cloud Storage bucket**: In the Cloud Shell terminal, use the `gsutil mb` command to create a new Google Cloud Storage bucket. The syntax is as follows:

   ```
   gsutil mb -l REGION gs://YOUR_BUCKET_NAME
   ```

3. Replace `REGION` with the desired location for your bucket (for example, us-central1) and `YOUR_BUCKET_NAME` with a globally unique name for your bucket.

   Here's an example:

   ```
   gsutil mb -l us-central1 gs://my-gcp-storage-bucket
   ```

4. **Set access control for the bucket (optional)**:

   By default, newly created buckets have private access. If you want to make your bucket publicly readable, you can set the ACL using the `gsutil` command:

   ```
   gsutil defacl set public-read gs://YOUR_BUCKET_NAME
   ```

   This command sets the default ACL for the bucket to allow public read access.

5. **Upload objects to the bucket**: You can use the `gsutil cp` command to upload files or objects to your bucket. The syntax is as follows:

   ```
   gsutil cp LOCAL_FILE_PATH gs://YOUR_BUCKET_NAME
   ```

   Replace `LOCAL_FILE_PATH` with the path of the file you want to upload and `YOUR_BUCKET_NAME` with the name of your bucket.

   Here's an example:

   ```
   gsutil cp my_file.txt gs://my-gcp-storage-bucket
   ```

6. **View the bucket's contents**: To see the contents of your bucket, use the `gsutil ls` command:

   ```
   gsutil ls gs://YOUR_BUCKET_NAME
   ```

   Here's an example:

   ```
   gsutil ls gs://my-gcp-storage-bucket
   ```

7. **Download objects from the bucket**: You can also download objects from the bucket to your Cloud Shell environment using the `gsutil cp` command:

```
gsutil cp gs://YOUR_BUCKET_NAME/REMOTE_FILE_PATH LOCAL_
DESTINATION_PATH
```

Replace `REMOTE_FILE_PATH` with the path of the file in your bucket and `LOCAL_DESTINATION_PATH` with the path where you want to save the file in Cloud Shell.

Here's an example:

```
gsutil cp gs://my-gcp-storage-bucket/my_file.txt ~/Downloads/
```

That's it! You've now set up Google Cloud Storage and performed basic operations with your bucket using the Cloud Shell utility. Remember to replace `YOUR_BUCKET_NAME` and `REGION` with your preferred values throughout the commands.

Azure Blob Storage

Azure Blob Storage is Microsoft Azure's object storage service that offers highly scalable and secure storage for unstructured data. Here are the key features and details of Azure Blob Storage:

- **Blob tiers**: Azure Blob Storage provides different storage tiers to accommodate varying access patterns and cost requirements. These tiers include Hot, Cool, and Archive, and they offer different levels of availability, latency, and cost.

- **Data replication**: Azure Blob Storage ensures data durability and availability through replication options. Users can choose between **locally redundant storage (LRS)**, **zone-redundant storage (ZRS)**, **geo-redundant storage (GRS)**, and **read-access geo-redundant storage (RA-GRS)** to meet their data protection needs.

Let's see how we can configure and add Azure Blob storage in the Azure cloud platform:

1. **Sign in to the Azure portal**:

   Log in to your Azure account using your credentials at `https://portal.azure.com/`.

2. **Create a resource group (optional)**:

3. If you want to organize your resources, you can create a new resource group. This step is optional, but it helps manage resources effectively. Go to **Resource groups** in the left-hand menu, click on **Add**, and provide a unique name and region for the resource group.

4. **Create a storage account**:

   Now, let's create the Azure storage account to host your Blob Storage. In the Azure portal, do the following:

   I.   Click on **Create a resource** in the left-hand menu.

II. Search for `Storage account` in the search bar and select **Storage account - blob, file, table, queue**.

III. Click on the **Create** button.

5. **Configure storage account settings**:

You will be prompted to configure various settings for your storage account:

I. **Basics**:

- **Subscription**: Choose the appropriate subscription (if you have multiple)

- **Resource group**: Select the resource group you created or use an existing one

- **Storage account name**: Provide a globally unique name for your storage account

- **Region**: Choose the region where you want your storage account to be located

- **Performance**: Select the desired performance level (Standard or Premium)

- **Account kind**: Choose **StorageV2** for general-purpose storage, which includes Blob Storage

II. **Replication**:

- Choose the replication strategy for your storage account. This determines how data is replicated across different data centers. Options include LRS, GRS, and ZRS.

III. **Networking**:

- Configure network settings for your storage account. By default, public access is disallowed, and you can allow access from specific networks or virtual networks if needed.

IV. **Data protection**:

- Configure advanced data protection options such as soft delete, Azure Backup, and more.

V. Once you've configured all the settings, click on the **Review + create** button.

6. **Review and create**:

Review the settings you've configured for your storage account, and if everything looks good, click on the **Create** button to create the storage account.

7. **Access your storage account**:

Once the storage account has been created, you can access it by navigating to **Storage accounts** in the Azure portal and clicking on the name of your newly created storage account.

8. **Create a blob container**:

    Inside the storage account, you need to create a container to store your blobs. A container is a way to organize and group related blobs. To create a container, do the following:

    I.   In your storage account overview, click on **Containers** in the left-hand menu.

    II.   Click on the + **Container** button.

    III.   Provide a unique name for your container, choose the access level (private, public read access, or public read and write access), and click on the **Create** button.

9. **Upload blobs to the container**:

    With the container created, you can now start uploading blobs (files) to it. There are various ways to upload blobs, including using the Azure portal, Azure Storage Explorer, the Azure CLI, or SDKs.

That's it! You've set up Azure Blob Storage and created a container to store your blobs. You can start using the storage account to store and manage your objects (blobs).

Integration with Azure services

Azure Blob Storage seamlessly integrates with other Azure services, such as Azure Functions, Azure Data Lake Storage, and Azure Data Factory, enabling users to build comprehensive data workflows and applications.

These three object storage services provide organizations with highly scalable, durable, and secure storage solutions in the cloud. By leveraging these services, businesses can store, manage, and retrieve their data efficiently, benefiting from the reliability, scalability, and flexibility offered by the leading cloud service providers.

Object storage is a versatile storage solution offered by cloud service providers, such as Amazon S3, Google Cloud Storage, and Azure Blob Storage. Its unique characteristics make it suitable for various use cases, including backup and archival, media storage, and content delivery.

One significant use case for object storage is backup and archival. Organizations generate massive amounts of data that needs to be stored securely and retained for long periods. Object storage provides the durability and scalability required for backup and archival purposes. With its high durability and redundancy features, object storage ensures data integrity and long-term preservation. Organizations can leverage object storage to create reliable data backup and archival solutions, eliminating the need for complex on-premises infrastructure.

Media storage is another prominent use case for object storage. In the digital age, media content such as images, videos, and audio files are critical assets for many businesses. Object storage's ability to handle large file sizes and its seamless scalability make it an ideal choice for storing media content. By utilizing object storage, organizations can store and manage vast libraries of media assets efficiently.

Content creators, media agencies, and streaming platforms can leverage object storage to store, retrieve, and distribute media content with ease.

Additionally, object storage plays a crucial role in content delivery. With the increasing demand for fast and reliable content delivery, object storage's distributed architecture and global accessibility make it well-suited for serving static content, such as images, videos, and documents, to users worldwide. CDNs can leverage object storage to cache and deliver content efficiently, ensuring low latency access and improved user experience. Object storage's scalability and ability to handle high volumes of concurrent requests make it a preferred choice for content delivery use cases.

Furthermore, object storage provides benefits such as cost-effectiveness and simplified management. Object storage services often offer flexible pricing models, allowing organizations to pay for storage consumed and reducing upfront infrastructure costs. The simplicity of object storage APIs and integration with various cloud services and tools make it easy to manage and integrate into existing workflows. Object storage is well suited for storing and managing unstructured data generated by big data analytics applications. It allows organizations to store and analyze massive datasets efficiently. Object storage's scalability and distributed architecture support data-intensive workloads, enabling faster and more cost-effective data analysis. IoT generates vast amounts of data from connected devices. Object storage provides a scalable and flexible storage solution for storing IoT data streams. It allows organizations to capture, store, and analyze IoT-generated data, facilitating real-time insights and decision-making.

In summary, object storage is a powerful storage solution with a wide range of use cases. It excels in backup and archival scenarios, offering durability and scalability for long-term data retention. Its ability to handle large media files makes it ideal for media storage applications. Additionally, object storage enables efficient content delivery through CDNs, ensuring fast and reliable access to static content. With its cost-effectiveness and simplified management, object storage provides organizations with a reliable and scalable solution for their storage needs in the cloud.

The next section, *Considerations and cost optimization strategies for compute and storage*, focuses on practical considerations and strategies for optimizing compute and storage resources in cloud computing. You can expect to learn about various factors that need to be taken into account when designing and provisioning compute and storage resources in the cloud. This includes considerations such as workload requirements, scalability, performance, availability, and data durability. This section also delves into cost optimization strategies, highlighting techniques to right-size compute and storage resources, utilize spot instances or reserved instances effectively, and leverage storage tiering and life cycle policies to optimize costs. You will gain insights into best practices for cost optimization, resource allocation, and performance tuning to achieve a balance between performance and cost efficiency in your cloud deployments. This section aims to provide you with practical guidance on making informed decisions and implementing effective strategies to optimize your compute and storage resources in the cloud, ultimately helping you achieve better cost efficiency and performance in your cloud-based applications and services.

Considerations and cost optimization strategies for compute and storage

In this section, we will explore the key factors to consider when designing and provisioning compute and storage resources in the cloud, along with effective strategies to optimize costs. By the end of this section, you will have a comprehensive understanding of the various considerations involved in selecting the right compute and storage resources for their workloads. You will learn how to analyze workload requirements, scale resources efficiently, ensure optimal performance, and enhance availability and data durability. Moreover, you will gain valuable insights into cost optimization techniques, such as rightsizing resources, leveraging pricing models, and implementing storage tiering and life cycle policies. Armed with this knowledge, you will be equipped to make informed decisions and implement strategies to optimize your compute and storage resources, achieving a balance between cost efficiency and performance in your cloud deployments.

One of the key considerations is workload requirements. It is essential to understand the specific needs of the workload, such as CPU and memory requirements, I/O demands, and storage capacity. By analyzing workload characteristics, organizations can identify the most suitable compute and storage options that align with their performance expectations.

Scalability is another vital aspect to consider. Cloud environments should be able to handle workload growth and fluctuations effectively. Elasticity, the ability to scale resources up or down based on demand, is a desirable feature to ensure efficient resource utilization and cost savings. Choosing compute and storage services that offer seamless scalability, such as auto-scaling groups or storage scaling policies, can facilitate the management of workload spikes and provide flexibility in resource allocation.

Availability and data durability are critical considerations for mission-critical applications. High availability can be achieved through redundant compute instances or storage solutions with built-in replication and backup capabilities. It is crucial to evaluate the **service-level agreements** (**SLAs**) provided by cloud providers to ensure they meet the required uptime and data durability requirements.

Cost optimization plays a significant role in cloud infrastructure decision-making. Organizations need to assess the cost implications of compute and storage options and identify opportunities for optimization. Rightsizing resources involves matching the resource allocation to the actual workload demands to avoid overprovisioning. This can lead to cost savings by eliminating unnecessary resources. Understanding pricing models, such as on-demand, reserved instances, or spot instances, and utilizing pricing calculators can help optimize costs. Additionally, implementing storage tiering and life cycle policies, where less frequently accessed data is moved to lower-cost storage tiers, can provide further cost optimizations.

Considerations for security and compliance are crucial in compute and storage selection. Organizations must assess the security features and controls offered by cloud providers, such as encryption, access management, and data protection mechanisms. Compliance requirements, such as industry-specific regulations or data residency, should also be taken into account.

Workload requirements analysis is a crucial aspect of selecting compute and storage resources in cloud infrastructure. It involves understanding and analyzing the specific needs and characteristics of the workloads that will be running in the cloud environment. This analysis helps determine the appropriate compute and storage resources that can effectively meet the workload demands.

To perform workload requirements analysis, several factors need to be considered:

- **Performance requirements**: It is essential to assess the performance needs of the workloads, such as CPU, memory, and storage requirements. Different workloads have varying performance demands, and understanding these requirements ensures that the chosen compute and storage resources can handle the workload efficiently.

- **Data storage and retrieval**: Workloads may have varying data storage and retrieval patterns. Some workloads may require high-speed access to data, while others may involve large-scale data processing or long-term archival. Assessing the data storage requirements helps determine the appropriate storage solutions, such as block storage, file storage, or object storage, that can efficiently handle the workload's data needs.

- **Compliance and security**: Depending on the nature of the workloads and industry regulations, compliance and security requirements may come into play. Workloads dealing with sensitive data or subject to specific compliance standards need to adhere to appropriate security measures. Evaluating the security capabilities of compute and storage resources ensures that the chosen options meet the workload's compliance and security requirements.

- **Cost optimization strategies**: These play a crucial role in managing expenses and maximizing the value derived from compute and storage resources in cloud infrastructure. These strategies aim to optimize costs while still meeting the workload requirements effectively. By implementing cost optimization strategies, organizations can achieve significant savings and ensure efficient resource utilization. Here are some common cost optimization strategies:

- **Rightsizing**: Rightsizing involves matching the compute and storage resources to the actual workload requirements. It entails analyzing the resource utilization patterns and identifying over-provisioned or under-utilized resources. By resizing or adjusting the allocated resources based on actual needs, organizations can eliminate unnecessary costs and optimize resource utilization.

- **Reserved instances or savings plans**: Cloud service providers often offer discounted pricing options for compute and storage resources through reserved instances or savings plans. These options allow organizations to commit to a specific usage level over a longer duration in exchange for lower rates. By utilizing reserved instances or savings plans effectively, organizations can achieve cost savings, especially for workloads with predictable or steady resource demands.

- **Spot instances or preemptible VMs**: Spot instances, also known as preemptible VMs in some cloud platforms, offer significant cost savings compared to on-demand instances. These instances are available at a lower price because they can be interrupted or reclaimed by the cloud provider when demand exceeds supply. Spot instances are ideal for fault-tolerant and flexible workloads that can handle interruptions or sudden termination.

- **Auto-scaling and load balancing**: Auto-scaling enables the dynamic adjustment of compute and storage resources based on workload demands. By automatically scaling resources up or down, organizations can align resource allocation with actual needs, eliminating unnecessary costs during periods of low demand. Load balancing distributes the workload across multiple resources to ensure efficient utilization and avoid resource bottlenecks.

- **Data life cycle management**: Analyzing data life cycle patterns and implementing appropriate storage tiers can optimize costs. Not all data requires high-performance storage, and by transitioning less frequently accessed or older data to lower-cost storage tiers such as object storage or archival storage, organizations can significantly reduce storage expenses while maintaining data accessibility.

- **Resource tagging and monitoring**: Implementing resource tagging and comprehensive monitoring allows organizations to gain insights into resource utilization, costs, and trends. By tracking resource usage and costs at a granular level, organizations can identify cost-intensive areas, optimize resource allocation, and make informed decisions for cost optimization.

- **Cloud cost management tools**: Utilizing cloud cost management tools and platforms provides visibility into resource usage, costs, and recommendations for cost optimization. These tools offer insights, cost allocation, budgeting capabilities, and recommendations to optimize resource usage and costs effectively.

Evaluating cloud provider offerings and SLAs is a critical step in selecting the right cloud provider for compute and storage services. It involves assessing various factors, including the provider's capabilities, reliability, performance guarantees, and support. Here are some key aspects to consider when evaluating cloud provider offerings and SLAs:

- **Service offerings**: Begin by examining the range of compute and storage services offered by the cloud provider. Understand the specific offerings such as virtual machines, storage types (block, file, and object), databases, and other specialized services. Evaluate whether these offerings align with your organization's requirements and can effectively support your workloads.

- **Pricing and cost transparency**: Examine the pricing models and cost structures of the cloud provider. Understand how compute and storage services are billed, including factors such as data transfer costs, storage costs, and any additional charges. Evaluate whether the provider offers transparent pricing and provides tools to monitor and manage costs effectively.

- **SLAs**: Carefully review the SLAs provided by the cloud provider for compute and storage services. SLAs define the provider's commitments regarding service availability, performance, response times, and issue resolution. Pay attention to factors such as uptime guarantees, service credits in case of SLA violations, and the provider's responsibilities during service disruptions or data loss.

- **Support and customer service**: Assess the provider's support offerings and customer service capabilities. Determine the level of support provided, such as 24/7 availability, response times, and communication channels. Consider the provider's reputation for customer service and their willingness to work closely with customers in resolving issues and providing technical assistance.

- **Storage tiering and life cycle policies**: These are essential aspects of managing data in cloud storage environments. They enable organizations to optimize storage costs, performance, and data accessibility by intelligently classifying and moving data across different storage tiers based on its value and usage patterns. Here's a detailed discussion of storage tiering and life cycle policies:

- **Storage tiering**: Storage tiering involves categorizing data into different tiers based on its characteristics and access requirements. Typically, storage tiers are defined by their performance, capacity, and cost. Higher-tier storage provides faster access and lower latency but comes at a higher cost, while lower-tier storage offers larger capacity and lower cost but with slower access. By tiering data, organizations can align storage costs with the value of the data and ensure that frequently accessed or critical data resides in higher-performing storage tiers.

- **Hot, warm, and cold data**: A common approach to storage tiering is to classify data into hot, warm, and cold categories. Hot data refers to frequently accessed and time-critical data that requires the highest performance. Warm data represents data that is accessed less frequently but still requires relatively fast access. Cold data includes data that is rarely accessed but may need to be retained for compliance or archival purposes. Each category is associated with a corresponding storage tier, with hot data residing in the fastest storage and cold data residing in the most cost-effective storage.

- **Life cycle policies**: Life cycle policies define rules for automatically moving data between different storage tiers based on predefined criteria. These policies consider factors such as data age, access frequency, business relevance, and compliance requirements. For example, a policy may specify that data that hasn't been accessed for a certain period should be automatically moved from a hot tier to a warm or cold tier. Life cycle policies streamline data management by automating the process of moving data to the appropriate storage tier based on its changing characteristics and access patterns.

Rightsizing compute and storage resources is a practice in cloud computing that involves optimizing the allocation of resources to match the actual needs of applications and workloads. It ensures that organizations are neither overprovisioning nor underprovisioning their compute and storage resources, leading to cost savings, improved performance, and better resource utilization. Let's discuss this topic in detail:

- **Understanding resource utilization**: Rightsizing begins with a thorough analysis of resource utilization. It involves assessing the current usage patterns of compute and storage resources, including CPU, memory, disk space, and I/O operations. By examining historical data and monitoring the workload's behavior, organizations can identify trends, peak usage periods, and resource bottlenecks.

- **Identifying overprovisioning**: Overprovisioning occurs when resources are allocated in excess of what is required. This can happen due to factors such as overestimating resource demands, deploying resources based on peak loads, or lack of visibility into application requirements. Overprovisioning leads to unnecessary costs and underutilization of resources.

- **Addressing underprovisioning**: Underprovisioning occurs when resources are insufficient to meet the demands of applications or workloads. This can result in degraded performance, application failures, and unhappy end users. Under-provisioning often happens when organizations are conservative in resource allocation or fail to anticipate sudden spikes in demand.

Rightsizing strategies:

- **Performance monitoring and analysis**: Implementing robust monitoring and performance analysis tools helps organizations gain visibility into resource usage and identify areas of overprovisioning or underprovisioning. By monitoring key performance metrics, such as CPU utilization, memory usage, and disk I/O, organizations can pinpoint resource bottlenecks and make informed decisions.

- **Rightsizing compute resources**: Rightsizing compute resources involves adjusting the allocated CPU and memory based on workload requirements. This can be achieved by analyzing historical usage patterns, identifying peak periods, and provisioning resources accordingly. Techniques such as vertical scaling (increasing or decreasing resource capacity within a single server) or horizontal scaling (adding or removing servers) can be employed to match resource needs.

- **Rightsizing storage resources**: For storage resources, rightsizing involves evaluating the amount of disk space, I/O performance, and data access patterns. It may involve resizing volumes, implementing data deduplication and compression techniques, or employing tiered storage solutions to match the storage requirements of different data types and access patterns.

- **Automation and autoscaling**: Leveraging automation and autoscaling capabilities provided by cloud service providers can help organizations dynamically adjust resource allocation based on real-time demand. Autoscaling allows resources to be automatically added or removed based on predefined thresholds, ensuring optimal performance and cost efficiency.

By accurately matching resources to workload requirements, organizations can achieve cost optimization, improved performance, and efficient resource utilization. It requires continuous monitoring, analysis, and the ability to adapt resources.

By considering all these factors when selecting compute and storage resources in cloud infrastructure, organizations can make informed decisions that align with their workload needs, scalability requirements, availability expectations, cost optimization goals, and security and compliance standards. This thoughtful approach ensures the efficient utilization of resources, optimal performance, and cost-effectiveness in cloud deployments.

Summary

This chapter covered various essential topics that provided a comprehensive understanding of two key components – compute and storage. It began with an introduction to compute and storage in cloud computing, explaining their significance and the role they play in enabling cloud-based services and applications.

The next section delved into cloud storage types, exploring the characteristics and use cases of different storage options. It covered block storage, which offers high-performance storage for applications with stringent performance requirements such as databases and high-performance computing. File storage was discussed, highlighting its shared access capabilities and its suitability for content management systems and shared file repositories. Object storage, known for its scalability and durability, was explored along with popular offerings such as Amazon S3, Google Cloud Storage, and Azure Blob Storage. Use cases for object storage, such as backup and archival, media storage, and content delivery, were also discussed.

This chapter also delved into considerations and cost optimization strategies for compute and storage. It covered important factors to consider when selecting compute and storage resources, including workload requirements analysis, cost optimization strategies, evaluating cloud provider offerings and SLAs, storage tiering and life cycle policies, and rightsizing compute and storage resources. These topics provided you with insights into making informed decisions about resource allocation, optimizing costs, and maximizing resource utilization in cloud environments.

Throughout this chapter, you gained knowledge about the fundamental concepts of compute and storage in cloud computing, explored different storage types and their use cases, and learned about important considerations and strategies for cost optimization. You also understood the significance of workload analysis, selecting the right storage tier, and efficiently managing compute resources. By the end of this chapter, you have developed a strong foundation in compute and storage concepts, enabling you to make informed decisions when designing and managing cloud architectures. You learned how to evaluate different storage options, optimize costs, and align resources with workload requirements, ultimately enhancing the efficiency and effectiveness of your cloud deployments.

The next chapter, *Networking – Cloud Perspective*, explores the crucial aspect of networking in cloud computing. It delves into the fundamentals of cloud networking, including the technologies, architectures, and considerations involved in establishing and managing networks in the cloud.

5
Networking

In this chapter, you will be presented with a comprehensive exploration of networking's vital role in cloud environments. The introduction lays the groundwork by explaining the significance of networking in facilitating seamless communication and data transfer among cloud resources. This chapter covers various networking types, including **virtual private cloud** (**VPC**), subnetting, load balancing, **content delivery networks** (**CDNs**), and **virtual private networks** (**VPNs**), providing insights into their functionalities and benefits. Crucial considerations for designing and managing efficient cloud networks will be discussed, encompassing aspects such as security, performance, scalability, and compliance. Furthermore, this chapter delves into cost optimization strategies for networking, focusing on resource allocation, autoscaling, network monitoring, and the utilization of reserved instances and pricing models. By the end of this chapter, you will have gained a comprehensive understanding of networking in cloud computing and be equipped with the knowledge to make informed decisions when implementing and managing networking solutions in cloud environments, ensuring both cost-effectiveness and high-performance networking.

The significance of networking is underscored as the backbone that enables seamless and efficient communication between various cloud resources, ensuring data exchange and service accessibility. Throughout this chapter, various networking types will be explored, shedding light on their specific applications and advantages. You will gain valuable insights into VPCs, which allow for the creation of isolated network environments with enhanced security controls. Additionally, the concept of subnetting and IP addressing will be elucidated, explaining how dividing large networks into smaller segments can improve manageability. The importance of load balancing in distributing incoming traffic across multiple servers for optimal resource utilization will be emphasized, as will the role of CDNs in enhancing content delivery to end users. Furthermore, this chapter delves into VPNs and their ability to establish secure connections between on-premises networks and cloud resources over the public internet.

Apart from exploring different networking types, this chapter will delve into the essential considerations for designing and managing robust cloud networks. Security remains a paramount concern, and you will learn about network segmentation, access controls, encryption, and intrusion detection as vital measures to protect data and resources from unauthorized access. The impact of network performance and latency on application responsiveness and user experience will also be discussed, emphasizing the need for low-latency and high-bandwidth networks. Scalability and elasticity are crucial elements, as cloud networks must be designed to accommodate dynamic resource demands effectively. This chapter also addresses the integration of on-premises networks with cloud-based networks, highlighting strategies for creating hybrid cloud architectures that ensure seamless and secure data flow between environments. Lastly, the significance of compliance with industry regulations and data protection laws will be underlined, especially when handling sensitive data within cloud networks.

Throughout this chapter, real-world use cases and examples will be provided to illustrate the practical application of networks in cloud infrastructure.

In this chapter, we will cover the following topics:

- Network types and services
- Considerations and cost optimization strategies for networks

By the end of the chapter, you will emerge with the knowledge and skills needed to make informed decisions when designing, managing, and optimizing networking solutions in cloud computing, fostering efficient, reliable, and budget-conscious cloud network infrastructures.

Technical requirements

To fully engage with the content of this chapter on cloud computing architecture, you should have a basic understanding of computer systems, networking concepts, and information technology.

Additionally, the following technical requirements are recommended:

- **Internet access**: You should have a reliable internet connection to access online resources, references, and examples related to cloud computing.

- **A computing device**: A desktop computer, laptop, tablet, or smartphone with a modern web browser is necessary to read this chapter's content and access any online materials.

- **A web browser**: The latest version of a modern web browser such as Google Chrome, Mozilla Firefox, Microsoft Edge, or Safari is recommended. This ensures compatibility and optimal viewing experience of web-based resources and interactive content.

- **Familiarity with cloud services**: Some familiarity with cloud services and their basic functionalities will enhance your understanding of this chapter. This includes knowledge of basic networking, operating systems, IP addresses, and servers.

Introduction to networks in cloud computing

This section serves as a comprehensive introduction to the fundamental concepts and importance of networks in the context of cloud infrastructure. In this section, you will gain a deep understanding of the crucial roles that networks play in enabling and supporting cloud-based services and applications.

In the dynamic landscape of modern computing, cloud technology has emerged as a transformative force, revolutionizing the way businesses and individuals manage and access data, applications, and services. Central to this technological revolution is networking, which serves as the backbone of cloud computing, facilitating seamless communication and data exchange among various cloud resources. Networking in cloud computing plays a pivotal role in enabling the delivery of on-demand computing resources over the internet, empowering organizations to scale their operations efficiently and achieve unprecedented levels of flexibility and agility.

At its core, cloud computing is a model that provides ubiquitous, convenient, and on-demand access to a shared pool of computing resources. These resources encompass computing power, storage, and networking capabilities, delivered as services that can be rapidly provisioned and released with minimal management effort. While computing and storage elements are essential components of cloud computing, it is networking that serves as the glue that binds these resources together into a cohesive, interconnected ecosystem.

Networking in cloud computing encompasses a broad range of functionalities, starting from the foundation of data centers and infrastructure that host the cloud services to the intricate interconnections between various cloud components. Cloud networking enables data and information to traverse vast distances across the globe, allowing users to access applications and services from virtually anywhere with internet connectivity. This global reach has shattered the barriers of physical location, making cloud computing a true enabler of global collaboration and accessibility.

VPCs are a fundamental aspect of cloud networking, providing organizations with private, isolated network environments within the cloud platform. VPCs offer enhanced security controls, allowing businesses to define custom network configurations and access rules. This isolation provides an additional layer of protection, assuring organizations that their sensitive data and resources remain segregated from other tenants on the same cloud infrastructure.

Another crucial networking concept in cloud computing is subnetting, where large networks are divided into smaller, more manageable segments called subnets. Subnetting not only improves network manageability but also enhances security and performance by creating logical boundaries for communication between resources.

Load balancing is an essential networking capability in cloud environments that involves distributing incoming network traffic across multiple servers. By doing so, load balancing ensures optimal utilization of computing resources and prevents individual servers from being overloaded, thereby enhancing the performance, responsiveness, and reliability of cloud-based applications.

CDNs are strategic solutions for enhancing content delivery and user experience. CDNs leverage a distributed network of servers, strategically placed in various geographical locations, to cache and serve content from locations that are closer to the end users. This approach reduces the latency in content delivery and minimizes the load on the origin server, resulting in faster load times and a better overall user experience.

VPNs are integral to establishing secure communication channels between on-premises networks and cloud resources over the public internet. VPNs utilize encryption and authentication mechanisms to ensure data privacy and integrity during transmission, allowing organizations to securely access and manage cloud-based resources while maintaining a seamless and protected connection.

As cloud computing continues to evolve, networking remains at the forefront of innovation, enabling cutting-edge technologies such as edge computing and serverless computing. Edge computing leverages the distribution of computing resources closer to the end users or devices, reducing data latency and enabling real-time processing of data. Serverless computing abstracts the server management layer, allowing developers to focus solely on writing and deploying code, while the cloud provider automatically handles the underlying infrastructure.

In conclusion, networking is the lifeblood of cloud computing, interconnecting resources, users, and services to create a cohesive, scalable, and globally accessible cloud ecosystem. As organizations increasingly embrace cloud technology, a solid understanding of cloud networking becomes paramount to designing, implementing, and managing efficient and secure cloud solutions. This chapter aims to equip you with comprehensive insights into the fundamentals of networking in cloud computing, covering various networking types, considerations, and cost optimization strategies, ultimately empowering you to make informed decisions when designing and managing cloud networks that meet the demands of the digital era.

In the upcoming section, *Exploring network options in cloud computing*, you will learn about the diverse array of networking options available to leverage the full potential of cloud environments. This section serves as a comprehensive guide, introducing you to various network types and configurations that are fundamental to cloud computing. You will gain a clear understanding of VPCs, which offer isolated and secure network environments within the cloud platform. You will explore the concepts of subnetting and IP addressing, which enhance network manageability and security. Additionally, you will discover the significance of load balancing in distributing incoming network traffic across multiple servers, ensuring optimal resource utilization and high application availability. This section will delve into the realm of CDNs and their role in improving content delivery by caching and serving content from strategically placed servers. Furthermore, you will explore VPNs and their importance in establishing secure connections between on-premises networks and cloud resources. By the end of this section, you will have a comprehensive grasp of the various network options available in cloud computing, empowering you to make informed decisions when designing and configuring cloud networks that cater to their specific needs and requirements.

Exploring network options in cloud computing

In this section, you will learn about diverse network types, including VPCs, subnetting, load balancing, CDNs, and VPNs. You will understand the benefits and applications of each option, enabling you to make informed decisions when configuring cloud networks to meet your specific needs.

Furthermore, you will discover the significance of load balancing, which optimizes resource utilization by efficiently distributing incoming network traffic across multiple servers. Load balancing ensures high availability and improved performance for cloud-based applications. The section also delves into CDNs and their role in enhancing content delivery by caching and serving content from strategically placed servers, reducing latency, and improving user experience. Moreover, you will explore VPNs and their vital function in establishing secure connections between on-premises networks and cloud resources, ensuring data privacy during transmission.

In cloud computing, various network options are available to facilitate seamless communication and data transfer between cloud resources and users. Let's list these network options and then discuss each of them in detail:

- VPC
- VPN
- Subnetting and IP addressing
- Load balancing
- CDNs

VPCs

VPCs are a fundamental networking option in cloud computing that allows users to create private, isolated, and customizable network environments within a cloud service provider's infrastructure. VPCs provide a high degree of control and security, akin to traditional on-premises networks, while harnessing the benefits of cloud computing. By creating a VPC, organizations can define their virtual network topology, IP address ranges, subnets, and routing tables, tailoring the network environment to their specific needs and requirements. The key features and benefits of VPCs are as follows:

- Isolation and security
- Customization
- Scalability
- Integration

Now, let's talk about the different types of VPCs:

- **Amazon Web Services** (**AWS**) **VPC**: AWS offers Amazon VPC, a versatile networking solution that enables users to create private, isolated networks in the AWS cloud environment. AWS VPC allows businesses to define custom IP address ranges, create subnets, and implement network access control policies using security groups and **network access control lists** (**NACLs**).

- **Google Cloud Platform** (**GCP**) **VPC**: GCP provides Google **Virtual Private Cloud** (**VPC**), which allows users to build private, global networks for GCP resources. GCP VPC offers automatic IP address allocation and flexible subnetting options, enabling seamless integration with other GCP services such as Google Compute Engine and Google Kubernetes Engine.

- **Microsoft Azure VNet**: Azure offers Azure **Virtual Network** (**VNet**), which enables users to create private, isolated networks in the Azure cloud environment. Azure VNet provides robust network security features, such as network security groups and route tables, allowing organizations to control traffic flow and implement security policies.

The next section explores the network offerings provided by different cloud vendors. In today's digital landscape, cloud service providers play a pivotal role in enabling organizations to build, scale, and manage their network infrastructure in the cloud. Each major cloud provider offers a range of network services and features that cater to various business needs and use cases.

Service providers

As the major cloud service providers, AWS, GCP, and Azure each offer VPC services, empowering users with a wide range of networking capabilities and features. These service providers continually enhance their VPC offerings to meet the evolving needs of businesses and to provide a secure and seamless networking experience in the cloud.

VPCs are a critical networking option in cloud computing, offering organizations the ability to create isolated and secure network environments tailored to their specific requirements. VPCs provide extensive control, scalability, and integration capabilities, enabling seamless extension of on-premises networks into the cloud. With offerings from leading cloud service providers such as AWS, GCP, and Azure, businesses have access to powerful networking tools that facilitate efficient communication and data transfer across cloud resources while ensuring the utmost security and privacy. *Figure 5.1* depicts a hybrid architecture where the AWS cloud environment interacts with an on-premises environment. The orange portion of the diagram depicts the VPC in AWS:

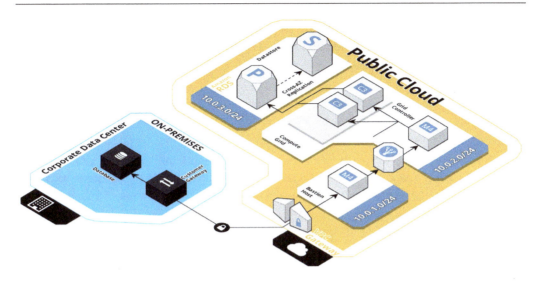

Figure 5.1 – Hybrid environment highlighting the VPC portion in orange

Let's understand how we can set up a VPC in the AWS cloud infrastructure. Setting up a VPC in AWS involves the following steps:

1. **Sign into the AWS Management Console**: Access the AWS Management Console using your AWS account credentials.

2. **Navigate to the VPC dashboard**: Once logged in, go to the AWS Management Console's main dashboard. In the search bar, type VPC or find **Networking & Content Delivery** and click on **VPC** to access the VPC dashboard.

3. **Create the VPC**: On the VPC dashboard, click on the **Create VPC** button to start the VPC creation process.

4. **Configure VPC settings**: In the **Create VPC** wizard, you will need to specify the following details:

   - **VPC Name**: Give your VPC a descriptive name to identify it easily.

   - **IPv4 CIDR Block**: Define the IP address range for the VPC using CIDR notation (for example, 10.0.0.0/16). This range will be used for all resources within the VPC.

5. **Configure subnet settings**: Next, you must create subnets within the VPC. Click on the **Add subnet** button and provide the following information for each subnet:

   - **Subnet Name**: Give the subnet a meaningful name (for example, "Public Subnet").

   - **Availability Zone**: Choose an Availability Zone in which the subnet will be located.

   - **IPv4 CIDR Block**: Specify the IP address range for the subnet using CIDR notation (for example, 10.0.1.0/24).

6. **Create an internet gateway (IGW)**: An IGW is required to enable communication between the VPC and the internet. Go to the **Internet Gateways** section in the VPC dashboard and click on **Create internet gateway**. Provide a name for the IGW, and then attach it to your VPC.

7. **Configure route tables**: To enable internet access for the subnets, you need to create and configure route tables. In the VPC dashboard, navigate to **Route Tables** and click on **Create route table**. Associate the route table with the public subnet, and then edit the routes to send all internet-bound traffic (0.0.0.0/0) to the IGW.

8. **Set up security groups**: Security groups act as virtual firewalls for your instances within the VPC. Go to the **Security Groups** section in the VPC dashboard and click on **Create security group**. Specify the inbound and outbound rules to control the traffic flow to and from instances.

9. **Launch instances and associate with subnets**: Now that the VPC, subnets, IGW, and security groups are set up, you can launch EC2 instances in the desired subnets. During the instance launch process, ensure that you associate the instances with the appropriate subnets.

10. **Test connectivity**: Finally, test the connectivity of your instances by accessing them through the public IP or **Elastic IP (EIP)**. Verify that your instances can access the internet for updates and that they can communicate with each other within the VPC.

If you were able to successfully execute all these steps, then congratulations! You have successfully set up a VPC in AWS, providing a private, isolated network environment with internet connectivity for your AWS resources. Remember to carefully manage your VPC settings and security groups to ensure a secure and well-functioning cloud infrastructure.

Now, if were to perform the same action using Cloud Shell, what would we need to do?

Setting up a VPC in AWS using Cloud Shell involves the following steps, along with the respective commands:

1. **Launch Cloud Shell**: Open AWS Cloud Shell from the AWS Management Console. It provides an integrated **command-line interface (CLI)** with the necessary tools pre-installed for managing AWS resources.

2. **Create a VPC**: Use the `aws ec2 create-vpc` command to create a VPC with a specified IPv4 CIDR block. Replace `<cidr_block>` with your desired IP address range in CIDR notation (for example, 10.0.0.0/16):

   ```
   aws ec2 create-vpc --cidr-block <cidr_block>
   ```

3. **Create subnets**: Create subnets within the VPC using the `aws ec2 create-subnet` command. Replace `<vpc_id>` with the VPC ID you obtained in *Step 2*, and `<subnet_cidr>` with the subnet's IP address range in CIDR notation (for example, 10.0.1.0/24):

   ```
   aws ec2 create-subnet --vpc-id <vpc_id> --cidr-block <subnet_cidr>
   ```

4. **Create an IGW**: Create an IGW using the `aws ec2 create-internet-gateway` command:

    ```
    aws ec2 create-internet-gateway
    ```

5. **Attach the IGW to the VPC**: Attach the IGW to the VPC using the `aws ec2 attach-internet-gateway` command. Replace `<igw_id>` with the IGW ID you obtained in *Step 4*, and `<vpc_id>` with the VPC ID you obtained in *Step 2*:

    ```
    aws ec2 attach-internet-gateway --internet-gateway-id <igw_id>
    --vpc-id <vpc_id>
    ```

6. **Create and configure a route table**: Create a new route table for the public subnet using the `aws ec2 create-route-table` command. Replace `<vpc_id>` with the VPC ID you obtained in *Step 2*:

    ```
    aws ec2 create-route-table --vpc-id <vpc_id>
    ```

7. **Add a route to the route table**: Add a route to the newly created route table that points all internet-bound traffic to the IGW. Use the `aws ec2 create-route` command. Replace `<route_table_id>` with the route table ID you obtained in *Step 6*, and `<igw_id>` with the IGW ID you obtained in *Step 4*:

    ```
    aws ec2 create-route --route-table-id <route_table_id>
    --destination-cidr-block 0.0.0.0/0 --gateway-id <igw_id>
    ```

8. **Associate the subnet with the route table**: Associate the public subnet you created in *Step 3* with the route table using the `aws ec2 associate-route-table` command. Replace `<route_table_id>` with the route table ID you obtained in *Step 6*, and `<subnet_id>` with the subnet ID you obtained in *Step 3*.

    ```
    aws ec2 associate-route-table --route-table-id <route_table_id>
    --subnet-id <subnet_id>
    ```

9. **Create a security group**: Create a security group using the `aws ec2 create-security-group` command. Replace `<group_name>` and `<vpc_id>` with your desired security group name and VPC ID, respectively:

    ```
    aws ec2 create-security-group --group-name <group_name>
    --description "My security group" --vpc-id <vpc_id>
    ```

10. **Set inbound and outbound rules for the security group**: Configure inbound and outbound rules for the security group using the `aws ec2 authorize-security-group-ingress` and `aws ec2 authorize-security-group-egress` commands. Replace `<security_group_id>` with the security group ID you obtained in *Step 9*:

    ```
    aws ec2 authorize-security-group-ingress --group-id <security_
    group_id> --protocol tcp --port 22 --cidr 0.0.0.0/0
    aws ec2 authorize-security-group-egress --group-id <security_
    group_id> --protocol all --cidr 0.0.0.0/0
    ```

If you were able to successfully execute all these steps, then congratulations! You have successfully set up a VPC in AWS using Cloud Shell. The VPC is now ready to host and manage your AWS resources with a private, isolated network environment and secure connectivity to the internet.

Now, let's understand how we can set up a VPC in GCP.

Setting up a VPC in GCP involves the following steps:

1. **Sign into the Google Cloud Console**: Access the Google Cloud Console using your GCP account credentials.

2. **Navigate to the VPC Network page**: Once logged in, navigate to the **VPC Network** page by clicking on **VPC Network** under the **Networking** section in the left-hand menu.

3. **Create a VPC network**: On the **VPC Network** page, click on the **Create VPC Network** button to start creating a new VPC.

4. **Configure VPC network details**: In the **Create a VPC network** form, you need to specify the following details:

   - **Name**: Give your VPC a descriptive name so that you can identify it easily (for example, my-vpc).

   - **Region**: Choose the region where you want to create the VPC (for example, us-central1).

   - **Subnet Creation Mode**: Select either **Automatic** or **Custom**. For simplicity, choose **Automatic**, which allows GCP to automatically create subnets in the VPC.

5. **Configure firewall rules**: You can set up firewall rules to control incoming and outgoing traffic to and from the instances within the VPC. Click on the **Firewall** tab, then click on **Create Firewall Rule**.

6. **Specify firewall rule details**: In the **Create a firewall rule** form, provide the following information:

   - **Name**: Give a descriptive name to the firewall rule

   - **Targets**: Choose **All instances in the network** to apply the rule to all instances in the VPC

   - **Source IP ranges**: Define the source IP ranges from which traffic is allowed (for example, 0.0.0.0/0 for all IP addresses)

   - **Protocols and ports**: Specify the protocol and port range to allow (for example, TCP: 80 for HTTP traffic)

7. **Create the firewall rule**: Click **Create** to create the firewall rule.

8. **Create subnets (optional)**: If you selected **Custom** as the subnet creation mode in *Step 4*, you could create subnets manually. Go to the **Subnets** tab and click on **Create Subnet**. Provide the required details, including subnet name, region, IP address range, and the VPC network it belongs to.

9. **Review and create the VPC**: Review all the configurations you made for the VPC and firewall rule. Click on **Create** to create the VPC and associated resources.

10. **Access the VPC**: Once the VPC has been created, you can access it through the **VPC Network** page. You can create and manage VM instances, storage buckets, and other resources within the VPC.

The VPC is now ready to host and manage your cloud resources in an isolated, secure, and customizable network environment.

VPN

As we discussed previously, a VPN is a secure networking technology that allows users to establish encrypted communication channels over the internet or any untrusted network. VPNs create a private and encrypted "tunnel" between the user's device (such as a computer, smartphone, or tablet) and a VPN server. This encrypted connection ensures that data transmitted between the user's device and the VPN server remains confidential and secure.

VPNs serve two primary purposes:

- **Data privacy**: VPNs encrypt the data transmitted over the internet, making it unreadable to anyone who might intercept it. This ensures that sensitive information, such as passwords, financial details, or business data, remains private and protected from potential eavesdroppers.

- **Anonymity and bypassing restrictions**: VPNs can also mask the user's IP address, effectively hiding their identity and location. This feature allows users to bypass geographic restrictions and access content or services that may be restricted or blocked in their region.

VPNs are widely used for various purposes, such as secure remote access to corporate networks, safeguarding online privacy, accessing geographically restricted content, and enhancing security while using public Wi-Fi networks.

Let's see how we can configure a VPN in an AWS environment.

Configuring a VPN in an AWS environment involves several steps. Here is a high-level overview of the process:

1. **Create a virtual private gateway (VGW)**: Start by creating a VGW in the AWS Management Console. The VGW serves as the entry and exit point for VPN traffic to and from your VPC.

2. **Set up a customer gateway (CGW)**: Next, set up a CGW on your on-premises network. The CGW represents the device or software that acts as the VPN endpoint on your side.

3. **Create a site-to-site VPN connection**: Create a site-to-site VPN connection in the AWS Management Console. This connection establishes the secure communication tunnel between the VGW in AWS and the CGW on your on-premises network.

4. **Configure VPN connection details**: For the site-to-site VPN connection configuration, specify the following details:

   - VGW ID

   - CGW IP address

   - A **pre-shared key (PSK)** for authentication

5. **Download configuration information**: After creating the VPN connection, download the configuration details for your CGW. This includes the configuration file and the pre-shared key.

6. **Configure your CGW**: On your on-premises network, use the downloaded configuration information to configure your CGW device or software. This step may vary depending on the CGW solution you are using.

7. **Enable route propagation (optional)**: If you want your AWS VPC to communicate with your on-premises network, enable route propagation from the VPN connection to the route tables in your VPC.

8. **Verify and monitor the VPN connection**: Once the VPN has been configured, verify the status of the VPN connection in the AWS Management Console. You can also monitor VPN performance and connection status using Amazon CloudWatch.

With these steps completed, you will have successfully configured a VPN connection between your AWS VPC and your on-premises network. This allows secure communication between the two environments, enabling data exchange and resource access as if they were part of the same private network.

Let's understand how we can accomplish the same using Cloud Shell.

Configuring a VPN in an AWS environment using Cloud Shell involves several steps. Here is a step-by-step guide to setting up a VPN:

1. **Launch Cloud Shell**: Open AWS Cloud Shell from the AWS Management Console. It provides an integrated CLI with the necessary tools pre-installed for managing AWS resources.

2. **Create a VGW**: Use the `aws ec2 create-vpn-gateway` command to create a VGW in AWS. This VGW will act as the entry and exit point for VPN traffic to and from your VPC:

   ```
   aws ec2 create-vpn-gateway --type ipsec.1 --tag-specifications
   'ResourceType=vpn-gateway,Tags=[{Key=Name,Value=my-vpn-
   gateway}]'
   ```

3. **Describe the VGW and note down its ID**: Use the `aws ec2 describe-vpn-gateways` command to get information about the VGW you just created. Note down the VGW ID; it will be needed in the following steps:

   ```
   aws ec2 describe-vpn-gateways --filters
   "Name=tag:Name,Values=my-vpn-gateway"
   ```

4. **Create a CGW**: Next, set up a CGW on your on-premises network. Use the `aws ec2 create-customer-gateway` command to create the CGW. Replace `<ip_address>` with the public IP address of your on-premises VPN device:

```
aws ec2 create-customer-gateway --type ipsec.1 --public-ip
<ip_address> --tag-specifications 'ResourceType=customer-
gateway,Tags=[{Key=Name,Value=my-customer-gateway}]'
```

5. **Describe the CGW and note down the ID**: Use the aws ec2 `describe-customer-gateways` command to get information about the CGW you just created. Note down the CGW ID as it will be needed in the following steps:

```
aws ec2 describe-customer-gateways --filters
"Name=tag:Name,Values=my-customer-gateway"
```

6. **Create a VPN connection**: Create a site-to-site VPN connection using the aws ec2 `create-vpn-connection` command. Replace `<vgw_id>` with the VGW ID you obtained in *Step 3*, and `<cgw_id>` with the CGW ID you obtained in *Step 5*:

```
aws ec2 create-vpn-connection --type ipsec.1 --customer-
gateway-id <cgw_id> --vpn-gateway-id <vgw_id>
--tag-specifications 'ResourceType=vpn-connection,Tags=[{Key=Nam
e,Value=my-vpn-connection}]'
```

7. **Describe the VPN connection and note down the configuration details**: Use the aws ec2 `describe-vpn-connections` command to get information about the VPN connection you just created. Note down the configuration details, including the pre-shared key and the configuration file, as you will need them to configure your CGW:

```
aws ec2 describe-vpn-connections --filters
"Name=tag:Name,Values=my-vpn-connection"
```

8. **Configure your CGW**: On your on-premises network, use the downloaded configuration information (pre-shared key and configuration file) to configure your CGW device or software.

9. **Verify and monitor the VPN connection**: Once the VPN has been configured, verify the status of the VPN connection in the AWS Management Console or using the aws ec2 `describe-vpn-connections` command. You can also monitor VPN performance and connection status using Amazon CloudWatch.

With these steps, you have successfully configured a VPN connection between your AWS VPC and your on-premises network using Cloud Shell. This enables secure communication and data exchange between the two environments as if they were part of the same private network.

Let's take another example and see how we can set up a VPN in the Azure cloud.

Configuring a VPN in an Azure environment involves several steps. Here is a high-level overview of the process:

1. **Sign in to the Azure portal**: Access the Azure portal using your Azure account credentials.

2. **Create a virtual network (VNet)**: Begin by creating a VNet in the Azure portal. This VNet will act as the hub for your VPN connections.

3. **Set up a local network gateway**: Create a local network gateway in the Azure portal. This represents the on-premises VPN device or software that acts as the VPN endpoint on your side.

4. **Create a VPN gateway**: Next, create a VPN gateway in the Azure portal. This VPN gateway will serve as the VPN endpoint in Azure and facilitate the secure communication tunnel between your VNet and the local network gateway.

5. **Configure the VPN gateway's settings**: In the VPN gateway configuration, specify the following details:

   - **VPN Type**: Choose the VPN type based on your requirements (route-based or policy-based)

   - **SKU**: Select the appropriate VPN gateway SKU based on your performance and feature needs

   - **Virtual Network**: Associate the VPN gateway with the VNet you created in *Step 2*

   - **Public IP Address**: Assign a public IP address to the VPN gateway

6. **Create a connection**: Create a connection between the VPN gateway and the local network gateway. This connection establishes the secure communication tunnel between Azure and your on-premises network.

7. **Configure the connection settings**: In the connection configuration, specify the following details:

   - **Connection Type**: Choose between site-to-site or ExpressRoute, depending on your use case

   - **Shared Key**: Set up a pre-shared key for authentication between the VPN gateway and the on-premises device

8. **Download the VPN configuration**: After creating the connection, download the VPN configuration file for your on-premises VPN device or software. This file includes the required settings and certificates.

9. **Configure your on-premises VPN device**: On your on-premises network, use the downloaded configuration file to configure your VPN device or software. This step may vary depending on the VPN solution you are using.

10. **Test and verify the VPN connection**: Once the VPN has been configured, test the connection to ensure secure communication between Azure and your on-premises network. You can verify the VPN status and connection details in the Azure Portal.

With these steps completed, you have successfully configured a VPN between your Azure environment and your on-premises network. This allows secure communication and data exchange between the two environments, extending your on-premises network into the Azure cloud.

Subnetting and IP addressing

Subnetting and IP addressing are fundamental concepts in computer networking that play a crucial role in the design and management of cloud computing environments. In cloud computing, virtualization and abstraction technologies allow for flexible allocation and utilization of resources. Subnetting and IP addressing are essential for effectively organizing and managing these resources within a cloud infrastructure. This section explores the concepts of subnetting and IP addressing in the context of cloud computing, discussing their importance, benefits, and best practices for their implementation.

Understanding subnetting in cloud computing

Subnetting involves dividing a larger network into smaller, more manageable segments called subnets. In the context of cloud computing, subnets are virtual network partitions that allow for logical isolation and efficient resource utilization. By creating subnets, cloud service providers and organizations can organize their cloud resources into distinct groups with their IP address ranges, routing tables, and security settings. This enables better network management, security, and scalability in cloud environments.

The following are the benefits of subnetting in cloud computing:

- **Network isolation**: Subnetting allows different sets of resources to be isolated from each other, preventing unauthorized access and minimizing the impact of security breaches or network issues on other subnets

- **Improved performance**: Subnetting can improve network performance by reducing broadcast traffic and allowing for more efficient use of network resources

- **Segregation of services**: Subnets facilitate the segregation of services based on their functional requirements, enabling easier management and troubleshooting

IP addressing in cloud computing

IP addressing involves assigning unique IP addresses to devices and resources connected to a network. In cloud computing, IP addressing plays a critical role in identifying and locating cloud resources and enabling communication between them.

The following types of IP addressing are available in cloud computing:

- **Public IP addressing**: Public IP addresses are routable over the internet and are used to expose resources to the public or connect cloud instances directly to the internet.

- **Private IP addressing**: Private IP addresses are non-routable over the internet and are used for internal communication within a cloud environment. Private IP addresses are commonly used for resources that do not need to be directly accessed from the internet.

- **Elastic IP addressing**: Elastic IP addresses are static public IP addresses that can be dynamically assigned to cloud resources. They allow for the reassignment of IP addresses between instances, enhancing availability and seamless service migration.

Let's look at the best practices for IP addressing in cloud computing:

- **Use private IP addressing**: Whenever possible, use private IP addressing for cloud resources to enhance security and reduce exposure to external threats

- **Implement network address translation** (**NAT**): NAT enables instances in private subnets to access the internet through a public IP address assigned to a NAT gateway, providing internet connectivity without exposing private IP addresses directly

- **Leverage IP address management** (**IPAM**) **tools**: IPAM tools help in managing IP address allocation, tracking, and resource discovery, streamlining IP address management in complex cloud environments

IPv4 and IPv6 considerations in cloud computing

With the depletion of IPv4 addresses, IPv6 adoption has become essential in cloud computing. IPv6 provides a vast address space, ensuring the continued growth and scalability of cloud infrastructures.

Let's look at the benefits of IPv6 in cloud computing:

- **Larger address space**: IPv6 provides a virtually unlimited address space, accommodating the proliferation of connected devices and resources in the cloud

- **Simplified addressing**: IPv6 uses a simplified and more efficient addressing format, making it easier to manage and configure IP addresses in cloud environments

- **Enhanced security**: IPv6 includes built-in security features, such as IPsec, which can improve the security of data transmitted over the network

Dynamic Host Configuration Protocol (DHCP) in cloud computing

DHCP is a network protocol that's used to dynamically assign IP addresses and other network configuration parameters to devices in a network. In cloud computing, DHCP can be used to automate the allocation of IP addresses to instances and other cloud resources.

Let's look at the benefits of DHCP in cloud computing:

- **Simplified IP address management**: DHCP automates the IP address assignment process, reducing the need for manual configuration and minimizing human errors

- **Scalability**: DHCP enables efficient IP address allocation in large-scale cloud environments, accommodating dynamic resource provisioning and deallocation
- **Resource optimization**: With DHCP, IP addresses are only assigned when needed, allowing for better resource utilization and avoiding IP address wastage

Let's see an example of setting up an IPV4 configuration in the AWS cloud.

To set up IPv4 configuration in AWS, you'll need to create a VPC and configure subnets, route tables, and security groups:

1. **Sign into the AWS Management Console**.

2. **Create a VPC**:

   - Navigate to the VPC dashboard from the AWS Management Console.

   - Click on **Create VPC**.

   - Provide a name for your VPC and specify an IPv4 CIDR block (for example, 10.0.0.0/16).

   - Click on **Create VPC** to create the VPC.

3. **Create subnets**:

   - In the VPC dashboard click on **Subnets**.

   - Click on **Create subnet**.

   - Choose the VPC you created in *Step 2*.

   - Specify a name for your subnet and select an Availability Zone.

   - Provide an IPv4 CIDR block for the subnet (for example, 10.0.1.0/24).

   - Click on **Create** to create the subnet.

4. **Create an IGW**:

   - In the VPC dashboard click on **Internet Gateways**.

   - Click on **Create internet gateway**.

   - Provide a name for the IGW and click on **Create internet gateway**.

   - Select the IGW and click on **Attach to VPC**.

   - Choose the VPC you created in *Step 2* and click on **Attach internet gateway**.

5. **Create a route table**:

   - In the VPC dashboard, click on **Route Tables**.

   - Click on **Create route table**.

- Provide a name for the route table and choose the VPC you created in *Step 2*.

- Click on **Create** to create the route table.

6. **Configure the route table for a public subnet**:

   - Select the route table you created in *Step 5* and click on the **Routes** tab.

   - Click on **Edit routes** and add a new route with a destination of 0.0.0.0/0 and the target as the IGW you created in *Step 4*.

   - Click on **Save routes** to update the route table.

7. **Associate subnets with route tables**:

   - In the **Subnets** section, select the public subnet you created in *Step 3*.

   - Click on **Actions**, then **Edit route table association**.

   - Choose the route table you created in *Step 5* and click on **Save**.

8. **Create security groups**:

   - In the EC2 dashboard, click on **Security Groups**.

   - Click on **Create security group**.

   - Provide a name and description for the security group.

   - Set inbound and outbound rules to allow traffic as per your requirements.

   - Click on **Create security group** to create the security group.

9. **Launch instances**:

   - In the EC2 dashboard, click on **Instances**.

   - Click on **Launch Instance** to create a new EC2 instance.

   - Choose an **Amazon Machine Image** (**AMI**) and configure the instance as needed.

   - In the **Configure Security Group** step, select the security group you created in *Step 8*.

   - Complete the instance launch process by following the prompts.

Your IPv4 configuration in AWS is now set up. The EC2 instance that's launched in the public subnet should have a public IPv4 address and be accessible from the internet. The private subnet can be used for instances that do not require direct internet access. Remember to configure the security group rules appropriately to control inbound and outbound traffic to the instances.

Let's look at the allocation of IP addresses in a cloud environment, as seen in *Figure 5.2*. The blue sections depict the IP addresses in a CIDR block:

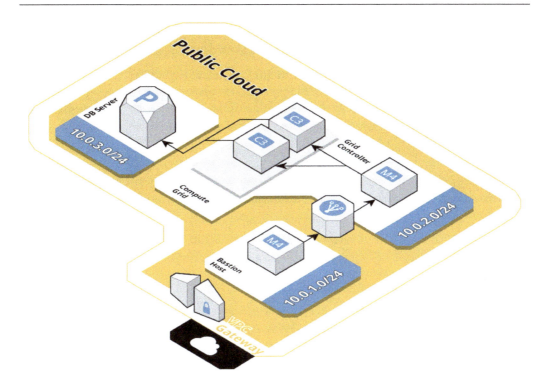

Figure 5.2 – The blue sections depict the IP addresses in a CIDR block

Subnetting and IP addressing are fundamental aspects of cloud computing that enable efficient resource management, network organization, and secure communication. By dividing networks into subnets and properly configuring IP addressing, cloud service providers and organizations can achieve better network isolation, performance, and scalability. Leveraging DHCP, IPv6, and IPAM tools further enhances IP address management in cloud environments. As cloud computing continues to evolve, subnetting and IP addressing will remain essential for building robust, secure, and scalable cloud infrastructures. Implementing best practices in subnetting and IP addressing ensures the optimal utilization of cloud resources and enables the seamless growth of cloud computing services.

Load balancing

This part is a section in itself and could be titled *Load balancing in cloud computing – optimizing performance and availability*.

Load balancing is a critical component of modern cloud computing architectures that aims to distribute network traffic evenly across multiple servers or resources. As cloud computing environments continue to grow in scale and complexity, load balancing becomes essential to ensure optimal performance, scalability, and high availability of cloud applications and services. This section explores the concept of load balancing in cloud computing, its benefits, various load balancing techniques, and the role it plays in enhancing the overall efficiency and reliability of cloud-based systems.

Load balancing is the process of efficiently distributing incoming network traffic across multiple resources, such as VMs, containers, or application instances, to avoid overloading any single resource. The goal is to ensure that each resource handles an equitable share of the traffic, preventing bottlenecks and ensuring that the cloud infrastructure operates efficiently and effectively.

Let's consider the benefits of load balancing in cloud computing:

- **Scalability**: Load balancing enables cloud services to scale horizontally by adding or removing resources based on demand, effectively handling increased or decreased traffic loads.

- **High availability**: By distributing traffic across multiple resources, load balancing improves system availability. If one resource fails or becomes unavailable, the load balancer redirects traffic to healthy resources, minimizing downtime and service disruption.

- **Performance optimization**: Load balancing ensures that each resource operates within its capacity, reducing response times and improving the overall performance of cloud-based applications.

Various load balancing techniques are employed in cloud computing to efficiently manage network traffic. Some of the commonly used load balancing algorithms are as follows:

- **Round robin**: In this technique, traffic is evenly sequentially distributed to each resource. Each incoming request is directed to the next resource in the list, ensuring a fair distribution of traffic.

- **Least connections**: In this approach, incoming requests are routed to the resource with the fewest active connections. It helps prevent heavily loaded resources from becoming overloaded.

- **Weighted round robin**: This technique assigns a weight to each resource based on its capacity or performance. Resources with higher weights receive a proportionally larger share of the traffic.

- **Least response time**: Load balancers direct requests to the resource that has the lowest response time. It helps in minimizing latency and optimizing user experience.

Load balancing is integrated into various cloud services to enhance their functionality and performance:

- **Application Load Balancer** (**ALB**): AWS ALB is a cloud service that distributes incoming application traffic across multiple targets (such as EC2 instances) within a region based on routing rules and content-based routing

- **Network Load Balancer** (**NLB**): AWS NLB provides ultra-low latency and high throughput for handling TCP, UDP, and TLS traffic, making it ideal for applications that require high performance

- **Load balancers for GCP**: GCP offers various load balancing services, including HTTP(S) Load Balancing, SSL Proxy Load Balancing, and TCP Proxy Load Balancing, catering to different application requirements

Load balancing works hand-in-hand with auto-scaling in cloud environments. Auto-scaling automatically adjusts the number of resources based on traffic demand, while load balancing efficiently distributes that traffic among the resources:

- **Dynamic resource provisioning**: Load balancers work in tandem with auto-scaling groups, adding or removing resources as needed to accommodate varying workloads

- **Elasticity**: Auto-scaling and load balancing together enable elasticity, allowing cloud infrastructures to flexibly expand or contract based on demand, optimizing resource utilization

Load balancing is a fundamental aspect of cloud computing that ensures optimal performance, scalability, and high availability of cloud-based applications and services. By evenly distributing incoming network traffic across multiple resources, load balancers prevent overload and improve the overall efficiency of cloud infrastructures. *Figure 5.4* depicts the functioning of a couple of load balancers in a cloud environment. The highlighted section in green shows the placement of a load balancer:

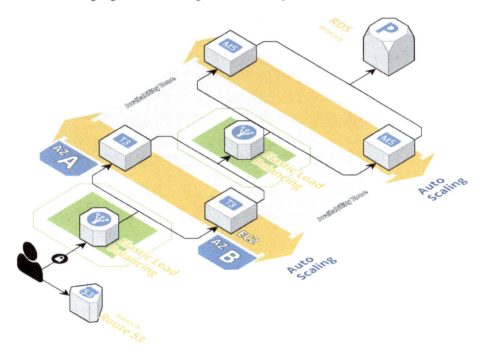

Figure 5.3 – A load balancer in a cloud environment (Elastic Load Balancer (ELB) in the case of AWS)

Various load balancing techniques and specialized load balancing services provided by cloud providers enhance the flexibility and responsiveness of cloud-based systems. As cloud computing continues to evolve, load balancing will remain a critical element in designing robust, scalable, and reliable cloud architectures, effectively meeting the demands of modern, data-driven applications.

CDNs

In today's interconnected digital world, where users demand instant access to content and seamless online experiences, CDNs have emerged as indispensable tools for improving website performance and ensuring global content delivery. CDNs are distributed networks of servers strategically positioned across the globe to deliver web content, such as images, videos, HTML files, and other media, to users from the nearest server location. This section delves into the concept of CDNs, their architecture, benefits, working principles, and their pivotal role in optimizing content delivery and enhancing the user experience in the digital landscape.

CDNs are geographically dispersed networks of proxy servers, referred to as edge servers or **points of presence** (**POPs**), that work in tandem to store and serve cached copies of web content. When a user requests content from a website, the CDN identifies the nearest edge server to the user's location and delivers the content from that server, minimizing latency and reducing the load on the website's origin server.

The following are the benefits of CDNs:

- **Improved website performance**: CDNs reduce the distance between users and content, resulting in faster loading times and improved page load performance

- **Global content accessibility**: CDNs enable businesses to serve content to users worldwide, irrespective of their geographical location, ensuring a consistent and efficient user experience

- **Enhanced scalability**: CDNs can handle sudden spikes in traffic by distributing the load across multiple edge servers, ensuring seamless content delivery during peak periods

Let's look at a CDN's architecture and working principles:

- **Edge servers**: The core building blocks of CDNs are edge servers, distributed across various geographic locations. These servers are strategically positioned in data centers and connected to the internet's backbone, ensuring close proximity to end users.

- **Content caching**: CDNs cache frequently accessed content, such as images, CSS files, and videos, on edge servers. When a user requests this content, the CDN delivers it from the nearest edge server, reducing latency and network congestion.

- **Content routing**: CDNs employ intelligent routing algorithms to direct user requests to the most appropriate edge server based on factors such as geographical proximity, server load, and network conditions.

- **Load balancing**: CDNs use load balancing techniques to evenly distribute traffic across multiple edge servers, preventing overloading on any individual server and optimizing resource utilization.

- **Dynamic content delivery**: In addition to static content, modern CDNs support dynamic content delivery by integrating with the website's application servers. This allows them to cache and deliver personalized and frequently changing content efficiently.

Let's see how a CDN is placed in a cloud network. *Figure 5.5* depicts the placement and connectivity of a CDN:

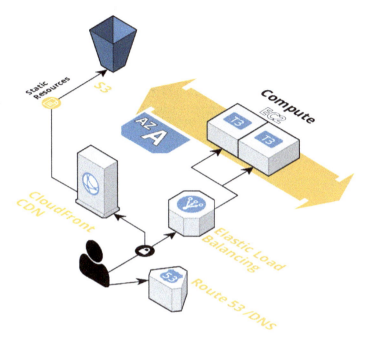

Figure 5.4 – A CDN/Cloud Front in an AWS environment

There are various types of CDNs:

- **Traditional CDNs**: These CDNs focus on caching and delivering static content, such as images, videos, and scripts, optimizing the delivery of fixed files.

- **Video streaming CDNs**: Video-focused CDNs are tailored to deliver high-quality video streams to end users, ensuring smooth playback and reducing buffering issues.

- **Application delivery CDNs**: These CDNs optimize the delivery of dynamic and interactive web applications, caching and serving personalized content.

The following are the leading CDN providers:

- **Akamai**: Akamai is one of the pioneers of CDNs, offering a broad range of CDN services and solutions to enhance web performance, security, and scalability

- **Cloudflare**: Cloudflare provides a powerful CDN integrated with web security features such as DDoS protection, SSL/TLS encryption, and firewall protection.
- **Amazon CloudFront**: Part of AWS, CloudFront is a widely used CDN service offering seamless integration with other AWS services.

Let's understand how we could deploy a CDN in the cloud. We shall use Azure Cloud for reference.

Deploying a CDS on Azure Cloud involves several steps to enable efficient content distribution and improved performance. Here's a step-by-step guide on how to set up a CDN on Azure:

1. **Sign into the Azure portal**: Access the Azure portal using your Azure account credentials.
2. **Create a CDN profile**:

   - In the Azure portal, click on + **Create a resource**.
   - Search for `Content Delivery Network` and select **Content Delivery Network**.
   - Click on **Create** to create a new CDN profile.
   - Provide a unique name for the CDN profile and choose the desired pricing tier (**Standard** or **Premium**).
   - Select the subscription, resource group, and region where you want to deploy the CDN profile.
   - Click on **Create** to create the CDN profile.

3. **Configure the CDN endpoint**:

   - Within the newly created CDN profile, click on **Endpoints**.
   - Click on **Add** to create a new endpoint.
   - Choose the desired endpoint type (**Web**, **Media**, or **Azure Storage**).
   - Select the origin type (**Custom Origin** or **Azure Resource**).
   - Configure the endpoint settings, including the origin hostname, protocol, and path.
   - Choose the pricing tier and set additional caching and rules as needed.
   - Click on **Create** to create the CDN endpoint.

4. **Configure custom domains (optional)**: If you want to use a custom domain for your CDN, you can configure it by following these steps:

   - In the CDN endpoint settings, click on **Custom domains**.
   - Click on + **Custom domain** and enter your custom domain name.
   - Configure the necessary DNS settings for the custom domain to point to the CDN endpoint.

5. **Validate the CDN configuration**: After setting up the CDN profile and endpoint, validate the CDN configuration to ensure that it is functioning as expected:

   - Access your CDN endpoint URL or custom domain to verify that content is being delivered via the CDN.

   - Use developer tools or online CDN testing tools to inspect response headers and confirm the CDN cache hits.

6. **Purge or invalidate the CDN cache (optional)**: If you have made changes to your origin content and want to update the CDN cache immediately, you can purge or invalidate the cache:

   - In the CDN endpoint settings, click on **Purge**.

   - Choose to purge the entire cache or specific files.

   - Click on **Purge** to remove the selected content from the CDN cache.

7. **Monitor and optimize CDN performance**: Monitor the performance of your CDN using Azure Monitor or other monitoring tools. Analyze CDN analytics to gain insights into usage patterns and optimize CDN performance:

   - In the CDN profile settings, click on **Analytics**.

   - Enable CDN analytics to track usage and performance metrics.

   - Use the analytics data to identify potential bottlenecks and optimize content delivery.

Setting up a CDN on Azure Cloud involves creating a CDN profile, configuring endpoints, and optionally configuring custom domains. Azure CDN provides an efficient and scalable way to deliver web content, media files, and other resources closer to end users, enhancing website performance and user experience. By following these steps and leveraging Azure's robust CDN capabilities, organizations can accelerate content delivery and ensure a seamless experience for users around the world.

The future of CDNs

As digital content consumption continues to grow, CDNs will play a pivotal role in shaping the future of the internet. Innovations such as edge computing, machine learning, and IoT integration will further optimize CDNs' performance and enable more personalized and context-aware content delivery.

CDNs have revolutionized the way content is delivered to users worldwide, improving website performance, reducing latency, and ensuring a seamless user experience. By distributing content across strategically placed edge servers, CDNs bring content closer to end users, optimizing load times and enabling global accessibility. With their ability to handle massive web traffic and support dynamic content delivery, CDNs have become an integral part of modern web infrastructures. As the digital landscape continues to evolve, CDNs will remain a crucial component in shaping a faster, more reliable, and user-centric internet experience for audiences around the globe.

The upcoming section, *Considerations and cost optimization strategies for networks*, focuses on key factors and approaches to designing, deploying, and managing networks in cloud computing. It covers network design principles, security measures, performance optimization techniques, and monitoring practices to ensure seamless communication, reliability, and low latency. Additionally, this section provides insights into cost optimization strategies, such as rightsizing network resources and optimizing data transfer costs, helping organizations achieve efficient and cost-effective cloud network infrastructures. By applying these considerations and strategies, you can enhance network performance, security, and cost efficiency in their cloud environments.

Considerations and cost optimization strategies for networks

The section focuses on the important factors and approaches that need to be taken into account while designing, deploying, and managing networks in cloud computing environments. As organizations increasingly rely on cloud services, the network plays a crucial role in ensuring seamless communication, security, and performance for various applications and services. This section explores the key considerations, challenges, and best practices to optimize network infrastructure in the cloud while also keeping an eye on cost efficiency.

In this section, you will gain insights into the following topics:

- **Network design considerations**: This part delves into the fundamental principles of network design in the cloud. It discusses topics such as VPC design, subnetting, IP addressing, and how to establish secure and reliable connectivity between cloud resources and on-premises environments. Additionally, you will learn about strategies to create redundant and highly available network architectures to avoid single points of failure.

- **Network security**: Security is a critical aspect of any network, especially in cloud computing where data traverses over the internet. This section covers various security measures, such as network access control, encryption, and implementing firewalls and intrusion detection systems. It emphasizes the importance of secure communication between cloud resources and the internet to safeguard sensitive information.

- **Performance optimization**: Optimizing network performance is essential to ensure low latency, reduced response times, and high bandwidth for delivering applications and services efficiently. This part explores techniques such as CDNs, edge caching, load balancing, and using dedicated network links for data-intensive workloads.

- **Cost optimization strategies**: Cloud resources can quickly escalate costs if not managed carefully. This part offers insights into cost optimization strategies specifically related to networking. It covers topics such as rightsizing network resources, leveraging spot instances, and optimizing data transfer costs between cloud regions.

Let's get started.

Network security

All providers support NACLs or **network security groups** (**NSGs**) for filtering network traffic at the subnet level. Additionally, they offer **distributed denial-of-service** (**DDoS**) protection to safeguard against attacks.

By considering these network design principles and cloud provider-specific features, organizations can create robust, secure, and scalable network architectures to support their cloud-based applications and services effectively.

Network security is a critical aspect of cloud computing, ensuring the protection of data, applications, and resources from unauthorized access, cyber threats, and data breaches. Each major cloud provider (AWS, Azure, and GCP) offers a set of network security features and services to safeguard their cloud environments. Let's explore network security considerations specific to each cloud provider:

- **AWS**:

  - **NACLs**: NACLs act as stateless firewalls at the subnet level, allowing or denying inbound and outbound traffic based on user-defined rules. They provide an additional layer of security to control traffic between subnets in a VPC.

  - **Security Groups**: AWS Security Groups are stateful firewalls that control inbound and outbound traffic for EC2 instances and other resources within a VPC. They allow fine-grained control over traffic by specifying rules based on protocols, ports, and IP addresses.

  - **AWS Web Application Firewall** (**WAF**): AWS WAF helps protect web applications from common web exploits and attacks, such as SQL injection, cross-site scripting, and more. It integrates with AWS CloudFront and Application Load Balancer for effective application-level security.

- **Microsoft Azure**:

  - **NSGs**: Azure NSGs provide inbound and outbound traffic filtering at the subnet and network interface level. Administrators can define rules based on source/destination IP addresses, ports, and protocols to control network traffic.

  - **Azure Firewall**: Azure Firewall is a fully managed, cloud-based firewall service that protects Azure resources and virtual networks. It provides centralized security policy enforcement and includes features such as application rules, network rules, and NAT rules.

  - **Azure DDoS Protection**: Azure DDoS Protection Standard provides enhanced DDoS mitigation capabilities for Azure resources, protecting against volumetric, protocol, and application layer attacks.

- **GCP**:

  - **Cloud Firewall rules**: GCP offers Cloud Firewall, allowing users to create and enforce stateful firewall rules to control traffic to and from instances. Firewall rules can be applied at the project or instance level.

- **Cloud Armor**: GCP Cloud Armor provides WAF capabilities to protect HTTP(S) load balancers against application-layer DDoS attacks and common web vulnerabilities.

- **VPC Service Controls**: GCP's VPC Service Controls allow users to define security perimeters around GCP resources, enabling granular control over data access and preventing data exfiltration.

The following are some common network security considerations across cloud providers:

- **Encryption**: All cloud providers offer encryption options for data at rest and data in transit, ensuring data confidentiality and integrity

- **Identity and Access Management** (**IAM**): IAM services provided by cloud providers enable granular control over user access to resources and ensure the principle of least privilege

- **Monitoring and logging**: Cloud providers offer various monitoring and logging solutions to detect and analyze security events and anomalies within the network

- **Compliance and certifications**: All major cloud providers comply with industry standards and certifications to ensure a secure environment for sensitive workloads, such as HIPAA, PCI DSS, and ISO

By leveraging these network security features and best practices from cloud providers, organizations can build robust and secure network architectures that protect their cloud resources and ensure data confidentiality and integrity.

Performance optimization

Performance optimization is crucial in cloud computing to ensure that applications and services deliver a fast and responsive user experience. Each major cloud provider (AWS, Azure, and GCP) offers various performance optimization techniques and services to enhance the speed, latency, and overall efficiency of network communication. Let's explore performance optimization considerations specific to each cloud provider:

- **AWS**:

  - **CDN**: AWS offers Amazon CloudFront, a fully managed CDN service that caches and delivers content from edge locations closer to end users. CloudFront reduces latency and improves load times for static and dynamic content, such as images, videos, scripts, and APIs.

  - **Elastic Load Balancing** (**ELB**): AWS ELB distributes incoming application traffic across multiple targets (for example, EC2 instances or containers) in multiple availability zones. ELB ensures high availability, fault tolerance, and optimal utilization of resources.

  - **Auto Scaling**: AWS Auto Scaling automatically adjusts the number of EC2 instances or other resources based on traffic demand. Auto Scaling ensures that the application can handle varying workloads efficiently.

- **AWS Global Accelerator**: This service provides static IP addresses that act as entry points to AWS's global network. It uses Anycast routing to direct user traffic to the nearest AWS edge location, reducing internet hops and improving performance.

- **Microsoft Azure**:

  - **CDN**: Azure CDN delivers content from Microsoft's global network of edge locations, reducing latency and improving content delivery for users worldwide.

  - **Load Balancer**: Azure Load Balancer distributes incoming traffic across multiple VMs or VM scale sets, ensuring high availability and optimized resource utilization.

  - **Application Gateway**: Azure Application Gateway is a web traffic load balancer that provides Layer 7 (application layer) load balancing, allowing for intelligent traffic distribution based on URL routing, session affinity, and SSL offloading.

  - **Azure Front Door**: This service provides a global application delivery platform that uses anycast to direct user traffic to the nearest Front Door point of presence, reducing latency and improving application performance.

- **GCP**:

  - **CDN**: GCP offers Cloud CDN, which caches and delivers content from Google's global network of edge locations. Cloud CDN reduces latency and optimizes content delivery for users worldwide.

  - **Load Balancing**: GCP Load Balancing distributes traffic across multiple instances or backend services, ensuring high availability and fault tolerance.

  - **Traffic Director**: GCP Traffic Director is a global traffic management service that routes traffic across backend services based on traffic type, performance, and health.

  - **Cloud Armor**: GCP's Cloud Armor provides WAF capabilities to protect HTTP(S) load balancers against application-layer DDoS attacks and common web vulnerabilities, enhancing application security and performance.

The following are common performance optimization considerations across cloud providers:

- **Edge caching**: All cloud providers offer edge caching capabilities to deliver content from the nearest edge location, reducing latency and improving content delivery

- **Content compression**: Compressing content before delivery helps reduce data transfer times and enhances overall performance

- **Database optimization**: Optimizing database performance, such as using caching mechanisms, read replicas, and database sharding, can significantly improve application responsiveness

- **Choosing the right instance types**: Selecting the appropriate instance types with sufficient compute resources can ensure optimal application performance

- **Database and application placement**: Placing databases and applications closer to each other can reduce latency and enhance performance

By implementing these performance optimization techniques and leveraging cloud provider-specific services, organizations can ensure that their cloud-based applications and services deliver high-speed, low-latency experiences to users, regardless of their geographical location.

Cost optimization

Cost optimization strategies are essential in cloud computing to manage expenses efficiently and maximize the return on investment. Each major cloud provider (AWS, Azure, and GCP) offers various cost optimization features and services to help organizations reduce their cloud spending without compromising performance or security. Let's explore cost optimization strategies specific to each cloud provider:

- **AWS**:

  - **Rightsizing instances**: AWS provides a wide range of instance types, and choosing the appropriate instance size based on workload requirements can help avoid overprovisioning and unnecessary costs.

  - **Spot instances**: AWS spot instances allow users to bid for spare EC2 capacity, enabling significant cost savings compared to on-demand or reserved instances. Spot instances are ideal for fault-tolerant, stateless, and non-production workloads.

  - **Savings plans and reserved instances (RIs)**: AWS offers savings plans and RIs that provide discounted pricing for long-term commitments. Choosing the right combination of savings plans and RIs can lead to substantial cost savings.

  - **AWS Cost Explorer**: This tool provides a comprehensive view of AWS costs and usage patterns, helping users identify cost-saving opportunities and make informed decisions.

- **Microsoft Azure**:

  - **Azure reserved VM instances**: Azure RIs offer significant discounts for committing to 1 or 3-year terms for VMs, resulting in cost savings compared to pay-as-you-go pricing

  - **Low-priority VMs**: Azure low-priority VMs offer cost savings for non-critical workloads by utilizing spare capacity at a significantly lower price

  - **Azure Advisor**: Azure Advisor provides recommendations to optimize resource utilization, cost management, security, and performance

  - **Azure Cost Management and Billing**: This tool helps users track, allocate, and optimize cloud costs across Azure services

- GCP:

  - **Committed Use Contracts (CUCs)**: GCP offers CUCs, which provide discounts for committed usage of VM instances over 1 or 3-year terms

  - **Preemptible VMs**: GCP preemptible VMs are short-lived instances that provide substantial cost savings, making them suitable for fault-tolerant and batch-processing workloads

  - **GCP Pricing Calculator**: This tool helps users estimate and compare the costs of GCP services based on usage and configuration parameters

Here are some common cost optimization considerations across cloud providers:

- **Resource tagging**: Tagging resources in the cloud allows for better cost allocation and tracking, ensuring that expenses are accurately attributed to specific projects or departments

- **Automatic scaling**: Implementing auto-scaling for resources helps align resource consumption with demand, preventing overprovisioning during periods of low traffic

- **Rightsizing databases**: Optimizing database instance sizes based on actual workload requirements can lead to significant cost savings

- **Data transfer costs**: Minimizing data transfer between regions and services within the cloud can help reduce data egress costs

- **Expiring unused resources**: Identifying and decommissioning unused or underutilized resources can help eliminate unnecessary expenses

By implementing these cost optimization strategies and leveraging cloud provider-specific cost management tools, organizations can effectively control their cloud expenses, ensuring that resources are utilized efficiently, and costs are optimized without compromising on performance, security, or availability.

In conclusion, this section delved into crucial aspects of designing, securing, and optimizing networks in cloud computing environments. You have gained insights into key considerations for VPC design, subnetting, and IP addressing. You also learned about essential network security measures, including NACLs, security groups, and DDoS protection. This section also explored performance optimization techniques, such as CDNs, load balancing, and global accelerators, to enhance network efficiency and user experience. Lastly, you gained knowledge of cost optimization strategies, including rightsizing instances, leveraging spot instances, and using reserved instance options, to manage cloud expenses effectively. By implementing these considerations and strategies, you can create robust, secure, and cost-efficient network infrastructures in the cloud, ensuring optimal performance, reliability, and cost-effectiveness for your cloud-based applications and services.

Summary

This chapter provided a comprehensive overview of networking in cloud computing, covering essential concepts, network types, services, considerations, and cost optimization strategies. First, you learned about VPC design, subnetting, IP addressing, connectivity options, and performance optimization techniques offered by major cloud providers such as AWS, Azure, and GCP. This equipped you with the skills to design secure and scalable network architectures. Next, we focused on network security measures, cost optimization strategies, and monitoring practices. You gained insights into NACLs, security groups, DDoS protection, cost-saving methods such as rightsizing instances, and analyzing network performance. By mastering this section, you acquired skills to ensure network resilience, enhance security, and optimize costs, resulting in efficient and cost-effective cloud networking solutions. Overall, this chapter equipped you with the knowledge and skills necessary to build robust, scalable, and budget-conscious cloud networks, ensuring seamless connectivity, high performance, and enhanced user experiences for your cloud-based applications and services.

The next chapter explores the crucial aspect of security in cloud computing. It delves into the fundamentals of cloud security, including the technologies, architectures, and considerations involved in establishing and managing security in the cloud.

Part 3:
Security, Compliance,
and Databases

This part covers the best practices for cloud security, offering you a comprehensive toolkit to strengthen your defenses. We also cover encryption, a fundamental pillar of data protection. Additionally, you will discover the significance of **identity and access management (IAM)**, secure API usage, network security, and secure coding practices for cloud-native applications. This part also explores the various database offerings available in the cloud. You can expect to learn about managed database services provided by major cloud providers.

This part has the following chapters:

- *Chapter 6, Security and Compliance 1: Cloud Perspective*
- *Chapter 7, Security and Compliance 2: Cloud Perspective*
- *Chapter 8, Database Services – Part 1*
- *Chapter 9, Database Services – Part 2*

6
Security and Compliance 1 – Cloud Perspective

Cloud computing has emerged as a transformative technology, enabling organizations and individuals to store, process, and access data and applications with unparalleled ease and scalability. However, this cloud-driven digital transformation brings with it unique security challenges that demand careful attention and comprehensive solutions. In this chapter, you can expect an in-depth exploration of the vital concepts surrounding security and compliance in cloud computing, equipping you with the knowledge and skills necessary to protect your cloud environment effectively.

One of the key focal points of this chapter lies in understanding the diverse range of security risks that cloud computing introduces. From data breaches and insider threats to data loss incidents and disruptive **denial-of-service (DoS)** attacks, you will gain valuable insights into the potential threats that could compromise the security of your cloud-based systems. Real-world examples and scenarios will illustrate the significant impact these risks can have on businesses, reinforcing the urgency of robust security measures.

To counter these risks, this chapter will delve into the best practices for cloud security, offering you a comprehensive toolkit to strengthen your defenses. Encryption, a fundamental pillar of data protection, will be explored in depth, emphasizing its role in safeguarding sensitive information from unauthorized access. Additionally, you will discover the significance of **Identity and Access Management (IAM)**, secure API usage, network security, and secure coding practices for cloud-native applications. Armed with these insights, you will be well-prepared to construct a multi-layered security strategy that fortifies your cloud infrastructure.

A fundamental aspect of cloud security is understanding the shared responsibility model, which clearly outlines the distribution of security responsibilities between cloud service providers and customers. By grasping this model, you will gain clarity on which security aspects fall under the purview of the cloud provider and which require active management on your part. This knowledge will empower you to make informed decisions and actively collaborate with your cloud service provider to establish a secure and compliant cloud environment.

This chapter will also shed light on the array of cloud security tools and technologies available to fortify cloud environments. **Intrusion detection systems (IDSs)**, **security information and event management (SIEM)** solutions, and cloud-native security services offered by major cloud providers will be covered to provide you with an arsenal of defensive capabilities.

This chapter seeks to empower you with a comprehensive understanding of the intricate relationship between security and cloud technology. By acquiring a strong foundation in cloud security principles, you will be poised to implement robust security measures, protect sensitive data, and confidently address the evolving challenges of cloud security. Through this knowledge, you will become adept at safeguarding cloud environments and ensuring the uninterrupted and secure operation of your cloud-based systems.

The security and compliance piece will be split into two separate chapters, namely *Security and Compliance 1* and *Security and Compliance 2*.

In this chapter, we will cover the following topics:

- *Understanding cloud security risks*: This chapter will elaborate on the unique security risks associated with cloud computing, including data breaches, insider threats, data loss, and DoS attacks. It will provide real-world examples and scenarios to illustrate the impact of these risks on businesses.

- *Cloud security tools and technologies*: You will learn about the different security tools and technologies available for securing cloud environments. This might include IDSs, SIEM solutions, and cloud-native security services provided by major cloud providers.

By the end of this chapter, you will emerge with the knowledge and skills needed to make informed decisions when designing, managing, and optimizing networking solutions in cloud computing, fostering efficient, reliable, and budget-conscious cloud network infrastructures.

Technical requirements

To fully engage with the content of this chapter on cloud computing architecture, you should have a basic understanding of computer systems, networking concepts, and information technology.

Additionally, the following technical requirements are recommended:

- **Internet access**: You should have a reliable internet connection to access online resources, references, and examples related to cloud computing.

- **A computing device**: A desktop computer, laptop, tablet, or smartphone with a modern web browser is necessary to read this chapter's content and access any online materials.

- **A web browser**: The latest version of a modern web browser such as Google Chrome, Mozilla Firefox, Microsoft Edge, or Safari is recommended. This ensures compatibility and optimal viewing experience of web-based resources and interactive content.

- **Familiarity with cloud services**: Some familiarity with cloud services and their basic functionalities will enhance your understanding of this chapter. This includes knowledge of basic network security, operating systems, encryption, and servers.

Introduction to security in cloud computing

Cloud technology has revolutionized the way businesses and individuals access and manage their data, but it has also introduced unique security challenges that require special attention.

Security in various cloud environments has undergone significant evolution over the years, adapting to the changing landscape of technology and cyber threats. Initially, cloud computing raised concerns about data privacy, data breaches, and the security of shared resources. However, cloud service providers recognized the urgency of addressing these concerns and invested heavily in robust security measures. As a result, modern cloud environments offer a wide array of security features, including encryption, IAM, network firewalls, and IDSs. Additionally, advancements in machine learning and artificial intelligence have empowered cloud security solutions to proactively detect and respond to emerging threats. With the implementation of strict compliance frameworks and regular security audits, cloud providers have instilled greater confidence in their customers' data protection. As the cloud landscape continues to evolve, security remains a top priority, and cloud environments are expected to adopt even more sophisticated security measures to stay ahead of evolving cyber threats and ensure the confidentiality, integrity, and availability of cloud resources and data.

By reading this section, you will have a comprehensive understanding of the diverse security risks prevalent in cloud computing. Armed with this knowledge, you will be better equipped to design and implement effective security measures that safeguard data, applications, and cloud resources from potential threats and vulnerabilities. The insights you will gain from this section will enable you to make informed decisions to protect your cloud environment, enhancing the overall security posture of your organization.

Understanding cloud security risks

In this section, we will dive into a comprehensive exploration of the various challenges and vulnerabilities that organizations may face when adopting cloud computing. Understanding these risks is essential for formulating robust security strategies and safeguarding sensitive data and applications hosted in the cloud. We will cover some of the key topics in the following sections.

Data breaches

Cloud environments store vast amounts of sensitive data from multiple users and organizations, making them attractive targets for cybercriminals. We will explore the factors contributing to data breaches, such as weak authentication, misconfigured permissions, and inadequate encryption practices. Understanding data breach risks will emphasize the need for strong security measures to protect valuable information from unauthorized access.

Data breaches in cloud environments are a significant concern for organizations and individuals alike. A data breach occurs when unauthorized individuals or entities gain access to sensitive or confidential information, resulting in the exposure, theft, or misuse of that data. Cloud computing, with its shared infrastructure and multi-tenant nature, introduces unique challenges that can potentially increase the risk of data breaches:

- **Causes and vulnerabilities**: Several factors contribute to data breaches in cloud environments. Misconfigurations in cloud services, weak access controls, and improper handling of data can expose critical information to unauthorized users. Inadequate encryption and data protection practices can also leave data vulnerable to interception and unauthorized access. Additionally, vulnerabilities in cloud service APIs or shared technology components might be exploited by attackers to gain access to sensitive data.

- **Impact and consequences**: The consequences of a data breach can be severe. For individuals, it can result in identity theft, financial loss, and reputational damage. For organizations, a data breach can lead to financial losses, regulatory penalties, and loss of customer trust. In some cases, the damage caused by a data breach can be irreparable and lead to the downfall of the affected business.

Insider threats

While cloud providers implement stringent security measures, internal employees or authorized users may pose significant threats to data security. We will discuss the importance of **privileged access management (PAM)**, monitoring user activities, and implementing measures to mitigate the risk of insider threats.

Insider threats pose a significant risk in cloud environments. Malicious or negligent actions by employees or authorized users with access to sensitive data can lead to data breaches. Organizations must implement strong access controls and monitoring mechanisms to detect and prevent insider threats.

An insider threat is defined as a security risk that originates from individuals within an organization, including employees, contractors, or business partners, who have legitimate access to the organization's systems, data, or facilities. These insiders may intentionally or unintentionally misuse their access privileges to compromise the confidentiality, integrity, or availability of sensitive information or critical assets.

Types of insider threats

Insider threats can be classified into three primary categories:

- **Malicious insiders**: These individuals intentionally and actively seek to harm the organization. Their motives may vary, such as revenge, financial gain, or espionage. They might steal sensitive data, disrupt operations, or introduce malware into the system.

- **Negligent insiders**: Negligent insiders are not malicious but inadvertently cause security incidents. They may fall victim to phishing attacks, mishandle data, or accidentally expose sensitive information, leading to data breaches.

- **Compromised insiders**: In this scenario, attackers gain unauthorized access to an insider's credentials or devices, using them as a front to carry out malicious activities within the organization.

Common insider threat scenarios

Insider threats can manifest in various ways, as follows:

- **Data theft**: Malicious insiders with access to valuable intellectual property or sensitive customer data may steal and leak it to competitors or on the dark web

- **Sabotage**: Disgruntled employees might deliberately disrupt operations, delete critical files, or introduce malware to cause damage

- **Unauthorized disclosure**: Insiders may inadvertently or intentionally share confidential information with unauthorized parties, leading to reputational and legal consequences

- **Insider fraud**: Employees with access to financial systems might engage in fraudulent activities, such as altering financial records or siphoning funds

Motives behind insider threats

Insider threats often stem from a combination of factors:

- **Financial gain**: Disgruntled employees seeking personal financial benefits may engage in fraud or theft

- **Revenge**: Former employees or individuals with a grudge against the organization may seek revenge through malicious actions

- **Whistleblowing**: Employees with grievances may leak sensitive information to expose wrongdoing within the organization

- **Carelessness**: Negligent employees may unknowingly expose sensitive data due to poor security practices

Detection and prevention strategies

Detecting insider threats requires a multi-layered approach that includes the following:

- **User behavior analytics**: Monitoring user activities and behavior to identify deviations from normal patterns and flag suspicious actions

- **Data loss prevention** (DLP): Implementing DLP solutions to prevent the unauthorized transmission of sensitive data outside the organization

- **PAM**: Restricting access to critical systems and data, ensuring only authorized users have privileged access

- **Security awareness training**: Providing regular security awareness training to employees to recognize and report suspicious activities

- **Regular auditing and monitoring**: Conducting regular security audits and monitoring user activities to detect anomalous behavior

Cultural and organizational aspects

Creating a positive and supportive work environment can mitigate insider threats. Encouraging open communication, providing employee assistance programs, and addressing grievances promptly can reduce the likelihood of malicious intent.

Data loss and recovery

Cloud service disruptions or hardware failures can lead to data loss if not adequately addressed. In this section, we will examine the risks associated with data loss, including accidental deletions, and explore data recovery and backup strategies to ensure business continuity.

Data loss and recovery are critical concerns in cloud computing, where vast amounts of sensitive information is stored and processed. Data loss can occur due to various factors, such as hardware failures, accidental deletions, cyberattacks, or natural disasters. In such scenarios, the ability to recover lost data efficiently is essential for ensuring business continuity and maintaining data integrity. Let's delve into the details of data loss and recovery in cloud environments:

- **Causes of data loss**: Data loss can result from both human errors and technical failures. Accidental deletions or overwrites, often caused by user mistakes, account for a significant portion of data loss incidents. Hardware failures, including disk crashes or server malfunctions, can lead to data loss at the infrastructure level. Cyberattacks, such as ransomware or destructive malware, can also encrypt or delete data, making recovery challenging.

- **Importance of data recovery**: The ability to recover lost data promptly is crucial for organizations to continue their operations without disruptions. Lost data may include critical business information, customer records, financial data, or proprietary intellectual property. A robust data recovery strategy helps organizations mitigate the potential financial losses, legal consequences, and reputational damage associated with data loss incidents.

- **Backup strategies**: Regular data backups are fundamental to data recovery in cloud environments. Organizations should implement backup strategies that include periodic backups of critical data to separate storage systems, either on-premises or in a different cloud region. Cloud providers often offer backup services or APIs to facilitate automated and scheduled backups.

- **Point-in-time snapshots**: Point-in-time snapshots are a useful feature provided by many cloud platforms, allowing organizations to create snapshots of their data at specific points in time. These snapshots serve as recovery points, enabling organizations to restore data to a previous state in case of data loss.

- **Replication and redundancy**: Cloud providers often offer data replication and redundancy options. Data replication ensures that data is stored in multiple locations, reducing the risk of complete data loss. Redundant storage systems and failover mechanisms help maintain data availability even in the event of hardware failures.

- **Recovery time objective (RTO) and recovery point objective (RPO)**: Organizations must define their RTO and RPO to set recovery goals. RTO specifies the maximum acceptable downtime before data recovery, while RPO defines the maximum data loss that can be tolerated during recovery.

- **Testing data recovery**: Periodic testing of data recovery processes is crucial to ensure the effectiveness of backup and recovery strategies. Organizations should perform recovery drills and simulations to verify the integrity and reliability of their backups and ensure they can restore data successfully.

- **Cloud disaster recovery services**: Some cloud providers offer disaster recovery services that automate data recovery processes, enabling organizations to restore data quickly and efficiently in the event of a catastrophic failure or disaster.

- **Hybrid and multi-cloud recovery**: Organizations with hybrid or multi-cloud environments must ensure their data recovery strategies span across all cloud environments and on-premises systems. Consistent recovery procedures and centralized management are essential for comprehensive data recovery.

- **Security and compliance considerations**: Data recovery processes should be aligned with security and compliance requirements. Encryption of backup data and secure access controls helps protect sensitive information during recovery.

Insecure APIs

APIs enable seamless communication between different cloud services. However, insecure APIs can be exploited by attackers to gain unauthorized access to cloud resources. We will explore the significance of secure API practices and how they contribute to a more secure cloud environment.

Insecure APIs pose a significant security risk in cloud computing environments. APIs serve as bridges that enable different software applications and services to communicate and exchange data seamlessly. However, when APIs are not adequately secured, they can become vulnerable points of entry for attackers to exploit, potentially leading to data breaches, unauthorized access, and other security incidents. Understanding the risks associated with insecure APIs is essential for ensuring the security and integrity of cloud-based systems, as we will see in the following sections.

API security risks

Several factors contribute to API security risks in cloud environments:

- **Weak authentication and authorization**: APIs with inadequate authentication mechanisms might allow unauthorized access to sensitive data and resources

- **Lack of input validation**: Failure to validate input data can lead to injection attacks, such as SQL injection or **cross-site scripting** (**XSS**), compromising the security of the application

- **Inadequate encryption**: Transmitting sensitive data over APIs without encryption can expose information to eavesdropping and data interception

- **Excessive permissions**: APIs with overly permissive access controls can grant attackers access to more data and functionality than necessary

- **Insecure error handling**: Revealing detailed error messages in API responses can provide attackers with valuable insights to exploit vulnerabilities

- **API rate limiting**: Failure to implement rate limiting can make APIs vulnerable to DoS attacks, where attackers overload the system with excessive requests

Securing API endpoints

To enhance API security, several best practices should be followed:

- **Strong authentication and authorization**: Implementing robust authentication methods, such as OAuth or API keys, ensures that only authorized users can access APIs

- **Input validation and sanitization**: Validating and sanitizing all input data prevents injection attacks and ensures that data transmitted via APIs is safe

- **Encryption**: Encrypting API communications using HTTPS (TLS/SSL) prevents data interception and ensures data privacy during transmission

- **Least privilege principle**: APIs should follow the principle of least privilege, granting users only the necessary permissions to access specific resources

- **Secure error handling**: Avoid exposing sensitive information in error messages and implement proper logging to monitor API activities

- **API rate limiting and throttling**: Implementing rate limiting and throttling mechanisms can help prevent DoS attacks by limiting the number of requests per user or IP address

API security testing and auditing

Regular security testing and auditing of APIs is critical to identifying vulnerabilities and ensuring ongoing security. Techniques such as penetration testing, code reviews, and vulnerability assessments help uncover weaknesses in APIs that require remediation.

API gateways and API management platforms

Organizations can use API gateways and API management platforms to provide an additional layer of security for APIs. These platforms can handle authentication, rate limiting, encryption, and other security features centrally, reducing the risk of vulnerabilities in individual APIs.

API versioning and life cycle management

Proper API versioning and life cycle management help maintain security by ensuring that deprecated or insecure API versions are retired and no longer accessible.

API security education and awareness

Ensuring that developers and API consumers are educated about API security best practices and potential risks fosters a security-first mindset and contributes to better overall API security.

Securing APIs is of paramount importance in cloud environments to protect against potential data breaches and security incidents. By implementing robust security measures, such as strong authentication, input validation, encryption, and proper error handling, organizations can enhance the security of their APIs. Regular security testing, API gateways, and proper life cycle management contribute to ongoing API security and help maintain the integrity and confidentiality of data exchanged through APIs. A comprehensive approach to API security is crucial for building trust with users and safeguarding cloud-based systems from external threats.

DoS attacks

Cloud services can become targets of DoS attacks, which aim to overwhelm resources and disrupt service availability. Understanding DoS attack risks will lead us to explore strategies for the detection, mitigation, and prevention of such attacks.

DoS attacks are malicious attempts to disrupt the normal operation of an online service, network, or cloud environment by overwhelming it with a massive volume of traffic or resource requests. The primary objective of a DoS attack is to render the target inaccessible to legitimate users, causing service downtime and disruption. These attacks can have severe consequences for businesses and organizations, leading to financial losses, damage to reputation, and loss of customer trust. Understanding the intricacies of DoS attacks is essential for implementing effective mitigation strategies and ensuring the resilience of cloud-based systems.

Types of DoS attacks

There are different types of DoS attacks:

- **Volume-based attacks**: These attacks flood the target with a high volume of traffic, consuming network bandwidth and overwhelming server resources

- **Protocol-based attacks**: These attacks exploit weaknesses in network protocols to consume server resources, leading to service degradation or unresponsiveness

- **Application layer attacks**: Also known as Layer 7 attacks, these target specific applications or services, such as web servers, by exploiting vulnerabilities and causing them to become unresponsive

- **Distributed denial-of-service (DDoS) attacks**: DDoS attacks involve multiple sources to coordinate and launch the attack simultaneously, making it more challenging to mitigate

The impact of DoS attacks

DoS attacks can have severe consequences:

- **Service disruption**: The primary goal of a DoS attack is to disrupt the target service, making it inaccessible to legitimate users

- **Financial losses**: Downtime resulting from DoS attacks can lead to financial losses for businesses, particularly those that rely on continuous online operations

- **Reputational damage**: Extended service disruptions can tarnish an organization's reputation, leading to loss of customer trust and loyalty

- **Opportunities for other attacks**: A successful DoS attack may serve as a distraction, providing an opportunity for other, more damaging cyberattacks

DDoS attacks and cloud environments

Cloud-based services are attractive targets for DDoS attacks due to their scalability and the potential to impact multiple customers hosted on the same infrastructure. DDoS attacks can be challenging to detect and mitigate in a cloud environment, as the traffic from multiple sources can be distributed and masked effectively.

DoS attack mitigation strategies

Let's look at some examples:

- **Traffic filtering**: Implementing traffic filtering mechanisms can help block malicious traffic and allow only legitimate traffic to reach the target

- **Rate limiting**: Rate limiting restricts the number of requests from a single IP address, preventing an attacker from overwhelming the system with excessive requests

- **Load balancing**: Distributing traffic across multiple servers can help distribute the load and prevent one server from becoming overwhelmed

- **Web Application Firewalls (WAFs)**: WAFs can identify and block malicious traffic targeting specific applications, helping protect against Layer 7 attacks

- **Anomaly detection**: Employing anomaly detection systems can help with identifying unusual traffic patterns and trigger proactive responses

The following figure depicts the WAF layout in the public cloud and shows how it interacts with AWS CloudFront:

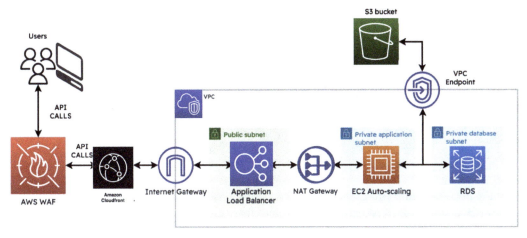

Figure 6.1 – WAF layout in AWS CloudFront

The preceding figure shows how the API calls interact with the AWS WAF service. Once they've gone through the WAF service, the API calls can interact with other AWS services. Please take note of the flow of the connection from the internet gateway to the application load balancer and then to other AWS services such as the EC2 instance.

Cloud-based DDoS protection services

Many cloud service providers offer DDoS protection services that leverage their distributed infrastructure to detect and mitigate DDoS attacks in real time. These services can effectively handle large-scale DDoS attacks and ensure minimal service disruption for customers.

Incident response and preparedness

Organizations must have a comprehensive incident response plan in place to detect and respond to DoS attacks promptly. Preparing for potential DoS attacks and conducting regular drills can improve the organization's ability to respond effectively.

DoS attacks are a serious threat to the availability and stability of cloud-based services. Understanding the different types of DoS attacks and implementing appropriate mitigation strategies is crucial for organizations to protect their cloud environments from disruption. Cloud-based DDoS protection services and proactive incident response planning are essential elements of a robust defense against DoS attacks. By investing in proper defenses and staying vigilant, organizations can ensure the resilience of their cloud-based systems and maintain uninterrupted service availability for their users.

Shared technology vulnerabilities

In a multi-tenant cloud environment, shared technology components may introduce vulnerabilities that can be exploited by attackers. In this section, we will examine the risks associated with the "noisy neighbor" effect and explore measures to ensure isolation and segregation between tenants.

Shared technology vulnerabilities refer to security weaknesses that arise in cloud computing environments due to the shared nature of underlying infrastructure and resources among multiple tenants (users or organizations). In a multi-tenant cloud environment, various users or organizations coexist on the same physical hardware and virtualized resources. While cloud providers implement strict isolation mechanisms to separate tenants logically, vulnerabilities in shared technology components can potentially lead to breaches of data confidentiality, integrity, and availability. Understanding shared technology vulnerabilities is essential for cloud users to assess and manage risks effectively:

- **The noisy neighbor effect**: The primary concern with shared technology vulnerabilities is the "noisy neighbor" effect. If one tenant consumes an excessive amount of resources or introduces malicious activities, it can impact the performance and availability of other neighboring tenants on the same infrastructure. For example, a resource-intensive application from one tenant might lead to degraded performance for others, affecting their ability to access and utilize resources effectively.

- **Virtualization vulnerabilities**: Virtualization, a core technology that enables multi-tenancy in the cloud, can introduce vulnerabilities. Flaws in the hypervisor or VM escape vulnerabilities could allow an attacker from one VM to access or compromise other VMs on the same physical host, potentially leading to data breaches and unauthorized access.

- **Insecure APIs and management interfaces**: Cloud providers offer APIs and management interfaces to facilitate interaction and control of cloud resources. If these interfaces are not adequately secured, attackers might exploit them to gain unauthorized access to tenant data or control cloud resources.

- **Cross-tenant data leakage**: In a shared infrastructure, improper data isolation or misconfigurations can lead to data leakage between tenants. A misconfigured storage bucket or database might expose one tenant's sensitive data to other tenants or the public, leading to compliance violations and privacy breaches.

- **Patching and software vulnerabilities**: Shared technology components, such as operating systems and software libraries, need regular updates and patches to address security vulnerabilities. Failure to promptly apply patches can expose tenants to known vulnerabilities, which attackers can exploit to gain unauthorized access.

- **Network vulnerabilities**: Inadequate network segmentation or security controls can lead to network-based attacks, where an attacker on one tenant's network attempts to infiltrate other tenants' resources or intercept their data.

- **Resource exhaustion**: If one tenant launches a DDoS attack or uses excessive resources, it can cause resource exhaustion for other tenants, resulting in service unavailability.

In this section, we delved into the multifaceted landscape of security challenges in cloud computing. We explored various risks that organizations face when leveraging cloud technology, including data breaches, insider threats, data loss and recovery, insecure APIs, DoS attacks, and shared technology vulnerabilities. By comprehensively analyzing these risks, you gained insights into the potential vulnerabilities that could compromise the confidentiality, integrity, and availability of your cloud-based resources and data.

Throughout this section, we emphasized the importance of implementing proactive security measures to mitigate these risks effectively. For data breaches, understanding the causes and impact allowed you to develop strong security practices, including encryption, access controls, and compliance with regulatory requirements. Regarding insider threats, you learned about the types of malicious actions, the significance of access management, and the need for security awareness training to minimize the risk of internal breaches.

The next section explores the diverse range of tools and technologies available to enhance the security of cloud computing environments. In this section, you will be introduced to a comprehensive array of security solutions designed to safeguard cloud resources, data, and applications from a variety of threats. We will cover a wide spectrum of topics, including IAM, encryption, firewalls, **intrusion detection and prevention systems** (**IDSs/IPSs**), SIEM, DLP, secure web gateways, and more. Each tool's functionality, benefits, and best practices for implementation will be discussed, enabling you to understand how these technologies contribute to a robust and resilient cloud security posture. By the end of this section, you will have gained valuable insights into the arsenal of cloud security tools at your disposal and how to strategically deploy them to effectively protect your cloud-based assets and combat emerging cyber threats.

Cloud security tools and technologies

In this comprehensive section, we will explore a wide range of cutting-edge tools and technologies specifically designed to bolster the security of cloud computing environments. As organizations increasingly adopt cloud services, the need for robust security measures has become paramount. In this section, we will delve into the various categories of cloud security tools, including IAM, encryption solutions, firewalls, IDS/IPS, SIEM, DLP, secure web gateways, and more. Each tool's functionalities, benefits, and practical implementation strategies will be thoroughly discussed to equip you with a comprehensive understanding of how these technologies can be harnessed to safeguard cloud resources, protect sensitive data, and fortify cloud-based applications from a myriad of threats. By the end of this section, you will have gained valuable insights into the wide array of cloud security tools available, empowering you to make informed decisions to enhance your cloud security posture and ensure the integrity, confidentiality, and availability of your cloud-based assets. Join us on this enlightening journey to explore the cutting-edge world of cloud security tools and technologies.

We will discuss several topics to provide a comprehensive understanding of the various tools and technologies available for securing cloud computing environments:

- *IAM*: We will explore IAM solutions and their role in managing user identities, access permissions, and authentication mechanisms to ensure that only authorized individuals can access cloud resources

- *Encryption and data protection*: We will discuss encryption techniques and technologies used to protect data at rest and in transit, ensuring data confidentiality and integrity in the cloud

- *Firewalls and network security*: We will examine the use of firewalls and network security solutions to control and monitor traffic entering and exiting cloud environments, preventing unauthorized access and cyber threats

- *IDS/IPS*: We will explore IDS and IPS tools that can detect and respond to potential security breaches and malicious activities in real time, enhancing cloud security

We will discuss these topics in detail now.

IAM

IAM is a crucial component of cloud security that focuses on managing user identities and controlling their access to resources within a cloud computing environment. IAM solutions are designed to ensure that only authorized individuals can access specific data, applications, or services, thereby enhancing data confidentiality, integrity, and overall cloud security. Let's delve into the details of IAM and some of the tools and services associated with it.

Let's look at some IAM components and features:

- **Identity management**: IAM solutions provide mechanisms to manage user identities, enabling administrators to create, modify, and delete user accounts. Each user is assigned a unique identity, and IAM systems maintain user attributes, roles, and permissions.

- **Authentication**: IAM ensures that users' identities are verified before granting access to resources. Common authentication methods include username and password, **multi-factor authentication (MFA)**, and integration with external identity providers (for example, SAML and OAuth).

- **Authorization and access control**: IAM allows fine-grained control over users' access privileges. Administrators can assign roles or permissions to users, determining what actions they are allowed to perform on specific resources.

- **Single sign-on (SSO)**: IAM often supports SSO, allowing users to access multiple cloud services with a single set of credentials. This enhances user convenience and reduces the risk of weak passwords or credentials reuse.

- **PAM**: IAM solutions offer PAM features to manage and monitor access to critical resources by privileged users. PAM ensures that privileged accounts are only used when necessary and with appropriate oversight.

IAM services

- **Amazon Web Services (AWS) IAM**: AWS IAM is a comprehensive IAM service for managing access to AWS resources. It enables users to create and manage AWS users, groups, and permissions, ensuring secure access to AWS services.

Setting up AWS IAM involves several key steps as you must create and manage user identities, access policies, and permissions within the AWS environment. IAM allows you to control who can access your AWS resources and what actions they can perform. Here's a step-by-step guide to setting up AWS IAM:

1. **Access the AWS Management Console**: Sign in to your AWS account using your root credentials (the initial account you created during the AWS registration process) and access the AWS Management Console.

2. **Create IAM users**: In the IAM dashboard, click on **Users** in the left navigation panel, and then click **Add user**. Enter a username and select an access type:

    - **Programmatic access**: For users that require API access.

    - **AWS Management Console access**: For users that require access to the AWS Management Console.

3. **Set user permissions**: Assign permissions to the user. You can either attach existing policies (predefined permission sets) or create custom policies. The best practice is to follow the principle of least privilege, granting users only the permissions they require for their specific tasks.

4. **Configure a user password and MFA**: For users with AWS Management Console access, set up a password or require them to set one during their first login. Additionally, enable MFA for an extra layer of security.

5. **Review and create a user**: Review the user's details and permissions, and then click **Create user** to complete the process. Users will receive an email with login details if they have AWS Management Console access.

6. **Create IAM groups (optional)**: To manage permissions more efficiently, you can create IAM groups and assign policies to groups rather than individual users. This simplifies access management, especially for users with similar roles.

7. **Attach users to groups (optional)**: Once IAM groups have been created, add users to the appropriate groups to grant them the required permissions.

8. **Enable and configure IAM roles (optional)**: IAM roles are used to delegate permissions to AWS services and external entities. If you need to grant permissions to services or applications, create and configure IAM roles accordingly.

9. **Manage IAM policies**: Regularly review and update IAM policies as your organization's requirements change. Ensure that users have the necessary permissions and that there are no unnecessary or overly permissive policies.

10. **Monitoring and auditing**: Enable AWS CloudTrail to log API activity and changes to IAM resources, providing an audit trail for security and compliance purposes. Additionally, set up AWS IAM Access Analyzer to review public and cross-account access to your resources.

Setting up AWS IAM using the AWS **Command-Line Interface** (**CLI**) involves using various AWS CLI commands to create users, groups, policies, and roles. Here are the steps to set up AWS IAM using the CLI:

1. **Install and configure the AWS CLI**: Ensure you have the AWS CLI installed on your local machine and configure it with your AWS credentials using the `aws configure` command.

2. **Create an IAM user**: Use the `create-user` command to create an IAM user. Replace <USERNAME> with the desired username:

   ```
   aws iam create-user --user-name <USERNAME>
   ```

3. **Create an IAM access key (for programmatic access)**: If the user requires programmatic access (access through API calls), create an access key using the `create-access-key` command. This will generate an access key ID and secret access key that the user will use to authenticate API requests:

   ```
   aws iam create-access-key --user-name <USERNAME>
   ```

4. **Create an IAM login profile (for AWS Management Console access)**: If the user requires access to the AWS Management Console, create a login profile using the `create-login-profile` command. This will allow the user to sign in to the AWS Management Console with a username and password:

   ```
   aws iam create-login-profile --user-name <USERNAME> --password
   <PASSWORD> --password-reset-required
   ```

5. **Attach IAM policies**: Attach an existing IAM policy to the user or create a custom policy and attach it. To attach an existing policy, use the `attach-user-policy` command, replacing <POLICY-ARN> with the ARN of the policy to attach:

   ```
   aws iam attach-user-policy --user-name <USERNAME> --policy-arn
   <POLICY-ARN>
   ```

6. **Create an IAM group (optional)**: To manage permissions more efficiently, create an IAM group using the `create-group` command:

   ```
   aws iam create-group --group-name <GROUP-NAME>
   ```

7. **Attach users to groups (optional)**: Use the `add-user-to-group` command to add the user to the group you created in the previous step:

   ```
   aws iam add-user-to-group --user-name <USERNAME> --group-name
   <GROUP-NAME>
   ```

8. **Create an IAM role (optional)**: To delegate permissions to services or applications, create an IAM role using the `create-role` command. Replace `<ROLE-NAME>` with the desired name for the role:

    ```
    aws iam create-role --role-name <ROLE-NAME> --assume-role-
    policy-document <TRUST-POLICY-DOCUMENT>
    ```

9. **Attach IAM policies to the role (optional)**: Attach policies to the role using the `attach-role-policy` command, just like you did for the IAM user:

    ```
    aws iam attach-role-policy --role-name <ROLE-NAME> --policy-arn
    <POLICY-ARN>
    ```

10. **Review and verify**: Use the appropriate commands, such as `list-users`, `list-groups`, and `list-roles`, to review and verify the IAM entities you have created.

By following these steps with the AWS CLI, you can effectively set up IAM users, groups, and roles, assign permissions, and control access to your AWS resources programmatically. The AWS CLI provides a powerful and scriptable way to manage IAM resources and ensure secure access management in your AWS environment.

Figure 6.2 depicts the relationship between IAM and IAM Policy, as well as how it works with the Lambda function:

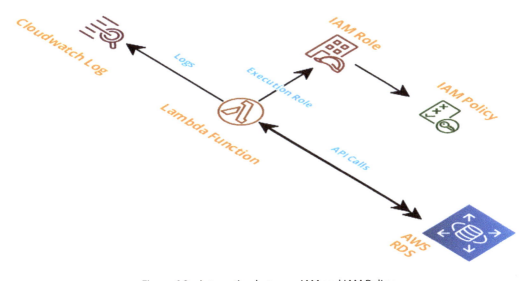

Figure 6.2 – Interaction between IAM and IAM Policy

- **Azure Active Directory (Azure AD)**: Microsoft's Azure AD is a cloud-based IAM service that offers identity management, SSO, MFA, and application access management for Microsoft cloud services and third-party applications

- **Google Cloud Identity and Access Management** (**Cloud IAM**): Cloud IAM is Google Cloud's IAM service, providing centralized control over access to **Google Cloud Platform** (**GCP**) resources and allowing fine-grained access management

- **Okta**: Okta is an identity management platform that offers SSO, MFA, life cycle management, and API access management for various cloud and on-premises applications

- **Ping Identity**: Ping Identity provides comprehensive IAM solutions, including identity federation, access management, and API security, enabling secure and seamless access to cloud and mobile applications

- **Microsoft Active Directory** (**AD**): While not specific to the cloud, Microsoft AD can integrate with cloud environments to manage on-premises and cloud-based user identities and provide centralized access control

- **Auth0**: Auth0 is an identity platform offering authentication and authorization services, including social identity providers, passwordless authentication, and extensible identity features for cloud and web applications

Encryption and data protection

Encryption and data protection are critical aspects of cloud security, aiming to safeguard sensitive information from unauthorized access, theft, and tampering. In the context of cloud computing, where data is stored, processed, and transmitted across networks, encryption plays a vital role in ensuring data confidentiality and integrity. Let's delve into the details of encryption and data protection in the cloud, along with some of the tools and services available for this purpose.

Encryption techniques:

- **Data-at-rest encryption**: This form of encryption ensures that data remains encrypted when it is stored in databases, disks, or other storage systems. Even if an attacker gains unauthorized access to the underlying storage, the data remains unreadable without the decryption key.

- **Data-in-transit encryption**: Data-in-transit encryption protects data while it is being transmitted between different cloud services or between cloud and on-premises environments. This ensures that data remains secure during transmission and cannot be intercepted by eavesdroppers.

- **End-to-end encryption**: End-to-end encryption ensures that data remains encrypted throughout its entire journey, from the source to the destination, without being decrypted at intermediate points. This approach provides the highest level of data protection.

Encryption tools and services:

- **AWS Key Management Service** (**KMS**): AWS KMS is a fully managed service that allows users to create and control encryption keys to protect their data stored in AWS services and custom applications. KMS offers both data-at-rest and data-in-transit encryption capabilities.

  Figure 6.3 depicts the usage of encryption (AWS KMS) in a cloud environment:

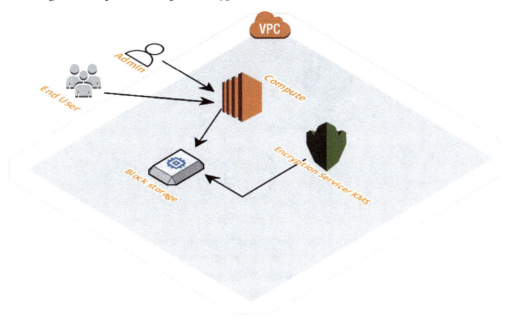

Figure 6.3 – Cloud environment with compute, storage, and encryption services

- **AWS CloudHSM**: AWS CloudHSM provides dedicated **Hardware Security Modules** (**HSMs**) to securely generate, store, and manage cryptographic keys, ensuring a higher level of security for sensitive data.

- **Azure Key Vault**: Azure Key Vault is a cloud-based service in Microsoft Azure that allows users to manage keys, secrets, and certificates used for encryption and authentication.

  Figure 6.4 depicts the usage of Azure Key Vault in an Azure cloud environment and how it can encrypt/decrypt the database layer:

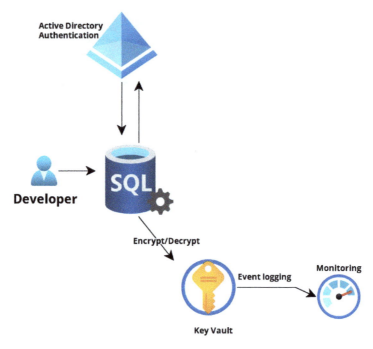

Figure 6.4 – Azure Key Vault in the Azure cloud

- **Google Cloud Key Management Service (KMS)**: Google Cloud KMS provides a centralized location to create, manage, and store cryptographic keys, offering a secure way to protect data in GCP. Let's see how we can set up KMS in Google Cloud.

Setting up Google Cloud KMS involves a few essential steps as you must create and manage cryptographic keys securely in GCP. Google Cloud KMS allows you to generate and control encryption keys, helping you protect your data and resources in the cloud. Here's a step-by-step guide to setting up Google Cloud KMS:

I.   **Create a Google Cloud project**: If you haven't already, create a new project on the Google Cloud Console. Go to the Google Cloud Console (`https://console.cloud.google.com/`), sign in with your Google account, and create a new project.

II. **Enable the Cloud KMS API**: On the Google Cloud Console, navigate to **APIs & Services > Library**. Search for `Cloud Key Management Service (KMS)` and click on it. Click the **Enable** button to enable the API for your project.

III. **Create a key ring**: In the Google Cloud Console, go to **Cloud KMS > Key rings**. Click the **Create Key Ring** button and provide a name for the key ring. Key rings are logical containers that hold cryptographic keys.

IV. **Create a crypto key**: After creating the key ring, click on it to access its details. Click the **Create Crypto Key** button to create a new cryptographic key within the key ring.

V.   **Configure the crypto key**: Provide a name for the crypto key and select the desired key algorithm and key purpose (encryption or signing). You can also choose to have Google Cloud KMS automatically rotate the key for added security.

VI. **Set IAM permissions**: By default, only project owners and editors have permissions to manage keys. To grant specific users or service accounts access to use the crypto key, go to **IAM & Admin** > **IAM** and add the appropriate roles for the desired users or service accounts.

VII. **Encrypt and decrypt data**: With the crypto key set up, you can now use the Cloud KMS API to encrypt and decrypt data in your applications. The encryption process will use the provided cryptographic key to protect your sensitive data, and decryption will require the appropriate permissions and the same key used for encryption.

VIII. **Manage key versions and rotation (optional)**: Google Cloud KMS allows you to manage key versions and rotation policies to enhance security. You can create new key versions to roll over encryption keys periodically or when required.

IX. **Audit logging and monitoring (optional)**: Enable audit logging and monitoring for your Google Cloud KMS activities. This will help you track key usage and changes, providing an audit trail for security and compliance purposes.

By following these steps, you can set up Google Cloud KMS and begin securing your data and resources with cryptographic keys in GCP. Google Cloud KMS provides a robust and scalable solution for managing encryption keys, enhancing the security of your cloud-based applications and data.

* **HashiCorp Vault**: Vault is an open source tool that provides a centralized solution for securely managing secrets, encryption keys, and other sensitive data.

* **OpenSSL**: OpenSSL is an open source toolkit that provides encryption, decryption, and cryptographic functions. It is widely used for securing data and communications.

* **TLS/SSL certificates**: **Transport Layer Security** (TLS) and **Secure Sockets Layer** (SSL) certificates are used to encrypt data during transit across networks, ensuring secure communication between clients and servers.

Firewalls and network security

Firewalls and network security play a pivotal role in safeguarding cloud environments by controlling and monitoring traffic entering and exiting the cloud infrastructure. These security measures are vital in preventing unauthorized access, mitigating cyber threats, and ensuring the confidentiality and integrity of data and resources. Let's delve into the details of firewalls and network security in the cloud, along with some of the tools and services available for robust network protection.

Firewalls in cloud environments:

- **Network firewalls**: Network firewalls act as a barrier between a trusted internal network (such as a VPC in AWS or a VNet in Azure) and untrusted external networks (such as the internet). They inspect network traffic and enforce security rules, allowing only authorized traffic to pass through while blocking or logging suspicious or malicious activities.

- **WAFs**: A WAF filters, monitors, and blocks HTTP/HTTPS requests between a web application and the internet. WAFs protect web applications from common web-based attacks such as SQL injection, XSS, and other OWASP Top 10 threats.

Figure 6.5 depicts how a WAF would function and be placed in a typical cloud environment:

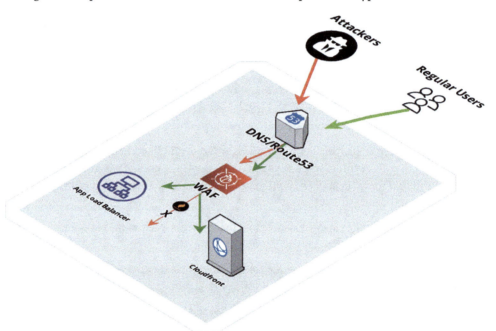

Figure 6.5 – WAF in a cloud environment

Network security tools and services:

- **AWS Network Firewall**: AWS Network Firewall is a managed firewall service that provides granular control over inbound and outbound network traffic at the protocol and port level. It integrates with AWS Security Groups and AWS Shield for comprehensive network security.

- **Azure Network Security Groups (NSGs)**: Azure NSGs are cloud-based firewalls that allow or deny traffic based on source and destination IP addresses, ports, and protocols. They provide network segmentation and isolation in Azure **Virtual Networks** (**VNets**).

- **Google Cloud Firewall Rules**: Google Cloud Firewall Rules enable you to control traffic at the instance level within GCP. They work similarly to traditional firewalls, filtering traffic based on IP addresses, protocols, and ports.

- **Cloud-based WAFs**: Cloud providers such as AWS, Azure, and GCP offer cloud-native WAF solutions that protect web applications from common web-based attacks. Third-party WAF services, such as Cloudflare and Imperva, can also be integrated with cloud environments.

- **Open source firewalls**: Tools such as iptables, nftables, and pfSense offer open source firewall solutions that can be deployed in cloud instances or virtual machines for more customized network security configurations.

- **Cloud-based DDoS protection**: Cloud providers such as AWS and Azure offer DDoS protection services that help defend against large-scale DDoS attacks, ensuring service availability.

The following are the benefits of firewalls and network security:

- **Access control**: Firewalls enable organizations to implement access control policies, allowing only authorized traffic to pass through and protecting against unauthorized access attempts

- **Threat mitigation**: Firewalls act as the first line of defense against cyber threats, preventing malicious traffic from reaching the cloud infrastructure and applications

- **Network segmentation**: Network firewalls and NSGs enable network segmentation, isolating different parts of the infrastructure and reducing the impact of potential breaches

- **Compliance and regulatory requirements**: Firewalls help organizations meet compliance and regulatory requirements by enforcing security policies and protecting sensitive data

- **Visibility and logging**: Firewalls provide logging and monitoring capabilities, allowing organizations to analyze network traffic and identify potential security incidents

Firewalls and network security are crucial components of cloud security, providing a secure perimeter and protecting cloud resources from external threats. Cloud providers offer native firewall services, and third-party tools complement these offerings, allowing organizations to tailor their network security measures to meet specific needs. By effectively implementing firewalls and network security measures, organizations can significantly enhance the overall security posture of their cloud environments, ensuring the confidentiality, integrity, and availability of their critical assets and data.

IDS/IPS

IDS and IPS are essential components of a comprehensive cloud security strategy. These systems are designed to monitor network traffic and detect potential security threats and intrusions in real time. IDS focuses on identifying suspicious activities, while IPS goes a step further by actively blocking or mitigating threats. Let's delve into the details of IDS/IPS in the cloud, along with some of the tools and services available for effective intrusion detection and prevention:

- **IDS**:

  - **Signature-based detection**: IDS uses a database of known attack signatures to identify malicious patterns in network traffic. When traffic matches a signature, IDS generates an alert for further investigation.

  - **Anomaly-based detection**: Anomaly-based IDS looks for deviations from normal network behavior. It establishes a baseline of typical network activity and raises alerts when traffic patterns deviate significantly from the norm.

  - **Network traffic analysis**: IDS inspects packets traversing the network, analyzing headers, payloads, and patterns to identify potential threats such as port scans, buffer overflows, or other suspicious activities.

Figure 6.6 depicts an example of IDS/IPS placement in an environment:

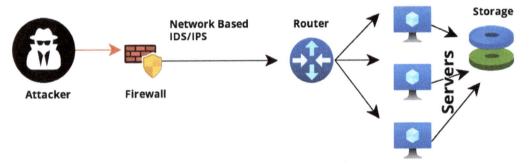

Figure 6.6 – IDS/IPS in an environment

- **IPS**:
- **Real-time blocking**: IPS not only detects intrusions such as IDS but can actively respond to threats. It can block malicious traffic or take preventive actions, such as resetting connections or sending alarms.

- **Automatic response**: IPS can trigger automatic responses based on predefined rules, such as blocking IP addresses or dropping packets from suspected malicious sources.

Now, let's look at some IDS/IPS tools and services:

- **AWS GuardDuty**: AWS GuardDuty is a managed threat detection service that continuously monitors AWS accounts for malicious activities, unauthorized behavior, and potential security threats.

  Setting up AWS GuardDuty is a straightforward process that involves a few simple steps. AWS GuardDuty is a managed threat detection service that continuously monitors AWS accounts for malicious activities, unauthorized behavior, and potential security threats. Here's a step-by-step guide on how to set up AWS GuardDuty:

  I.   **Access the AWS Management Console**: Sign in to your AWS account using your root credentials or an IAM user with administrative privileges. Then, access the AWS Management Console.

  II. **Navigate to AWS GuardDuty**: In the AWS Management Console, navigate to the **GuardDuty** service by either searching for `GuardDuty` in the search bar or finding it under the **Security, Identity, & Compliance** section.

  III. **Enable GuardDuty for your AWS region**: In the GuardDuty dashboard, click on the **Get Started** button. You will be prompted to enable GuardDuty for the AWS region in which you are currently working.

  IV. **Choose a detector name**: Enter a name for your GuardDuty detector. The detector is a logical entity that represents your GuardDuty setup in a specific AWS region.

  V.   **Enable CloudTrail (optional)**: If you already have AWS CloudTrail enabled, you can choose to enable CloudTrail data ingestion for GuardDuty. CloudTrail logs provide additional context for threat analysis.

  VI. **Enable VPC Flow Logs (optional)**: If you have VPC Flow Logs enabled in your AWS environment, you can choose to enable VPC Flow Logs data ingestion for GuardDuty. VPC Flow Logs provides network traffic visibility for analysis.

  VII. **Review your settings and create the detector**: Review your settings, such as CloudTrail and VPC Flow Logs, and click on the **Create** button to create the GuardDuty detector.

  VIII. **Wait for detector activation**: After creating the detector, GuardDuty will start analyzing the AWS CloudTrail logs and VPC flow logs (if enabled) for potential threats. The activation process may take a few minutes to complete.

  IX. **Review and act on your findings**: Once GuardDuty is activated, it starts generating findings based on its analysis. You can view these findings in the GuardDuty dashboard, along with details about the severity of the findings, affected resources, and recommended actions.

  X.   **Configure notifications and remediation (optional)**: Optionally, you can configure CloudWatch Events to send notifications based on GuardDuty findings. You can also set up automated remediation actions through AWS Lambda based on specific findings.

  XI. **Monitor GuardDuty regularly**: Regularly monitor the GuardDuty dashboard to stay aware of potential security threats and take appropriate actions to address them.

By following these steps, you can effectively set up AWS GuardDuty in your AWS account to continuously monitor for security threats and potential security issues. GuardDuty provides proactive security monitoring and alerts, helping you enhance your overall cloud security posture and safeguard your AWS resources from potential threats and malicious activities.

- **Azure Security Center**: Azure Security Center provides a unified security management and advanced threat protection solution for Azure cloud resources. It includes built-in IDS/IPS capabilities to detect and prevent attacks.

- **Google Cloud IDS**: Google Cloud IDS is an IDS that monitors network traffic for suspicious activities and alerts administrators about potential threats in GCP environments.

- **Snort**: Snort is a popular open source IDS/IPS system known for its signature-based detection. It can be deployed in cloud environments to provide network security.

- **Suricata**: Suricata is another open source IDS/IPS tool that offers both signature-based and anomaly-based detection, making it suitable for detecting a wide range of threats.

- **Cisco Firepower**: Cisco Firepower is an advanced IPS solution that provides real-time threat intelligence and automatic response capabilities.

Now, let's consider the benefits of IDS/IPS in cloud environments:

- **Early threat detection**: IDS/IPS systems enable early detection of security incidents, helping organizations respond promptly to potential threats before they escalate.

- **Real-time protection**: IPS actively blocks malicious traffic, preventing attacks from reaching their targets and minimizing the impact of security breaches.

- **Compliance and auditing**: IDS/IPS solutions assist organizations in meeting compliance requirements by providing continuous monitoring and generating detailed security logs.

- **Security automation**: IDS/IPS tools offer automation, reducing the burden on security teams and enabling faster response times to security incidents.

- **Proactive security posture**: By deploying IDS/IPS in the cloud, organizations can maintain a proactive security posture, fortifying their cloud infrastructure against emerging threats.

IDS and IPS are crucial components of cloud security, providing continuous monitoring and real-time protection against potential intrusions and threats. Cloud providers offer native IDS/IPS services, and third-party tools complement these offerings, enabling organizations to implement robust security measures tailored to their specific cloud environments. By leveraging IDS/IPS tools and services, organizations can enhance their overall security posture and ensure the integrity and availability of their cloud-based assets and data.

Summary

The chapter has been an illuminating journey, offering a comprehensive understanding of the critical aspects of security in cloud computing. By exploring cloud security risks, you have become well-versed in the various vulnerabilities that can threaten cloud environments, including data breaches, insider threats, data loss, insecure APIs, DoS attacks, and shared technology vulnerabilities. Armed with this knowledge, you are now empowered to proactively identify and address potential risks, fortifying your cloud assets and safeguarding sensitive data.

In the *Cloud security tools and technologies* section, you were exposed to a wide array of solutions, from IAM to encryption, firewalls, IDS/IPS, and beyond. This comprehensive overview equipped you with a broad spectrum of tools to enhance your cloud security. Moreover, you learned how to implement best practices, manage access control, and orchestrate encryption measures, ensuring data confidentiality, integrity, and availability in your cloud environments.

By completing this chapter, you have acquired vital skills, such as being able to perform a cloud security risk assessment, incident detection and response, compliance implementation, tool selection, integration, and security automation. Armed with this knowledge, you are now well-equipped to navigate the complexities of cloud security, making informed decisions to protect your cloud infrastructure from potential threats and maintaining compliance with industry regulations. Overall, this chapter has provided a solid foundation for you to build and maintain secure, compliant, and resilient cloud environments, ensuring the utmost protection for your data and services in the dynamic realm of cloud computing.

The next chapter, *Security and Compliance 2 – Cloud Perspective*, explores some important aspects of security in cloud computing. It delves into compliance and legal considerations, incident response, the evolving threat landscape, managing cloud security at scale, and cloud security best practices.

7

Security and Compliance 2 – Cloud Perspective

This is the second part of the previous chapter. In this chapter, readers will explore critical aspects of security in cloud computing, gaining insights into compliance and legal considerations, cloud security best practices, **incident response (IR)**, cloud forensics, managing cloud security at scale, and the evolving threat landscape. First, they will understand the regulatory landscape surrounding cloud operations, ensuring compliance with frameworks such as the **General Data Protection Regulation (GDPR)**, the **Health Insurance Portability and Accountability Act (HIPAA)**, and the **Payment Card Industry Data Security Standard (PCI DSS)**. Next, readers will be equipped with a comprehensive set of best practices to fortify their cloud environments, including encryption, **identity and access management (IAM)**, secure API usage, network security, and cloud-native application security. The chapter will also cover crafting effective IR procedures and the significance of cloud forensics in investigating breaches. For organizations operating at scale, strategies for managing security across multiple cloud regions and accounts will be provided. Lastly, readers will explore emerging threats and attack vectors in the cloud, fostering a proactive security approach.

In this chapter, we will cover the following topics:

- **Compliance and legal considerations**: The chapter will delve into various compliance frameworks and regulations relevant to cloud computing, such as the GDPR, HIPAA, and PCI DSS. Readers will gain an understanding of how these regulations impact their cloud operations and the steps needed to ensure compliance.

- **IR and cloud forensics**: The chapter will cover IR procedures specific to cloud incidents and the importance of cloud forensics in investigating and analyzing security breaches. This knowledge will help readers develop effective response plans to address security incidents promptly.

- **Managing cloud security at scale**: For readers dealing with large-scale cloud deployments, the chapter will discuss strategies for managing security across multiple cloud regions, accounts, and services efficiently.

- **Evolving threat landscape**: Readers can anticipate insights into current and emerging threats in the cloud computing environment. Understanding the evolving threat landscape is vital to staying ahead of potential security risks.

- **Cloud security best practices**: Readers will learn about industry-leading security practices and strategies designed to mitigate cloud-related risks. This will include topics such as encryption, IAM, secure API usage, network security, and secure coding practices for cloud-native applications.

At the end of the chapter, readers will emerge with the knowledge and skills needed to make informed decisions around cloud best practices when designing, managing, and optimizing security solutions in cloud computing, fostering efficient, reliable, and budget-conscious cloud infrastructures.

Technical requirements

To fully engage with the content of this chapter on cloud computing architecture, readers should have a basic understanding of computer systems, networking concepts, and information technology.

Additionally, the following technical requirements are recommended:

- **Internet access**: Readers should have a reliable internet connection to access online resources, references, and examples related to cloud computing.

- **Computing device**: A desktop computer, laptop, tablet, or smartphone with a modern web browser is necessary to read the chapter content and access any online materials.

- **Web browser**: The latest version of a modern web browser such as Google Chrome, Mozilla Firefox, Microsoft Edge, or Safari is recommended. This ensures compatibility and optimal viewing experience of web-based resources and interactive content.

- **Familiarity with cloud services**: Some familiarity with cloud services and their basic functionalities will enhance the understanding of the chapter. This includes knowledge of basic network security, O/S, encryption, and servers.

Compliance and legal considerations

The section delves into the crucial aspect of ensuring cloud environments adhere to relevant industry regulations, legal requirements, and data protection laws. In the cloud computing landscape, organizations are responsible for complying with a myriad of regulatory frameworks, depending on their industry and geographical location. This section sheds light on the significance of compliance in cloud computing, the potential consequences of non-compliance, and the measures needed to meet various regulatory standards.

Compliance and legal considerations in cloud technology are paramount due to increasing reliance on cloud computing for business operations and data storage. Organizations that utilize cloud services must navigate a complex landscape of regulatory frameworks, data protection laws, and industry-specific standards. Failing to meet these requirements can lead to severe consequences, including financial penalties, reputational damage, and legal liabilities. Hence, understanding and addressing compliance and legal considerations are crucial aspects of cloud security and risk management. Let's understand some of the top legal and compliance considerations that are critical from a security standpoint:

- **Data protection laws and regulations**: Compliance with data protection laws is a primary concern for cloud users, especially when dealing with sensitive and personal data. Laws such as the GDPR in the **European Union (EU)**, the **California Consumer Privacy Act (CCPA)**, and the HIPAA in the healthcare sector impose stringent requirements for data privacy and security. Organizations must ensure that data stored in the cloud adheres to the specific data protection requirements mandated by relevant laws.

- **Data residency and cross-border data transfers**: Data residency requirements may dictate that certain data must remain within specific geographical regions or countries. Cloud providers should offer data centers located in these regions to comply with such regulations. Additionally, cross-border data transfers may necessitate additional safeguards, such as data encryption and contractual commitments, to ensure compliance during data movement between different jurisdictions.

- **Industry-specific compliance standards**: Various industries have their own compliance standards. For instance, organizations processing credit card transactions must adhere to PCI DSS. Healthcare providers handling electronic health records must comply with the HIPAA. **Cloud service providers (CSPs)** should offer specialized services and configurations to meet these industry-specific requirements.

- **Audits and documentation**: Maintaining comprehensive documentation and conducting regular audits are essential components of compliance. Organizations need to demonstrate that they have implemented the necessary security controls, policies, and procedures to protect data and maintain compliance. Cloud providers often offer compliance reports and certifications that can be shared with auditors and regulatory bodies to verify adherence to industry standards.

- **CSP compliance assurance**: When selecting a CSP, organizations must ensure that the provider adheres to relevant compliance standards. The cloud vendor should be transparent about their compliance measures and offer contractual commitments to protect customer data in accordance with applicable regulations.

- **Cloud security controls and governance**: Effective cloud security controls and governance practices are vital for maintaining compliance. Organizations should implement robust IAM, encryption, monitoring, and logging mechanisms to protect data and detect potential security incidents. They must also enforce proper data retention and disposal policies to comply with data protection laws.

In the realm of cloud technology, several tools and services are available to assist organizations in addressing compliance and legal considerations. These tools and services are designed to help organizations meet regulatory requirements, manage data privacy, and maintain the necessary documentation to demonstrate compliance.

As we delve into the intricacies of cloud technology, it's imperative to explore AWS Artifact, a pivotal service offered by **Amazon Web Services** (**AWS**). This section focuses on compliance and regulatory dimensions of cloud computing, shedding light on how AWS Artifact serves as a cornerstone in meeting these essential requirements. From providing access to crucial compliance documents to offering a user-friendly interface for seamless navigation, AWS Artifact plays a key role in instilling trust and transparency in the cloud environment.

AWS Artifact

AWS Artifact is a service provided by AWS that offers on-demand access to compliance reports and security documentation. It provides customers with access to various compliance documents, including AWS's certifications, attestations, and agreements. Organizations can use AWS Artifact to demonstrate compliance with various regulatory standards.

Key features of AWS Artifact include the following:

- **Compliance reports and certifications**: AWS Artifact offers a comprehensive collection of compliance reports and certifications related to various AWS services. These documents cover a wide range of industry standards and regulations, including the GDPR, **International Organization for Standardization** (**ISO**) *27001*, **System and Organizational Controls** (**SOC**) reports, the HIPAA, and more.

- **Agreements and contracts**: Customers can access and review agreements and contracts relevant to their use of AWS services. These agreements include the AWS Customer Agreement, **Business Associate Addendum** (**BAA**), and the AWS Service Terms.

- **On-demand access**: AWS Artifact allows customers to obtain compliance documents on demand, reducing the need for manual requests and ensuring timely access to the latest compliance reports.

- **Download of audit reports**: Customers can download compliance reports and use them during internal audits or regulatory assessments. The reports provide valuable insights into AWS's security and compliance controls.

- **Security and compliance documentation**: AWS Artifact hosts a variety of security and compliance-related documents, such as whitepapers, best practice guides, and security FAQs. These resources help customers understand AWS's security measures and best practices.

Using and deploying AWS Artifact in the AWS cloud is a straightforward process that allows AWS customers to access compliance-related documents, agreements, and security reports. Here's a step-by-step guide on how to use and deploy AWS Artifact:

1. **Sign in to the AWS Management Console**: Sign in to your AWS account using your root credentials or an IAM user with sufficient permissions to access AWS Artifact.

2. **Access AWS Artifact**: In the AWS Management Console, navigate to the **Security, Identity & Compliance** section. Under this section, you will find AWS Artifact. Click on **AWS Artifact** to access the service.

3. **Choose a compliance report or document**: Within AWS Artifact, you can search for the compliance report, agreement, or security document you need. These documents are categorized based on regulatory standards or AWS services. Browse the available reports and select one that meets your compliance needs.

4. **Review and download the document**: Once you select a compliance document, you can review its details and contents. The document is typically available in PDF format. Download the report to your local machine.

5. **Use the compliance report**: With the compliance report downloaded, you can use it for various purposes. For internal reviews, audits, or regulatory assessments, the report provides valuable insights into AWS's security and compliance controls. Ensure that you comply with the necessary requirements based on the information in the report.

Here are some additional considerations:

- **Frequent updates**: AWS regularly updates the compliance documents in AWS Artifact to ensure customers have access to the most current information. As a best practice, check for updates regularly to stay informed about changes and improvements in AWS security and compliance measures.

- **Role-based access control (RBAC)**: Ensure that IAM users in your AWS account have appropriate permissions to access AWS Artifact. Limit access to only users who need to review or download compliance documents.

- **Data protection**: Keep compliance reports and downloaded documents secure. Use secure channels for document transfer and storage to protect sensitive information.

Azure Compliance Manager

Microsoft Azure Compliance Manager is a tool that enables organizations to assess and track their compliance with various regulatory standards, including the GDPR, ISO *27001*, the HIPAA, and more. It provides a dashboard to monitor compliance progress and offers guidance and recommendations for improving compliance. It also enables users to assess their cloud workloads against a broad range of regulatory controls, monitor compliance progress, and generate compliance reports. Azure Compliance Manager simplifies the process of achieving and maintaining compliance within the Azure cloud environment.

Key features of Azure Compliance Manager include the following:

- **Comprehensive compliance assessments**: Azure Compliance Manager provides a library of industry-specific regulatory standards and frameworks, such as the GDPR, ISO *27001*, the **National Institute of Standards and Technology** (**NIST**), HIPAA, and more. Users can select the relevant regulations and assess their Azure workloads against specific controls of those standards.

- **Continuous monitoring and progress tracking**: Organizations can continuously monitor their compliance progress through the Compliance Manager dashboard. This feature enables users to identify gaps, track improvements, and stay up to date on the status of their compliance efforts.

- **Control documentation and evidence gathering**: Azure Compliance Manager allows users to upload and manage evidence of their compliance efforts, such as policies, procedures, and audit reports. It simplifies the process of gathering, organizing, and maintaining documentation required for compliance assessments.

- **Automated compliance control testing**: Compliance Manager automates the testing of various controls by using predefined assessment questions. This automation helps streamline the compliance evaluation process and reduces the manual effort required for compliance assessments.

- **Guidance and recommendations**: The tool offers guidance and recommendations for implementing controls and best practices to improve compliance. It provides valuable insights into areas where organizations can enhance their security and compliance posture.

- **Built-in assessments and third-party assessments**: Compliance Manager supports both built-in assessments and third-party assessments. Built-in assessments are performed by Microsoft, while third-party assessments can be carried out by external auditors. Users can access the results of both types of assessments through the dashboard.

Using and deploying Azure Compliance Manager in the Azure cloud involves a few straightforward steps. This tool helps organizations assess, track, and improve their compliance with various regulatory standards and industry-specific requirements. Here's a step-by-step guide on how to use and deploy Azure Compliance Manager:

1. **Sign in to the Azure portal**: Sign in to the Azure portal using your Azure account credentials. Ensure that you have appropriate permissions to access and deploy Azure Compliance Manager.

2. **Access Azure Compliance Manager**: Once signed in, navigate to the **Compliance Manager** service. You can find it by searching for `compliance manager` in the search bar or by navigating to the **Security + Compliance** section and selecting **Compliance Manager** from the list of services.

3. **Select compliance standards**: In the Azure Compliance Manager dashboard, start by selecting compliance standards and frameworks that apply to your organization. These standards cover various regulations such as the GDPR, ISO *27001*, NIST, HIPAA, and more. Choose ones that align with your industry and geographical location.

4. **Evaluate compliance controls**: For each selected compliance standard, Compliance Manager will present a set of controls that need to be assessed. Answer the predefined assessment questions for each control to evaluate your organization's compliance status. The tool will automatically test and analyze the controls based on your responses.

5. **Upload evidence and documentation**: As part of the assessment process, you may need to upload evidence and documentation to support your compliance efforts. This documentation can include policies, procedures, audit reports, and any other relevant evidence. Organize and manage these documents within Compliance Manager.

6. **Review recommendations and guidance**: Compliance Manager provides guidance and recommendations for improving compliance. Review these suggestions to enhance your security and compliance posture. Implement the recommended best practices to strengthen your compliance efforts.

7. **Monitor compliance progress**: Use the Compliance Manager dashboard to monitor your compliance progress. It provides a centralized view of your organization's compliance efforts and status. Regularly review the dashboard to track improvements and stay informed about your compliance status.

8. **Generate compliance reports**: Compliance Manager allows you to generate compliance reports summarizing your organization's compliance efforts and status. These reports can be used for internal reviews, audits, or regulatory assessments. Download and share the reports as needed.

Here are some additional considerations:

- **Regular updates**: Keep track of updates and changes to compliance standards and frameworks. Regularly review and adjust your compliance assessments to reflect any updates.

- **Collaboration**: Collaborate with relevant stakeholders and teams within your organization to ensure accurate and comprehensive compliance assessments.

- **Third-party assessments**: Consider engaging external auditors for third-party assessments to obtain independent verification of your organization's compliance efforts. Let's dig deeper into some of the services that are available from different cloud vendors that address compliance-related issues:

  - **Google Cloud compliance**: Google Cloud provides various resources, including whitepapers, compliance guides, and compliance packages, to help organizations understand and meet their compliance obligations. Google Cloud's compliance offerings cover a wide range of regulatory standards, such as the GDPR, ISO *27001*, PCI DSS, and HIPAA.

  - **Cloud-based data protection solutions**: Many CSPs offer data protection and encryption services that help organizations comply with data protection laws. These services include encryption at rest and in transit, key management services, and **data loss prevention (DLP)** tools.

  - **Compliance automation platforms**: Some third-party companies offer compliance automation platforms that help organizations streamline compliance processes. These platforms can automate compliance assessments, generate compliance reports, and provide continuous monitoring to ensure ongoing compliance.

- **Data classification and protection tools**: Data classification tools help organizations categorize and label data based on its sensitivity. These tools can automatically apply appropriate data protection measures based on the classification, ensuring compliance with data protection laws.

- **Third-party auditing and certification services**: Third-party auditing and certification services can help organizations conduct independent assessments of their compliance efforts. These audits and certifications can provide validation of compliance and build trust with customers and partners.

- **Cloud security and governance solutions**: Comprehensive cloud security and governance solutions include features that facilitate compliance management. These solutions often provide IAM controls, access monitoring, audit logging, and reporting capabilities to help organizations maintain compliance with industry standards.

- **Cloud-based eDiscovery and legal hold services**: For organizations that need to comply with legal hold requirements, some cloud providers offer eDiscovery and legal hold services that facilitate legal data preservation and discovery processes.

In this section, we delved into key tools such as AWS Artifact and Azure Compliance Manager. AWS Artifact emerged as a crucial service from AWS, facilitating easy access to compliance documents and enhancing transparency. Azure Compliance Manager, as another notable tool, was discussed in the context of Microsoft's Azure cloud platform, offering capabilities for assessing and managing compliance risks. The section highlighted the significance of these tools in navigating complex regulatory landscapes, ensuring secure cloud environments, and fostering trust between CSPs and their clients.

The next section, *IR and cloud forensics*, delves into critical aspects of handling security incidents and conducting digital forensics in cloud environments. IR is the process of identifying, managing, and mitigating cybersecurity incidents, such as data breaches, unauthorized access, or **denial-of-service** (**DoS**) attacks, to minimize the impact on an organization's operations and reputation. Cloud forensics, on the other hand, focuses on the collection, preservation, and analysis of digital evidence in cloud environments to understand the scope and cause of security incidents and support legal investigations.

IR and cloud forensics

This section delves into the crucial realm of handling security incidents and conducting digital forensics in cloud environments. IR is the disciplined approach of detecting, managing, and mitigating cybersecurity incidents to minimize their impact on an organization. Within the context of cloud computing, IR becomes even more complex, requiring specialized strategies to address the dynamic nature of cloud resources and distributed data. Cloud forensics, on the other hand, focuses on the collection, preservation, and analysis of digital evidence from cloud platforms to understand the scope and cause of security incidents and support legal investigations. This section explores the fundamental principles of IR, best practices for handling cloud-related incidents, and the tools and techniques used in cloud forensics. Through this knowledge, readers will gain the necessary skills to develop effective **IR plans** (**IRPs**) and conduct cloud forensics investigations, bolstering their organization's resilience against cybersecurity threats in the cloud.

IR and cloud forensics are critical components of cloud technology, ensuring the effective handling of security incidents and the preservation of digital evidence in cloud environments. As businesses increasingly migrate to the cloud, the need for robust IR and forensics practices becomes paramount to safeguarding sensitive data and maintaining **business continuity (BC)**. Let's look at this more closely:

- **IR in cloud technology**: IR in cloud technology follows a systematic approach to detect, analyze, contain, eradicate, and recover from cybersecurity incidents. This involves setting up IRPs specific to cloud environments, defining roles and responsibilities, and establishing communication protocols. IR teams need to be well versed in the nuances of cloud computing, as the distributed nature of cloud resources and data can pose unique challenges. Organizations must also collaborate with CSPs to ensure seamless coordination in case of incidents affecting cloud assets.

- **Cloud forensics**: Cloud forensics is the process of collecting, preserving, and analyzing digital evidence from cloud platforms to investigate security incidents, determine the root cause, and support legal proceedings if necessary. It involves understanding the intricacies of cloud architecture, data storage, and access logs to reconstruct events and identify the source and impact of security breaches. Cloud forensics requires specialized tools and expertise to handle complex multi-tenant environments and maintain the integrity of digital evidence.

Navigating the landscape of IR and cloud forensics requires a keen understanding of the tools and services at our disposal. In this subsection, we'll explore key resources that empower organizations to effectively detect, respond to, and investigate security incidents within the dynamic realm of cloud computing. From real-time monitoring tools to advanced forensics services, this section sheds light on the arsenal available for fortifying cloud security and responding swiftly to potential threats.

Tools and services for IR and cloud forensics

In this section, we delve into the fundamental aspects of cloud security, focusing on essential tools such as AWS CloudTrail, Azure Monitor, and Google Cloud Logging and Monitoring. These tools are at the forefront of enabling robust security practices within cloud environments. AWS CloudTrail offers comprehensive auditing capabilities, Azure Monitor provides insights into performance and application health, and Google Cloud Logging and Monitoring ensures visibility and control across services. Let's unravel the capabilities of each, understanding how they contribute to effective security, monitoring, and IR in the dynamic landscape of cloud computing.

AWS CloudTrail

AWS CloudTrail provides detailed logs of API activity across AWS services, enabling organizations to monitor and investigate security incidents in the cloud.

AWS CloudTrail is a service provided by AWS that enables organizations to monitor and log all activity within their AWS accounts. It provides detailed event history for actions taken by users, services, or applications, allowing users to gain insights into who did what and when in their AWS environment. CloudTrail helps enhance security, compliance, and operational auditing by providing an audit trail of actions taken in the AWS Management Console, the AWS **Command Line Interface (CLI)**, and AWS SDKs.

Figure 7.1 depicts the interaction and placement of CloudTrail with various other AWS services' system managers and end users:

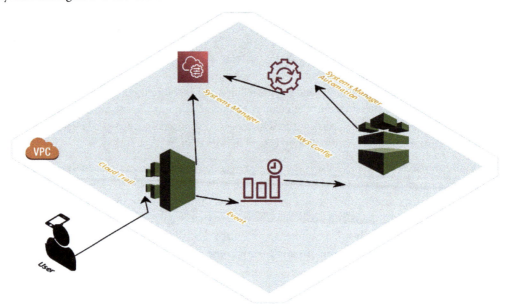

Figure 7.1 – CloudTrail in AWS

In the preceding diagram, we can see how the user connects with the CloudTrail service, which records every API call made through the user within an AWS cloud account, and how the CloudTrail service integrates with the CloudWatch service.

Key features of AWS CloudTrail include the following:

- **Detailed logging**: CloudTrail captures and records every API call made within an AWS account, including the identity of the entity making the call, the time of the call, the source IP address, and other relevant details.

- **Multi-region support**: CloudTrail can be enabled in multiple AWS regions, ensuring that all activity across different regions is centrally logged and monitored.

- **Integration with CloudWatch**: CloudTrail can be configured to deliver its log data to Amazon CloudWatch Logs. This enables users to set up alarms and notifications based on specific API activity, helping them to detect and respond to potential security threats in real time.

- **Encryption and data integrity**: CloudTrail logs are encrypted to ensure data confidentiality. Additionally, the integrity of the logs is maintained by using digital signatures to detect any unauthorized changes.

- **Log file integrity validation**: AWS CloudTrail provides log file integrity validation, enabling users to verify the authenticity of log files and ensure they have not been tampered with.

- **Simple Storage Service (S3) bucket integration**: CloudTrail logs can be stored in an S3 bucket of the user's choice, providing flexibility and scalability for log storage.

- **Integration with AWS Config**: CloudTrail can be integrated with AWS Config to provide a more comprehensive view of AWS resource changes and configurations.

Use cases of AWS CloudTrail include the following:

- **Security and compliance monitoring**: CloudTrail provides essential insights into activity and changes made within an AWS account, helping organizations monitor for unauthorized access, security misconfigurations, and compliance violations

- **Troubleshooting and debugging**: CloudTrail logs can be valuable for troubleshooting operational issues, as they contain a detailed history of API calls, enabling users to identify the root cause of problems quickly

- **Incident investigation**: In the event of a security incident, CloudTrail logs can be used to conduct forensic investigations, providing a detailed audit trail of actions taken by users or services

- **Resource change tracking**: CloudTrail logs can be used in conjunction with AWS Config to track changes to AWS resources and maintain a historical record of configuration changes

Setting up AWS CloudTrail in an AWS cloud environment involves several steps. The process involves creating a new CloudTrail trail or modifying an existing one to capture and log the desired AWS API activity. Next is a step-by-step guide to setting up AWS CloudTrail:

1. **Sign in to the AWS Management Console**: Sign in to the AWS Management Console using your AWS account credentials.

2. **Open the CloudTrail service**: In the AWS Management Console, navigate to the **Management & Governance** section and select **CloudTrail**.

3. **Click Create Trail**: If you are setting up CloudTrail for the first time, click on **Create Trail**. If you already have a trail and want to modify it, select the existing trail from the list and click on **Edit**.

4. **Specify trail details**: In the **Create Trail** or **Edit Trail** form, specify the following details:

   - **Trail Name**: Provide a unique name for the trail to identify it in the console.

   - **Apply trail to all regions**: Choose whether the trail should apply to all regions or specific regions.

   - **Storage Location**: Select the S3 bucket where CloudTrail logs will be stored. You can either choose an existing bucket or create a new one.

   - **Enable Log File Validation**: Decide whether to enable log file integrity validation to detect any tampering with log files.

   - **CloudWatch Logs**: Optionally, configure the CloudWatch Logs integration to receive real-time notifications of API activity.

5. **Choose event settings**: Select the AWS API events you want to log for the trail. You can log all API events or choose specific ones based on your requirements.

6. **Configure data events** (*optional*): You have the option to log data events for S3 and Lambda. Data events provide additional visibility into read and write operations on these resources.

7. **Enable Insights** (*optional*): You can enable CloudTrail Insights, which provides high-level summaries of unusual API activity patterns.

8. **Create or update trail**: After specifying the trail details and event settings, click on **Create** (for new trails) or **Save** (for existing trails) to create or update a CloudTrail trail.

9. **Start logging**: Once a trail is created or updated, CloudTrail starts logging the specified API activity in your AWS environment.

10. **Review log files**: Log files will be delivered to the S3 bucket specified in the trail configuration. You can review and analyze these log files using the AWS Management Console or export them for further analysis and monitoring.

By following these steps, you can successfully set up AWS CloudTrail in your AWS cloud environment, enabling you to monitor and audit API activity, enhance security, and support compliance requirements.

By providing detailed logging and monitoring capabilities, CloudTrail enables organizations to maintain an audit trail of AWS activity, detect and respond to security incidents, and ensure compliance with industry standards and regulatory requirements.

Azure Monitor

Azure Monitor offers centralized monitoring and logging capabilities, assisting IR teams in detecting and responding to security events in Microsoft Azure.

Azure Monitor is a comprehensive monitoring and observability service provided by Microsoft Azure that allows users to collect, analyze, and act on telemetry data from various Azure resources and applications. It provides insights into the performance, availability, and health of Azure services and applications, helping organizations proactively identify and address issues before they impact users.

Key features of Azure Monitor include the following:

- **Metrics collection**: Azure Monitor collects performance metrics from Azure resources such as **virtual machines** (**VMs**), databases, storage accounts, and more. These metrics provide real-time information on resource utilization and health.

- **Log Analytics**: Azure Monitor offers Log Analytics, which enables users to collect and analyze log data from Azure resources and applications. It supports custom log data, making it possible to centralize logs from various sources.

- **Alerting and notifications**: Azure Monitor allows users to set up alerts based on specific metric thresholds or log query results. When an alert condition is met, it can trigger notifications via email, SMS, or integration with other services such as Microsoft Teams.

- **Application Insights**: Application Insights, a part of Azure Monitor, is used for application performance monitoring. It provides detailed telemetry data and insights into the usage and behavior of web applications, APIs, and other components.

- **Diagnostics and troubleshooting**: Azure Monitor facilitates troubleshooting with diagnostic logs that offer detailed information on resource operations and potential issues.

- **Autoscale**: Azure Monitor integrates with Autoscale, enabling automatic scaling of resources based on predefined conditions, such as CPU utilization or queue length.

Use cases of Azure Monitor include the following:

- **Resource monitoring**: Azure Monitor helps monitor the performance and health of various Azure resources, such as VMs, databases, virtual networks, and storage accounts. It enables users to track metrics, set alerts, and diagnose issues.

- **Application performance monitoring (APM)**: With Application Insights, Azure Monitor provides in-depth monitoring of web applications and APIs. It helps identify slow response times, track user interactions, and pinpoint performance bottlenecks.

- **Infrastructure monitoring**: Azure Monitor allows for monitoring the health and performance of infrastructure components such as VMs, **Azure Kubernetes Service** (**AKS**) clusters, and Azure functions.

- **Alerting and incident management (IM)**: Users can configure alerts in Azure Monitor to notify teams about critical conditions or service disruptions. This aids in proactive IM and quick issue resolution.

- **Capacity planning**: By analyzing performance metrics and trends, Azure Monitor helps organizations plan resource capacity to optimize cost and performance.

- **Security and compliance**: Azure Monitor can be used to track and analyze security-related events and logs, enhancing security monitoring and compliance efforts.

- **Integration with third-party monitoring tools**: Azure Monitor supports integration with various third-party monitoring tools and solutions, allowing users to consolidate monitoring data from multiple sources.

Azure Monitor is a powerful tool that enables organizations to gain visibility into the performance, availability, and health of their Azure resources and applications. With its wide range of features, Azure Monitor aids in proactive monitoring, diagnostics, and IM, helping organizations optimize resource utilization, enhance application performance, and maintain a high level of service reliability in the Azure cloud environment.

Setting up Azure Monitor in the Azure cloud involves several steps to start collecting telemetry data, setting up alerts, and gaining insights into the performance and health of your resources. Next is a step-by-step guide to help you set up Azure Monitor:

1. **Sign in to the Azure portal**: Sign in to the Azure portal using your Azure account credentials.

2. **Create a Log Analytics workspace** (*optional*): If you want to use Log Analytics to collect and analyze log data, you need to create a Log Analytics workspace first. Go to the **Create a resource** page and search for **Log Analytics**. Follow the steps to create a new workspace.

3. **Enable diagnostics settings for Azure resources** (*optional*): For resources such as VMs, databases, and other supported Azure services, you can enable diagnostics settings to stream telemetry data to Azure Monitor. This step is optional but highly recommended for comprehensive monitoring. Follow this process:

   - Navigate to the resource you want to monitor

   - Under **Monitoring**, select **Diagnostics settings**

   - Enable diagnostics settings and choose the target Log Analytics workspace or other monitoring destinations

4. **Set up metrics collection** (*optional*): If you want to monitor performance metrics for specific resources, follow these steps:

   - In the Azure portal, go to the **Monitoring** section and select **Metrics**

   - Choose the Azure resource type you want to monitor

   - Select a specific resource and metric you want to add to the chart

   - Customize the chart as needed and save it

5. **Create Azure Monitor alerts**: To create alerts based on metric data or log queries, follow these steps:

   - In the Azure portal, go to the **Monitoring** section and select **Alerts**

   - Click on **New alert rule** to create a new alert

   - Configure the alert rule, specifying the condition, threshold, frequency, and actions (such as sending email notifications or triggering Azure functions)

   - Save the alert rule

6. **Application Insights** (*optional*): If you want to monitor the performance of your applications, set up Application Insights:

    - In the Azure portal, go to the **Create a resource** page and search for **Application Insights**

    - Follow the steps to create a new Application Insights instance

    - Integrate Application Insights into your application code

7. **View monitoring data and insights**: After setting up Azure Monitor, you can view monitoring data, charts, and insights in the Azure portal. Explore the **Monitoring** section for metrics, alerts, and logs. Use the **Application Insights** section to view application performance and user interactions.

8. **Configure additional monitoring and integration** (*optional*): Depending on your requirements, you can further configure additional monitoring solutions, such as Azure Monitor for containers, Azure Monitor for VMs, or integrating with third-party monitoring tools.

By following these steps, you can successfully set up Azure Monitor in your Azure cloud environment, allowing you to monitor the performance, health, and usage of your resources and applications. Azure Monitor helps you gain valuable insights, detect issues proactively, and optimize the performance of your Azure-based solutions.

Google Cloud Logging and Monitoring

Google Cloud Logging and Monitoring provides real-time analysis of logs and metrics, aiding in **incident detection and response (IDR)** within **Google Cloud Platform (GCP)**. Use cases include the following:

- **Security information and event management (SIEM) tools**: SIEM tools such as Splunk, the Elasticsearch, Logstash, Kibana (ELK) Stack, and Sumo Logic can be integrated with cloud platforms to aggregate, correlate, and analyze security event data for IR

- **Digital forensics tools**: Tools such as Volatility, Autopsy, and AWS Artifact can be utilized to conduct cloud forensics investigations, helping collect and analyze digital evidence from cloud environments

- **Third-party cloud security platforms**: Several vendors offer cloud security platforms that encompass IR and forensics capabilities, streamlining IM and investigation processes in cloud environments

- **Cloud-based IR automation**: Cloud-based automation platforms, such as Demisto (now part of Palo Alto Networks), enable organizations to automate IR workflows, ensuring rapid and consistent responses to security incidents

- **Cloud IR playbooks**: Organizations can develop IR playbooks tailored for cloud-specific scenarios, guiding response teams in handling cloud-related incidents efficiently

In this section, readers explored critical tools and services integral to securing and monitoring cloud environments. AWS CloudTrail, Azure Monitor, and Google Cloud Logging and Monitoring were spotlighted for their pivotal roles. AWS CloudTrail emerged as a key auditing tool, ensuring transparency and compliance. Azure Monitor was presented as a comprehensive solution for performance insights and application health monitoring. Google Cloud Logging and Monitoring stood out for providing visibility and control across services. Readers gained a nuanced understanding of how these tools contribute to robust security practices, effective monitoring, and streamlined IR in the dynamic realm of cloud computing.

The next section, *Managing cloud security at scale*, focuses on challenges and best practices for ensuring robust security across large and complex cloud environments. As organizations scale up their cloud operations, managing security becomes increasingly intricate due to the growing number of resources, users, and potential threats. This section explores strategies for implementing centralized security controls, automating security processes, and using cloud-native tools to streamline security management across the entire cloud infrastructure. It also addresses the importance of RBAC, continuous monitoring, and IR automation to maintain a secure and compliant cloud environment at scale. By the end of this section, readers will have gained insights into how to effectively manage security in large-scale cloud deployments, bolstering their organization's defense against evolving cyber threats and compliance challenges.

Managing cloud security at scale

This section delves into critical aspects of maintaining robust security practices across large and complex cloud environments. As organizations expand their cloud operations, managing security becomes more challenging due to the increased number of resources, users, and potential risks. This section explores strategies for implementing centralized security controls, automating security processes, and leveraging cloud-native tools to streamline security management at scale. It will cover topics such as RBAC, continuous monitoring, IR automation, and security best practices for large-scale cloud deployments. By the end of this section, readers will have gained valuable insights into effectively managing security in complex cloud infrastructures, enhancing their organization's ability to tackle evolving cybersecurity threats and compliance requirements.

Managing cloud security at scale is a critical aspect of cloud computing, especially for large enterprises and organizations with extensive cloud deployments. As cloud environments grow in complexity and size, ensuring robust security becomes more challenging due to the proliferation of resources, data, and potential threats. Effectively managing security at scale requires a combination of centralized controls, automation, and the utilization of cloud-native tools and services. Let's explore some key strategies, tools, and services used in managing cloud security at scale:

- **Centralized IAM**: Implementing a centralized IAM strategy is crucial for managing security at scale. RBAC is commonly used to define granular access permissions for users and resources. With RBAC, organizations can assign roles to users based on their responsibilities, ensuring that users have the necessary permissions to perform their duties without granting excessive access.

- **Cloud security posture management (CSPM) tools**: CSPM tools, such as AWS Config and Azure Policy, play a vital role in managing security at scale. These tools continuously assess cloud resources against security best practices, compliance frameworks, and organizational policies. They provide real-time insights into potential misconfigurations or security risks, helping organizations maintain a secure cloud posture.

Setting up AWS Config involves a series of steps to enable the service, configure the required resources, and start capturing configuration data for your AWS environment. Here's a step-by-step guide on how to set up and use the AWS Config service from the AWS console:

1. **Sign in to the AWS Management Console**: Sign in to the AWS Management Console using your AWS account credentials.

2. **Navigate to AWS Config**: In the AWS Management Console, navigate to the **Management & Governance** section and select **AWS Config**.

3. **Enable AWS Config**: Click on the **Get started** button to begin the setup process. Choose whether you want to use the default settings or customize the setup based on your requirements.

4. **Configure AWS Config rules** (*optional*): If you want to set up AWS Config rules to evaluate the compliance of your AWS resources against desired configurations, you can configure the rules at this stage. AWS Config provides some predefined rules, and you can also create custom rules.

5. **Select AWS resources to monitor**: Choose AWS resources you want AWS Config to monitor and track configuration changes. You can select specific resource types or monitor all supported resources.

6. **Choose an S3 bucket for configuration history**: Select an S3 bucket where AWS Config will store the configuration history of your resources. This bucket will be used to retain a snapshot of your resource configurations over time.

7. **Enable AWS Config Rules** (*optional*): If you have chosen to configure AWS Config rules, you can enable them at this stage to start evaluating the compliance of your resources.

8. **Review and confirm**: Review the settings you have configured and ensure they align with your requirements. Once you are satisfied, click on the **Confirm** button to enable AWS Config.

9. **Verify AWS Config status**: After enabling AWS Config, it may take a few minutes to start capturing configuration data. You can check the status on the AWS Config dashboard to verify that the service is active and operational.

10. **Explore AWS Config dashboard and configuration history**: Once AWS Config is operational, you can explore the AWS Config dashboard to view your resources' current configurations and configuration history. You can also use the dashboard to assess compliance with AWS Config rules if you have enabled them.

With these steps, you will have successfully set up AWS Config, and it will start capturing configuration data and monitoring changes to your AWS resources. AWS Config allows you to maintain a historical record of your resource configurations, track compliance with desired configurations, and detect any unintended changes, helping you maintain a secure and compliant AWS environment. The following is the multifaceted landscape of advanced security strategies and tools within cloud environments. **Cloud access security brokers** (**CASBs**) take the spotlight, serving as intermediaries that fortify security by enforcing policies, preventing data exfiltration, and providing visibility into cloud usage. The discussion expands to SIEM tools, which analyze security event logs for threat detection and IR. Cloud-native security services offered by providers such as AWS and Azure are explored, showcasing tools such as Amazon GuardDuty, Azure Security Center, and others. Automation and orchestration, facilitated by **Infrastructure-as-Code** (**IaC**) tools, demonstrate their pivotal role in ensuring consistent and repeatable security configurations. **Continuous security monitoring** (**CSM**), IR automation, and cloud governance and compliance practices round out this exploration, offering readers a holistic understanding of how to manage security effectively at scale within dynamic cloud environments:

- **CASBs**: CASBs act as intermediaries between users and cloud services, providing an additional layer of security. These solutions enforce security policies, detect and prevent data exfiltration, and offer visibility into cloud usage. CASBs are especially valuable for organizations with multiple cloud providers, allowing them to implement consistent security policies across different cloud environments.

- **SIEM tools**: SIEM tools aggregate and analyze security event logs from various sources, including cloud platforms, network devices, and applications. They enable organizations to detect security incidents, identify patterns of suspicious activity, and respond to threats effectively.

- **Cloud-native security services**: Cloud providers offer a range of cloud-native security services that organizations can leverage to manage security at scale. For example, AWS provides services such as Amazon GuardDuty for threat detection, AWS Shield for **distributed DoS** (**DDoS**) protection, and AWS **Web Application Firewall** (**WAF**) for WAF capabilities. Azure offers Azure Security Center, Azure DDoS Protection, and Azure WAF for similar purposes.

- **Automation and orchestration**: Automating security processes is essential for managing security at scale efficiently. IaC tools such as AWS CloudFormation and **Azure Resource Manager** (**ARM**) enable organizations to define security configurations as code, ensuring consistency and repeatability in deploying secure resources.

- **CSM**: Implementing CSM is crucial for detecting and responding to security threats promptly. Organizations can set up automated monitoring and alerting using cloud-native services such as AWS CloudWatch and Azure Monitor, helping them stay vigilant against potential security incidents.

- **IR automation**: Automation plays a crucial role in IR at scale. Tools such as AWS Lambda and Azure Functions can be utilized to trigger automated IR workflows when security events are detected, enabling rapid mitigation and response to threats.

- **Cloud governance and compliance**: Implementing effective cloud governance practices and maintaining compliance with industry standards and regulations are critical components of managing security at scale. Cloud providers' governance services, along with third-party solutions, can help organizations ensure adherence to security policies and compliance requirements.

Managing cloud security at scale requires a combination of centralized controls, automation, and the use of cloud-native tools and services. Organizations must implement robust IAM practices, leverage CSPM tools, CASBs, and SIEM solutions, and take advantage of cloud providers' security offerings. Automation and continuous monitoring are essential for maintaining a secure cloud posture, and adherence to cloud governance and compliance standards is crucial to safeguarding cloud environments against evolving cyber threats.

In this section, we delved into challenges and strategies associated with maintaining robust security practices in large and complex cloud environments. As organizations expand their cloud operations, the section emphasized the increasing difficulty of managing security due to a higher number of resources, users, and potential risks. Key topics covered included strategies for implementing centralized security controls, the importance of automating security processes, and the utilization of cloud-native tools to streamline security management. Specifically, the section explored concepts such as RBAC, continuous monitoring, IR automation, and security best practices tailored for large-scale cloud deployments. The goal was to provide readers with valuable insights and practical approaches to effectively manage security in intricate cloud infrastructures, thereby enhancing their ability to address evolving cybersecurity threats and comply with regulatory requirements. This comprehensive discussion aimed to equip readers, particularly those in large enterprises, with the knowledge needed to navigate the complexities of securing expansive cloud deployments.

The next section, *Evolving threat landscape*, explores the dynamic nature of cybersecurity threats and the challenges they pose to cloud environments. As technology evolves, so do the tactics and techniques used by threat actors. This section delves into the latest trends and emerging threats targeting cloud infrastructures and applications. It discusses the importance of staying vigilant and proactive in adopting security measures to mitigate potential risks. Readers will gain insights into understanding the ever-changing threat landscape, the importance of **threat intelligence** (**TI**), and the significance of continuous monitoring and IR to safeguard cloud assets against evolving cyber threats.

Evolving threat landscape

This section examines the dynamic and constantly changing nature of cybersecurity threats in the context of cloud computing. This section provides an overview of the latest trends, attack vectors, and techniques used by cybercriminals to target cloud environments. Readers will gain insights into the significance of staying updated on emerging threats, understanding the impact of evolving cyber risks, and the importance of adopting proactive security measures to protect cloud assets. By understanding the evolving threat landscape, readers can bolster their organization's security posture, enhance IR capabilities, and implement effective strategies to safeguard their cloud infrastructures and applications against ever-changing cyber threats.

Let's explore this topic in detail, along with the tools and services available to address the challenges posed by the evolving threat landscape:

1. **Emerging threats and attack vectors**: As organizations increasingly rely on cloud services, understanding the evolving landscape of cybersecurity threats and attack vectors becomes paramount. This may include ransomware, **advanced persistent threats** (**APTs**), insider threats, supply chain attacks, and zero-day vulnerabilities. Understanding these evolving threats is crucial for organizations to assess their risk exposure and adopt appropriate security measures.

2. **TI services**: TI services, both from third-party vendors and cloud providers, provide real-time information about current and emerging threats. These services offer insights into the **tactics, techniques, and procedures** (**TTPs**) used by threat actors. By leveraging TI, organizations can proactively detect and respond to potential threats before they cause significant damage.

3. **Cloud-native security services**: Leading cloud providers such as AWS, Azure, and Google Cloud offer a range of cloud-native security services to address the evolving threat landscape. These services include Amazon GuardDuty, Azure Security Center, and Google Cloud Security Command Center, which provide continuous monitoring, threat detection, and security analytics tailored for cloud environments.

An integral component in the defense against emerging threats in cloud environments is Amazon GuardDuty. GuardDuty is a managed threat detection service by AWS designed to identify malicious activity and unauthorized behavior within AWS accounts. Leveraging **machine learning** (**ML**) and anomaly detection, GuardDuty analyzes vast amounts of data, including CloudTrail logs, VPC flow logs, and DNS logs. It provides real-time insights into potential security risks, such as compromised instances, unauthorized access, or communication with known malicious IP addresses. By incorporating Amazon GuardDuty into cloud security strategies, organizations enhance their ability to proactively detect and respond to evolving threats, fortifying their overall cybersecurity posture. Let's discuss this service in some depth.

Amazon GuardDuty is a managed threat detection service provided by AWS that helps users protect their AWS cloud environments from security threats and vulnerabilities. It continuously monitors and analyzes AWS resources and account activity to identify and alert users about potential malicious activities and suspicious behavior.

Key features of Amazon GuardDuty include the following:

- **Intelligent threat detection**: GuardDuty uses ML and anomaly detection techniques to identify unusual and potentially malicious behavior in your AWS environment

- **Continuous monitoring**: GuardDuty continuously monitors AWS CloudTrail event logs, VPC flow logs, and DNS logs to detect security threats in real time

- **Multiple detection techniques**: GuardDuty employs a wide range of detection techniques, including IP reputation lists, known attack patterns, and behavior analysis to identify various types of threats

- **Centralized management**: GuardDuty provides a centralized dashboard where users can view and analyze findings across multiple AWS accounts and regions

- **Automated remediation**: GuardDuty integrates with AWS Lambda and CloudWatch Events, enabling automated responses to detected threats, such as triggering Lambda functions for IR

- **Easy integration**: GuardDuty can be easily enabled for AWS accounts without requiring any additional software or agents to be installed

Types of threats detected by Amazon GuardDuty include the following:

- **Unauthorized access**: Detects unauthorized attempts to access AWS resources, including compromised credentials, brute-force attacks, and account-hijacking attempts

- **Instance compromise**: Identifies activities associated with potential compromise of **Elastic Compute Cloud** (EC2) instances, such as communication with known malicious IPs or domains

- **Data exfiltration**: Detects attempts to exfiltrate data from AWS resources, including unusual data transfer patterns

- **Suspicious behavior**: Flags activities that deviate from normal behavior, such as unusual API calls, unauthorized resource creation, and unusual data access patterns

Usage and benefits of Amazon GuardDuty include:

- **Improved security posture**: GuardDuty enhances the security posture of AWS environments by providing real-time threat detection and alerting, allowing organizations to respond promptly to potential security incidents

- **Cost-effective**: As a fully managed service, GuardDuty eliminates the need for additional infrastructure or software, making it a cost-effective solution for threat detection in AWS

- **Ease of use**: It is easy to set up and configure GuardDuty, requiring minimal effort to start monitoring and protecting AWS resources

- **Centralized monitoring**: GuardDuty's centralized dashboard provides a consolidated view of security findings across multiple AWS accounts and regions, simplifying security management

Overall, Amazon GuardDuty is a valuable tool for organizations using AWS, providing intelligent and continuous threat detection to safeguard cloud environments from a wide range of security threats. By leveraging GuardDuty, AWS customers can bolster their cloud security strategy and mitigate potential risks proactively.

In conclusion, this topic highlights the importance of staying informed about emerging threats and the various tools and services available to address these challenges. By leveraging TI, cloud-native security services, automation, and robust monitoring, organizations can proactively defend against ever-changing cyber threats and maintain a secure cloud environment.

The next section, *Cloud security best practices*, focuses on providing essential guidelines and recommendations to ensure robust security in cloud environments. This section highlights industry-proven strategies for securing cloud resources, data, and applications effectively. It covers various aspects, including IAM, encryption, network security, data protection, IR, and compliance. By adhering to these best practices, readers can enhance the security posture of their cloud deployments, mitigate risks, and maintain a secure and compliant cloud environment.

Cloud security best practices

This section offers a concise overview of essential guidelines to establish robust security in cloud environments. Readers will gain insights into proven strategies covering IAM, encryption, network security, data protection, IR, and compliance. By following these best practices, readers can strengthen their cloud security, mitigate risks, and maintain a secure and compliant cloud environment.

Cloud security best practices is a crucial topic that provides guidance on implementing robust security measures in cloud environments. These practices are essential for ensuring the confidentiality, integrity, and availability of data and resources hosted in the cloud. Let's explore some key best practices, along with the tools and services available to support them.

Cloud users can ensure that they are following best practices for cloud security by taking a proactive and comprehensive approach. Here are some steps to help cloud users adhere to best practices:

1. **Educate and train personnel**: Provide training and awareness programs to employees and teams responsible for managing the cloud environment. Ensure they understand cloud security best practices and potential risks associated with misconfigurations or negligence.

   It involves providing comprehensive training and awareness programs to employees and teams responsible for managing and using cloud infrastructure and services. Here's a detailed explanation of why education and training are essential and how they contribute to a secure cloud environment:

   A. **Understanding cloud security risks**: Education and training help employees understand the unique security risks associated with cloud computing. They become aware of potential threats, such as data breaches, misconfigurations, insider threats, and unauthorized access, that can impact cloud resources and sensitive data. It is a good idea to regularly read the latest blogs and articles written by industry professionals. There are a few blogs written by me that one could follow at `https://blogs.oracle.com/authors/divit-gupta`. Look for the security blog written by me that covers zero-trust architecture.

   B. **Awareness of best practices**: Training sessions introduce employees to cloud security best practices and industry standards. They learn how to implement IAM, data encryption, network security, and IR protocols effectively.

   C. **Handling cloud resources securely**: Training ensures that employees know how to handle cloud resources securely and adhere to the organization's security policies. They become proficient in creating and managing secure cloud configurations, access controls, and permissions.

D. **Recognizing social engineering attacks**: Personnel education covers social engineering threats such as phishing and spear-phishing attacks. Employees learn to recognize suspicious emails, links, and requests for sensitive information, reducing the risk of successful attacks.

E. **IR preparedness**: Training prepares employees to respond promptly and effectively to security incidents. They understand the importance of reporting incidents, following the IRP, and minimizing the impact of security breaches.

F. **Continuous learning**: Cloud security is an ever-evolving domain. Regular training sessions and continuous learning opportunities help employees stay up to date with the latest security trends, new attack vectors, and emerging best practices.

G. **Establishing a security culture**: Education and training foster a security-conscious culture within the organization. Employees become more proactive in addressing security concerns and play an active role in maintaining a secure cloud environment.

H. **Reducing human errors**: Human errors, such as misconfigurations and accidental data exposure, are common causes of security incidents. Proper training can significantly reduce these errors by equipping employees with the knowledge and skills needed to work securely in the cloud.

I. **Compliance and regulatory requirements**: Education ensures that employees understand the importance of complying with relevant security regulations and industry standards. This helps the organization avoid potential compliance violations and associated penalties.

J. **Building a strong security team**: By providing ongoing training, organizations can build a skilled and knowledgeable security team that can effectively address security challenges and protect cloud resources proactively.

2. **Implement IAM**: Enforce strong authentication mechanisms, implement the **principle of least privilege (PoLP)**, and regularly review and update IAM policies. Ensure that only authorized users have access to critical resources. We already discussed this point previously.

3. **Secure data with encryption**: Encrypt sensitive data both in transit and at rest. Use encryption services provided by the cloud provider and manage encryption keys securely.

4. **Network security and segmentation**: Implement network security measures such as network access controls, firewalls, and segmentation to control traffic flow between resources and restrict access to specific subnets.

5. **Monitor and log activities**: Enable logging and monitoring of cloud resources. Regularly review logs and analyze security events to detect and respond to potential threats promptly. We will discuss monitoring and logging in detail in chapters to follow.

6. **Use cloud-native security services**: Leverage cloud-native security services offered by the cloud provider, such as AWS Security Hub, Azure Security Center, and Google Cloud Security Command Center, to gain insights and ensure compliance.

7. **Regularly perform security assessments**: Conduct regular security assessments, audits, and vulnerability scans to identify potential weaknesses and address them promptly. These assessments are essential for identifying vulnerabilities, weaknesses, and potential security gaps, allowing organizations to proactively address and mitigate security risks. Let's delve deeper into the significance of conducting regular security assessments:

    A. **Identify security vulnerabilities**: Security assessments involve thorough evaluations of the cloud infrastructure, applications, and configurations. By conducting vulnerability scans and penetration testing, organizations can identify potential security weaknesses that could be exploited by attackers.

    B. **Assess compliance and adherence to best practices**: Security assessments help assess the organization's compliance with relevant security standards, industry regulations, and internal security policies. They also ensure adherence to cloud security best practices recommended by cloud providers and security experts.

    C. **Proactive risk mitigation**: By identifying and understanding security risks early on, organizations can take proactive measures to address vulnerabilities before they are exploited. This proactive approach reduces the likelihood of security incidents and data breaches.

    D. **Incident prevention and detection**: Security assessments help improve incident prevention and detection capabilities. By discovering weaknesses and addressing them promptly, organizations can better protect cloud resources and detect potential security breaches early in their life cycle.

    E. **Improve security posture**: Regular security assessments enable organizations to continuously improve their security posture. Acting on assessment findings allows them to bolster their defenses, enhance security controls, and strengthen overall security practices.

    F. **Optimize security investments**: Conducting security assessments helps organizations prioritize security investments effectively. They can allocate resources to address high-risk areas, making their security investments more efficient and impactful.

    G. **Increase stakeholder confidence**: Regular security assessments demonstrate the organization's commitment to maintaining a secure cloud environment. This, in turn, increases stakeholder confidence, including customers, partners, and regulatory bodies.

    H. **Meet compliance requirements**: Many industries have specific compliance requirements regarding security and data protection. Regular security assessments help organizations meet these compliance obligations and avoid potential penalties.

    I. **Continuous improvement**: Security assessments are not a one-time effort; they should be conducted regularly to keep pace with the evolving threat landscape and changes in the cloud environment. Insights gained from these assessments drive continuous improvement in security practices.

    J. **IR preparedness**: By conducting security assessments, organizations can validate the effectiveness of their IRP. Regular assessments help identify areas for improvement in IR procedures and allow for the testing of response capabilities.

8. **Follow compliance requirements**: Understand and adhere to relevant compliance requirements, industry standards, and regulations applicable to the organization's cloud environment.

9. **IR planning**: Develop and maintain an IRP that outlines the steps to be taken in case of security incidents. Conduct periodic drills and simulations to ensure preparedness.

10. **CASBs**: Consider integrating CASBs into the cloud environment to enhance visibility, control, and security over cloud activities and data.

    CASBs are security solutions that act as intermediaries between cloud users and CSPs, providing an additional layer of security and control over cloud activities. Let's explore the key features and benefits of CASBs:

    A. **Visibility and control**: CASBs offer visibility into cloud usage and activities, providing organizations with insights into who is accessing cloud resources, from where, and with which devices. They enable organizations to set granular access controls and enforce security policies for cloud applications.

    B. **Data protection and leakage prevention**: CASBs help prevent data leakage and data loss by enforcing data protection policies. They can encrypt data at rest and in transit, apply DLP rules, and prevent unauthorized sharing of sensitive information.

    C. **Threat detection and protection**: CASBs use advanced threat detection techniques to identify and prevent various types of cyber threats. They can detect and block malware, phishing attempts, and other malicious activities targeting cloud environments.

    D. **Shadow IT discovery**: CASBs help identify and manage shadow IT, which refers to unauthorized cloud services used by employees within an organization. By discovering shadow IT applications, organizations can ensure that only approved and secure cloud services are used.

    E. **Compliance and regulatory compliance**: CASBs assist organizations in meeting compliance requirements by providing security controls and enforcing policies to protect sensitive data and ensure adherence to industry regulations.

    F. **Adaptive access control**: CASBs can apply adaptive access controls, such as context-aware authentication and risk-based access, to assess the user's behavior and grant appropriate access based on the risk level.

    G. **Cloud-to-cloud visibility**: CASBs offer visibility and control across multiple cloud platforms, allowing organizations to manage security consistently across various cloud providers.

    H. **IR and forensics**: CASBs can play a role in IR and forensics by logging and monitoring cloud activities, which can be invaluable when investigating security incidents.

    I. **API integration**: CASBs can integrate with CSP APIs to gain real-time visibility and control over cloud activities and apply security policies effectively.

    J. **Securing mobile and remote access**: With the increasing use of mobile devices and remote work, CASBs help secure cloud access from outside the corporate network, ensuring that data remains protected even when accessed from untrusted devices and locations.

11. **Cloud security reviews**: Conduct regular reviews and assessments of the cloud infrastructure and configurations to identify and rectify any potential security gaps or misconfigurations.

12. **Stay updated on cloud security**: Stay informed about the latest security threats, vulnerabilities, and cloud security best practices. Follow security blogs, attend webinars, and engage in the security community.

By following these steps and adopting a proactive security mindset, cloud users can ensure that they are adhering to cloud security best practices effectively. Regularly reviewing and improving security measures will help protect cloud environments from potential threats and ensure the safety of data and resources in the cloud.

Summary

This chapter provided an in-depth exploration of essential topics to ensure robust security and adherence to regulatory requirements in cloud computing. It covered *compliance and legal considerations* that enlightened you about the importance of meeting compliance standards and legal obligations in cloud environments. The *IR and cloud forensics* section equiped readers with the knowledge to effectively detect, respond to, and investigate security incidents in the cloud. The *Managing cloud security at scale* section imparted skills to implement and manage security measures across large cloud infrastructures. The *Evolving threat landscape* section familiarized readers with the dynamic nature of cybersecurity threats and the tools to combat emerging risks. Lastly, the *Cloud security best practices* section offered industry-proven guidelines to secure cloud resources, data, and applications effectively. By the end of this chapter, you will have gained a comprehensive understanding of cloud security principles, IR strategies, and compliance requirements. You will have enhanced skills in implementing best practices, managing security at scale, and staying vigilant against evolving cyber threats, empowering you to create and maintain secure and compliant cloud environments.

The next chapter, *Database Services*, provides a concise overview of managed database solutions in the cloud, including relational databases, NoSQL databases, and data warehousing services. You will learn about database types, use cases, and benefits, enabling you to make informed decisions for your applications. The chapter will empower you with the knowledge and skills to effectively leverage cloud-based databases, ensuring data integrity, scalability, and optimal performance for your cloud-based applications. Whether you are a developer, database administrator, or IT professional, this chapter equips you with the tools to make informed decisions and successfully implement database solutions in the cloud.

8
Database Services - Part 1

This chapter is dedicated to exploring the various database offerings available in the cloud. Readers can expect to learn about managed database services provided by major cloud providers, such as **Amazon Web Services** (**AWS**), Microsoft Azure, and **Google Cloud Platform** (**GCP**). The chapter will delve into different types of databases, including relational databases, NoSQL databases, and data warehousing services.

Readers will gain insights into the benefits and use cases of each database type, helping them make informed decisions when selecting the most suitable option for their specific applications and workloads. The chapter will cover essential concepts such as data modeling, schema design, data indexing, and query optimization.

Database services is a vast topic, and it has been divided into two chapters: *Database Services 1* and *Database Services 2*.

In this chapter, we will cover the following topics:

- Overview of database services in the cloud
- Types of databases – relational and NoSQL
- Data warehousing services in the cloud
- Databases beyond the traditional realm

The goal of this chapter is to provide readers with a comprehensive understanding of database services in the cloud. It begins with an overview of cloud-based database services, exploring the fundamental concepts and advantages they offer. The chapter then delves into the types of databases, comparing and contrasting relational and NoSQL databases and elucidating their use cases, strengths, and weaknesses. Moving forward, readers will explore data warehousing services in the cloud, understanding how these specialized databases cater to analytical and **business intelligence** (**BI**) needs. The chapter concludes by venturing into databases beyond the traditional realm, introducing readers to innovative database solutions and their applications. By the end of this chapter, readers will have a well-rounded knowledge of the diverse landscape of database services available in the cloud, enabling them to make informed decisions based on their specific requirements and use cases.

Technical requirements

To fully engage with the content of this chapter on cloud computing architecture, readers should have a basic understanding of computer systems, networking concepts, databases, and information technology.

Additionally, the following technical requirements are recommended:

- **Internet access**: Readers should have a reliable internet connection to access online resources, references, and examples related to cloud computing.

- **Computing device**: A desktop computer, laptop, tablet, or smartphone with a modern web browser is necessary to read the chapter content and access any online materials.

- **Web browser**: The latest version of a modern web browser such as Google Chrome, Mozilla Firefox, Microsoft Edge, or Safari is recommended. This ensures compatibility and optimal viewing experience of web-based resources and interactive content.

- **Familiarity with cloud services**: Some familiarity with cloud services and their basic functionalities will enhance the understanding of the chapter. This includes knowledge of basic database concepts, O/S, encryption, and servers.

Overview of database services in the cloud

This section provides a comprehensive and detailed understanding of the diverse range of database offerings available in cloud computing environments. Cloud providers offer managed database services that simplify database administration by handling tasks such as provisioning, configuration, patching, backups, and scaling. Two major categories of database services are covered: relational databases and NoSQL databases. Relational databases follow a structured schema and store data in tables with rows and columns, making them ideal for structured data. Managed relational database services such as Amazon **Relational Database Service (RDS)**, Azure SQL Database, and Google Cloud SQL support popular engines such as MySQL, PostgreSQL, Oracle, and SQL Server. On the other hand, NoSQL databases are designed for flexible and schema-less data storage, making them suitable for unstructured or semi-structured data. Cloud providers offer managed NoSQL database services such as Amazon DynamoDB, Azure Cosmos DB, and Google Cloud Firestore, catering to various use cases such as real-time data storage, document databases, key-value stores, and graph databases. Additionally, data warehousing services are optimized for processing and analyzing large volumes of data, providing insights for BI. Managed data warehousing services such as Amazon Redshift, Azure Synapse Analytics, and Google BigQuery offer features such as columnar storage, parallel processing, and data integration capabilities. Cloud database services prioritize scaling and **high availability (HA)**, supporting automatic scaling to handle demand fluctuations and offering features such as read replicas and multi-region deployments. Security and compliance are also emphasized, with cloud database services providing robust encryption, **identity and access management (IAM)**, and adherence to industry standards and regulations. Data migration and integration tools help users seamlessly transition from on-premises databases to the cloud and integrate data with other cloud services. Ultimately, understanding the features and capabilities of various cloud database services empowers organizations to make informed decisions, optimize costs, and build scalable and efficient applications that leverage the power and flexibility of cloud-based databases. Cloud providers offer a wide range of managed database services that cater to various application requirements and workloads. Let's delve into the details of this topic:

1. **Managed database services**: Cloud providers offer managed database services that handle various aspects of database administration, such as provisioning, configuration, patching, backups, and scaling. With managed database services, users can focus on their applications and data while leaving database management tasks to the cloud provider.

    Managed database services in the cloud are a category of cloud offerings that handle various aspects of database administration, reducing the burden on users and allowing them to focus on their applications and data. These services abstract the underlying infrastructure and automate routine database management tasks, such as software installation, patching, backups, and scaling. By choosing managed database services, organizations can benefit from enhanced scalability, availability, and performance without the need for extensive database management expertise. Let's explore this point in detail, along with examples and reasoning.

    Here are some examples of managed database services:

    *   **Amazon RDS**: Amazon RDS offers managed relational database services supporting popular database engines such as MySQL, PostgreSQL, Oracle, and SQL Server. Users can easily launch, configure, and scale these databases with just a few clicks through the AWS Management Console.

    *   **Azure SQL Database**: Azure SQL Database is a managed relational database service offered by Microsoft Azure. It provides automatic backups, automated patching, and built-in HA, ensuring robust performance for SQL Server-based applications.

    *   **Google Cloud Firestore**: Google Cloud Firestore is a managed NoSQL database service suitable for real-time data storage, enabling seamless data synchronization across web and mobile applications.

    *   **Amazon DynamoDB**: Amazon DynamoDB is a fully managed NoSQL database service known for its fast and predictable performance at any scale. It provides automatic scaling based on demand and supports low-latency access to data.

    Let's look at the advantages and reasoning for using managed database services:

    A. **Simplified management**: Managed database services abstract the complexity of database administration, allowing users to focus on developing applications. This reduces the operational overhead, as the cloud provider handles routine maintenance tasks such as backups and software updates.

B.   **Scalability and elasticity**: These services offer automatic scaling capabilities, enabling databases to grow or shrink based on workload demands. This elasticity ensures that applications can handle varying levels of traffic without manual intervention.

C.   **HA**: Managed database services often provide built-in HA and **fault tolerance (FT)** mechanisms, such as automated backups and **multi-Availability Zone (multi-AZ)** deployments, which ensure data durability and minimal downtime in case of hardware failures.

D.   **Security and compliance**: Cloud providers implement robust security measures to protect data stored in managed databases. Features such as encryption at rest and in transit, IAM, and auditing help organizations meet compliance requirements.

E.   **Cost-effectiveness**: Managed database services follow a pay-as-you-go pricing model, where users are charged based on usage. This allows organizations to optimize costs by provisioning resources according to actual demand.

2.   **Relational databases**: Relational databases are traditional database systems that use a structured schema to store data in tables with rows and columns. Cloud providers offer managed relational database services such as Amazon RDS, Azure SQL Database, and Google Cloud SQL, which support popular database engines such as MySQL, PostgreSQL, Oracle, and SQL Server.

3.   **NoSQL databases**: NoSQL databases, on the other hand, offer a schema-less or flexible schema data model suitable for unstructured or semi-structured data. Managed NoSQL databases include Amazon DynamoDB, Azure Cosmos DB, and Google Cloud Firestore, which cater to different use cases such as real-time data storage, document databases, key-value stores, and graph databases.

4.   **Data warehousing services**: Data warehousing services are optimized for processing and analyzing large volumes of data to derive business insights. Managed data warehousing services such as Amazon Redshift, Azure Synapse Analytics, and Google BigQuery offer features such as columnar storage, parallel processing, and built-in data integration.

5.   **Scaling and HA**: Cloud database services support automatic scaling to handle fluctuations in demand. They offer features such as read replicas (read replicas are copies of a primary database in a cloud environment, designed to handle read-intensive workloads by distributing read requests across multiple instances, thereby enhancing performance and scalability), multi-region deployments, and automated backups to ensure HA and data durability.

6.   **Cost-effectiveness**: Managed database services often adopt a pay-as-you-go pricing model, allowing users to scale resources based on demand, thus optimizing costs.

7.   **Security and compliance**: Cloud database services provide robust security features, including encryption at rest and in transit, IAM, and compliance with industry standards and regulations.

8.   **Data migration and integration**: Cloud providers offer tools and services to facilitate data migration from on-premises databases to the cloud and support data integration with other cloud services.

9. **Integration with application ecosystem**: Managed database services seamlessly integrate with cloud-native application services, allowing developers to build scalable and highly available applications.

10. **Vendor lock-in considerations**: While using managed database services offers convenience, it's essential to consider potential vendor lock-in and evaluate strategies for portability between cloud providers.

Understanding the characteristics, strengths, and limitations of different database types empowers users to make informed decisions when choosing the most suitable database service for their applications and data storage needs in the cloud. Leveraging these managed database services allows organizations to focus on their core competencies while benefiting from the scalability, flexibility, and cost-effectiveness of cloud-based databases.

The upcoming section, *Types of databases – relational and NoSQL*, delves into the two primary categories of databases that shape data storage and management in modern computing environments. This section provides readers with a concise yet comprehensive overview of the key differences, strengths, and use cases of relational databases and NoSQL databases. By exploring the characteristics and functionalities of these database types, readers will gain a solid foundation for understanding how to select the most appropriate database solution to match specific application requirements and data management needs.

Types of databases – relational and NoSQL

In this section, readers can expect an in-depth exploration of the fundamental database categories that underpin data storage and retrieval strategies. They will learn about essential characteristics, advantages, and use cases of both relational databases and NoSQL databases. The section will provide a clear distinction between these two types of databases, discussing their data models, scalability capabilities, performance considerations, and suitability for various application scenarios. Readers will gain insights into the strengths and limitations of each database type, enabling them to make informed decisions when choosing the right database solution for their specific projects. By the end of this section, readers will have a comprehensive understanding of the core differences between relational and NoSQL databases, empowering them to align their data management choices with the unique requirements of their applications. Let's take a closer look.

1. **NoSQL databases**:

    NoSQL databases, also known as *not only SQL* databases, represent a diverse category of database systems designed to handle unstructured, semi-structured, and complex data in a flexible and scalable manner. Unlike traditional relational databases that rely on structured schemas, NoSQL databases offer a schema-less or dynamic schema model, making them ideal for applications where data structures can evolve over time. Let's delve into this topic in more detail.

Here are some examples of NoSQL databases:

1. **MongoDB**: MongoDB is a widely used document-oriented NoSQL database. It stores data in flexible, **JavaScript Object Notation (JSON)**-like **Binary JSON (BSON)** documents, allowing for easy storage of diverse and hierarchical data structures.

2. **Cassandra**: Apache Cassandra is a distributed and highly available NoSQL database. It's suitable for handling massive amounts of data across multiple nodes while maintaining low latency and high performance.

3. **Redis**: Redis is an in-memory key-value store that excels in caching, real-time analytics, and session management. Its fast data retrieval capabilities make it popular for applications requiring high-speed data access.

4. **Couchbase**: Couchbase is a NoSQL database that combines the flexibility of a JSON document store with the speed of a memory-first architecture, making it suitable for real-time applications.

5. **DynamoDB**: Amazon DynamoDB is a NoSQL database. It falls under the category of document-oriented NoSQL databases. DynamoDB is a fully managed NoSQL database service provided by AWS. It offers a highly scalable, high-performance, and fully managed platform for storing and retrieving data. DynamoDB is particularly well suited for applications that require low-latency and high-throughput data access, making it a popular choice for various use cases, including real-time applications, gaming, e-commerce, and more. It uses a schema-less data model, allowing developers to store and retrieve data in flexible and dynamic ways without the constraints of a fixed schema. DynamoDB stores data in tables, where each item in a table can have a different set of attributes, offering great flexibility in handling diverse data structures.

Let's understand how we can set up DynamoDB in AWS.

Setting up Amazon DynamoDB in AWS involves several steps. Here's a high-level overview of the process:

1. **Sign in to the AWS console**:

    Log in to your AWS Management Console using your AWS account credentials.

2. **Open the DynamoDB console**:

    Once logged in, navigate to the DynamoDB service by selecting it from the list of available services.

3. **Create a table**:

    - Click on the **Create table** button
    - Specify a table name

4. Define a primary key, which consists of a partition key (and, optionally, a sort key) to uniquely identify items in the table.

5. **Configure provisioned throughput**:

   - Set the desired provisioned read and write capacity units. These determine the throughput of your table.

   - You can adjust these values later based on your application's needs.

6. **Define additional settings**:

   Configure optional settings such as auto-scaling, encryption at rest, and global secondary indexes.

   Global secondary indexes allow you to query data using alternate attributes.

7. **Create a table**:

   Review your settings and click the **Create** button.

   DynamoDB will create a table and allocate the specified provisioned throughput.

8. **Access your table**:

   Once the table is created, you can access it from the DynamoDB console.

   Here, you can add, modify, or delete items using the AWS Management Console.

9. **Use SDKs/APIs**:

   To interact with DynamoDB programmatically, you can use AWS SDKs or API calls in your preferred programming language.

   AWS SDKs offer libraries and tools for various programming languages to make it easier to work with DynamoDB.

10. **Configure access control**:

    Set up AWS IAM roles and policies to control who can access and modify your DynamoDB resources.

    This ensures proper security and authorization.

11. **Monitor and optimize**:

    Use Amazon CloudWatch to monitor the performance of your DynamoDB tables.

    Adjust provisioned throughput or consider using on-demand capacity mode based on your application's usage patterns.

Setting up DynamoDB in AWS provides you with a powerful and scalable NoSQL database solution that can handle various workloads. It's important to consider your application's requirements, data modeling, and access patterns when configuring DynamoDB tables to ensure optimal performance and cost-effectiveness.

Setting up Amazon DynamoDB using the **AWS Command-line Interface** (**AWS CLI**) involves a series of commands. Here's a step-by-step guide:

1. **Install and configure the AWS CLI**: If you haven't already, install the AWS CLI and configure it with your AWS credentials using the `aws configure` command.

2. **Create a DynamoDB table**: Use the `aws dynamodb create-table` command to create a new DynamoDB table. Replace the placeholders with your desired values:

```
aws dynamodb create-table \
   --table-name YourTableName \
   --attribute-definitions
AttributeName=PartitionKey,AttributeType=S \
   --key-schema AttributeName=PartitionKey,KeyType=HASH \
   --provisioned-throughput
ReadCapacityUnits=5,WriteCapacityUnits=5
```

3. **Wait for table creation**: After executing the `create-table` command, the table creation is asynchronous. You can wait for the table to be active using the following command:

```
aws dynamodb wait table-exists --table-name YourTableName
```

4. **Put items into the table**: You can use the `aws dynamodb put-item` command to insert items into the table. Replace the placeholders with your actual data:

```
aws dynamodb put-item \
   --table-name YourTableName \
   --item '{"PartitionKey": {"S": "Value1"}, "Attribute2": {"S":
"Value2"}}'
```

5. **Query and scan data**: Use the `aws dynamodb query` and `aws dynamodb scan` commands to retrieve data from the table based on your requirements:

```
aws dynamodb query \
   --table-name YourTableName \
   --key-condition-expression "PartitionKey = :val" \
   --expression-attribute-values '{":val":{"S":"Value1"}}'
```

6. **Delete the table** (*optional*): If you want to delete the table, you can use the `aws dynamodb delete-table` command:

```
aws dynamodb delete-table --table-name YourTableName
```

Remember to replace placeholders such as `YourTableName` and attribute values with actual values specific to your use case. These commands allow you to manage DynamoDB resources programmatically using the AWS CLI, enabling automation and integration with your application deployment processes.

The following diagram depicts the basic setup of DynamoDB in the AWS cloud:

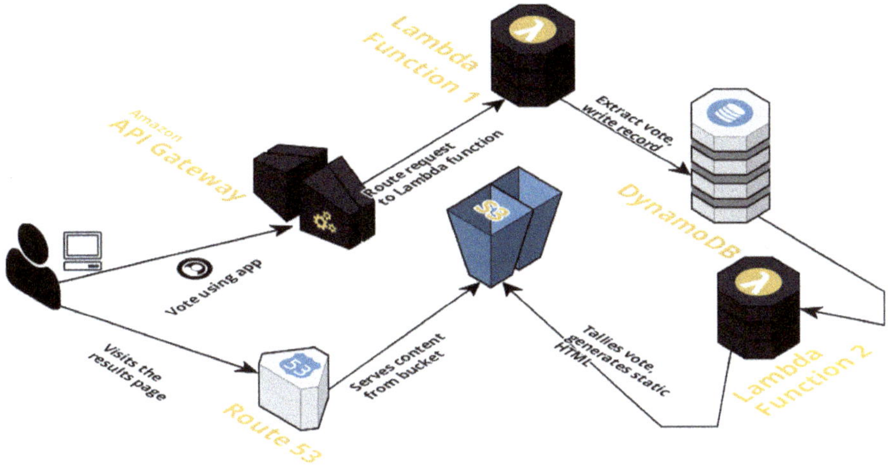

Figure 8.1: DynamoDB and Lambda functions in the AWS cloud

Now let's understand the major differences between some popular NoSQL databases such as MongoDB, Redis, and DynamoDB. We will focus on elucidating the significant distinctions among popular NoSQL databases, specifically MongoDB, Redis, and DynamoDB. Readers can anticipate an insightful comparison covering various aspects such as data models, query languages, scalability, and use cases. This exploration aims to provide a nuanced understanding, helping readers make informed decisions when choosing a NoSQL database based on their specific requirements and preferences:

1. **MongoDB**:

   - **Data model**: MongoDB is a document-oriented NoSQL database that stores data in flexible, JSON-like BSON documents. Each document can have a different structure.

   - **Use cases**: MongoDB is suitable for a wide range of use cases, including **content management systems (CMSs)**, e-commerce platforms, catalog management, and real-time analytics.

   - **Example**: Storing product information in an e-commerce application where each product has various attributes such as name, price, description, and images.

2. **Redis**:

   - **Data model**: Redis is an in-memory key-value store that supports various data structures such as strings, lists, sets, hashes, and more.

   - **Use cases**: Redis is ideal for caching, real-time analytics, session management, message queues, and leaderboards.

   - **Example**: Caching frequently accessed database queries or storing user sessions in a web application.

3. **DynamoDB**:

- **Data model**: DynamoDB is a managed NoSQL database provided by AWS. It uses a schema-less model with tables and items. Each item can have a different set of attributes.

- **Use cases**: DynamoDB is suitable for applications requiring high-speed, low-latency data access, such as gaming leaderboards, real-time applications, and IoT data storage.

- **Example**: Storing user preferences in a mobile app where each user has different attributes such as favorite genres, watch history, and ratings.

Major differences:

- **Data structure**:

  - MongoDB uses flexible, schema-less documents.

  - Redis employs a key-value structure with various data types.

  - DynamoDB uses tables and items with flexible attributes.

- **Data persistence**:

  - MongoDB provides both in-memory and on-disk storage options.

  - Redis is an in-memory database but supports disk persistence.

  - DynamoDB is a managed service with data automatically persisted.

- **Scalability**:

  - MongoDB supports horizontal scaling through sharding.

  - Redis and DynamoDB offer automatic horizontal scaling.

- **Query language**:

  - MongoDB offers a powerful query language.

  - Redis provides simple key-based queries.

  - DynamoDB uses Query and Scan operations for data retrieval.

- **Consistency and availability**:

  - MongoDB offers tunable consistency levels.

  - Redis supports eventual consistency.

  - DynamoDB provides strong consistency by default but allows eventual consistency for read operations.

- **Complex transactions**:

  - MongoDB and DynamoDB offer multi-document transactions.

  - Redis supports transactions on multiple commands, but not ACID transactions.

Benefits of NoSQL databases:

- **Flexible data models**: NoSQL databases accommodate various data structures, including key-value, document, column-family, and graph models. This flexibility allows developers to store diverse data types within the same database.

- **Scalability**: NoSQL databases are designed to scale horizontally, distributing data across multiple servers or nodes. This makes them well suited for handling large volumes of data and high traffic loads.

- **High performance**: Many NoSQL databases, such as in-memory stores, offer fast data retrieval and processing. This is particularly beneficial for applications that require real-time analytics or rapid responses.

- **Schema evolution**: NoSQL databases don't enforce rigid schemas, allowing data structures to evolve over time. This flexibility is advantageous when dealing with changing or unpredictable data requirements.

- **Distributed architecture**: NoSQL databases often employ distributed architectures that provide HA and FT. Data is replicated across nodes to ensure data durability and availability.

- **Horizontal partitioning**: NoSQL databases enable data to be partitioned and distributed across nodes, reducing the need for complex join operations and enhancing performance.

- **Support for large data volumes**: NoSQL databases are designed to handle large amounts of data efficiently, making them suitable for applications dealing with big data.

- **Use cases**: NoSQL databases are well suited for various use cases, including real-time analytics, CMSs, social media applications, IoT data storage, and more.

- **Simplified development**: The schema-less nature of NoSQL databases simplifies the development process, allowing developers to focus on building applications rather than managing complex schema designs.

- **Cloud compatibility**: NoSQL databases align well with cloud-native architectures and provide options for easy deployment and scaling in cloud environments.

NoSQL databases offer a powerful and flexible approach to data storage, particularly for applications requiring agility, scalability, and efficient handling of diverse and unstructured data. The benefits of NoSQL databases make them a preferred choice for modern applications that demand rapid development, high performance, and the ability to accommodate evolving data requirements.

Relational databases are a type of **database management system (DBMS)** that uses a structured data model based on tables to store and manage data. These databases follow the principles of the relational model, introduced by Edgar F. Codd in the 1970s. In this model, data is organized into rows and columns, and relationships between tables are established using keys.

Here are some examples of relational databases:

- **MySQL**: An open source **relational DBMS (RDBMS)** widely used for web applications and various software projects.
- **PostgreSQL**: A powerful open source RDBMS known for its extensibility and support for advanced data types.
- **Microsoft SQL Server**: A commercial RDBMS by Microsoft, offering various editions for different use cases.
- **Oracle Database**: A commercial RDBMS with a long history in enterprise applications.

Now, let's look at the benefits of relational databases:

- **Structured data model**: Relational databases enforce a structured data model, ensuring data consistency and integrity through the use of predefined schemas.
- **Data integrity**: They provide constraints such as primary keys, foreign keys, and unique constraints to maintain data accuracy.
- **ACID transactions**: Relational databases offer **Atomicity, Consistency, Isolation, and Durability** (**ACID**) properties, ensuring data reliability and consistency even in the face of failures.
- **Query language (SQL): SQL** allows for the powerful querying, filtering, and manipulation of data.
- **Normalization**: Relational databases support data normalization, which reduces data redundancy and ensures efficient storage.
- **Complex queries**: They handle complex queries and reporting efficiently due to the inherent structure of the data.
- **Data integrity**: Foreign keys establish relationships between tables, ensuring data integrity and referential integrity.
- **Multi-user support**: Relational databases offer concurrent access to multiple users, enabling collaborative data management.
- **Mature technology**: Relational databases have been around for decades, resulting in a mature ecosystem of tools, libraries, and resources.

Let's look at some use cases of relational databases:

- **E-commerce platforms**: Storing product details, customer orders, and sales transactions.

- **Financial applications**: Managing financial data, account balances, and transaction history.

- **Human resources management**: Storing employee records, payroll information, and attendance data.

- **CMS**: Organizing and retrieving content for websites and blogs.

- **Inventory management**: Tracking inventory levels, stock movements, and supplier information.

Relational databases offer a structured approach to data storage and management, ensuring data consistency and integrity through predefined schemas. They are particularly beneficial for applications that require well-defined relationships between data entities. The ACID properties provide strong guarantees for data reliability, making relational databases suitable for critical and transactional applications. SQL enables developers to perform complex queries, aggregate data, and retrieve information efficiently.

The normalization process in relational databases helps minimize data redundancy and maintain data integrity. Relationships between tables are established using primary keys and foreign keys, ensuring accurate data associations. Multi-user support allows simultaneous access to data, making relational databases suitable for collaborative environments.

Relational databases offer a structured, reliable, and mature approach to data management. Their benefits in terms of data integrity, powerful querying capabilities, and established best practices make them an excellent choice for applications that require structured data storage and management, especially when the relationships between data entities are well defined.

Let's delve into the details of the top relational databases: MySQL, PostgreSQL, Microsoft SQL Server, Oracle Database, Amazon RDS (a cloud database service), and SQLite. We'll compare their differences and provide use cases for each:

1. **MySQL**:

   Features: MySQL is known for its speed, reliability, and ease of use.

   Differences: It's open source and versatile, used for web applications and data-driven apps.

   Use case: MySQL is suitable for small-to-medium-sized applications.

2. **PostgreSQL**:

   Features: PostgreSQL is an advanced open source RDBMS with support for complex queries and JSON data.

   Differences: It's versatile with advanced features and suitable for applications requiring complex data manipulation.

   Use case: PostgreSQL is great for applications with complex data structures and advanced analytics.

3. **Microsoft SQL Server**:

    Features: Offers multiple editions catering to various use cases.

    Differences: Ideal for Windows-centric environments and businesses using Microsoft technologies.

    Use case: Used in enterprise apps, BI solutions, and large-scale data warehousing.

4. **Oracle Database**:

    Features: Known for robustness, scalability, and extensive features.

    Differences: Ideal for large-scale, high-performance applications and data warehousing.

    Use case: Used in enterprise-level applications and scenarios requiring high scalability and availability.

5. **Amazon RDS**:

    Features: Managed database service by AWS offering multiple RDBMS options, including MySQL, PostgreSQL, SQL Server, Oracle, and MariaDB.

    Differences: Fully managed service with automated backups, scaling, and maintenance.

    Use case: Suitable for various use cases, from small apps to large-scale enterprise solutions.

    Incorporating Amazon RDS into the comparison, it's important to note that while it doesn't replace traditional databases such as MySQL or PostgreSQL, it provides a managed service for these databases along with others such as SQL Server, Oracle, and MariaDB. This allows users to leverage the benefits of these databases in a fully managed cloud environment.

6. **SQLite**:

    Features: Self-contained, serverless, file-based RDBMS designed to be embedded in applications.

    Differences: Lightweight local database option.

    Use case: Used in mobile apps, desktop applications, and embedded systems.

Now, let's discuss how we can set up a popular database service on the cloud. We will pick Amazon RDS in this example. Setting up Amazon RDS in the AWS cloud involves several steps.

Here's a guide to help you get started:

1. **Sign in to the AWS console**: Log in to your AWS Management Console using your AWS account credentials.

2. **Open the Amazon RDS console**: Once logged in, navigate to the Amazon RDS service by selecting it from the list of available services.

3. **Create a database instance**:

    Click on the **Create database** button.

    Choose the database engine you want to use, such as MySQL, PostgreSQL, SQL Server, Oracle, and so on.

4. **Specify the database details**:

   Choose the appropriate version of the database engine.

   Set the database instance class, which determines the CPU, memory, and storage capacity.

   Provide the database instance identifier and master username/password.

5. **Configure additional settings**:

   Configure advanced settings such as storage, backup, maintenance, and connectivity options.

   You can choose to enable automated backups, set the backup retention period, and enable multi-AZ deployment for HA.

6. **Network and security**:

   Choose the VPC and subnet where you want the database instance to be launched.

   Configure security group settings to control inbound and outbound traffic.

7. **Database authentication**:

   Set the master username and password for the database.

   Optionally, you can enable IAM database authentication for enhanced security.

8. **Backup and maintenance**:

   Configure automated backups and specify the backup window.

   Choose the preferred maintenance window for system updates and patches.

9. **Finalize and create**:

   Review the configuration settings and click the **Create database** button.

   Amazon RDS will provision the database instance according to your specifications.

10. **Monitor and manage**:

    Once the database instance is created, you can monitor its performance using Amazon CloudWatch.

    You can manage the database through the Amazon RDS console, the AWS CLI, or an API.

11. **Connecting to the database**:

    Obtain the endpoint (hostname) of the database instance from the Amazon RDS console.

    Use your preferred database client or programming language to connect to the database using the provided endpoint and credentials.

12. **Scaling and maintenance**:

    As your application grows, you can scale your RDS instance up or out to handle increased load.

    Amazon RDS also provides features such as automated backups, automated software patching, and HA options.

The following diagram depicts the basic setup of the Amazon RDS service in AWS. Please notice the diagram also shows primary and secondary RDS services for HA:

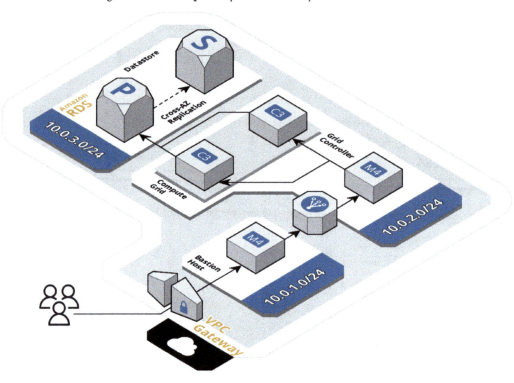

Figure 8.2: Basic Amazon RDS service setup

Setting up Amazon RDS offers a fully managed relational database service, making it easier to deploy, operate, and scale databases in the AWS cloud. The steps outlined previously provide a general guideline for creating and configuring an RDS instance, but remember to tailor the settings to your specific application requirements.

In a broader discussion of database options available in cloud environments, we are now shifting our attention from the setup of AWS RDS to the configuration of an Oracle database in **Oracle Cloud Infrastructure (OCI)**. This transition allows us to explore the specific features, considerations, and steps involved in establishing and managing an Oracle database within the Oracle Cloud environment. Now, let's understand how we can set up an Oracle database in OCI Oracle Cloud.

Setting up OCI

Setting up an Oracle database in OCI involves several steps. Here's a guide to help you get started:

1. **Sign in to the Oracle Cloud console**: Log in to your Oracle Cloud account using your credentials.

2. **Open the Oracle Database service**: Once logged in, navigate to the Oracle Database service in the OCI console.

   Create a database:

   Click on the **Create Database** button.

   Choose the workload type that best fits your use case (OLTP, Data Warehouse, Free Tier, and so on).

3. **Configure database details**:

   Choose the Oracle Database version and edition you want to use (Standard Edition, Enterprise Edition, and so on).

   Set the name for your database and select the VM shape for the compute resources.

4. **Configure networking**:

   Choose the **virtual cloud network** (**VCN**) where the database will be deployed.

   Configure subnet and private IP settings.

5. **Set a security and SSH key**:

   Configure the SSH key for secure access to the compute instance.

   Set up SSH key details and other security settings.

6. **Choose storage options**:

   Configure storage options including block volume size, backup options, and the option to enable automatic backups.

7. **Set up a database connection**:

   Provide a password for the Oracle Database administrative user (SYS, SYSTEM).

   Optionally, you can enable SQL*Net access and specify network access rules.

8. **Configure backup and recovery**:

   Set up backup and recovery options, including automated backups and data retention settings.

9. **Review and create**:

   Review the configuration settings.

   Click the **Create** button to initiate the database creation process.

10. **Monitor and manage**:

   Once the database is provisioned, you can monitor its performance and manage it through the OCI console.

   You can also use Oracle Cloud's monitoring and management tools.

11. **Connect to the database**:

   Obtain the public IP or private IP of the compute instance.

   Use SSH to connect to the instance, and then use Oracle SQL*Plus or another database client to connect to the Oracle database.

Setting up an Oracle database in OCI offers a scalable and fully managed solution with various configuration options. The steps provided here offer a general overview, but the specifics may vary based on the Oracle Cloud console interface and updates. Be sure to refer to Oracle's official documentation for the most up-to-date and detailed instructions.

The next section delves into the powerful capabilities of cloud-based data warehousing solutions. In this section, readers will explore how cloud technology has transformed the way businesses handle and analyze large volumes of data. Data warehousing services in the cloud offer scalable, managed environments for efficiently storing, managing, and processing vast datasets. From understanding the fundamentals of data warehousing to exploring advanced analytics and reporting, this section guides readers through the features, benefits, and best practices of leveraging cloud-based data warehousing solutions to uncover valuable insights and drive informed decision-making.

Data warehousing services in the cloud

Data warehousing services in the cloud provide organizations with scalable, high-performance, and managed environments to store, manage, and analyze large volumes of data. Traditional data warehousing solutions often required significant upfront investments in hardware, software, and maintenance. Cloud-based data warehousing has revolutionized this approach by offering flexible, pay-as-you-go models that eliminate the need for upfront capital expenditures and reduce the complexities of infrastructure management.

Key aspects and benefits of data warehousing services include the following:

- **Scalability**: Cloud data warehousing services allow you to scale your storage and compute resources up or down based on your data needs. This elasticity ensures optimal performance during both peak and off-peak times.

- **Managed services**: Cloud providers manage the infrastructure, backups, patches, and updates, allowing your team to focus on data analysis and business insights rather than routine maintenance.

- **Cost efficiency**: Cloud data warehousing operates on a pay-as-you-go model, meaning you only pay for the resources you use. This eliminates the need for overprovisioning and reduces operational costs.

- **Integration**: Cloud data warehousing services often integrate seamlessly with other cloud-based services, analytics tools, and BI platforms, enhancing the overall analytical ecosystem.

- **Performance**: These services offer high-performance processing capabilities, allowing for complex queries and rapid data analysis to drive actionable insights.

- **Security and compliance**: Cloud providers implement robust security measures and compliance standards to protect your data. Data encryption, access controls, and auditing features are often built in.

- **Global accessibility**: Cloud data warehousing enables remote access and collaboration from different locations, making it suitable for global organizations.

Use cases include the following:

- **BI**: Organizations can centralize data from various sources to create a **single source of truth** (**SSOT**) for reporting and analysis

- **Advanced analytics**: Cloud data warehousing supports data science initiatives, enabling the application of **machine learning** (**ML**) algorithms and predictive analytics to historical and real-time data

- **E-commerce analysis**: E-commerce platforms can analyze customer behavior, sales trends, and inventory data to optimize product offerings and marketing strategies

- **Supply chain optimization**: Data warehousing aids in tracking and analyzing supply chain data to improve inventory management and reduce operational costs

- **Financial analytics**: Financial institutions use cloud data warehousing to analyze transactional data, detect fraud, and gain insights into customer spending patterns

Here are some examples of cloud data warehousing services:

- **Amazon Redshift**: A fully managed data warehousing service by AWS, offering fast query performance and integration with various analytics tools.

- **Google BigQuery**: A serverless, highly scalable data warehouse by Google Cloud that enables super-fast SQL queries using the processing power of Google's infrastructure.

- **Azure Synapse Analytics (formerly SQL Data Warehouse)**: Microsoft's cloud data warehousing service that combines big data and data warehousing into a single platform for analytics.

- **Oracle Autonomous Data Warehouse**: Oracle's cloud-based data warehousing service that leverages AI and automation for self-driving, self-securing, and self-repairing capabilities, enabling high performance and minimal maintenance.

One of the most popular cloud data warehousing services is AWS Redshift. The decision to delve into setting up Amazon Redshift in the AWS cloud is driven by the prominence and significance of Amazon Redshift as a powerful data warehousing solution within the AWS ecosystem. Amazon

Redshift stands out for its capability to handle large-scale data analytics with speed and efficiency. It is a fully managed, scalable, and cost-effective data warehouse that integrates seamlessly with other AWS services. By focusing on the setup process for Amazon Redshift, readers can gain practical insights into leveraging this robust data warehousing solution within the AWS cloud, understanding its features, configurations, and best practices for optimal performance. This choice aligns with the widespread use of Amazon Redshift for analytical workloads and underscores its relevance in the AWS data management landscape.

Let's understand how we can set up Amazon Redshift in the AWS cloud.

Setting up Amazon Redshift

Setting up Amazon Redshift, a cloud-based data warehousing solution, in AWS involves several steps. Here's a general guide to help you get started:

1. **Sign in to the AWS console**: Log in to your AWS Management Console using your AWS account credentials.

2. **Open the Amazon Redshift console**: Once logged in, navigate to the Amazon Redshift service by selecting it from the list of available services.

3. **Create a cluster**:

    Click on the **Create Cluster** button.

    Choose the standard Redshift cluster type or Redshift Spectrum for data warehousing and analytics.

4. Configure cluster details.

5. Provide a unique cluster identifier.

6. Choose the node type and number of nodes based on your performance and scalability requirements.

7. **Set database options**:

    Choose the database name, master user, and master password.

    Optionally, you can enable enhanced VPC routing and IAM database authentication for added security.

8. **Configure cluster permissions**:

    Specify the security group or VPC settings for network access.

    You can also configure parameter groups and snapshot settings.

9. **Choose additional configuration**:

    Configure additional settings such as maintenance windows, automated backups, and automated snapshot retention.

10. **Set up encryption**:

    Choose whether to encrypt data in transit and data at rest.

    You can use AWS **Key Management Service** (**KMS**) to manage encryption keys.

11. **Review and launch**:

    Review your configuration settings.

    If everything looks good, click the **Launch Cluster** button to create the Redshift cluster.

12. **Monitor and manage**:

    Once the cluster is created, you can monitor its performance using Amazon CloudWatch and manage it through the Amazon Redshift console.

13. **Connect to the cluster**:

    Obtain the cluster endpoint (hostname) from the Amazon Redshift console.

    Use a SQL client tool, such as SQL Workbench or other compatible tools, to connect to the cluster using the endpoint and provided credentials.

14. **Load data and query**:

    Load data into your Redshift cluster using tools such as AWS Data Pipeline, AWS Glue, or the `COPY` command.

    Start writing SQL queries to analyze and extract insights from your data.

Remember that the preceding steps provide a general outline, and actual setup steps might vary based on your specific requirements and the current AWS interface.

Setting up Google BigQuery

Let's understand how we can set up Google BigQuery in the GCP cloud:

1. **Sign in to the Google Cloud console**: Log in to your Google Cloud console using your GCP account credentials.

2. **Open the Google BigQuery console**: Once logged in, navigate to the Google BigQuery service by selecting it from the list of available services.

3. **Create a new dataset**:

   Click on the **Create Dataset** button.

   Choose a unique dataset ID, and specify the default location and data expiration settings.

4. **Create a new table**:

   Inside your dataset, click on the **Create Table** button.

   Choose to create the table from a file, manually, or from another table.

5. **Configure the table schema**:

   Define the schema for your table by specifying column names, data types, and optional descriptions.

6. **Load data into the table**:

   If you choose to create the table from a file, upload the file from Google Cloud Storage or from your local machine.

   Configure the load options, such as data format and delimiter.

7. **Set up access control**:

   Configure access control to determine who can access the dataset and tables.

   You can set access at the dataset level or individual table level.

8. **Run queries**:

   After loading data, you can run SQL queries in the BigQuery console to analyze and retrieve insights from your data.

9. **Review Query Editor and results**:

   Use the Query Editor to compose and execute SQL queries.

   Review and analyze query results, and even save results to new tables.

10. **Monitoring and logging**:

    Monitor your BigQuery usage, performance, and costs using Google Cloud **Monitoring and Logging.**

11. **Integrate with other GCP services**:

    BigQuery integrates seamlessly with other GCP services such as Google Data Studio, allowing you to visualize and share your data.

12. **Scheduled queries and automations**:

    Use features such as scheduled queries and automations for routine data processing and analysis.

Remember that the preceding steps provide a general outline, and actual setup steps might vary based on your specific requirements and the current GCP interface.

The next section explores the diverse landscape of modern database systems that depart from the conventional relational database model. This topic delves into the array of database types that have emerged to address specific data management challenges and varying application requirements. Beyond the structured tables and rows of traditional databases, these alternative models include document databases, graph databases, in-memory databases, columnar databases, key-value stores, time-series databases, and more. Each of these database types offers unique strengths suited to specific use cases, such as handling complex relationships, optimizing for rapid data access, accommodating varied data structures, or enabling efficient analytics. By understanding the characteristics and use cases of these non-relational database models, businesses and developers can select the most appropriate solution for their specific data management and application needs.

Databases beyond the traditional realm

In a landscape where data has become increasingly diverse and complex, this topic explores innovative solutions that have emerged to accommodate various data structures, relationships, and use cases. From NoSQL databases such as document stores and graph databases to specialized models such as in-memory databases, time-series databases, and more, this topic illuminates the versatility and flexibility offered by these modern database types. By embracing these alternatives, businesses can harness the power of data in new and dynamic ways, adapting their data management strategies to the evolving requirements of today's digital landscape.

There are various types of databases beyond the traditional relational model. Here are some examples of different database types, along with a brief description and an example for each.

Document database

Document databases store, retrieve, and manage data in a flexible, semi-structured format using documents (for example, JSON or BSON) instead of tables and rows.

Unlike the rigid structure of relational databases, document databases allow each document to have its own unique schema, accommodating dynamic and evolving data models. This flexibility is especially useful in scenarios where data structures can change frequently or where data is unstructured or semi-structured.

JSON functionality

JSON is a widely used format for structuring data. In the context of document databases, JSON provides a way to represent and store data in a hierarchical format, making it easy to store and retrieve complex data structures.

Key features of JSON in document databases include the following:

- **Hierarchical data**: JSON allows the nesting of data, creating a hierarchy of attributes and values within a single document. This makes it suitable for representing nested and complex data structures.

- **Flexibility**: JSON documents can have varying fields and structures, enabling easy adaptation to changing data requirements without altering the overall database schema.

- **Arrays**: JSON supports arrays, allowing multiple values to be stored within a single field. This is useful for scenarios such as storing a list of items or comments.

- **Serialization and deserialization**: JSON data can be easily serialized (converted to a string) and deserialized (parsed from a string), making it straightforward to work with in programming languages.
- **Schema-less**: JSON documents in document databases do not require a fixed schema like traditional relational databases. This flexibility simplifies data modeling and adaptation to evolving requirements.

Advantages of document databases include the following:

- **Flexibility**: The schema-less nature of document databases allows for easy adaptation to changing data models without significant changes to the database structure
- **Semi-structured data**: Document databases are well suited for storing semi-structured or unstructured data, making them suitable for applications such as CMSs, e-commerce catalogs, and user-generated content
- **Performance**: Document databases provide fast read and write operations, especially when retrieving entire documents or subsets of data
- **Scalability**: Many document databases are designed to scale horizontally, distributing data across multiple nodes to handle increased data volumes and traffic
- **Developer-friendly**: The JSON format is widely used and familiar to developers, simplifying data manipulation and integration with various programming languages and frameworks

MongoDB is a popular example of a document database. It stores data in JSON-like BSON format and provides powerful querying and indexing capabilities for efficient data retrieval. MongoDB is used in a range of applications, including CMSs, real-time analytics, IoT applications, and more.

In conclusion, document databases leverage JSON functionality to provide a flexible, adaptable, and developer-friendly approach to storing and managing data. Their capability to handle semi-structured and dynamic data makes them a valuable choice for modern applications with evolving data needs.

In-memory database

An in-memory database is a type of database system that stores and manages data primarily in the main memory (RAM) of a computer, as opposed to traditional databases that store data on disk. This approach offers significantly faster data access and retrieval compared to disk-based systems, as memory access times are orders of magnitude faster than disk access times. In-memory databases are particularly well suited for applications that require rapid and low-latency data processing, such as real-time analytics, caching, and high-frequency transaction processing.

Functions of in-memory databases include the following:

- **Data storage**: In-memory databases load data directly into the main memory upon request or during database startup. This data is stored in data structures optimized for quick access, such as hash tables or trees.

- **Data retrieval**: When a query or operation is performed, the database engine retrieves data directly from the main memory, eliminating the need to access disk storage. This results in significantly reduced latency and faster query performance.

- **Indexes**: In-memory databases use indexes to quickly locate and retrieve data. These indexes are stored in memory and enable the database engine to efficiently navigate through the data.

- **No disk I/O**: In-memory databases minimize or eliminate disk I/O operations, which are a major source of latency in traditional databases. This absence of disk I/O contributes to the high-speed performance of in-memory databases.

- **Data durability**: In-memory databases often implement techniques to ensure data durability, such as periodic data persistence to disk or replication to other servers. This prevents data loss in case of system failures.

Advantages of in-memory databases include the following:

- **Speed**: In-memory databases offer blazing-fast data access and query performance due to the absence of disk I/O

- **Low latency**: With data residing in memory, there's minimal delay in retrieving and processing data, making them ideal for real-time applications

- **Complex queries**: In-memory databases excel in executing complex queries and analytical operations, as the data is readily available for computation

- **Caching**: In-memory databases can serve as powerful caching layers, reducing the load on backend systems and enhancing overall application performance

- **Real-time analytics**: In-memory databases enable businesses to perform real-time data analysis and generate insights without waiting for data to be read from disk

- **High throughput**: In-memory databases can handle a high volume of transactions and queries simultaneously, making them suitable for high-concurrency scenarios

Use cases include the following:

- **Financial services**: In-memory databases are used for high-frequency trading, fraud detection, risk analysis, and portfolio optimization

- **E-commerce**: Online retailers utilize in-memory databases for real-time inventory management, personalized recommendations, and rapid order processing

- **Gaming**: In-memory databases support real-time analytics, player profile management, and leaderboard updates in online gaming platforms

- **Telecommunications**: In-memory databases help manage call records, network optimization, and real-time billing for telecommunications providers

- **IoT applications**: In-memory databases handle real-time data streams from IoT devices, enabling instant monitoring, alerts, and analytics

Here are a couple of examples of in-memory databases:

- **SAP HANA**: An in-memory database platform that supports real-time data processing and analytics, used in **enterprise resource planning** (**ERP**) systems and business applications

- **Redis**: While Redis is often used as an in-memory data store for caching, its capabilities extend to data structures and real-time analytics, making it suitable for various use cases

In conclusion, in-memory databases leverage the speed of main memory to deliver lightning-fast data access and query performance. Their ability to handle high-throughput, low-latency scenarios makes them valuable in applications where real-time data processing and analysis are crucial.

Graph database

A graph database is a type of database designed to efficiently store, manage, and query data that represents complex relationships between entities. Unlike traditional relational databases that primarily focus on tabular data, graph databases organize data in nodes (entities) and edges (relationships), creating a visual representation of interconnected data. Graph databases excel at modeling and querying scenarios where relationships between data points are crucial, such as social networks, recommendation engines, fraud detection, and knowledge graphs.

Functions of graph databases include the following:

- **Nodes and edges**: In a graph database, data is represented as nodes (entities) and edges (relationships). Nodes hold properties, and edges define connections between nodes.

- **Indexing**: Graph databases build indexes on nodes and edges to enable efficient traversal of the graph. These indexes optimize queries to quickly locate nodes and relationships.

- **Traversals**: A traversal is a fundamental operation in graph databases. It involves moving through nodes and edges based on specific criteria and uncovering relationships and patterns in the data.

- **Graph algorithms**: Graph databases often include built-in graph algorithms that allow for advanced analyses, such as finding shortest paths, community detection, and recommendation generation.

- **Query language**: Graph databases use specialized query languages, such as Cypher for Neo4j or Gremlin for Apache TinkerPop, to express graph-based queries and traversals.

Advantages of graph databases include the following:

- **Relationship focus**: Graph databases excel at representing and querying complex relationships between data points, enabling rich insights and deep analyses

- **Flexible schema**: Graph databases support dynamic and evolving data models, making them suitable for scenarios with changing relationships

- **Efficient queries**: Graph databases are optimized for traversals and relationship-based queries, delivering fast and efficient results

- **Pattern recognition**: Graph databases excel at identifying patterns and connections within data, which is invaluable for applications such as fraud detection and recommendation systems

- **Hierarchical data**: Graph databases can model hierarchical structures as well as complex interconnections

- **Performance**: For relationship-heavy workloads, graph databases outperform traditional databases that require complex joins and subqueries

Use cases include the following:

- **Social networks**: Graph databases power social networks by efficiently storing and querying relationships between users, posts, likes, and comments

- **Recommendation engines**: Graph databases enable personalized recommendations by analyzing connections between users, products, and preferences

- **Fraud detection**: In fraud detection systems, graph databases identify suspicious patterns by analyzing connections between transactions, users, and entities

- **Knowledge graphs**: Graph databases construct knowledge graphs to organize and query vast amounts of interconnected information, enhancing search and discovery

- **Supply chain management**: Graph databases model and optimize complex supply chain networks, tracking relationships between suppliers, products, and logistics

Here are a couple of examples of graph databases:

- **Neo4j**: One of the most well-known graph databases, Neo4j uses the Cypher query language and is used in a wide range of applications involving relationship-driven data modeling and analysis.

- **Amazon Neptune**: A managed graph database service by AWS that supports both the Property Graph and RDF graph models, providing flexibility for various use cases.

Graph databases specialize in managing and analyzing complex relationships, making them ideal for scenarios where understanding connections and patterns is crucial. They offer a unique way to model and explore data in applications ranging from social networks to recommendation engines and knowledge graphs.

Columnar database

A columnar database is a type of DBMS optimized for storing and querying data by column, rather than by row, as in traditional relational databases. In a columnar database, each column of data is stored separately, allowing for efficient compression and faster query performance for analytical workloads. Columnar databases are particularly well suited for applications that involve heavy analytical and reporting tasks, as they can significantly improve query speeds and data compression.

Functions of columnar databases include the following:

- **Data storage**: In a columnar database, data is stored column-wise rather than row-wise. Each column forms a separate structure that contains all the values of that particular attribute.

- **Compression**: Columnar databases often employ specialized compression techniques tailored for column storage. Since columns usually contain similar or repetitive values, compression ratios are higher, reducing storage requirements.

- **Query optimization**: For analytical queries, columnar databases can process data more efficiently. They read only the columns needed for a query, minimizing I/O operations and improving query speed.

- **Aggregation**: Aggregation operations, such as SUM, COUNT, and AVG, are faster in columnar databases due to the storage format, which allows grouping and calculation on a per-column basis.

- **Data loading**: Columnar databases excel at bulk data loading and inserts, making them well suited for scenarios that require frequent updates and inserts along with analytical querying.

Advantages of columnar databases include the following:

- **Analytical performance**: Columnar databases are designed for analytical workloads, where queries involve aggregations, reporting, and data analysis. Their column-oriented storage accelerates these operations.

- **Compression efficiency**: Columnar databases achieve high compression ratios due to the similarity of values within a column, reducing storage costs.

- **Reduced I/O**: Columnar databases read only the necessary columns for a query, reducing I/O and improving query performance.

- **Parallel processing**: Columnar databases can leverage parallel processing to perform operations on multiple columns simultaneously, further boosting query performance.

- **Schema evolution**: Columnar databases support schema evolution, allowing you to add new columns or modify existing ones without interrupting service.

Use cases include the following:

- **Data warehousing**: Columnar databases are ideal for data warehousing scenarios where large amounts of historical data need to be stored and analyzed

- **BI**: For BI and analytics platforms, columnar databases accelerate query response times for complex analytical queries

- **Log analysis**: Columnar databases are effective for log analysis, where users need to query and analyze vast amounts of log data efficiently

- **Financial analysis**: Financial institutions use columnar databases for analyzing large volumes of transactional and market data in real time

Here are a couple of examples of columnar databases:

- **Amazon Redshift**: A popular columnar database service by AWS designed for data warehousing and analytics, supporting large-scale data storage and high-performance querying

- **Google BigQuery**: A serverless, highly scalable columnar database service by Google Cloud that enables super-fast SQL queries and analytical processing

Columnar databases optimize data storage and retrieval for analytical workloads by storing data in a column-wise manner, allowing for efficient compression and faster query performance. Their strengths lie in their ability to handle large-scale analytics, reporting, and complex queries with speed and efficiency.

Key-value store

A key-value store database is a type of NoSQL database that stores data as a collection of key-value pairs. Each key is a unique identifier for a piece of data, and the corresponding value can be of various data types, including strings, numbers, objects, or even binary data. Key-value databases are designed for high-speed data retrieval and storage, making them suitable for scenarios that require rapid access to data without complex querying.

Functions of key-value store databases include the following:

- **Data structure**: Key-value databases store data in a simple structure: keys and associated values. Each key is unique within the database.

- **Data storage**: Data is stored in an associative array or hash table format, where keys are hashed to determine their storage location.

- **Data retrieval**: To retrieve data, the database uses the provided key to look up the corresponding value. This operation is highly efficient and results in constant-time ($O(1)$) retrieval.

- **Scalability**: Many key-value databases are designed to scale horizontally, distributing data across multiple nodes for increased capacity and FT.

- **Operations**: Key-value databases typically support basic operations such as insert (put), retrieve (get), update, and delete (remove).

Advantages of key-value store databases include the following:

- **High performance**: Key-value databases excel at rapid data retrieval and storage, making them ideal for caching and frequently accessed data

- **Simplicity**: The simple structure of key-value pairs makes these databases easy to understand, deploy, and use

- **Scalability**: Key-value databases are often designed for distributed architectures, allowing for horizontal scalability to handle growing data volumes

- **Flexibility**: The value associated with a key can be of various types, accommodating different data structures within the same database

- **Caching**: Key-value databases are commonly used as caching layers to reduce the load on primary databases and improve application performance

Use cases include the following:

- **Caching**: Key-value databases are widely used for caching frequently accessed data, reducing the need to repeatedly query backend databases

- **Session management**: Storing user sessions and session-related data in key-value stores ensures quick access and session persistence

- **User profiles**: Storing user profiles and preferences, such as settings and preferences, in key-value stores facilitates rapid retrieval

- **Real-time analytics**: Key-value databases support real-time analytics by storing temporary data, counters, and real-time event tracking

Here are a couple of examples of key-value store databases:

- **Redis**: One of the most popular key-value store databases, Redis provides advanced features such as data types (strings, hashes, lists, and sets) and support for more complex operations

- **Amazon DynamoDB**: A managed key-value and document database service by AWS that offers seamless scalability and low-latency performance

Key-value store databases offer simplicity, speed, and efficient data retrieval by storing information as key-value pairs. They excel in scenarios that require fast data access, such as caching, session management, and real-time analytics.

Time-series database

A time-series database is a specialized type of database designed to store and manage data that is indexed and organized by time. It is optimized for handling data points collected at specific time intervals, such as sensor readings, log entries, stock prices, and other time-stamped data. Time-series databases offer efficient storage, retrieval, and analysis of chronological data, making them valuable for applications that require historical data analysis and monitoring.

Functions of time-series databases include the following:

- **Time-ordered storage**: Time-series databases store data points in chronological order, typically using a timestamp as the primary index. This allows for the efficient querying and retrieval of data within specified time ranges.

- **Data compression**: To optimize storage, time-series databases often employ data compression techniques that exploit patterns in the data to reduce its size.

- **Aggregation**: Time-series databases support various aggregation functions, allowing users to retrieve summarized data over specific time intervals, such as hourly, daily, or monthly.

- **Retention policies**: Time-series databases often incorporate retention policies to automatically manage data retention and deletion based on predefined criteria, such as age or storage capacity.

- **High write throughput**: Time-series databases are designed to handle high write throughput, making them suitable for applications with frequent data updates.

Advantages of time-series databases include the following:

- **Efficient storage**: Time-series databases efficiently store large volumes of timestamped data by optimizing storage and compression techniques

- **Rapid retrieval**: These databases excel at fast data retrieval based on time intervals, making them ideal for real-time analytics and monitoring

- **Analytical capabilities**: Time-series databases often provide built-in support for time-based aggregations, calculations, and analytics

- **Historical analysis**: Time-series databases are essential for historical data analysis, trend identification, and forecasting

- **IoT and monitoring**: They are widely used in IoT applications and monitoring systems where timestamped sensor data is crucial

Use cases include the following:

- **IoT monitoring**: Time-series databases are used to store and analyze sensor data from IoT devices, enabling real-time monitoring and insights

- **Financial data**: Stock market data, trading activity, and financial transactions are stored in time-series databases for historical analysis

- **Log management**: Time-series databases help manage and analyze log data from various sources, allowing for easy troubleshooting and debugging

- **Energy management**: Utilities use time-series databases to monitor energy consumption patterns and optimize usage

Here are a couple of examples of time-series databases:

- **InfluxDB**: A popular open source time-series database that provides high write and query performance along with built-in support for visualization and analytics

- **Prometheus**: An open source monitoring and alerting toolkit that uses a time-series database to store and analyze metric data collected from applications and infrastructure

Time-series databases are tailored for storing and retrieving timestamped data efficiently. Their focus on chronological organization and optimized storage makes them essential for applications that require historical analysis, real-time monitoring, and trend identification.

Converged database

A converged database is a type of database system that combines multiple data models and processing capabilities into a single platform. Unlike traditional databases that focus on a specific data model (for example, relational or NoSQL), converged databases provide a unified environment for storing and processing structured, semi-structured, and unstructured data. This approach simplifies data management, reduces data silos, and enables versatile analytics across diverse data types.

Functions of converged databases include the following:

- **Unified platform**: Converged databases integrate various data models, including relational, document, graph, and more, within a single platform. This allows different data structures to coexist and be queried together.

- **Data flexibility**: Converged databases accommodate structured, semi-structured, and unstructured data, eliminating the need to transform or preprocess data before analysis.

- **Data processing**: These databases offer diverse processing capabilities, enabling users to perform analytics, querying, and reporting on various data models without switching platforms.

- **Unified query language**: Converged databases often provide a single query language that supports all supported data models, simplifying data retrieval and analysis.

- **Scalability**: Many converged databases offer scalability options, allowing users to expand their data processing and storage capabilities as their needs grow.

Advantages of converged databases include the following:

- **Reduced complexity**: Converged databases streamline data management by providing a single platform for different data models, reducing the need for data transformation and integration

- **Versatile analytics**: Users can perform complex analytics and queries across different data types without the need for separate tools or systems

- **Data agility**: Converged databases allow organizations to adapt to changing data requirements and structures without migrating data between different systems

- **Cost efficiency**: By consolidating data storage and processing on a single platform, converged databases can reduce infrastructure and operational costs

- **Holistic insights**: Converged databases enable organizations to gain holistic insights by analyzing relationships between different data types

Use cases include the following:

- **Enterprise data lakes**: Converged databases are used in building enterprise data lakes, where data from various sources is ingested, stored, and analyzed in a unified environment

- **Multi-model applications**: Applications that require different data models, such as relational and graph, can benefit from converged databases that support both models within a single platform

- **Content management**: Organizations managing diverse types of content, such as images, videos, and documents, can benefit from a converged database to manage and analyze their content

Here are a couple of examples of converged databases:

- **Oracle Database**: Oracle offers a converged database that supports various data models, including relational, document, and graph, along with advanced analytics capabilities

- **SAP HANA**: SAP HANA provides a converged in-memory database platform that supports both relational and columnar storage, enabling real-time analytics on a variety of data types

Converged databases provide a unified platform for storing, managing, and analyzing various data models within a single system. Their ability to handle diverse data types and processing capabilities offers organizations greater agility, efficiency, and insights across their data landscape.

Wide-column store

A wide-column store database is a type of NoSQL database that stores data in columns rather than traditional rows. It is optimized for handling large-scale distributed data storage and retrieval, making it suitable for scenarios that require efficient data processing, scalability, and HA. Wide-column stores are commonly used in big data and analytical applications where fast query performance is crucial.

Functions of wide-column store databases include the following:

- **Column-oriented storage**: In a wide-column store, data is grouped and stored by columns, allowing for more efficient storage and retrieval of specific data attributes.

- **Column families**: Data in a wide-column store is organized into column families, which group related columns together. Each column family can have a different set of columns.

- **Data compression**: Wide-column store databases often use compression techniques to reduce storage requirements, as column values within a family are often similar.

- **Scalability**: These databases are designed for horizontal scalability, allowing organizations to distribute data across multiple nodes or clusters to handle large volumes of data.

- **Data modeling flexibility**: Wide-column store databases allow flexibility in data modeling, accommodating evolving data schemas and diverse data types.

Advantages of wide-column store databases include the following:

- **Scalability**: Wide-column stores scale horizontally by adding more nodes, enabling efficient handling of large amounts of data

- **Query performance**: These databases are optimized for analytical queries and are particularly efficient in retrieving and aggregating specific columns

- **Schema flexibility**: Wide-column stores accommodate changing data models and evolving schema requirements without significant disruptions

- **HA**: With data distribution and replication, wide-column store databases offer HA and FT

- **Aggregation**: These databases are well suited for scenarios requiring data aggregation, reporting, and analytics

Use cases include the following:

- **Big data analytics**: Wide-column stores are commonly used in big data analytics platforms where data needs to be processed, queried, and analyzed quickly

- **Time-series data**: Applications that manage time-series data, such as sensor readings, logs, and metrics, can benefit from efficient columnar storage

- **Content management**: Systems that manage large volumes of diverse content, such as media libraries, can utilize wide-column stores for efficient data storage

Here are a couple of examples of wide-column store databases:

- **Apache Cassandra**: One of the most well-known wide-column store databases, Cassandra provides HA, FT, and scalability for handling large-scale data

- **HBase**: Built on top of the **Hadoop Distributed File System** (**HDFS**), HBase is a distributed wide-column store database that excels in handling large volumes of sparse data

Wide-column store databases optimize data storage and retrieval by organizing data into columns and column families. Their strengths lie in horizontal scalability, efficient analytical queries, and flexible schema designs, making them suitable for applications involving big data analytics, content management, and time-series data.

In this section, we've explored a diverse array of database types that cater to the evolving needs of modern data management. From document databases to in-memory databases, and graph databases to wide-column stores, these specialized database models offer unique solutions for a wide range of applications. By embracing these versatile options, organizations can harness the power of tailored data storage and retrieval methods to optimize their operations, enhance analytics, and drive innovation across various domains.

Summary

This chapter, *Database Services 1 – Cloud Perspective*, dove into the dynamic landscape of database technologies in the cloud environment. It started with an *overview of database services in the cloud*, highlighting the fundamental role that databases play in modern computing, especially within cloud infrastructures. Moving forward, the chapter investigated the dichotomy between *relational and NoSQL databases*, offering insight into the strengths and applications of both models. It further explored the realm of *data warehousing services in the cloud*, showcasing how cloud-based solutions empower organizations to efficiently manage and analyze vast datasets for enhanced BI.

The chapter reached its pinnacle with a comprehensive examination of *databases beyond the traditional realm*. Here, it uncovered the intricacies of emerging database models such as document databases, in-memory databases, graph databases, and wide-column stores. These unconventional database paradigms present unique solutions for diverse data management needs, fostering adaptability and innovation across various sectors. Together, the chapters present a comprehensive journey through the evolving world of database services, offering readers a nuanced understanding of the various database models available in the cloud and their potential applications.

The next chapter, *Database Services 2 – Cloud Perspective*, provides a concise overview of managed database solutions in the cloud, including relational databases, NoSQL databases, and data warehousing services. Readers will learn about database types, use cases, and benefits, enabling them to make informed decisions for their applications. The chapter will empower readers with the knowledge and skills to effectively leverage cloud-based databases, ensuring data integrity, scalability, and optimal performance for their cloud-based applications. Whether readers are developers, database administrators, or IT professionals, this chapter equips them with the tools to make informed decisions and successfully implement database solutions in the cloud.

In the upcoming chapter, we will delve deeper into the intricate aspects of database management in the cloud environment. We'll start by exploring *data modeling and schema design*, unraveling the art of structuring data for optimal efficiency and usability. Moving forward, we'll uncover the mechanics of *database provisioning and configuration*, delving into the process of setting up and fine-tuning databases to align with specific requirements.

Security will take center stage as we delve into *database security best practices*, illuminating strategies to safeguard sensitive data in the cloud. The chapter will then explore *data migration and synchronization strategies*, guiding readers through seamless data movement and ensuring consistency across distributed databases.

The theme of resilience continues with a focus on *HA and scalability features*, shedding light on techniques to maintain data access and handle increasing workloads. We'll then explore the intricate realm of *database performance optimization*, providing insights into techniques to fine-tune database operations for lightning-fast responses.

The chapter will uncover the critical aspect of *backup and restore mechanisms*, ensuring data recoverability in the face of unexpected challenges. Finally, we will delve into *managing data durability and redundancy*, where we will explore strategies to maintain data integrity and redundancy, even in the face of disruptions.

9
Database Services – Part 2

This chapter is dedicated to exploring the various database offerings available in the cloud. You can expect to learn about managed database services provided by major cloud providers, such as **Amazon Web Services** (**AWS**), Microsoft Azure, and **Google Cloud Platform** (**GCP**). The chapter will delve into different types of databases, including relational databases, NoSQL databases, and data warehousing services. The chapter encompasses a wide array of critical topics aimed at enhancing your understanding and proficiency in handling databases effectively. It commences with a deep dive into *Data modeling and schema design*, emphasizing the foundational importance of structuring data optimally.

The chapter then explores the complexities of *Database provisioning and configuration*, providing insights into the setup and fine-tuning of databases to align them to specific needs. Security takes the forefront with *Database security best practices*, where strategies to protect sensitive data within the cloud are unveiled.

You will gain insights into the benefits and use cases of each database type, helping you make informed decisions when selecting the most suitable option for your specific applications and workloads. The chapter will cover essential concepts such as data modeling, schema design, data indexing, and query optimization.

Key topics covered in this chapter include the following:

- Data modeling and schema design
- Database provisioning and configuration
- Database security best practices
- High-availability and scalability features
- Database performance optimization

By the end of this chapter, readers will have a comprehensive understanding of the various database services available in the cloud, their respective strengths and weaknesses, and best practices for effectively implementing and managing cloud-based databases. Whether readers are developers, database administrators, or IT professional, this chapter equips you with the knowledge and skills needed to leverage database services in the cloud and optimize the performance and scalability of your applications. This chapter also equips readers with the knowledge and skills needed to effectively architect, secure, optimize, and manage databases, enabling you to navigate complex database challenges with confidence and proficiency.

Technical requirements

To fully engage with the content of this chapter on cloud computing architecture, readers should have a basic understanding of computer systems, networking concepts, and information technology.

Additionally, the following technical requirements are recommended:

- **Internet access**: You should have a reliable internet connection to access online resources, references, and examples related to cloud computing.

- **Computing device**: A desktop computer, laptop, tablet, or smartphone with a modern web browser is necessary to read the chapter content and access any online materials.

- **Web browser**: The latest version of a modern web browser such as Google Chrome, Mozilla Firefox, Microsoft Edge, or Safari is recommended. This ensures compatibility and an optimal viewing experience of web-based resources and interactive content.

- **Familiarity with cloud services**: Some familiarity with cloud services and their basic functionalities will enhance the understanding of the chapter. This includes knowledge of basic network concepts, basic database concepts, O/S, encryption, and servers.

Data modeling and schema design

In this section, we will delve into the foundational principles of structuring data effectively within database systems. It explores the process of defining data models and creating schemas that optimize data storage, retrieval, and manipulation. Readers will learn about the importance of selecting appropriate data types, creating relationships between entities, and establishing constraints to ensure data integrity.

This section delves into both conceptual and physical data modeling, guiding readers through the steps of conceptualizing the data structure and translating it into a concrete database schema. It covers normalization techniques to reduce data redundancy and improve database efficiency. Moreover, readers will gain insights into denormalization strategies for specific performance optimization needs.

Through real-world examples and best practices, this section equips readers with the skills to design databases that align with the specific requirements of applications and analytical needs. By grasping the intricacies of data modeling and schema design, readers will be empowered to create efficient, well-organized, and adaptable databases that form the foundation of successful data management within the cloud environment.

Data modeling and schema design are critical steps in creating a well-structured and efficient database system. Data modeling involves creating a conceptual representation of the data and its relationships, while schema design translates this conceptual model into a physical database structure. These processes are fundamental in ensuring data accuracy, integrity, and efficient retrieval.

Let's look at the key concepts in the following sections.

Conceptual data model

This high-level representation defines the entities, attributes, and relationships within the data without concerning itself with implementation details.

A conceptual data model is a high-level representation of an organization's data, emphasizing the relationships between various entities without delving into the technical details of how the data will be stored or implemented in a database. It provides a clear visualization of the business concepts and their interactions, serving as a bridge between business requirements and the eventual database schema.

The key components of a conceptual data model are as follows:

- **Entities**: Entities are the major objects or concepts within the organization's domain. They represent things such as customers, products, employees, and orders.

- **Attributes**: Attributes define the characteristics or properties of entities. For example, a *Customer* entity might have attributes such as *Name, Email*, and *Phone Number*.

- **Relationships**: Relationships illustrate the connections between entities. They signify how entities interact and can be one-to-one, one-to-many, or many-to-many.

- **Cardinality**: Cardinality specifies the quantity of related entities in a relationship. It clarifies how many instances of one entity are connected to instances of another entity.

- **Business rules**: Conceptual data models often incorporate high-level business rules that dictate the behavior and interactions between entities.

The purposes and benefits of conceptual data models are as follows:

- **Clarity**: Conceptual data models provide a clear visual representation of the organization's data landscape, fostering a shared understanding among stakeholders

- **Requirements gathering**: They serve as a foundation for gathering and validating business requirements before moving into the technical implementation phase

- **Communication**: Conceptual data models facilitate effective communication between business analysts, developers, and other stakeholders by providing a common reference point
- **Design alignment**: A well-constructed conceptual data model ensures that the eventual database schema aligns closely with the organization's needs

The following is needed to create a conceptual data model:

- **Requirements gathering**: Engage with stakeholders to identify the major entities, attributes, and relationships relevant to the business.
- **Entity-relationship diagrams (ERDs)**: ERDs visually represent entities, attributes, relationships, and their cardinalities. This graphical tool is commonly used to create conceptual data models.
- **Simplified complexity**: Focus on the key concepts and relationships while avoiding technical implementation details.
- **Validation**: Review the conceptual data model with stakeholders to ensure that it accurately captures the business's understanding and requirements.

Example:

Consider an e-commerce platform. The conceptual data model might feature entities such as *Customer*, *Product*, and *Order*. The *Customer* entity could have attributes such as *Name*, *Email*, and *Address*. *Relationships* might involve *Customers* placing *Orders*, with each *Order* consisting of multiple *Products*.

In essence, a conceptual data model acts as a blueprint for designing the database schema. It guides the subsequent phases of data modeling, ultimately leading to a well-structured and efficiently organized database that aligns precisely with the business's needs.

Physical data model

This translates the conceptual model into a concrete database schema, including tables, columns, data types, constraints, and indexes. A **physical data model (PDM)** is a detailed blueprint that represents how data is stored, organized, and accessed within a **database management system (DBMS)**. It is a technical representation of the logical design created during the data modeling process. Unlike conceptual or conceptual-physical models, a physical data model is closely tied to the specific database platform's implementation details.

The key components of a PDM are as follows:

- **Tables and columns**: A PDM defines the actual tables and their corresponding columns that will hold the data. Columns are defined with specific data types and constraints.
- **Primary and foreign keys**: A PDM specifies which columns will be primary keys (unique identifiers) and establishes relationships through foreign keys.

- **Indexes**: Indexes are used to speed up data retrieval by providing efficient access paths to data. A PDM determines which columns need indexing.

- **Constraints**: Data integrity constraints such as NOT NULL, UNIQUE, and CHECK are defined to ensure data quality and consistency.

- **Triggers and stored procedures**: A PDM might include triggers and stored procedures that automate specific database actions or enforce business rules.

Its purposes and benefits are as follows:

- **Implementation guide**: A PDM acts as a detailed implementation guide for database developers and administrators, ensuring a consistent and accurate database structure

- **Performance optimization**: By defining indexes, constraints, and data types, a PDM helps optimize database performance

- **Data integrity**: A PDM enforces data integrity by specifying rules and constraints that data must adhere to

- **Database maintenance**: A PDM serves as a reference for ongoing database maintenance tasks, such as backups, updates, and modifications

The following is needed to create a PDM:

- **A logical design**: A PDM is derived from a logical data model, taking the high-level entities, attributes, and relationships and mapping them onto the specific database platform's structures.

- **A choice of database platform**: Choose the DBMS that the physical model will be implemented on. Different DBMSs have varying storage and indexing mechanisms.

- **Defintions of columns and constraints**: Define the columns, data types, and constraints for each table based on the logical model.

- **Relationships and keys**: Specify primary keys, foreign keys, and indexes to ensure data integrity and efficient querying.

- **Normalization and denormalization**: Consider normalization and, if necessary, denormalization techniques to optimize data storage and retrieval.

Example:

For an e-commerce platform, the PDM might detail tables such as *Customers*, *Orders*, and *Products*, defining the columns within each table, relationships, indexes, and constraints.

In essence, a PDM provides the technical specifics required to turn a well-designed logical model into a functional database system. It serves as a crucial guide for implementing, maintaining, and optimizing the database within the chosen DBMS.

Normalization

This technique eliminates data redundancy by organizing data into related tables and minimizing data duplication. Normalization is a database design technique that aims to minimize data redundancy and maintain data integrity by organizing data into separate tables based on their logical relationships. The process involves breaking down a single large table into smaller, related tables that store specific types of data, reducing data duplication and potential anomalies. Normalization ensures efficient data storage, query performance, and updates while avoiding anomalies such as insertion, update, and deletion anomalies.

The key concepts of normalization are as follows:

- **Functional dependency**: Functional dependency indicates that one attribute's value is dependent on another attribute's value. It forms the basis for normalization.

- **Normalization forms**: There are several **normal forms (NFs)** that represent increasing levels of data normalization. Commonly used ones include **first normal form (1NF)**, **second normal form (2NF)**, **third normal form (3NF)**, and **Boyce-Codd normal form (BCNF)**:

  - **1NF**: Each table cell should contain only atomic (indivisible) values, and each column should have a unique name

  - **2NF**: Building upon 1NF, all non-key attributes must be fully functionally dependent on the primary key

  - **3NF**: Building upon 2NF, 3NF eliminates transitive dependencies, where a non-key attribute depends on another non-key attribute through the primary key

  - **BCNF**: An extension of 3NF, BCNF ensures that there are no non-trivial dependencies between candidate keys and non-key attributes

The benefits of normalization are as follows:

- **Data integrity**: Normalization minimizes data redundancy and eliminates update anomalies, ensuring that data remains consistent

- **Storage efficiency**: Smaller, well-organized tables lead to efficient storage utilization

- **Query performance**: Normalization can improve query performance by reducing the need for complex joins and aggregations

- **Scalability**: Normalized tables can be efficiently expanded without disrupting the existing structure

Its considerations and limitations include the following:

- **Balance**: Over-normalization can lead to complex queries and performance issues, so it's essential to strike a balance between normalization and query efficiency

- **Application context**: The level of normalization should align with the application's data access patterns and usage scenarios
- **Denormalization**: In certain cases, controlled denormalization might be appropriate to enhance query performance

Example:

Consider a library management system. The initial unnormalized table might contain columns for both book and author information. Through normalization, the data could be divided into separate tables for books and authors, reducing redundancy and improving data integrity.

Normalization is a fundamental process in database design that ensures data accuracy, integrity, and efficiency. By systematically eliminating data redundancy and organizing data logically, normalization sets the foundation for well-structured and maintainable databases.

Denormalization

In contrast to normalization, denormalization involves intentionally introducing redundancy to improve query performance, especially in read-heavy scenarios. Denormalization is a database design technique that involves intentionally introducing redundancy into a normalized database schema. This process aims to improve query performance by reducing the need for complex joins and aggregations, especially in scenarios where read operations are more frequent than writes. Denormalization can lead to duplication of data, but it serves as a trade-off between data redundancy and query efficiency.

The key concepts of denormalization are as follows:

- **Redundancy**: Denormalization introduces redundant data by storing information in multiple places. This contrasts with normalization, where redundancy is minimized.
- **Query performance**: Denormalization focuses on optimizing query performance by reducing the number of joins and simplifying data retrieval.

The benefits of denormalization are as follows:

- **Query efficiency**: Complex queries that involve multiple joins can become simpler and faster due to reduced join operations
- **Read-heavy workloads**: Denormalization is particularly useful for applications with a heavy emphasis on read operations, such as reporting or analytics
- **Aggregation performance**: Aggregations and calculations are more efficient when data is pre-joined and pre-calculated

Its considerations and trade-offs include the following:

- **Data redundancy**: Denormalization introduces redundancy, which can lead to data inconsistency if updates are not managed carefully

- **Write performance**: While read performance improves, write performance can suffer due to increased data modification complexity

- **Maintenance complexity**: Managing redundant data requires careful maintenance to ensure data consistency across denormalized copies

When to consider denormalization:

- **Reporting and analytics**: Systems that involve extensive reporting and analytical queries can benefit from denormalization

- **Real-time applications**: Applications where real-time data access is critical might opt for denormalization to reduce query complexity

- **Data warehousing**: Data warehouses often denormalize data to optimize query performance for analytical purposes

Strategies for denormalization include the following:

- **Combining tables**: Join-intensive queries can be optimized by combining multiple normalized tables into a single denormalized table

- **Pre-joined data**: Creating tables that already have data joined can accelerate query performance

- **Caching and materialized views**: Storing pre-computed results in materialized views or cache can enhance query efficiency

Example:

In an e-commerce platform, denormalization might involve duplicating customer information in the order table to avoid joins between customer and order tables when retrieving order history.

In conclusion, denormalization is a deliberate trade-off between data redundancy and query efficiency. It is employed to enhance read-heavy workloads and optimize query performance, particularly in scenarios where complex joins hinder data retrieval speed. Careful consideration and balance between normalized and denormalized data structures are crucial to maintaining data consistency while reaping the benefits of improved query performance.

Benefits of data modeling and schema design

This section delves into the fundamental principles that underpin effective database architecture. Data modeling and schema design play pivotal roles in shaping the structure, organization, and relationships within a database. A well-crafted data model not only defines how data is stored but also influences system performance, scalability, and ease of maintenance. This section aims to elucidate the advantages of thoughtful data modeling and schema design, emphasizing their impact on data integrity, query efficiency, and the overall agility of database systems. By understanding these benefits, readers will gain essential insights into creating robust and optimized databases that align with the specific requirements and objectives of your applications.

Let's discuss the benefits of data modeling and schema design in more depth:

- **Data integrity**: Proper data modeling and schema design enforce data integrity through constraints, ensuring that data remains accurate and consistent

- **Efficient retrieval**: A well-designed schema optimizes data retrieval, reducing the need for complex joins and enhancing query performance

- **Adaptability**: A thoughtful schema design allows for easier modifications and adaptations as application requirements evolve

Its considerations are as follows:

- **Application requirements**: Schema design should align with the specific needs of the application, taking into account the types of queries, data relationships, and usage patterns

- **Normalization level**: The appropriate level of normalization depends on the trade-off between data integrity and query performance

- **Data types**: Choosing appropriate data types is crucial to efficient storage and accurate representation of data

- **Indexing**: Selectively applying indexes enhances query performance, but excessive indexing can lead to overhead

Best practices include the following:

- **Start with conceptual design**: Begin by understanding the business requirements and creating a conceptual data model

- **Normalize prudently**: Normalize data to a level that balances data integrity and query performance, considering the usage patterns

- **Denormalize with caution**: Use denormalization judiciously for specific performance optimization needs

- **Optimize indexing**: Apply indexes strategically to improve query performance while minimizing overhead

Use cases

A retail application might model customers, orders, and products, requiring careful schema design to support efficient order tracking and inventory management.

An analytics platform might focus on aggregating data, necessitating a schema design that facilitates complex aggregations and reporting.

Data modeling and schema design are foundational steps in creating efficient and adaptable database systems. By following best practices, understanding application requirements, and striking a balance between normalization and denormalization, professionals can ensure that their database structures efficiently store and retrieve data, supporting the needs of diverse applications and analytical processes.

The following *Database provisioning and configuration* section delves into the process of setting up and configuring databases within a cloud environment. It covers various aspects of provisioning, including selecting the appropriate database types, sizing resources, defining configurations, and establishing security measures. Readers will gain insights into the steps required to effectively provision and configure databases to meet specific application needs, ensuring optimal performance, security, and scalability within the cloud environment.

Database provisioning and configuration

Database provisioning and configuration is a crucial aspect of managing databases within a cloud environment. Provisioning involves setting up the necessary resources, while configuration focuses on optimizing database settings to ensure performance, security, and reliability. In this section, readers will explore the key considerations when selecting the right database types, sizing resources appropriately, and configuring database settings to align with the requirements of your applications. Additionally, this section will delve into security measures that need to be implemented during provisioning and configuration to safeguard sensitive data. By the end of this section, readers will have a comprehensive understanding of how to provision and configure databases effectively to meet the demands of your applications while optimizing performance and ensuring data integrity in the cloud environment. This topic delves into the key considerations and steps involved in these processes.

Database provisioning

Database provisioning stands as a pivotal component in the realm of managing databases within a cloud environment. It encompasses the essential process of setting up the requisite resources to ensure optimal functionality and performance. Let's discuss some critical aspects of database provisioning:

- **Resource selection**: The process begins with selecting the appropriate database type based on the application's requirements. Factors such as data structure, access patterns, and scalability needs influence this decision.

- **Resource allocation**: Determining the right amount of computing resources, such as CPU, memory, and storage, is essential to optimal performance. Over-provisioning can lead to unnecessary costs, while under-provisioning can result in poor performance.

- **Cloud services:** Cloud providers offer managed database services that simplify provisioning. These services handle tasks such as resource allocation, scalability, and backups, reducing administrative overhead.

- **Automated provisioning**: Automation tools and scripts can streamline provisioning by quickly setting up databases with predefined configurations. This ensures consistency and reduces human error.

Database configuration

Database configuration serves as a critical facet in the effective management of databases within a cloud environment. Once the necessary resources are provisioned, the focus shifts to optimizing database settings to ensure optimal performance, security, and reliability. This topic delves into the intricacies of database configuration, exploring key considerations and steps involved in fine-tuning settings to align with the unique requirements of various applications. Let's discuss some critical aspects of database configuration:

- **Database settings**: Configuring database settings is crucial to achieving desired performance and reliability. Parameters such as cache sizes, buffer pools, and query optimization settings need to be fine-tuned based on workload characteristics.

- **Security configuration**: Security is paramount. Access controls, encryption, and regular security patching are key elements. Compliance with industry regulations must also be considered.

- **Backup and recovery**: Establishing backup and recovery strategies is vital to safeguarding data. Determining backup frequency, retention policies, and mechanisms for restoring data in case of failure are essential.

- **High availability**: Configuring high-availability mechanisms such as failover clusters ensures that the database remains accessible even during hardware or software failures.

- **Scalability configuration**: As data and user loads grow, databases must scale accordingly. Vertical scaling involves adding more resources to a single instance, while horizontal scaling involves distributing data across multiple instances.

- **Performance monitoring**: Regularly monitoring database performance using tools and metrics helps identify bottlenecks and performance issues. This data guides further configuration adjustments.

Benefits of effective provisioning and configuration

In the dynamic landscape of cloud-based database management, the effective provisioning and configuration of databases play a pivotal role in shaping the performance, security, and reliability of an organization's data infrastructure. Proper provisioning involves setting up the necessary resources, while configuration focuses on fine-tuning database settings to meet the specific needs of applications:

- **Optimized performance**: Proper provisioning and configuration lead to improved database performance, ensuring responsive and efficient data access

- **Enhanced security**: Effective security measures and configurations protect sensitive data from unauthorized access and breaches

- **Scalability**: Well-configured databases can handle increased workloads and scale seamlessly as demand grows

- **Reliability**: High-availability setups and backup strategies ensure data durability and availability, minimizing downtime

- **Cost efficiency**: Proper resource allocation prevents unnecessary costs while ensuring the database meets performance requirements

Example of database provisioning in the cloud – e-commerce platform

Let's consider an example of setting up a relational database for an e-commerce platform in a cloud environment, specifically using AWS. This step-by-step methodology outlines the process of provisioning a database instance:

1. *Sign in to the AWS console*: Log in to your AWS account and access the AWS Management Console.

2. *Choose Relational Database Service*: Navigate to Amazon RDS, which offers managed relational databases. Click on **Create Database**.

3. *Select database engine*: Choose the preferred database engine (e.g., MySQL, PostgreSQL, SQL Server, or Oracle). Each engine has specific features and compatibility considerations.

4. *Specify database details*: Provide details such as DB instance class (CPU and memory), allocated storage, database identifier, and master username/password for initial setup.

5. *Configure advanced settings*: Configure advanced settings such as VPC, subnet group, security groups, and availability zones. These settings dictate network access and high availability.

6. *Database authentication*: Choose the authentication method, either password authentication or IAM database authentication.

7. *Database connectivity*: Configure options such as public accessibility, if required. This determines whether the database can be accessed over the internet.

8. *Database backup and maintenance*: Configure automated backups, specifying retention periods and backup window timings. Set up maintenance preferences for system updates.

9. *Additional configuration*: Depending on the database engine, configure specific settings such as encryption, parameter groups, and performance enhancements.

10. *Review and launch*: Review your configuration settings to ensure accuracy. Once confirmed, click **Create Database**.

11. *Database provisioning*: AWS will initiate the database provisioning process. It creates the specified instance, allocates resources, sets up network connectivity, and applies configurations.

12. *Database availability*: Once provisioning is complete, the database instance will be available and accessible through the provided endpoint.

13. *Data population*: Import or create the necessary database schema and tables and populate them with relevant data.

14. *Application integration*: Update your application's configuration to point to the newly provisioned database endpoint. Test the integration thoroughly.

Benefits:

- **Ease of use**: Cloud platforms such as AWS simplify the provisioning process, providing user-friendly interfaces and automation

- **Scalability**: As your e-commerce platform grows, you can easily scale resources to accommodate increased traffic

- **Reliability**: Cloud providers ensure high availability, automated backups, and maintenance, reducing operational concerns

- **Security**: Cloud databases offer encryption at rest and in transit, enhancing data security

- **Cost control**: Cloud providers offer pay-as-you-go pricing, allowing you to match costs with resource utilization

By following this methodology, an e-commerce platform can quickly provision a reliable and scalable database in the cloud, enabling efficient data storage and retrieval to support its operations.

Example of database provisioning in the cloud – healthcare patient management

Let's explore another use case of setting up a cloud database, specifically using GCP, for a healthcare patient management system. Here's a step-by-step methodology for provisioning the database:

1. *Sign in to GCP console*: Log in to your Google Cloud account and access the Google Cloud console.

2. *Choose Cloud SQL*: Navigate to the Cloud SQL service, which offers managed databases. Click on **Create instance**.

3. *Select database engine*: Choose the preferred database engine (e.g., MySQL, PostgreSQL, SQL Server) that suits your application's requirements.

4. *Configure instance details*: Specify instance ID, password, and instance type (CPU and memory). Choose the database version and storage capacity.

5. *Choose connectivity settings*: Configure network connectivity options such as private or public IP addresses, and choose whether to enable SSL encryption for data in transit.

6. *Configure access control*: Set up authorized networks to control which IP addresses can connect to the database instance. You can also choose to use IAM for access control.

7. *Choose high availability*: Opt for high availability by enabling failover replicas in a different zone for automatic failover in case of an outage.

8. *Backup and maintenance*: Configure automated backups and specify the retention period. Schedule maintenance windows for updates and patches.

9. *Additional configuration*: Depending on the chosen database engine, configure additional settings such as custom flags, user-defined parameters, and instance tiers.

10. *Review and create*: Review your configuration settings to ensure accuracy. Once validated, click **Create** to initiate the database provisioning process.

11. *Database provisioning*: Google Cloud will create the database instance, allocate resources, configure network settings, and apply the chosen configurations.

12. *Database access and integration*: Once provisioned, you'll receive connection details such as instance IP and credentials. Use these details to integrate your healthcare application with the database.

13. *Data migration and population*: Import or create the necessary tables and schema to store patient information securely in the database.

14. *Application testing*: Thoroughly test your healthcare application's functionality and data integration with the newly provisioned cloud database.

Benefits:

- **Managed service**: Google Cloud SQL offers automated management, backups, and scaling, reducing administrative overhead

- **Security**: Google Cloud provides encryption at rest and in transit, ensuring data security and compliance

- **Scalability**: Cloud SQL allows you to easily scale resources vertically by adjusting instance types

- **High availability**: Failover replicas and regional availability enhance application reliability

- **Pay as you go**: Google Cloud's pricing model aligns costs with usage, providing cost efficiency

By following this methodology, a healthcare organization can set up a robust, secure, and highly available cloud database on GCP, effectively managing patient data while adhering to compliance requirements.

Example of database provisioning in the cloud – e-learning platform

In this scenario, we'll consider provisioning a database for an e-learning platform using the Microsoft Azure cloud. We'll use Azure's **command-line interface** (**CLI**) to illustrate the process. Here's a step-by-step methodology:

1. *Install the Azure CLI*: If it's not already installed, download and install the Azure CLI onto your local machine.

2. *Log in to Azure account*: Open a terminal or command prompt and run the following command to log in to your Azure account:

    ```
    az login
    ```

3. *Create a resource group*: Create a resource group to contain your resources. Replace `<resource-group-name>` with a suitable name:

    ```
    az group create --name <resource-group-name> --location
    <location>
    ```

4. *Create a SQL database*: Use the following command to create an Azure SQL Database instance. Replace placeholders with actual values:

    ```
    az sql server create --name <server-name> --resource-group
    <resource-group-name> --location <location> --admin-user <admin-
    username> --admin-password <admin-password>
    ```

5. *Configure firewall rules*: Allow your IP address to access the database server:

    ```
    az sql server firewall-rule create --resource-group <resource-
    group-name> --server <server-name> --name AllowYourIP --start-
    ip-address <your-ip-address> --end-ip-address <your-ip-address>
    ```

6. *Create a database*: Create a database within the SQL server instance:

    ```
    az sql db create --resource-group <resource-group-name> --server
    <server-name> --name <database-name> --edition GeneralPurpose
    --family Gen5 --capacity 2 --zone-redundant false
    ```

7. *Connect to the database*: Retrieve the connection string to connect your application to the Azure SQL database:

    ```
    az sql db show-connection-string --name <database-name> --server
    <server-name> --client ado.net
    ```

8. *Data migration and population*: Use SQL Server Management Studio or another tool to import your e-learning platform's schema and data into the newly created Azure SQL database.

9. *Application integration*: Update your e-learning platform's configuration to use the Azure SQL Database connection string.

In this illustrative example of provisioning a database for an e-learning platform on Microsoft Azure, we've employed the Azure CLI for a step-by-step walkthrough. Beginning with the installation of Azure CLI and logging in to the Azure account, the process involves creating a resource group, establishing an Azure SQL Database instance, configuring firewall rules, and ultimately connecting the database to the e-learning platform. This detailed methodology ensures a seamless provision of resources tailored to the specific needs of the e-learning application.

Effectively provisioning a database in the cloud is not just about allocating resources; it's a strategic process that ensures optimal performance, security, and scalability. In this example, using Microsoft Azure, we've demonstrated how each step, from creating a resource group to configuring firewall rules and connecting the database to the application, contributes to a well-orchestrated provisioning workflow. By following such meticulous steps, organizations can not only establish a robust database infrastructure for their applications, but also enhance efficiency and maintain best practices in cloud-based data management. This example serves as a practical guide, showcasing the importance of thoughtful database provisioning in the cloud and providing a blueprint for similar implementations in diverse scenarios.

Benefits:

- **Azure CLI efficiency**: Using the Azure CLI streamlines resource creation and management through scripting

- **Managed service**: Azure SQL Database is fully managed, handling maintenance, backups, and scaling

- **Security**: Azure provides advanced security features such as threat detection and encryption

- **Scalability**: Azure SQL Database supports automatic and manual scaling to handle changing workloads

- **Geo-redundancy**: Azure offers built-in redundancy for data protection and disaster recovery

By following this methodology, an e-learning platform can swiftly provision and configure an Azure SQL database to store and manage user data, providing a robust foundation for their application's backend infrastructure.

In the following figure, we can see the basic setup of a database in a cloud environment:

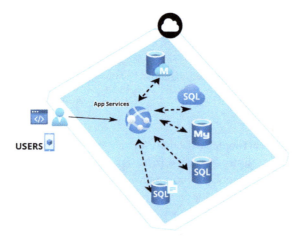

Figure 9.1: App services interacting with various databases and database services

In this section, we explored two vital facets of managing databases in the cloud. Starting with provisioning, the section detailed the essential steps and considerations for allocating resources efficiently. Real-world examples, including e-commerce, healthcare patient management, and e-learning platforms, showcased practical methodologies on platforms such as Microsoft Azure. Transitioning to configuration, the focus shifted to fine-tuning database settings for optimal performance and security. These insights, coupled with hands-on examples, provide readers with a comprehensive understanding of crafting robust, efficient, and secure database environments in diverse cloud scenarios.

The following *Database security best practices* section delves into essential strategies and measures to ensure the security of databases within a cloud environment. It focuses on safeguarding sensitive data, preventing unauthorized access, and maintaining data integrity. Readers will learn about a range of security practices, including access controls, encryption, auditing, and monitoring. This section aims to equip readers with the knowledge to implement comprehensive security measures to protect your databases from various threats and vulnerabilities.

Database security best practices

Database security is paramount in ensuring the confidentiality, integrity, and availability of critical data. In a cloud environment, where databases are accessible from anywhere, implementing robust security practices is crucial to mitigate risks. This section covers a range of measures to fortify database security.

Access control

Implement fine-grained access controls to restrict database access to authorized users only. Use **role-based access control** (**RBAC**) to assign permissions based on user roles. For example, a healthcare system might grant doctors access to patient records while limiting administrative access. Access control is a fundamental aspect of database security that regulates who can access what data and perform which actions within a database system. It prevents unauthorized users from gaining access to sensitive information and helps maintain data confidentiality and integrity. We will delve into each of these access control models—RBAC, **discretionary access control** (**DAC**), **mandatory access control** (**MAC**), and **attribute-based access control** (**ABAC**)—in detail, exploring their functionalities, advantages, and considerations in shaping secure and efficient data access within diverse environments.

RBAC

RBAC is a widely used method in access control. It assigns roles to users, and each role has specific permissions associated with it. Users are then assigned roles rather than having individual permissions. This simplifies the management of permissions and reduces the risk of granting excessive access.

DAC

DAC allows the owner of the data to decide who can access it. Owners can grant or revoke permissions on objects such as tables, views, or stored procedures. This model can lead to difficulties in managing permissions for large databases.

MAC

MAC enforces access based on a predefined security policy. Data is classified, and users are assigned security labels. Access is granted based on matching labels and permissions.

ABAC

ABAC evaluates access decisions based on attributes such as user attributes, resource attributes, and context. This allows for more dynamic and fine-grained access control based on various factors.

Popular tools and methods for access control

We will list the tools and methods central to access control that play a pivotal role in ensuring secure data environments. The focus areas include RBAC tools such as Amazon IAM, Google Cloud IAM, and Azure RBAC. DBMS access control will be explored through MySQL, PostgreSQL, and Microsoft SQL Server Management Studio. **Identity and access management (IAM)** solutions such as Okta and OneLogin will be highlighted, along with ABAC tools such as Axiomatics. Additionally, we'll cover data masking and redaction tools such as Oracle Data Masking and Subsetting, database auditing tools such as IBM Guardium, and the possibility of custom application development for tailored access control solutions. These tools can be segregated as follows:

1. **RBAC tools**:

    *   **Amazon IAM for AWS**: Amazon IAM serves as a comprehensive access control solution for AWS. It enables the management of users and their permissions, allowing organizations to finely control access to AWS resources.

    *   **Google Cloud IAM for GCP**: Google Cloud IAM provides robust access control for GCP resources. It allows organizations to define and manage roles, granting precise permissions to users and service accounts across Google Cloud services.

    *   **Azure RBAC for Microsoft Azure**: Azure RBAC is a central component for access management in Microsoft Azure. It enables the assignment of roles to users, regulating access to Azure resources with granularity.

2. **DBMS access control**:

    *   **MySQL**: MySQL utilizes GRANT and REVOKE statements for access control, offering a flexible mechanism to manage user privileges. Organizations can precisely define what actions users are allowed to perform on specific database objects.

- **PostgreSQL**: PostgreSQL employs GRANT and REVOKE statements, providing extensive control options for managing user access. This includes fine-grained control over individual tables, schemas, and other database elements.

- **Microsoft SQL Server**: Microsoft SQL Server leverages SQL Server Management Studio for configuring user roles and permissions. This graphical tool facilitates the management of access rights, allowing administrators to define and modify user roles effectively.

3. **IAM solutions**:

- **Okta**: Okta is an IAM solution that centralizes identity management and access control across various applications and databases. It simplifies **single sign-on** (**SSO**) and ensures secure and seamless access to resources.

- **OneLogin**: OneLogin specializes in SSO and identity management, providing a unified approach to access control for various services. It streamlines authentication processes while enhancing security.

4. **ABAC tools**:

- **Axiomatics**: Axiomatics offers ABAC solutions, enabling fine-grained access control and dynamic authorization. ABAC evaluates access decisions based on attributes, providing a flexible and context-aware approach to access management.

5. **Data masking and redaction tools**:

- **Oracle Data Masking and Subsetting**: Masks sensitive data to protect its confidentiality. Oracle's solution for data masking and subsetting is designed to protect sensitive data by masking it. It ensures confidentiality by replacing real data with fictitious, yet realistic, data.

6. **Database auditing tools**:

- **IBM Guardium**: IBM Guardium offers **database activity monitoring** (**DAM**) and auditing for compliance. It is a robust database auditing tool that provides activity monitoring and auditing. It helps organizations ensure compliance by tracking database activity, detecting anomalies, and facilitating forensic analysis.

7. **Custom application development**:

- For specific requirements, organizations might develop custom access control mechanisms using programming languages and frameworks. This approach allows tailored solutions aligned with unique business needs and security considerations.

The benefits of effective access control are as follows:

- **Data confidentiality**: Access control prevents unauthorized users from accessing sensitive data, protecting its confidentiality

- **Data integrity**: Only authorized users can modify data, ensuring its integrity and accuracy

- **Regulatory compliance**: Access control helps meet compliance requirements by limiting access to authorized personnel

- **Minimized insider threats**: Access control reduces the risk of insider threats, as users are restricted to their defined roles

- **Improved accountability**: Auditing user activity ensures accountability for any unauthorized actions

Effective access control ensures that only authorized users have access to the right data at the right time, enhancing overall database security within a cloud environment.

Encryption

Implement encryption for data at rest and in transit. Use **transparent data encryption** (TDE) to encrypt data files, preventing unauthorized access to data even if the storage media is compromised. Additionally, enable SSL/TLS to encrypt data transmitted between clients and the database server. Encryption is a critical security measure that converts plaintext data into ciphertext using cryptographic algorithms. This process ensures that even if an unauthorized entity gains access to the data, it won't be able to understand it without the decryption key. Encryption is essential to protecting data confidentiality, both at rest and in transit.

Types of encryption include the following:

- **Symmetric encryption**: In symmetric encryption, the same key is used for both encryption and decryption. While it's efficient, securely distributing the key to all parties can be challenging.

- **Asymmetric encryption (public key encryption)**: Asymmetric encryption uses a pair of keys: a public key for encryption and a private key for decryption. Public keys can be openly shared, while private keys are kept secret.

- **Hybrid encryption**: This combines both symmetric and asymmetric encryption. Data is encrypted with a symmetric key, and then the symmetric key is encrypted with the recipient's public key.

In the realm of data security, two fundamental aspects play a critical role—encryption at rest and encryption in transit. Encrypting data at rest involves securing information stored on various media, such as hard drives and databases, safeguarding it from unauthorized access in scenarios of theft or compromise. On the other hand, encryption in transit ensures the protection of data during its transmission between systems or over networks, thwarting potential eavesdropping and interception threats. These encryption practices are foundational in fortifying data integrity and confidentiality across storage and communication channels, contributing significantly to overall data security protocols.

Encryption at rest

Encrypting data at rest involves encrypting data stored on storage media such as hard drives, databases, and cloud storage. This prevents unauthorized access to data in case the physical storage medium is stolen or compromised.

Encryption in transit

Encryption in transit ensures that data is protected while being transmitted between different systems or over networks. This prevents eavesdropping and data interception during transmission.

Popular encryption algorithms

In the landscape of cybersecurity, the deployment of robust encryption algorithms is paramount for ensuring the confidentiality and integrity of sensitive information. Among the most widely adopted encryption algorithms, some of them are as follows:

- **Advanced Encryption Standard** (**AES**): This symmetric encryption algorithm is extensively utilized for securing data both at rest and in transit, offering a high level of protection.

- **Rivest-Shamir-Adleman** (**RSA**): As an asymmetric encryption algorithm, RSA plays a crucial role in secure key exchange and the implementation of digital signatures, providing a foundation for secure communication.

- **Diffie-Hellman**: Serving as a key exchange protocol, Diffie-Hellman plays a pivotal role in securely sharing symmetric encryption keys across potentially insecure channels, contributing to the establishment of secure connections. These encryption algorithms form the backbone of modern cryptographic practices, underlining their significance in safeguarding digital assets.

Methods and tools for encryption

In the ever-evolving landscape of cybersecurity, the implementation of effective encryption methods and tools is pivotal for safeguarding sensitive data across diverse domains. Notable solutions encompass the following:

- **Database encryption**: Oracle Transparent Data Encryption and Microsoft SQL Server Always Encrypted ensure the confidentiality of sensitive data within Oracle and SQL databases, both at rest and in transit. Amazon RDS Encryption extends encryption options across various Amazon RDS database engines.

  - **Oracle Transparent Data Encryption**: Encrypts sensitive data in Oracle databases

  - **Microsoft SQL Server Always Encrypted**: Encrypts data at rest and in transit

  - **Amazon RDS encryption**: Provides options to encrypt data in various Amazon RDS database engines

- **File and disk encryption**: BitLocker for Windows and FileVault for Mac stand as robust solutions encrypting entire disks to fortify data protection on these platforms.

  - **BitLocker (Microsoft)**: Encrypts entire disks to protect data on Windows systems
  - **FileVault (Apple)**: Encrypts Mac disks to safeguard data

- **Network encryption**: TLS/SSL protocols play a critical role in securing internet communication, with HTTPS for web traffic and IMAPS for email, ensuring confidentiality in transit.

  - **TLS/SSL**: Provides secure communication over the internet using protocols such as HTTPS for web traffic and IMAPS for email

- **Cloud encryption services**: AWS **Key Management Service (KMS)** and Google KMS centrally manage encryption keys, enhancing security across various cloud services.

  - **AWS KMS**: Manages encryption keys for various AWS services
  - **Google Cloud KMS**: Offers centralized key management for GCP

- **Endpoint encryption**: Solutions such as Microsoft BitLocker for Windows devices and VeraCrypt, an open source disk encryption software, provide a shield for data stored on endpoints. These encryption methods and tools collectively contribute to a comprehensive cybersecurity posture, fortifying data integrity and confidentiality at various layers of digital infrastructure.

  - **Microsoft BitLocker**: Encrypts data on Windows devices
  - **VeraCrypt**: Open source disk encryption software

Benefits of encryption include the following:

- **Data confidentiality**: Encrypted data remains confidential even if unauthorized access occurs
- **Compliance**: Encryption helps meet regulatory requirements for data protection
- **Safe data sharing**: Encrypted data can be shared securely with authorized parties
- **Mitigation of data breaches**: In case of data breaches, encrypted data remains unreadable without the decryption key

Encryption is a powerful tool for safeguarding sensitive data in various contexts, and its implementation is crucial in maintaining data security within cloud environments.

This section on popular tools and methods for access control provides an insightful exploration of key tools and methodologies crucial to ensuring robust access control and securing data environments. It encompasses RBAC tools such as Amazon IAM, Google Cloud IAM, and Azure RBAC, offering precise access management for cloud resources. DBMS access control is examined through MySQL, PostgreSQL, and Microsoft SQL Server Management Studio, providing flexible control over user privileges. IAM solutions such as Okta and OneLogin, along with ABAC tools such as Axiomatics, add layers of security. Data masking and redaction tools, such as Oracle Data Masking and Subsetting, and database auditing tools such as IBM Guardium, contribute to a comprehensive security posture. The section concludes by highlighting the significance of effective access control in maintaining data confidentiality, integrity, regulatory compliance, and mitigating insider threats.

Moving to the topic of encryption, the section underscores its pivotal role in fortifying data security. It distinguishes between encryption at rest, securing stored data, and encryption in transit, protecting data during transmission. The introduction of popular encryption algorithms such as AES, RSA, and Diffie-Hellman emphasizes their fundamental role in safeguarding digital assets. The subsequent discussion on methods and tools for encryption delves into solutions such as database encryption (Oracle TDE, Microsoft SQL Server Always Encrypted), file and disk encryption (BitLocker, FileVault), network encryption (TLS/SSL), and cloud encryption services (AWS KMS, Google Cloud KMS). The section concludes by highlighting the benefits of encryption, including data confidentiality, regulatory compliance, secure data sharing, and the mitigation of data breaches. Encryption emerges as a powerful tool essential to maintaining data security in various contexts, particularly within cloud environments.

Auditing and monitoring

Enable auditing to track user activity and changes to the database. Regularly review audit logs to identify suspicious activities. Implement real-time monitoring to detect unusual patterns or unauthorized access attempts. For instance, financial institutions monitor transactions to identify fraudulent activities. Auditing and monitoring are essential components of database security that involve tracking and recording database activities, user actions, and changes to the database. These practices help detect unauthorized access, ensure data integrity, and facilitate compliance with regulatory requirements.

Auditing

Auditing involves recording database activities and user actions to create an audit trail. This trail can be used to track who accessed the database, what actions they performed, and when these actions occurred. Auditing is crucial to identifying security breaches and investigating suspicious activities.

Monitoring

Monitoring involves real-time tracking of database activities and events. It allows for immediate detection of abnormal behaviors or security incidents. Monitoring can include activities such as user logins, data modifications, and failed access attempts.

The benefits of auditing and monitoring are as follows:

- **Security incident detection**: Auditing and monitoring help identify security breaches and unauthorized access attempts promptly
- **Regulatory compliance**: Many regulations require organizations to maintain audit logs and demonstrate control over their data

- **Accountability**: Auditing and monitoring hold users accountable for their actions within the database

- **Data integrity**: Monitoring helps ensure that data remains consistent and accurate, detecting unauthorized changes

- **Forensics and investigation**: Audit trails aid in forensic investigations to understand the sequence of events during a security incident

Popular tools and methods for auditing and monitoring

In the dynamic landscape of cybersecurity, robust auditing and monitoring are integral components for maintaining the integrity and security of databases. We need to shed some light on the diverse strategies and tools designed to fortify this critical aspect. Most modern DBMSs come equipped with built-in auditing features, allowing for comprehensive monitoring at various levels. Oracle Database Auditing, a key player, enables the tracking and recording of database activities and user actions. DAM solutions such as Imperva and IBM Guardium provide real-time monitoring, identifying potential threats. **Security information and event management (SIEM)** systems, including Splunk and Elastic Stack, contribute to intelligent log analysis. The section also sheds light on custom scripts and triggers, illustrating how organizations can tailor monitoring to capture specific events. Cloud providers offer dedicated tools such as Amazon CloudWatch and Google Cloud Operations Suite for monitoring resources, emphasizing a multi-faceted approach.

Let's look at some of the solutions around this aspect:

1. **DBMS audit features**:

   - Most modern DBMSs offer built-in auditing features that allow you to enable auditing at various levels (e.g., database, schema, table)

   - **Oracle Database Auditing**: Allows tracking and recording of database activities and user actions

2. **DAM solutions**:

   - **Imperva DAM**: Monitors and audits database activities to identify threats and vulnerabilities

   - **IBM Guardium**: Offers real-time monitoring and alerts for database events

3. **SIEM systems**:

   - **Splunk**: Collects and analyzes log data to identify patterns and detect security incidents

   - **Elastic Stack (formerly ELK Stack)**: Combines Elasticsearch, Logstash, and Kibana for log analysis

4. **Custom scripts and triggers**:

   - Organizations might develop custom scripts or triggers to capture specific events and log them

5. **Cloud provider monitoring tools**:

   - **Amazon CloudWatch**: Provides monitoring and alerting for AWS resources, including databases
   - **Google Cloud Operations Suite**: Offers monitoring, logging, and alerting for GCP resources

6. **User and privilege monitoring**:

   - Some tools focus on monitoring user activities, privilege escalation, and access patterns

Follow these steps to implement auditing and monitoring:

1. *Enable auditing*: Configure the DBMS to enable auditing on relevant database objects and actions.

2. *Configure alerts*: Set up alerts and notifications for specific events or patterns that could indicate security incidents.

3. *Regular review*: Regularly review audit logs and monitor data to detect anomalies and potential threats.

4. *Automated responses*: Consider setting up automated responses to certain events, such as blocking an IP address after multiple failed login attempts.

By implementing comprehensive auditing and monitoring practices, organizations can proactively detect and respond to security threats, ensuring the integrity and security of their databases within cloud environments. Please note that this section about auditing and monitoring is brief and we will be discussing these topics in detail in the chapters that follow.

Least-privilege principle

The **least-privilege principle** (**LPP**) is a fundamental security concept that revolves around granting users and processes only the minimum access necessary to perform their tasks. It's based on the idea that users should have the least amount of privilege required to complete their work, which reduces potential risks and exposure in case of a security breach.

Follow the principle of least privilege, granting users only the permissions necessary for their tasks. This minimizes the impact of a compromised account and reduces the attack surface.

Key aspects of the LPP are as follows:

- **Minimized attack surface**: By limiting access to only what's necessary, potential attack vectors and points of vulnerability are significantly reduced

- **Mitigation of insider threats**: Even if a user with malicious intent gains access, their ability to cause damage is restricted to the privileges they have

- **Accidental error prevention**: Users with limited access are less likely to accidentally modify or delete critical data or settings

- **Granular access control**: The principle promotes finely-tuned control over access, allowing organizations to align permissions with specific job roles

- **Need-to-know basis**: Users are granted access only to the data and resources essential to their tasks, preventing overexposure

Implementing the LPP entails the following:

- **RBAC**: Assign permissions based on job roles rather than individuals. Users are grouped into roles, each with predefined access levels.

- **Just-in-time access**: Provide temporary access for a limited period when needed and then revoke it automatically.

- **Privilege elevation**: Implement mechanisms that temporarily elevate a user's privileges only when necessary.

- **Regular review**: Periodically review and audit user permissions to ensure alignment with current roles and responsibilities.

- **Separation of duties (SoD)**: Divide tasks in a way that no single user has full control over a critical process.

Tools and methods to establish least privilege include the following:

1. **Cloud IAM**:

   - Amazon IAM: Controls access to AWS resources

   - Google Cloud IAM: Manages access to GCP services

   - Azure RBAC: Defines permissions for Azure resources

2. **Privilege management solutions**:

   - CyberArk: Manages and monitors privileged access

   - BeyondTrust Privilege Management: Controls elevated privileges

3. **Database access control**:

   - Utilize RBAC within databases to manage access to different schema, tables, or views

4. **Application-level access control**:

   - Implement RBAC within applications to ensure that users only have access to features they need

5. **API access control**:

   - Use API gateways and tokens to enforce controlled access to APIs

6. **File system permissions**:

   - Set file and directory permissions based on user roles

Implementing the LPP requires careful analysis of user roles, a comprehensive understanding of their tasks, and robust access control mechanisms. By adhering to this principle, organizations can significantly enhance their security posture and minimize potential vulnerabilities.

Secure configuration

Secure configuration refers to the practice of setting up systems, applications, and devices in a way that minimizes security risks and vulnerabilities. It involves configuring settings, permissions, and access controls to align with security best practices and industry standards. By implementing secure configurations, organizations reduce the attack surface and enhance the overall security posture of their IT infrastructure.

Configure databases according to security best practices provided by the database vendor. Disable unnecessary features, default accounts, and unused services. Regularly update and patch the DBMS to address security vulnerabilities.

Key aspects of secure configuration are as follows:

- **Hardening systems**: Removing unnecessary components, features, and services from systems to minimize potential vulnerabilities
- **Applying patches and updates**: Regularly updating software, operating systems, and applications to fix known vulnerabilities and security issues
- **Default settings**: Changing default settings, passwords, and configurations to avoid using easily guessable credentials or open access points
- **LPP**: Configuring systems to grant users and processes only the necessary privileges required for their tasks
- **Network security**: Configuring firewalls, intrusion detection systems, and access controls to protect the network from unauthorized access

Implementing a secure configuration is done as follows:

1. *Baseline configuration*: Develop a standard configuration baseline for systems and applications that reflects security best practices.
2. *Regular audits*: Perform regular security audits to identify deviations from the baseline configuration and address them promptly.

3. *Configuration management tools*: Use tools to automate configuration management and ensure consistency across systems.

4. *Vulnerability assessment*: Regularly scan systems for vulnerabilities and misconfigurations to identify areas that need attention.

Tools and methods for secure configuration include the following:

1. **Configuration management tools**:

   - Ansible: Automates configuration management and deployment

   - Puppet: Manages and enforces configurations across systems

   - Chef: Configures and manages infrastructure as code

2. **Vulnerability scanning tools**:

   - Nessus: Identifies vulnerabilities and misconfigurations across systems

   - OpenVAS: Open source vulnerability scanner for discovering security issues

3. **System hardening guides**:

   - **Center for Internet Security (CIS)** benchmarks: Offers best practice guides for securely configuring systems

4. **SIEM systems**:

   - Splunk: Collects and analyzes log data to detect and respond to security incidents

   - Elastic Stack (ELK Stack): Offers log analysis and monitoring capabilities

5. **Container security tools**:

   - Docker Bench for Security: Scans Docker containers against best practices

   - Kubernetes security context: Configures security settings for Kubernetes pods

By adhering to secure configuration practices, organizations can significantly reduce the risk of security breaches, unauthorized access, and data exposure. It's an essential aspect of maintaining a robust and resilient security posture within cloud environments.

Regular backups

Regular backups are a crucial aspect of data and system security. They involve creating copies of data, applications, and system configurations at regular intervals to ensure data recovery in case of data loss, disasters, or cyberattacks. Backups provide a safety net against accidental deletion, hardware failures, ransomware attacks, and other unforeseen events that can compromise data integrity.

Frequently back up the database and test the restoration process. Backups ensure data recovery in case of data loss due to hardware failures, software bugs, or security incidents.

Key aspects of regular backups are as follows:

- **Data integrity**: Backups ensure that data can be restored to its original state before data loss or corruption occurred

- **Disaster recovery**: In case of system failures or disasters, backups enable organizations to recover critical systems and services quickly

- **Ransomware protection**: Backups provide a means by which to restore data without being forced to pay a ransom in the event of ransomware attacks

- **Compliance**: Many regulatory frameworks require organizations to maintain backups as part of data protection and continuity measures

Backup strategies include the following:

- **Full backups**: Complete copies of all data and files are created at regular intervals

- **Incremental backups**: Only changes made since the previous backup are saved, reducing storage requirements

- **Differential backups**: Backs up changes since the last full backup, making restoration faster than incremental backups

Implementing regular backups:

1. *Backup frequency*: Determine the appropriate frequency based on data criticality and potential for changes.

2. *Backup retention*: Decide how long backups should be retained, considering compliance and disaster recovery needs.

3. *Automated backup*: Utilize backup solutions that automate the process, reducing the risk of human error.

Tools and methods for regular backups include the following:

1. **Cloud backup services**:

   - Amazon S3: Provides scalable object storage for backups

   - Google Cloud Storage: Offers secure and durable cloud storage

   - Azure Backup: Enables backup and recovery for Azure resources

2. **Backup software**:

   - Veeam Backup & Replication: Offers data protection and disaster recovery solutions
   - Acronis True Image: Provides data backup, storage, and recovery options

3. **On-premises solutions**:

   - **Network-attached storage (NAS)** devices: Can serve as local backup storage
   - External hard drives: Physical backups for critical data

4. **Database backup tools**:

   - mysqldump: Creates backups of MySQL databases
   - pg_dump: Backs up PostgreSQL databases

5. **Virtual machine backup**:

   - VMware vSphere Data Protection: Backs up virtual machines in VMware environments
   - Hyper-V Backup: Provides backup solutions for Hyper-V virtual machines

Regular backups are an essential part of an organization's disaster recovery and data protection strategy. By ensuring the availability and integrity of backups, organizations can recover from data loss scenarios and maintain business continuity within cloud environments. Please note that this section about backups is brief and we will be discussing backups in detail in the chapters to follow.

Data masking and redaction

Data masking and redaction are techniques used to protect sensitive information by obscuring or replacing it with fictional or anonymized data. These techniques are especially important when sharing or using sensitive data for non-production purposes, such as development, testing, or analytics, while ensuring that the original data remains confidential.

Sensitive data should be masked or redacted to prevent unauthorized exposure. For instance, credit card numbers can be masked to display only a subset of digits to non-authorized users.

Key aspects of data masking and redaction are as follows:

- **Confidentiality**: Data masking and redaction help preserve the confidentiality of sensitive information, preventing unauthorized access
- **Privacy compliance**: These techniques assist in adhering to privacy regulations by ensuring that sensitive data is not exposed
- **Data utility**: While securing data, data masking and redaction aim to retain the usefulness of the data for testing and analysis purposes

Data masking

Data masking involves modifying sensitive data in such a way that the original value is replaced with a fictitious but consistent value. The goal is to ensure that the masked data retains the same format, structure, and relationships as the original data.

Data redaction

Data redaction goes a step further by not only changing the content of sensitive data but also altering its format or structure. This ensures that even metadata or contextual information related to sensitive data is obscured.

Implementing data masking and redaction involves the following:

1. *Identify sensitive data*: Determine which data elements are sensitive and require masking or redaction.

2. *Define masking rules*: Develop rules that dictate how sensitive data should be transformed while retaining data consistency.

3. *Testing and validation*: Verify that masked or redacted data maintains its usefulness for testing or analytics purposes.

Tools and methods for data masking and redaction include the following:

1. **Database masking tools**:

   - Delphix: Offers data masking and virtualization capabilities

   - Informatica Data Masking: Provides masking and redaction solutions

2. **Database redaction features**:

   - Oracle Database Redaction: Built-in feature for redacting sensitive data in Oracle databases

   - SQL Server Dynamic Data Masking: Masks sensitive data in SQL Server databases

3. **Anonymization tools**:

   - ARX Data Anonymization: Offers privacy-preserving data anonymization solutions

4. **Custom scripting**:

   - Organizations might develop custom scripts or applications to apply data masking and redaction

5. **Database views and synonyms**:

   - Create views or synonyms that present masked or redacted data instead of original data

Data masking and redaction are valuable techniques for protecting sensitive data while maintaining its utility for various purposes. By applying these techniques, organizations can balance the need for data security and data usability within cloud environments.

Multi-factor authentication (MFA)

Multi-factor authentication (**MFA**), also known as **two-factor authentication** (**2FA**), is a security mechanism that requires users to provide two or more forms of authentication before granting access to a system or application. MFA adds an additional layer of security beyond traditional username-and-password combinations, significantly enhancing the protection of sensitive data and accounts.

It is important to implement MFA for database access, which means that users need to provide an additional form of authentication, such as a code from a mobile app, along with their password. This prevents unauthorized access even if passwords are compromised.

The following figure depicts the basic setup of MFA on the AWS cloud:

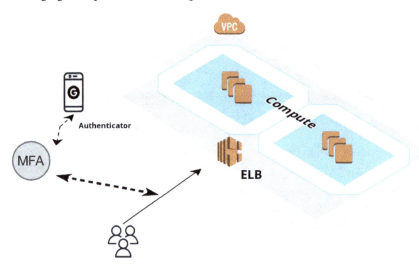

Figure 9.2: MFA setup on the AWS cloud

The preceding diagram shows how users are able to access the cloud system using the MFA service that is closely coupled with the authenticator, which could be a device such as a user's phone.

Key aspects of MFA are as follows:

- **Enhanced security**: MFA reduces the risk of unauthorized access by requiring multiple forms of verification

- **Mitigation of credential theft**: Even if passwords are compromised, the additional authentication factors provide an extra barrier against unauthorized access

- **Adaptive authentication**: Some MFA systems use adaptive techniques to adjust authentication requirements based on user behavior and risk profiles

Authentication factors are as follows:

- **Something you know**: This is typically a password or PIN

- **Something you have**: This includes a physical device such as a smartphone, security token, or smart card

- **Something you are**: This refers to biometric factors such as fingerprints, facial recognition, or voice recognition

Implementing MFA involves the following:

- **Selecting MFA methods**: Choose appropriate authentication factors based on the level of security required and user convenience

- **User enrollment**: Guide users through the process of enrolling their chosen authentication methods

- **Authentication process**: When accessing a system, users are prompted to provide multiple forms of authentication

Tools and methods for MFA include the following:

1. **Authentication apps**:

    - Google Authenticator: Generates **time-based one-time passwords (TOTP)**

    - Microsoft Authenticator: Provides TOTP and push-based authentication

2. **Hardware tokens**:

    - YubiKey: Hardware security token that supports multiple authentication methods

    - RSA SecurID: Provides hardware tokens for MFA

3. **Biometric authentication**:

    - Apple Face ID and Touch ID: Use facial recognition and fingerprint scanning for authentication

    - Windows Hello: Provides biometric authentication for Windows devices

4. **SMS and email codes**:

    - Authentication codes are sent via SMS or email for users to enter during login

5. **Adaptive MFA**:

    - Azure Active Directory Conditional Access: Adjusts MFA requirements based on user behavior

6. **Cloud identity providers**:

    - AWS IAM: Supports MFA for securing AWS accounts
    - Google Cloud Identity Platform: Provides MFA for Google Cloud services

MFA is a powerful tool for preventing unauthorized access, especially in cloud environments where remote access is common. By requiring multiple forms of authentication, MFA significantly reduces the risk of data breaches resulting from compromised passwords or credentials.

By adhering to these database security best practices and customizing them to the specific requirements of the organization, businesses can mitigate risks, comply with regulations, and build a secure foundation for their cloud-based data storage and management.

The following *Database high-availability and scalability features* section delves into the critical considerations and techniques for ensuring that databases hosted in the cloud are highly available and capable of scaling to meet evolving demands. In today's data-driven landscape, databases form the backbone of applications, making their availability and scalability paramount. This section explores concepts such as database replication, clustering, sharding, and autoscaling, which empower organizations to maintain continuous access to their data and adapt to changing workloads without compromising performance. By understanding these strategies and leveraging cloud-native tools, readers will be equipped to design and manage robust and responsive database systems that align with modern application requirements.

Database high-availability and scalability features

In this section, we will explore concepts such as database replication, failover, load balancing, and scaling techniques that are pivotal for enhancing database performance, reliability, and responsiveness. By mastering these concepts and leveraging cloud-native tools, we will be well equipped to architect and manage databases that can seamlessly adapt to changing demands and deliver an optimal user experience.

Database high availability and scalability are essential to ensuring that cloud-hosted databases can handle increasing workloads and maintain consistent access to data, even in the face of failures or spikes in traffic. Cloud providers offer a range of tools and features to achieve these goals, allowing organizations to design resilient and responsive database systems. Let's look at these concepts in detail in the following sections.

High availability

In the realm of cloud-based database management, achieving high availability is paramount to guarantee seamless access to data and safeguard against potential disruptions. This section introduces the crucial concept of database replication, a cornerstone technique for data synchronization and system resilience. Cloud providers offer replication options, allowing the creation of database copies across different geographic regions or availability zones. This strategic duplication ensures that if one instance encounters a failure, traffic can seamlessly be directed to a healthy replica, minimizing downtime. Database replication emerges as a versatile tool addressing various operational needs, from enhancing read performance to fortifying data resilience. Within a cloud environment, its significance is heightened, contributing to high availability, disaster recovery, and optimized performance. Organizations are encouraged to meticulously plan replication strategies, factoring in considerations such as data consistency, replication lag, and failover mechanisms to architect responsive and robust database architectures. By the end of this section, readers will be equipped with the knowledge to strategically leverage database replication in the cloud, fostering robust architectures that enhance performance, resilience, and data accessibility. Let's discuss some of the aspects of high availability in detail.

Database replication

Cloud providers offer replication options to create copies of databases across different geographic regions or availability zones. If one instance fails, traffic can be seamlessly routed to a healthy replica.

Database replication is a data synchronization process that involves creating and maintaining multiple copies of a database in different locations, ensuring data consistency and availability. It's a fundamental technique for achieving high availability, disaster recovery, and load distribution. In a cloud environment, where reliability and performance are critical, replication plays a crucial role in ensuring seamless data access and system resilience.

Types of database replication include the following:

- **Master-slave replication**: One database serves as the master where all write operations occur, and changes are then replicated to one or more slave replicas for read queries

- **Multi-master replication**: Multiple databases act as both masters and slaves, allowing writes on any node and ensuring changes are propagated to other nodes

- **Bi-directional replication**: Changes made on any replica are allowed to be synchronized with other replicas, ensuring consistency across multiple nodes

Replication methods include the following:

- **Snapshot-based replication**: This method periodically takes a snapshot of the master database and copies it to replicas. It's simple but can lead to delays in data synchronization.

- **Log-based replication**: Changes made to the database's transaction log are captured and replicated, ensuring near real-time data synchronization.

- **Statement-based replication**: This method replicates SQL statements from the master to replicas, executing the same statements on replica databases.

Cloud database replication:

- **Amazon RDS replication**: Amazon RDS offers read replicas and Multi-AZ deployments for MySQL, PostgreSQL, and more

- **Azure SQL Database replication**: Azure provides geo-replication for disaster recovery and read replicas for scaling

- **Google Cloud SQL replication**: Google Cloud SQL supports read replicas and external replication for MySQL instances

Database replication is a versatile technique that addresses various operational needs, from improving read performance to ensuring data resilience. In a cloud environment, it's a valuable tool for maintaining high availability, disaster recovery, and optimized performance. Organizations should carefully plan their replication strategies, considering factors such as data consistency, replication lag, and failover mechanisms to design robust and responsive database architectures.

Automatic failover

Cloud platforms offer automated failover mechanisms that swiftly redirect traffic to a standby instance if the primary database becomes unavailable. Automatic failover is a critical component of high-availability strategies, ensuring that services remain operational even in the event of hardware or software failures. In the context of databases and cloud environments, automatic failover involves seamlessly shifting user traffic from a primary instance to a standby instance when the primary becomes unavailable. This process minimizes downtime and maintains continuous service availability for users.

The key aspects of automatic failover are as follows:

- **Detection of failure**: Monitoring mechanisms continuously monitor the health of the primary instance. If a failure is detected, such as hardware issues, network problems, or software crashes, the automatic failover process is initiated.

- **Promotion of standby instance**: The standby instance, often kept synchronized with the primary instance through replication, is promoted to become the new primary.

- **Traffic redirect**: Once the standby instance is promoted, incoming user traffic is automatically redirected to the new primary instance.

- **Data consistency**: To ensure data consistency, changes that were in progress on the primary instance but not yet replicated to the standby are typically rolled forward.

- **Minimized downtime**: Automatic failover aims to minimize the time during which the service is unavailable, offering seamless continuity for users.

Cloud provider implementations include the following:

- **Amazon RDS Multi-AZ**: Amazon RDS provides Multi-AZ deployments for database instances, ensuring automatic failover to a standby replica in a different availability zone

- **Azure SQL Database failover groups**: Azure SQL Database offers failover groups that automatically redirect traffic to a standby database in a different region in the event of a failure

- **Google Cloud SQL high availability**: Google Cloud SQL offers automatic failover to a standby instance in the same region

The benefits of automatic failover include the following:

- **Minimal downtime**: By swiftly switching to a standby instance, automatic failover ensures minimal disruption to users

- **Continuous service**: Users experience uninterrupted access to applications and data, even during failures

- **Reliability**: The automated nature of failover reduces the potential for human error in critical situations

- **Disaster recovery**: Automatic failover serves as a component of disaster recovery strategies, safeguarding against unexpected outages

Automatic failover is a crucial component of high-availability architectures, ensuring that cloud-based services and databases maintain their operational integrity. By quickly detecting and responding to failures, automatic failover reduces downtime and offers users a consistent and reliable experience, aligning with the demands of modern applications and user expectations.

Multi-AZ deployments

Many cloud providers allow the deployment of databases in multiple availability zones, ensuring redundancy and minimizing downtime.

Multi-**availability zone** (**AZ**) deployments are a high-availability feature provided by cloud service providers, especially in database services such as Amazon RDS, Azure SQL Database, and Google Cloud SQL. Multi-AZ deployments involve creating and maintaining synchronized copies of a primary database instance in multiple availability zones within a cloud region. The goal is to enhance data availability and resilience by ensuring that if one availability zone experiences an outage or failure, traffic can be automatically directed to a standby instance in another zone.

The key aspects of Multi-AZ deployments are as follows:

- **Availability zones**: Availability zones are physically separate data centers within a cloud region. Each zone has its own power, cooling, and network infrastructure to minimize the risk of correlated failures.

- **Synchronous replication**: In a Multi-AZ deployment, the primary database instance is synchronously replicated to a standby instance in a different availability zone.

- **Automatic failover**: If the primary instance becomes unavailable due to hardware or software issues, the cloud platform initiates an automatic failover to the standby instance.

- **Data consistency**: During automatic failover, any pending changes in the primary instance's transaction log are applied to the standby to maintain data consistency.

The benefits of Multi-AZ deployments include the following:

- **High availability**: Multi-AZ deployments offer improved availability by ensuring that there's always a healthy instance to handle user requests

- **Automated failover**: In case of a failure in the primary zone, the cloud platform automatically promotes the standby to become the new primary, minimizing downtime

- **Disaster recovery**: Multi-AZ deployments serve as a disaster recovery solution, safeguarding against data center outages or catastrophic failures

- **Enhanced reliability**: Redundancy across multiple availability zones improves overall system reliability and reduces the impact of single points of failure

Multi-AZ deployments offer a simple yet effective way to enhance the availability and reliability of cloud-hosted databases. By synchronously replicating data across multiple availability zones and automating failover processes, organizations can ensure a seamless user experience, even in the face of infrastructure failures.

The following figure depicts high availability on EC2 instances, Multi-AZ deployment, and autoscaling, as well as database high availability (primary and secondary RDS):

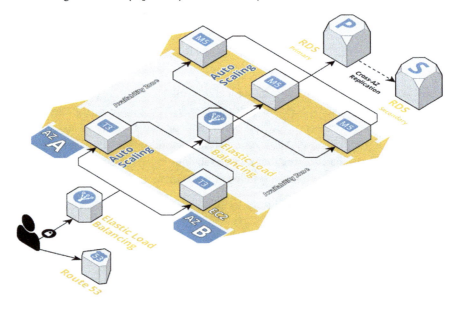

Figure 9.3: Highly available, scalable architecture

This section was a comprehensive exploration of crucial concepts for ensuring robust database performance in cloud environments. It delves into the principles of high availability, emphasizing the importance of database replication to maintain data consistency and system resilience. The section covers various types of replications, including master-slave, multi-master, and bi-directional, highlighting their specific use cases. Furthermore, it introduces readers to different replication methods such as snapshot-based, log-based, and statement-based, offering insights into their strengths and considerations. The discussion extends to cloud-specific solutions from major providers, including Amazon RDS replication, Azure SQL Database replication, and Google Cloud SQL replication. The section also touches upon failover mechanisms and Multi-AZ deployments, providing readers with a well-rounded understanding of strategies for ensuring high availability and scalability in cloud-based database architectures.

The next section is a concise exploration of essential concepts in optimizing database performance in the cloud. It introduces readers to various types of scaling, focusing on vertical scaling (increasing the power of existing hardware) and horizontal scaling (adding more machines or nodes to a system). The section outlines the significance of scaling in enhancing database capabilities and discusses how cloud environments provide diverse scaling deployment options. Readers will gain insights into the strategic considerations involved in choosing between vertical and horizontal scaling based on your specific performance and resource requirements. The section serves as a foundational guide for those looking to effectively scale their databases in cloud environments for improved performance and responsiveness.

Scalability

Scalability in the context of cloud databases refers to the ability of a database system to accommodate varying workloads and growing demands while maintaining optimal performance and responsiveness. It's a critical aspect of modern applications that experience unpredictable spikes in traffic or need to handle increasing amounts of data without sacrificing the user experience. Scalability can be achieved through two main approaches: vertical scaling (scaling up) and horizontal scaling (scaling out).

Vertical scaling (scaling up)

Vertical scaling involves adding more resources to a single database instance to handle increased workload. This typically includes increasing CPU power, memory, storage capacity, or other system resources. Vertical scaling is suitable for scenarios where a database's performance bottlenecks are related to the limitations of individual resources.

The benefits of vertical scaling are as follows:

- **Simplicity**: Vertical scaling is relatively simple to implement, requiring changes to a single instance
- **Cost-effective for small workloads**: It can be cost-effective for smaller workloads that don't require extreme scalability

The limitations of vertical scaling include the following:

- **Diminished returns**: There's a limit to how much a single instance can be scaled before diminishing returns set in
- **Single points of failure**: Since all resources are concentrated in a single instance, there's a higher risk of a single point of failure

Horizontal scaling (scaling out)

Horizontal scaling involves adding more instances to distribute the workload. This is often done by using database replication or sharding techniques to split the data across multiple instances. Horizontal scaling is suitable for scenarios where the workload cannot be efficiently handled by a single instance.

The benefits of horizontal scaling are as follows:

- **Unlimited scalability**: Horizontal scaling allows for almost unlimited scalability by adding more instances as needed
- **High availability**: By distributing the workload, horizontal scaling enhances availability and reliability

The limitations of horizontal scaling include the following:

- **Complexity**: Horizontal scaling can introduce complexity due to managing multiple instances and ensuring data consistency
- **Data sharding challenges**: Sharding introduces challenges in maintaining data integrity and consistency across multiple instances

Cloud vendor approaches available on the market include the following:

1. **AWS**:

   - **Amazon RDS Multi-AZ**: Provides automatic failover to a standby replica in another availability zone
   - **Amazon Aurora global databases**: Replicates data across multiple AWS Regions for global availability
   - **Amazon DynamoDB autoscaling**: Automatically adjusts capacity based on traffic patterns

2. **Microsoft Azure**:

   - **Azure SQL Database failover groups**: Offers automatic failover to a standby database in a different region

- **Azure Cosmos DB global distribution**: Replicates data globally for low-latency access

- **Azure Database for PostgreSQL Hyperscale**: Scales out horizontally to accommodate growing workloads

3. **GCP**:

- **Google Cloud SQL high availability**: Provides automated failover to a standby instance

- **Google Cloud Spanner**: Offers global distribution and horizontal scaling for consistent performance

- **Google Cloud Firestore autoscaling**: Automatically adjusts capacity based on usage

Each cloud provider offers various features to ensure high availability and scalability, with differences in terminology and implementation. Organizations need to assess their specific requirements, workload characteristics, and budget to select the appropriate approach for their cloud-hosted databases. The goal is to design database architectures that combine redundancy, failover mechanisms, and scaling capabilities to deliver reliable and responsive data services in the cloud.

The following *Database performance optimization* section takes us into the intricate art of fine-tuning database systems to achieve optimal speed, responsiveness, and efficiency. In the realm of cloud computing, where dynamic workloads and varying demands are the norm, understanding and implementing performance optimization strategies are essential to ensuring a seamless user experience and efficient resource utilization. This section explores key aspects of database performance enhancement, from query optimization and indexing to caching and resource allocation. By harnessing cloud provider tools and features, as well as adhering to best practices, organizations can unlock the full potential of their cloud databases and deliver consistently high-quality services to their users.

Database performance optimization

Database performance optimization is a continuous process of enhancing the efficiency, responsiveness, and overall speed of a database system to ensure an optimal user experience and efficient resource utilization. In the context of cloud databases, where dynamic workloads and changing demands are common, performance optimization is critical to delivering consistently high-quality services.

The key aspects of database performance optimization are as follows:

- **Query optimization**: Ensuring that database queries are structured and executed in the most efficient way to minimize response times

- **Indexing**: Creating appropriate indexes on columns that are frequently queried, improving query performance

- **Caching**: Utilizing caching mechanisms to store frequently accessed data in memory, reducing the need to retrieve data from the disk

- **Compression**: Employing data compression techniques to reduce storage requirements and enhance I/O performance
- **Partitioning**: Partitioning large tables into smaller segments based on certain criteria to improve query performance
- **Resource allocation**: Properly allocating CPU, memory, and storage resources to prevent resource bottlenecks
- **Data modeling**: Designing an efficient data model that minimizes redundant data and maximizes query performance

Cloud provider tools and features to help with database performance optimization include the following:

- **Amazon RDS Performance Insights**: Amazon RDS provides insights into database performance, query execution times, and recommendations for optimization.

  Amazon RDS Performance Insights is a powerful tool that provides deep visibility into the performance of Amazon RDS databases. It offers a comprehensive view of query performance, helping users identify and troubleshoot performance bottlenecks. Performance Insights provides detailed information about query execution times, throughput, and resource utilization. It also helps in pinpointing the root causes of performance issues by highlighting the most resource-intensive queries. This tool empowers users to optimize database workloads effectively, leading to enhanced application performance. It's particularly beneficial in cloud environments where dynamic workloads can impact database performance.

- **Azure SQL Database performance recommendations**: Azure SQL Database offers intelligent performance recommendations to enhance database performance.

  Performance recommendations in Azure SQL Database is a feature that offers intelligent insights into the performance of Azure SQL databases. It analyzes historical database performance data and provides actionable recommendations to optimize query performance. These recommendations cover areas such as indexing, query design, and resource allocation. By following these recommendations, users can improve the efficiency and responsiveness of their Azure SQL databases. This tool is valuable for organizations leveraging Azure services, as it assists in maintaining optimal database performance and ensuring a seamless user experience.

- **Google Cloud SQL Performance Insights**: Google Cloud SQL provides real-time performance insights, query analysis, and recommendations.

  Google Cloud SQL Performance Insights is a monitoring and analysis tool for Google Cloud SQL databases. It provides real-time performance visibility into query execution times, resource consumption, and query patterns. Performance Insights offers graphical representations of database activity, making it easier to spot performance anomalies and bottlenecks. It also allows users to analyze individual queries to identify areas for optimization. With its user-friendly interface and actionable insights, Google Cloud SQL Performance Insights empowers users to enhance database performance and responsiveness, ensuring efficient operations in a cloud environment.

Using Google Cloud SQL Performance Insights involves several steps to monitor and optimize the performance of your Google Cloud SQL databases. Here's a general overview of the process:

1. **Enable Performance Insights**:

   - Log in to your Google Cloud console

   - Navigate to the Google Cloud SQL instance you want to monitor

   - In the left-hand menu, select **Performance**

   - Click on **Enable Performance Insights** to activate the feature for that instance

2. **View performance data**:

   - Once Performance Insights is enabled, you'll be able to see performance data on the Performance Insights page

   - The dashboard displays graphs of key performance metrics, including CPU usage, memory usage, query latency, and more

3. **Analyze query performance**:

   - Click on the **Queries** tab to access detailed query performance data

   - You can view a list of queries along with metrics such as average latency, CPU usage, and number of executions

   - Sort and filter queries based on different criteria to identify problematic queries

4. **Identify performance anomalies**:

   - Look for queries with high latency, excessive resource usage, or unusual execution patterns

   - Performance Insights highlights potential issues to help you quickly identify problematic queries

5. **Optimize queries**:

   - Select a query to see a detailed analysis

   - Performance Insights provides recommendations to optimize queries, such as adding indexes, rewriting queries, or changing configuration settings

6. **Apply recommendations**:

   - Based on the recommendations, you can make changes to your database configuration, query structure, or indexing strategy

7. **Monitor and iterate**:

- Regularly monitor the Performance Insights dashboard to track improvements and identify new performance challenges

- Continuously optimize queries and database settings to ensure optimal performance

  Remember that Google Cloud SQL Performance Insights is a powerful tool for monitoring and optimizing database performance. It's essential to review and act on the insights provided to improve the efficiency and responsiveness of your Google Cloud SQL databases.

The best practices for database performance optimization are as follows:

- **Monitor regularly**: Continuously monitor database performance metrics to identify bottlenecks and potential areas for improvement

- **Analyze query performance**: Use query analyzers to identify slow-performing queries and optimize them for better execution

- **Use indexes wisely**: Strategically create indexes on columns frequently used in queries to speed up data retrieval

- **Cache appropriately**: Implement caching mechanisms, such as in-memory caching, to reduce the need for repeated database queries

- **Regular maintenance**: Perform routine maintenance tasks such as updating statistics, compacting databases, and defragmenting indexes

- **Scale resources**: Scale resources up or out as needed to handle increasing workloads without sacrificing performance

- **Benchmarking**: Regularly benchmark your database's performance to track improvements and identify areas needing attention

Database performance optimization is an ongoing effort that requires a deep understanding of the database system, the application's requirements, and the specific workload patterns. By applying optimization techniques, leveraging cloud provider tools, and adhering to best practices, organizations can ensure that their databases deliver responsive, efficient, and reliable services to users, ultimately contributing to a positive user experience.

Summary

In this chapter, we delved into the critical aspects of modern database management, offering insights into fine-tuning, securing, and optimizing database systems within the dynamic landscape of cloud computing. It began by exploring the intricacies of data modeling and schema design, highlighting the significance of designing efficient and adaptable database structures. The chapter then navigated through the processes of database provisioning and configuration, emphasizing the importance of setting up databases optimally to cater to specific workload demands. Subsequently, it unveiled the world of database security best practices, shedding light on access control, encryption, auditing, and other measures crucial to safeguarding sensitive data.

Moreover, the chapter delved into the realm of high availability and scalability, discussing techniques such as database replication, automatic failover, and Multi-AZ deployments that are essential to ensuring consistent performance, even under varying workloads and potential outages. Furthermore, it examined the strategies and tools to optimize database performance, covering query optimization, indexing, caching, and more. Throughout the chapter, readers gained a comprehensive understanding of how to design, configure, secure, scale, and optimize databases effectively in the cloud environment, ensuring both reliability and efficiency in your database systems.

From this chapter, readers have gained essential skills to proficiently manage database services in the cloud. The chapter has equipped you with best practices to secure databases using access control, encryption, and auditing measures. Readers have also developed expertise in implementing high-availability and scalability features, ensuring uninterrupted database services. Lastly, you have learned strategies to optimize database performance, including query optimization, indexing, and caching, enhancing the responsiveness and efficiency of your database systems.

The next chapter, *Monitoring and Management*, is a comprehensive exploration of the tools, techniques, and practices essential to effectively monitoring and managing database systems in the cloud. Readers can expect to gain insights into various monitoring methodologies, including real-time performance tracking, resource utilization analysis, and alerting mechanisms. The chapter will delve into cloud-specific management strategies, covering tasks such as database backups, restoration, and updates. With a focus on ensuring optimal database performance, availability, and security, the chapter will equip readers with the skills needed to proactively manage and maintain your database environments in the dynamic cloud landscape.

Part 4:
Monitoring, Backup, and Restore

This part provides a comprehensive understanding of the tools, practices, and techniques required to monitor databases in real time, track resource utilization, and respond to potential issues promptly. This part also offers a step-by-step walk-through of essential procedures for data backup and restoration within cloud environments. You can expect a thorough exploration of various backup and restoration strategies, techniques, and best practices tailored to the cloud environment.

This part has the following chapters:

- *Chapter 10, Monitoring and Management*
- *Chapter 11, Backup and Restore Mechanisms*
- *Chapter 12, Backup and Restore Procedures*

10

Monitoring and Management

This chapter, *Monitoring and Management*, delves into the critical aspects of overseeing and maintaining database systems in the cloud. In today's fast-paced technological landscape, effective monitoring and management are essential to ensure databases function optimally, remain secure, and deliver reliable performance. This chapter provides a comprehensive understanding of the tools, practices, and techniques required to monitor databases in real time, track resource utilization, and respond to potential issues promptly.

You will learn the art of real-time monitoring and understand how to track database performance metrics, resource utilization, and user activity. You will gain insights into setting up alerting mechanisms that proactively notify administrators about potential issues, allowing timely interventions.

Cloud-specific management strategies are a highlight of this chapter. You will discover how to execute tasks such as database backups to safeguard data against unforeseen events. You will grasp the intricacies of database restoration, ensuring data integrity in case of failures. Furthermore, this chapter will explore how to manage updates and patches, keeping databases current while minimizing disruption.

The following key topics will be covered in this chapter:

- Real-time monitoring and alerts:

  - The importance of real-time monitoring in cloud databases

  - Metrics to monitor – performance, latency, throughput, resource utilization, and more

  - Setting up alerts to proactively identify and address issues

- Cloud-specific monitoring tools:

  - An overview of cloud provider-specific monitoring tools and dashboards

  - AWS CloudWatch, Azure Monitor, Google Cloud Monitoring, and others

  - Monitoring database health, availability, and scaling in a cloud environment

  - Automated scaling and resource management

- Utilizing auto-scaling capabilities to adjust resources based on demand
- Managing CPU, memory, and storage resources dynamically in response to workload changes

- Updates and patching:

  - The importance of keeping databases and other components up to date for security and performance
  - Scheduled updates and patches without disrupting services

By exploring these key topics, this chapter will equip you with a comprehensive understanding of monitoring and managing databases within a cloud environment, ensuring optimal performance, security, and resource utilization.

Technical requirements

To fully engage with the content of this chapter on cloud computing architecture, you should have a basic understanding of computer systems, networking concepts, and information technology.

Additionally, the following technical requirements are recommended:

- **Internet access**: You should have a reliable internet connection to access online resources, references, and examples related to cloud computing.

- **A computing device**: A desktop computer, laptop, tablet, or smartphone with a modern web browser is necessary to read this chapter's content and access any online materials.

- **A web browser**: The latest version of a modern web browser such as Google Chrome, Mozilla Firefox, Microsoft Edge, or Safari is recommended. This ensures compatibility and an optimal viewing experience of web-based resources and interactive content.

- **Familiarity with cloud services**: Some familiarity with cloud services and their basic functionalities will enhance your understanding of this chapter. This includes knowledge of basic monitoring tools, basic database and networking concepts, operating systems, and servers.

Real-time monitoring and alerts

This section on real-time monitoring and alerts explores the significance of continuously monitoring database performance, resource utilization, and other critical metrics in a cloud environment. Real-time monitoring enables administrators to promptly identify and address issues before they impact the user experience. This section delves into the key metrics to monitor, such as query response times, throughput, CPU and memory usage, and network latency. Additionally, it emphasizes the importance of setting up proactive alerts that notify administrators when predefined thresholds are breached, allowing for swift intervention and optimization. By mastering real-time monitoring and alerts, database administrators can ensure optimal performance and responsiveness, enhancing the overall reliability of their cloud-based database systems.

Real-time monitoring and alerts are essential practices in managing databases effectively within a cloud environment. They enable administrators to stay ahead of potential issues, maintain optimal performance, and ensure a seamless user experience. Here's a more detailed look at this topic:

- **The importance of real-time monitoring**:

  - Cloud databases are subject to dynamic workloads and changing demands. Real-time monitoring provides a continuous insight into their performance, enabling timely interventions.

  - Monitoring helps in detecting and addressing issues such as high query latency, resource spikes, and sudden drops in throughput.

- **Key metrics for monitoring**:

  - **Performance metrics**: Tracking query response times, transaction rates, and overall database performance

  - **Resource utilization**: Monitoring CPU usage, memory consumption, disk I/O, and network traffic to ensure efficient resource allocation

  - **User activity**: Observing user access patterns and identifying potential security threats or unusual behavior

Monitoring key metrics is a fundamental practice in ensuring the optimal performance and reliability of databases within a cloud environment. By tracking these metrics, administrators gain insights into the health of their database systems and can make informed decisions to address potential issues. Here's an in-depth look at the key metrics for monitoring:

- **Performance metrics**:

  - **Query response time**: Measuring the time it takes for the database to process and respond to queries. Slow response times could indicate performance bottlenecks.

  - **Throughput**: Monitoring the rate at which the database processes transactions or queries. High throughput signifies efficient performance.

- **Resource utilization**:

  - **CPU usage**: Tracking the percentage of CPU capacity utilized by the database. High CPU usage can lead to performance degradation.

  - **Memory consumption**: Monitoring the amount of memory used by the database. Inadequate memory can result in increased disk I/O and slower performance.

  - **Disk I/O**: Measuring the rate of read and write operations to the storage. High disk I/O can impact query performance and response times.

  - **Network traffic**: Monitoring data transfer rates between the database and clients. Excessive network traffic can lead to latency issues.

- **User activity**:

  - **Active sessions**: Counting the number of active user sessions or connections. Monitoring this metric helps in managing resource allocation.

  - **Lock waits**: Identifying instances where queries are waiting for resources to be released. Excessive lock waits can hinder performance.

- **Storage metrics**:

  - **Storage usage**: Tracking the amount of storage space consumed by the database and ensuring adequate storage prevents unexpected outages.

  - **Input/output operations per second (IOPS)**: Measuring the rate of read and write operations to the storage. High IOPS can lead to performance issues.

- **Latency metrics**:

  - **Query latency**: Calculating the time taken for queries to execute and monitoring query latency helps maintain fast response times

  - **Replication latency**: In replicated databases, this involves tracking the delay between data changes and replication to secondary nodes

- **Error and exception metrics**:

  - **Error rates**: Measuring the frequency of errors or exceptions encountered during database operations. High error rates indicate potential issues.

- **Use cases**:

  - **E-commerce platform**: Monitoring performance metrics such as query response time and throughput ensures smooth online shopping experiences during peak periods

  - **Healthcare system**: Tracking active sessions and storage usage ensures the efficient processing of patient data in real time

Proactive alerting

Alerts are set up based on predefined thresholds. When these thresholds are breached, notifications are sent to administrators or automated response systems.

Alerts can be configured for various metrics, such as CPU exceeding a certain percentage or a sudden increase in query latency.

Proactive alerting is a critical component of effective database management, enabling administrators to stay ahead of potential issues and take timely actions to maintain optimal performance and availability. This practice involves setting up alerts that notify administrators when specific predefined thresholds are breached. Here's a more detailed look at proactive alerting:

- **The importance of proactive alerting**:

  - Traditional reactive approaches to issue resolution can lead to downtime and user dissatisfaction. Proactive alerting helps prevent problems before they escalate.

  - Timely intervention minimizes the impact of potential disruptions, ensuring a smoother user experience.

- **Setting thresholds**:

  - Administrators define specific thresholds for different metrics based on acceptable performance ranges and critical values.

  - For example, a threshold could be set for CPU usage at 80%. If the usage crosses this limit, an alert is triggered.

- **Alert conditions**:

  - Alerts can be triggered for a variety of conditions, including high resource utilization, slow query response times, low disk space, and more

  - Complex conditions can be configured by combining multiple metrics or values

- **Notification channels**:

  - Administrators can choose various channels for receiving alerts, such as email, SMS, instant messaging, or integration with collaboration tools

  - Multi-channel notifications ensure timely awareness, even when administrators are not actively monitoring dashboards

- **Escalation and severity levels**:

  - Alerts can be assigned different severity levels based on the potential impact of the issue

  - Escalation policies can be defined to ensure alerts are directed to appropriate personnel based on severity

- **Use cases**:

  - **E-commerce site**: If CPU utilization crosses a threshold during a sale event, an alert is sent to administrators, allowing them to allocate more resources

  - **Financial platform**: An alert is triggered when the transaction response time exceeds a set limit, enabling immediate investigation

- **Benefits**:

  - **Proactive issue mitigation**: Alerting allows administrators to address issues before they impact users, reducing downtime and service disruptions

  - **Resource optimization**: By acting on alerts, administrators can optimize resource allocation and prevent overutilization

- **Best practices**:

  - **Set appropriate thresholds**: Thresholds should reflect acceptable performance ranges and potential risk points

  - **Avoid alert fatigue**: Configure alerts thoughtfully to avoid overwhelming administrators with excessive notifications

  - **Regular review**: Continuously reassess and adjust thresholds based on changing workload patterns

Proactive alerting empowers administrators to maintain the health and availability of their database systems by identifying and addressing potential issues in real time. By implementing effective alerting strategies, organizations can ensure a responsive, reliable, and efficient database environment within the cloud.

Cloud provider tools

Cloud providers offer a range of monitoring and alerting tools to help users effectively manage their database environments within the cloud. These tools provide real-time insights, enable proactive issue detection, and enhance overall operational efficiency. This section will provide an in-depth exploration of cloud provider tools from popular vendors.

AWS CloudWatch (Amazon Web Services)

Amazon CloudWatch is a comprehensive monitoring and management service offered by AWS. It plays a crucial role in monitoring the health, performance, and operational aspects of various AWS resources, including databases. CloudWatch gathers data from different AWS services, presents it in a unified interface, and provides insights that empower users to optimize their applications and resources. Let's have a deeper look at AWS CloudWatch.

The following are its key features and functionality:

- **Metrics collection**: CloudWatch collects metrics from AWS resources, including databases, in real time. These metrics cover a wide range of aspects, such as CPU utilization, memory usage, disk I/O, and more, and are stored for future analysis and can be used to create custom dashboards and alerts.

- **Dashboards**: CloudWatch allows users to create customizable dashboards that provide a visual representation of key metrics. These dashboards enable quick and easy monitoring of the health and performance of your database environment.

- **Alarms and alerts**: CloudWatch allows you to set up alarms based on specific metric thresholds. When a metric breaches or crosses a parameter defined in the metric – that is, a defined threshold – an alarm triggers and sends alerts to designated recipients via various notification methods such as email, SMS, and more.

- **Logs and insights**: CloudWatch also provides capabilities for collecting, storing, and analyzing logs. CloudWatch Logs Insights allows you to query and analyze log data efficiently, aiding in troubleshooting and identifying patterns.

- **Anomaly detection**: CloudWatch uses machine learning algorithms to detect anomalies in metrics. This feature helps in identifying unusual behavior that may not be captured by traditional static thresholds.

- **Automated actions**: CloudWatch can trigger automated actions based on alarm states. For example, you can set up automatic scaling of your database instances in response to high CPU utilization.

- **Integration**: CloudWatch seamlessly integrates with various AWS services, including Amazon RDS, Amazon DynamoDB, Amazon Redshift, and more. This ensures comprehensive monitoring of your AWS database resources.

Here's why AWS CloudWatch is popular:

- **Comprehensive monitoring**: CloudWatch provides a single platform for monitoring various AWS services, making it a centralized solution for managing different resources.

- **Real-time insights**: CloudWatch provides real-time visibility into the health and performance of your resources. This immediacy enables timely responses to potential issues.

- **Automation**: The integration of alarms with automated actions enables proactive and responsive management. For example, automatic scaling helps maintain optimal performance under varying workloads.

- **Customization**: CloudWatch offers the flexibility to create custom dashboards and alarms based on specific requirements. This customization ensures that you monitor what matters most to your application.

- **Scalability**: CloudWatch is designed to handle large-scale environments. It can efficiently manage a vast number of metrics and resources, making it suitable for both small and large applications.

- **Cost-efficiency**: CloudWatch's pay-as-you-go pricing model ensures that users only pay for the metrics they collect and the features they use, making it a cost-effective solution.

- **Ease of use**: CloudWatch provides an intuitive user interface, making it accessible to users with varying levels of technical expertise.

AWS CloudWatch is popular among users because it empowers them to monitor, manage, and optimize their AWS resources effectively. Its diverse set of features, real-time insights, and seamless integration with various AWS services make it a go-to choice for organizations seeking comprehensive monitoring and management capabilities within their cloud environments.

Figure 10.1 depicts the integration of CloudWatch and CloudAlarm in AWS and how it facilitates sending email alerts:

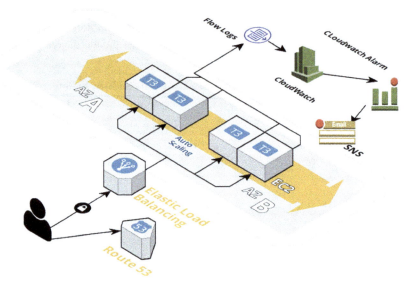

Figure 10.1: The CloudWatch, CloudAlarm, and SNS services in AWS

Azure Monitor (Microsoft Azure)

Azure Monitor is Microsoft Azure's comprehensive monitoring and management solution that helps users gain insights into the performance, availability, and health of their applications and resources within the Azure cloud ecosystem. It offers a unified platform for collecting, analyzing, and acting on telemetry data from various Azure services, including databases. Let's take a closer look at the key features and functionalities of Azure Monitor.

The following are its key features and functionality:

- **Metrics and logs collection**: Azure Monitor collects performance metrics, activity logs, and diagnostic logs from Azure resources, providing a holistic view of resource behavior.

- **Custom dashboards**: Users can create customized dashboards using Azure Monitor to visualize relevant metrics, logs, and insights. These dashboards can be tailored to specific needs and shared across teams.

- **Alerts and notifications**: Azure Monitor enables users to define alert rules based on metric thresholds, log query results, or activity log events. When conditions are met, alerts can trigger notifications through various channels.

- **Application Insights**: Azure Monitor offers Application Insights, a feature that provides detailed insights into the performance and usage of applications, helping developers identify bottlenecks and optimize user experiences.

- **Log Analytics**: Azure Monitor's Log Analytics allows users to query and analyze logs collected from various Azure resources. This feature aids in troubleshooting, root cause analysis, and identifying trends.

- **Diagnostics and troubleshooting**: Azure Monitor helps diagnose issues with interactive query capabilities and log analysis. It also provides insights into potential problems and suggests remediation steps.

- **Automated actions**: Users can configure automated actions in response to alerts. These actions can include scaling Azure resources or invoking Azure Logic Apps to trigger workflows.

- **Integration**: Azure Monitor seamlessly integrates with various Azure services, including Azure SQL Database, Azure Cosmos DB, and Azure Cache for Redis, providing comprehensive monitoring capabilities.

Let's take a look at why Azure Monitor is popular:

- **Unified platform**: Azure Monitor serves as a central hub for monitoring Azure resources, thus streamlining the monitoring process and providing a consistent experience.

- **Granular insights**: Azure Monitor allows users to drill down into specific resources, services, or components to gain granular insights into their behavior and performance.

- **Customization**: Users can build tailored dashboards, alerts, and queries to suit their specific needs. This customization ensures that users monitor what is most relevant to their applications.

- **Scalability**: Azure Monitor is built to handle large-scale environments, making it suitable for applications of all sizes, from small startups to enterprise-level deployments.

- **Predictive insights**: With the use of machine learning, Azure Monitor can identify unusual patterns and anomalies in metrics, helping users predict and prevent potential issues.

- **Integration with DevOps**: Azure Monitor seamlessly integrates with Azure DevOps, allowing developers to gain insights into application performance and identify areas for improvement.

- **Rich data visualization**: The visualization capabilities of Azure Monitor help users quickly understand and communicate performance trends, issues, and improvements.

Azure Monitor's comprehensive monitoring capabilities, real-time insights, and integration with various Azure services make it a popular choice for organizations seeking to optimize the performance, availability, and health of their applications and resources within the Azure cloud environment.

Setting up Azure Monitor in the Azure cloud involves several steps so that you can start collecting and analyzing telemetry data from your resources. Here's a general overview of the process:

1. **Access the Azure portal**: Log in to the Azure portal (`https://portal.azure.com/`) using your Azure account credentials.

2. **Create a Log Analytics workspace**:

   A. In the Azure portal, click on + **Create a resource** and search for `Log Analytics Workspace`.

   B. Select the appropriate subscription, resource group, and region for your workspace.

   C. Provide a unique name for the workspace, configure other settings as needed, and click **Review + Create** to create the workspace.

3. **Enable monitoring for resources**:

   A. Once your Log Analytics workspace has been created, navigate to the resource you want to monitor (for example, an Azure VM or Azure SQL database).

   B. Under the **Monitoring** section of the resource's menu, select **Enable** to enable monitoring for that resource.

4. **Configure data collection**:

   A. Depending on the resource, you must configure data collection settings. For example, for an Azure VM, you can configure performance counters, event logs, and diagnostics settings.

   B. Choose which types of data you want to collect and analyze for the selected resource.

5. **Configure alerts**:

   A. To set up alerts, navigate to the **Alerts** section in the Azure Monitor menu.

   B. Create alert rules based on specific conditions, such as CPU usage exceeding a threshold, and define actions to be taken when the alert triggers (for example, sending an email notification).

6. **Create dashboards**:

   A. Navigate to the **Dashboards** section in the Azure Monitor menu.

   B. Create custom dashboards by adding tiles that display metrics, charts, and other visualizations from your monitored resources.

7. **Configure Log Analytics queries**:

   A. In the Log Analytics workspace, you can create and run queries to analyze the data collected from your resources.

    B.   Use the **Kusto Query Language** (**KQL**) to write queries that help you gain insights into your data.

8. **Visualize insights**:

    A.   Use the insights gained from your monitoring and queries to identify trends, troubleshoot issues, and optimize your resources' performance.

9. **Integrate with Azure DevOps**:

    A.   You can integrate Azure Monitor with Azure DevOps to gain insights into application performance and align monitoring with your DevOps practices.

10. **Explore additional features**:

    A.   Azure Monitor offers features such as Application Insights for application performance monitoring and Azure Security Center for enhanced security insights.

Please note that the exact steps may vary, depending on the type of resource you are monitoring and the specific features you are utilizing within Azure Monitor.

Google Cloud Monitoring (Google Cloud Platform)

Google Cloud Monitoring is a powerful and flexible monitoring solution provided by **Google Cloud Platform** (**GCP**). It allows users to collect, visualize, and analyze metrics and data from various GCP resources, helping organizations ensure the health, performance, and availability of their applications and services. Let's take an in-depth look at the key features and functionalities of Google Cloud Monitoring.

Here are its key features and functionality:

- **Metrics collection and visualization**:

  - Google Cloud Monitoring collects metrics from various GCP services and resources, such as virtual machines, databases, and storage.

  - Users can create custom dashboards using Google Cloud Monitoring's flexible and intuitive interface. Dashboards provide real-time visualizations of metrics, charts, and widgets.

- **Alerting and notifications**:

  - Google Cloud Monitoring enables users to set up alerting policies based on specific metric thresholds or conditions

  - When an alert condition is met, notifications can be sent through various channels, including email, SMS, PagerDuty, and Google Chat

- **Uptime monitoring**:

  - Google Cloud Monitoring offers uptime checks to monitor the availability and performance of HTTP(S) endpoints and other services

  - Users can configure how frequently checks are performed and define expected response codes

- **Custom metrics and logs**:

  - In addition to built-in metrics, Google Cloud Monitoring allows users to create and collect custom metrics using the Monitoring API

  - Users can also export logs to Google Cloud Logging for in-depth analysis and correlation with metrics

- **Integrations**:

  - Google Cloud Monitoring seamlessly integrates with various GCP services, such as Google Compute Engine, Google Kubernetes Engine, Google Cloud Storage, and more

  - It also supports integration with third-party monitoring tools through open source agents

- **Multi-cloud monitoring**:

  - Beyond GCP, Google Cloud Monitoring offers support for multi-cloud environments, allowing users to monitor AWS resources using CloudWatch integration

- **Automated insights**:

  - Google Cloud Monitoring uses machine learning to provide automated insights into anomalies, helping users detect and address issues proactively

- **Advanced analytics**:

  - Google Cloud Monitoring provides advanced querying capabilities using **Monitoring Query Language (MQL)** for detailed analysis of metrics and logs

Here's why Google Cloud Monitoring is popular:

- **Native integration**: Google Cloud Monitoring is seamlessly integrated with GCP services, making it easy to set up and monitor resources within the Google Cloud ecosystem

- **Customization**: The platform offers customizable dashboards, alerts, and metrics, allowing users to tailor monitoring to their specific needs

- **Automation**: Automated insights and anomaly detection help users identify issues and performance bottlenecks without manual intervention

- **Multi-cloud support**: The ability to monitor AWS resources through Google Cloud Monitoring provides a unified view for multi-cloud environments

- **Scalability**: Google Cloud Monitoring is designed to handle large-scale environments, making it suitable for businesses of all sizes

- **Machine learning insights**: The use of machine learning enables Google Cloud Monitoring to provide predictive and actionable insights

- **Cost control**: Users pay only for the metrics they collect, ensuring cost efficiency

Google Cloud Monitoring empowers users to maintain the health and performance of their GCP resources and applications through comprehensive monitoring, actionable insights, and seamless integration with various GCP services.

Setting up Google Cloud Monitoring using the **command-line interface** (CLI) involves several steps as you must configure monitoring and start collecting metrics from your GCP resources. Here's a general overview of the process:

1. **Install and authenticate the Google Cloud SDK**:

   A. If you haven't already, install the Google Cloud SDK on your local machine

   B. Authenticate the SDK by running the `gcloud auth login` command and following the prompts to log in to your GCP account

2. **Enable the Monitoring API**:

   - Use the following command to enable the Google Cloud Monitoring API:

   ```
   gcloud services enable monitoring.googleapis.com
   ```

3. **Create a workspace**:

   - A workspace is a logical container for your monitoring data. Use the following command to create a workspace:

   ```
   gcloud monitoring dashboards create --config-from-file=[PATH_TO_
   DASHBOARD_CONFIG]
   ```

4. **Set up uptime checks**:

   - Configure uptime checks to monitor the availability and performance of your HTTP(S) endpoints:

   ```
   gcloud monitoring uptime-checks create [CHECK_NAME] \
   --project=[PROJECT_ID] --display-name=[DISPLAY_NAME] \ --http-
   check 'request_method="GET", use_ssl=true, path="/"'
   ```

5. **Create alerting policies**:

    - Set up alerting policies to receive notifications when specific conditions are met. For example, to create a policy for high CPU utilization, you can use the following code:

    ```
    gcloud alpha monitoring policies create [POLICY_NAME]
    \ --project=[PROJECT_ID] \ --conditions=[CONDITIONS] \
    --notification-channels=[CHANNELS]
    ```

6. **Add resources for monitoring purposes**:

    - Add the GCP resources you want to monitor to the workspace:

    ```
    gcloud alpha monitoring dashboards create [DASHBOARD_ID]
    \ --title=[DASHBOARD_TITLE] \ --project=[PROJECT_ID] \
    --gauges=[RESOURCES_TO_MONITOR]
    ```

7. **Custom metrics and monitoring agents**:

    - If you want to collect custom metrics or use monitoring agents, consult the GCP documentation for detailed instructions based on your use case

Please note that the commands provided are examples and may need to be customized based on your specific project, resource names, and requirements.

Oracle Cloud Infrastructure Monitoring (Oracle Cloud)

Oracle Cloud Infrastructure (**OCI**) Monitoring is a comprehensive solution provided by Oracle Cloud for monitoring the health, performance, and availability of resources and services within the Oracle Cloud environment. It enables users to collect, analyze, and visualize metrics, alerts, and logs to ensure optimal performance of their cloud-based applications and infrastructure. Let's take a closer look at the key features and functionalities of OCI Monitoring.

Here are its key features and functionality:

- **Metrics collection and visualization**:

    - OCI Monitoring collects metrics from various Oracle Cloud services, such as compute instances, databases, storage, and networking components

    - Users can create custom dashboards using OCI Monitoring's user-friendly interface, allowing real-time visualization of metrics and data

- **Alerting and notifications**:

    - Users can define alerting rules based on metric thresholds or conditions using OCI Monitoring

    - When alerts are triggered, notifications can be sent through multiple channels, including email, SMS, and Oracle Cloud Notification Service

- **Integration with other tools**:

  - OCI Monitoring seamlessly integrates with other Oracle Cloud services, such as Oracle Cloud Infrastructure Notifications and Oracle Cloud Infrastructure Events

- **Log analytics**:

  - OCI Monitoring allows users to integrate with Oracle Cloud Infrastructure Logging, enabling the collection and analysis of logs for monitoring and troubleshooting.

- **Service-level agreement (SLA) monitoring**:

  - Users can set SLA-based alerting rules to ensure compliance with predefined SLAs.

- **Automation and orchestration**:

  - OCI Monitoring enables the automation of actions based on alerts through integration with Oracle Cloud Infrastructure Events, allowing users to trigger actions and workflows

- **Advanced analytics**:

  - Users can perform advanced analytics and queries on collected metrics using Oracle Cloud Infrastructure MQL

- **Cross-compartment monitoring**:

  - OCI Monitoring supports monitoring resources across different compartments within your Oracle Cloud Infrastructure tenancy

Here's why OCI Monitoring is popular:

- **Oracle ecosystem integration**: As part of the Oracle Cloud Infrastructure suite, OCI Monitoring offers seamless integration with other Oracle Cloud services and resources

- **Custom dashboards**: The user-friendly dashboard creation tool allows users to create visualizations and charts that match their specific monitoring needs

- **Alerting flexibility**: OCI Monitoring's customizable alerting system provides flexibility in setting up alerts based on specific metric conditions

- **Native logging integration**: Integration with Oracle Cloud Infrastructure Logging allows for comprehensive analysis of metrics and logs in one place

- **Unified platform**: Oracle Cloud Infrastructure offers a unified platform for managing, monitoring, and securing resources, simplifying cloud management

- **SLA monitoring**: The ability to monitor SLAs ensures compliance and consistent performance of critical resources

- **Query language**: MQL enables advanced querying for in-depth analysis of metric data

OCI Monitoring plays a crucial role in maintaining the performance and availability of Oracle Cloud resources and applications, providing insights and alerts that help organizations optimize their cloud deployments.

IBM Cloud Monitoring (IBM Cloud)

IBM Cloud Monitoring is a comprehensive monitoring solution offered by IBM Cloud that allows users to monitor and manage the health, performance, and availability of their cloud resources and applications. It provides a set of tools and features to collect, analyze, and visualize metrics, logs, and events from various IBM Cloud services and infrastructure components. Let's take a closer look at the key features and functionalities of IBM Cloud Monitoring.

Here are its features and functionality:

- **Metrics collection and visualization**:

  - IBM Cloud Monitoring collects metrics from a wide range of IBM Cloud services, virtual machines, containers, and other resources

  - Users can create customized dashboards with visualizations, charts, and graphs to monitor the metrics in real time

- **Alerting and notifications**:

  - Users can set up alerting rules based on metric thresholds or specific conditions using IBM Cloud Monitoring

  - When alerts are triggered, notifications can be sent through various channels, including email, SMS, and integrations with external notification services

- **Integrations and APIs**:

  - IBM Cloud Monitoring offers integrations with other IBM Cloud services and tools, enabling seamless data flow between various cloud components

  - It provides APIs for programmatic access to metric and monitoring data, allowing users to build custom monitoring solutions

- **Log analysis**:

  - IBM Cloud Monitoring allows users to collect and analyze logs from different sources, helping with troubleshooting and root cause analysis

- **Automated insights**:

  - The platform uses machine learning to provide automated insights and anomaly detection to help users identify performance issues

- **Custom dashboards**:

  - Users can create personalized dashboards that display the most relevant metrics and visualizations for their specific needs

- **Service integration**:

  - IBM Cloud Monitoring integrates with other IBM Cloud services, such as IBM Cloud Functions, for triggering actions based on alerts

- **Tagging and grouping**:

  - Users can tag and group resources to organize and manage monitoring data more efficiently

Here's why IBM Cloud Monitoring is popular:

- **IBM ecosystem integration**: IBM Cloud Monitoring seamlessly integrates with other IBM Cloud services, providing a unified platform for monitoring and managing cloud resources

- **Customization**: The ability to create customized dashboards and alerts allows users to tailor monitoring to their specific requirements

- **Automated insights**: Automated anomaly detection and insights help users identify and address issues proactively

- **Log analysis**: The integration of log analysis with monitoring data assists in comprehensive troubleshooting and analysis

- **Multi-cloud support**: IBM Cloud Monitoring can monitor resources across different cloud environments, enhancing its usefulness for hybrid and multi-cloud scenarios

- **Scalability**: IBM Cloud Monitoring is designed to handle large-scale environments, making it suitable for businesses of varying sizes

- **API access**: The availability of APIs allows users to build custom monitoring solutions and integrate monitoring data into their existing workflows

- **Machine learning**: The use of machine learning helps in identifying patterns and anomalies for effective monitoring

IBM Cloud Monitoring empowers users to maintain optimal performance and availability of their IBM Cloud resources and applications by providing comprehensive monitoring, actionable insights, and integration with various IBM Cloud services.

Alibaba Cloud CloudMonitor (Alibaba Cloud)

Alibaba Cloud CloudMonitor is a monitoring and management service provided by Alibaba Cloud, a leading cloud service provider in Asia and beyond. CloudMonitor offers a suite of tools and capabilities to help users monitor, manage, and optimize the performance, availability, and security of their Alibaba Cloud resources and applications. Let's take a comprehensive look at the key features and functionalities of Alibaba Cloud CloudMonitor.

Here are its key features and functionality:

- **Metrics collection and visualization**:

  - CloudMonitor collects real-time metrics from various Alibaba Cloud services, including compute instances, databases, storage, and networking components

  - Users can create customized dashboards with visualizations and charts to monitor metrics and performance data

- **Alerting and notifications**:

  - Users can define alerting rules based on predefined metric thresholds or conditions in CloudMonitor

  - When alerts are triggered, notifications can be sent through various channels, such as email, SMS, and Alibaba Cloud Message Service

- **Application performance management (APM)**:

  - CloudMonitor provides application performance insights through transaction tracing and application diagnostics

- **Log service integration**:

  - Integration with Alibaba Cloud Log Service enables users to correlate logs and metrics for comprehensive analysis and troubleshooting

- **Custom dashboards**:

  - Users can create personalized dashboards to visualize key performance indicators and metrics

- **Automation and event triggers**:

  - CloudMonitor can trigger Alibaba Cloud Function Compute or Alibaba Cloud Resource Orchestration Service actions based on metric alerts

- **Integration with cloud services**:

  - CloudMonitor integrates with other Alibaba Cloud services, such as Auto Scaling and Elastic Compute Service, to enable automatic scaling based on monitoring data

Here's why Alibaba Cloud CloudMonitor is popular:

- **Alibaba Cloud integration**: CloudMonitor is deeply integrated with Alibaba Cloud's services, making it well-suited for monitoring Alibaba Cloud resources
- **Real-time monitoring**: The real-time collection and visualization of metrics allow users to quickly identify and respond to performance issues
- **Customization**: Users can customize dashboards and alerts to meet their specific monitoring needs
- **Alerting flexibility**: CloudMonitor provides flexible alerting and notification options for proactive issue resolution
- **Application insights**: The available APM features help users gain insights into application performance, diagnose bottlenecks, and optimize applications
- **Log and metric correlation**: Integration with Log Service enables users to analyze both metrics and logs for more effective troubleshooting
- **Multi-channel notifications**: Users can receive notifications through various channels, ensuring timely awareness of critical events
- **Event-driven automation**: CloudMonitor's event-triggered automation allows users to perform actions automatically in response to alerts

Alibaba Cloud CloudMonitor plays a crucial role in ensuring the optimal performance and availability of Alibaba Cloud resources and applications. Its comprehensive monitoring and management capabilities, which are integrated with Alibaba Cloud's ecosystem, empower users to monitor, diagnose, and resolve issues efficiently.

Best practices

Let's understand the best practices for monitoring:

- **Explore and familiarize**: Understand the capabilities of each cloud provider's monitoring tools and their integration with database services
- **Customize alerts**: Tailor alerting policies so that they align with specific performance requirements and business needs
- **Integrate with automation**: Utilize alert notifications to trigger automated responses or scaling actions

Here are some in-depth best practices to consider:

- **Understand tool capabilities**:

  - Thoroughly explore the features and functionalities of your cloud provider's monitoring tools. Understand the metrics they collect, the visualization options available, and how to set up alerts.

- Familiarize yourself with the tools' integration with different database services and other cloud resources.

- **Define relevant metrics**:

  - Identify the key metrics that are critical for monitoring the health and performance of your database. These could include metrics related to CPU utilization, memory usage, disk I/O, query response time, and more.

  - Avoid monitoring metrics that are not directly relevant to your use case, as excessive metrics can clutter dashboards and alerts.

- **Set up custom dashboards**:

  - Create custom dashboards that provide a consolidated view of essential metrics and insights. Tailor the dashboards to suit your specific monitoring requirements.

  - Visualize metrics in charts, graphs, and other formats that help you quickly identify trends and anomalies.

- **Define alerting policies**:

  - Establish alerting policies based on predetermined thresholds. Ensure that alerts are set at levels that indicate a potential issue without generating unnecessary alerts due to normal variations.

  - Differentiate between warning-level and critical-level alerts, and establish appropriate actions or responses for each.

- **Leverage automated actions**:

  - Integrate alerts with automated actions to streamline responses to specific triggers. For instance, an alert on high CPU usage could trigger an automatic scaling action.

  - Automate responses to address common issues swiftly and reduce the need for manual intervention.

- **Regularly review and adjust**:

  - Continuously assess the effectiveness of your alerting and monitoring strategy. Regularly review the metrics, thresholds, and alerts to ensure they align with changing workload patterns and business needs.

  - Adjust thresholds and policies as your application's requirements evolve.

- **Monitor for anomalies**:

  - Leverage anomaly detection capabilities provided by some cloud provider tools. These can help you identify abnormal behavior patterns that might not be covered by predefined thresholds.

  - Investigate and address anomalies promptly to prevent potential disruptions.

- **Collaborate and share insights**:

  - Share dashboards and insights with relevant team members, including database administrators, developers, and operations personnel. Collaboration ensures everyone is on the same page and can take informed actions.

- **Training and documentation**:

  - Provide training to your team members on how to use the monitoring tools effectively. Create documentation or guides that outline best practices, usage scenarios, and troubleshooting steps.

- **Stay up to date**:

  - Keep track of updates and improvements to your cloud provider's monitoring tools. New features and functionalities could enhance your monitoring capabilities and overall experience.

By following these best practices, you can maximize the benefits of cloud provider monitoring tools, ensuring a proactive approach to managing your database environment and maintaining optimal performance and availability.

These cloud provider monitoring tools empower users to gain deep insights into their cloud-based databases, ensuring proactive issue detection, efficient resource utilization, and enhanced operational efficiency. By leveraging these tools, organizations can maintain robust and performant database environments within the cloud.

Real-time monitoring and alerts are foundational to maintaining the health and performance of databases in the cloud. By mastering this practice, administrators can ensure seamless operations, timely issue resolution, and an optimized user experience.

The next section, *Automated scaling and resource management*, delves into the strategies, tools, and practices related to automatically adjusting the allocation of cloud resources based on demand. We will explore how cloud providers offer mechanisms for dynamically scaling resources to match workload fluctuations, optimizing cost efficiency, performance, and user experience. You will learn about concepts such as auto-scaling, load balancing, and resource orchestration, along with real-world scenarios and best practices for effectively managing resources in a dynamic cloud environment. The next section focuses on empowering you to create efficient and responsive infrastructures that automatically adapt to varying workloads while ensuring consistent performance and cost-effectiveness.

Automated scaling and resource management

Automated scaling and resource management are critical components of cloud infrastructure management that allow businesses to dynamically adjust the allocation of resources in response to changes in workload demand. This section explores various strategies, tools, and practices that enable cloud environments to efficiently scale resources up or down to optimize performance, cost, and user experience.

Here's a comprehensive look at the key aspects that will be covered in this section:

- **Auto-scaling**: Auto-scaling involves automatically adjusting the number of compute resources, such as virtual machines or containers, based on changes in demand. This ensures that the application can handle varying levels of traffic without manual intervention. Auto-scaling policies can be configured to trigger scaling actions based on metrics such as CPU utilization, memory usage, or network traffic.

- **Load balancing**: Load balancing evenly distributes incoming network traffic across multiple resources to prevent any single resource from being overwhelmed. Load balancers ensure optimal resource utilization, improve fault tolerance, and enhance the overall performance and availability of applications.

- **Elastic Load Balancing (ELB)**: Cloud providers offer ELB services that automatically distribute incoming traffic across multiple instances. This helps optimize application availability and performance by distributing traffic evenly and directing it to healthy instances.

- **Auto-scaling groups**: Auto-scaling groups are sets of resources that are managed collectively. These groups automatically adjust the number of instances based on defined conditions. As demand increases, new instances are launched, and as demand decreases, instances are terminated.

- **Resource orchestration**: Resource orchestration involves managing the deployment and scaling of resources through automation. **Infrastructure as Code (IaC)** tools such as AWS CloudFormation, Azure Resource Manager, and Google Cloud Deployment Manager enable users to define and manage resources using code.

- **Serverless computing**: Serverless computing abstracts infrastructure management by allowing developers to focus solely on writing code. Cloud providers automatically manage the resources required to run functions or applications, scaling them based on incoming events or requests.

- **Container orchestration**: Container orchestration platforms such as Kubernetes automate the process of deploying, scaling, and managing containerized applications. They ensure that containers are efficiently scheduled and scaled based on application needs.

- **Benefits**:

  - **Efficiency**: Automated scaling optimizes resource utilization, eliminating over-provisioning and reducing costs during periods of low demand

  - **Resilience**: Load balancing and auto-scaling improve application availability and fault tolerance by distributing traffic and resources effectively

  - **Performance**: Scaling resources up during high demand maintains optimal performance for end users

  - **Cost Savings**: Auto-scaling eliminates the need for manual intervention, optimizing resource usage and cost-effectiveness

- **Elasticity**: Applications can easily accommodate varying workloads without manual intervention, ensuring a seamless user experience

- **Real-world examples**:

  - During a major online sale, an e-commerce platform uses auto-scaling groups to launch additional instances to handle increased traffic, ensuring a smooth shopping experience for users

Imagine an e-commerce platform gearing up for a highly anticipated online sale event, where thousands of customers are expected to flock to the website looking for deals. In this scenario, the platform employs auto-scaling strategies to ensure a seamless shopping experience for users while effectively managing its resources and costs:

1. **Scenario**: A highly anticipated sale event on an e-commerce website.

2. **Preparation**: Before the sale event, the e-commerce platform predicts a significant increase in traffic and prepares by setting up an auto-scaling group in their cloud infrastructure.

3. **Auto-scaling policies**: The platform defines auto-scaling policies based on metrics such as CPU utilization and incoming requests. They determine that if the CPU utilization crosses a certain threshold, new instances will be launched automatically.

4. **Event launch**: As the sale event begins, user traffic starts to surge, causing CPU utilization to increase rapidly.

5. **Auto-scaling trigger**: The auto-scaling policies are triggered, and the platform's cloud environment recognizes the need for additional resources to handle the traffic influx.

6. **Instance launch**: The auto-scaling group launches new instances of the application to accommodate the increased load. These new instances are quickly provisioned and integrated into the application pool.

7. **Balanced traffic**: The load balancer seamlessly distributes incoming traffic across all instances, ensuring that no single instance becomes overwhelmed and that users experience consistent performance.

8. **Traffic subsides**: As the sale event ends and user traffic subsides, the auto-scaling group detects the decrease in demand.

9. **Instance termination**: The auto-scaling group scales down by terminating the unnecessary instances, thereby saving costs by only utilizing the resources needed.

10. **Benefits and insights**:

    - **Seamless user experience**: Auto-scaling ensures that users experience quick load times and minimal downtime, even during peak traffic periods

    - **Cost efficiency**: The platform avoids over-provisioning resources, only paying for the resources consumed during the peak period

- **Resource optimization**: Auto-scaling effectively manages resource allocation, preventing underutilization during off-peak times

- **Easy management**: The entire process is automated, reducing the need for manual intervention and allowing the platform's team to focus on other aspects of the event

This real-world example demonstrates the effectiveness of auto-scaling in handling sudden spikes in demand, such as during online sales or promotional events. By dynamically adjusting resources to match traffic fluctuations, businesses can provide an optimal user experience while maintaining cost efficiency and operational ease. For example, a video streaming service might leverage serverless computing to automatically scale its backend functions based on incoming requests, optimizing resource usage and reducing operational overhead.

Consider a ride-sharing application that experiences varying levels of user activity throughout the day. To efficiently handle the fluctuating demand and ensure seamless user experiences, the application leverages serverless computing in its cloud environment:

1. **Scenario**: A ride-sharing application with varying levels of user activity.

2. **Architecture design**: The application is designed using a serverless architecture. Instead of provisioning and managing traditional virtual machines or containers, the application consists of individual serverless functions.

3. **Function deployment**: Different functions are created to handle various aspects of the application, such as user authentication, ride booking, and driver matching.

4. **Event-driven scaling**: The serverless functions are event-driven, meaning they are invoked in response to specific events, such as user requests.

5. **Scaling mechanism**: When user activity is low, only a few serverless functions are active. As the number of user requests increases, the serverless platform automatically scales out by deploying additional instances of the functions.

6. **Resource allocation**: Each function instance is allocated resources (CPU, memory, and so on) on demand. The cloud provider manages the resource allocation process, ensuring optimal performance and resource utilization.

7. **Peak periods**: During peak hours, such as rush hour or weekends, the application experiences a surge in ride requests.

8. **Dynamic scaling**: The serverless platform detects the increase in incoming events and scales out by launching multiple instances of the functions to handle the higher load.

9. **Load balancing**: Incoming requests are distributed across the available function instances through load balancing, ensuring even distribution of traffic.

10. **Auto-scaling**: As the demand decreases during non-peak hours, the serverless platform scales in by reducing the number of function instances.

11. **Benefits and insights**:

- **Cost optimization**: The application pays only for the actual compute time and resources used by the functions, leading to cost savings during periods of low activity

- **High scalability**: The serverless architecture allows the application to scale effortlessly in response to spikes in user demand, ensuring consistent performance

- **Automatic management**: The cloud provider handles the underlying infrastructure, allowing the application developers to focus solely on writing code

- **Resilience**: The application's auto-scaling capabilities make it resilient to sudden traffic spikes, preventing performance bottlenecks or downtimes

- **Efficient resource utilization**: Serverless functions are only active when invoked, making efficient use of resources and reducing waste

This real-world example showcases how serverless computing provides an ideal solution for applications with unpredictable workloads. By automatically scaling resources based on event-driven triggers, the application can provide optimal performance and cost-efficiency, even during varying levels of user activity.

Various cloud providers offer tools and services to facilitate efficient resource utilization and scaling. Let's take a quick look at the tools and services provided by different cloud vendors.

AWS:

- **Auto Scaling**: AWS Auto Scaling allows users to configure automatic scaling for multiple services, such as Amazon EC2 instances, Amazon ECS tasks, and more. It uses predefined scaling policies or custom metrics to adjust resources based on demand. The following figure depicts how to autoscale EC2 compute instances in AWS. Here, T3 is the EC2 compute instance type, which receives connections through the Elastic Load Balancer:

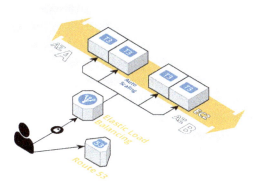

Figure 10.2: Autoscaling in AWS cloud

- **ELB**: AWS ELB distributes incoming traffic across multiple instances, ensuring availability and fault tolerance. It includes **Application Load Balancers** (**ALBs**) and **Network Load Balancers** (**NLBs**).

- **Amazon EC2 Auto Scaling**: This service automatically adjusts the number of EC2 instances in a scaling group based on conditions defined by the user. It helps maintain application availability and allows scaling in and out.

Microsoft Azure:

Azure Autoscale: Azure Autoscale enables users to automatically adjust the number of virtual machine instances in a scale set or an app service plan based on predefined conditions or metrics.

Setting up Azure Autoscale involves configuring autoscaling rules for your Azure resources based on specific metrics or schedules. Here's a step-by-step guide to setting up Azure Autoscale:

1. **Sign into the Azure portal**: Log in to the Azure portal (`https://portal.azure.com/`) using your credentials.

2. **Navigate to your resource**: Select the resource you want to enable Autoscale for. This could be a Virtual Machine Scale Set, an App Service Plan, or a Cloud Service, among others.

3. **Configure Autoscale**: Inside the resource's blade, find and select the **Autoscale** option in the left-hand menu.

4. **Add a rule**: Click on the + **Add a rule** button to create a new Autoscale rule.

5. **Configure the necessary conditions**:

   - **Name**: Give your Autoscale rule a meaningful name.

   - **Metric Source**: Choose the metric source (such as CPU utilization, memory usage, and so on).

   - **Condition**: Define the conditions that trigger scaling. For example, you might set a threshold such as **Increase instances by 1 if CPU > 70%.**

   - **Direction**: Specify whether the rule should scale out (increase instances) or scale in (decrease instances).

   - **Instance Limits**: Set upper and lower limits for the number of instances.

6. **Add a second rule (optional)**: You can add multiple Autoscale rules for different metrics or conditions.

7. **Configure scaling actions**:

   - **Scale out**: Define how many instances to add when scaling out

   - **Scale in**: Define how many instances to remove when scaling in

- **Advanced configuration (optional)**: Depending on the resource type, you might have additional configuration options, such as cooldown periods or schedule-based scaling

- **Notifications (optional)**: Set up notifications so that you receive alerts when autoscaling events occur

8. **Review and save**: Review your configuration settings and then click the **OK** or **Save** button to apply the Autoscale rules.

9. **Enable Autoscale**: Once the rules have been created and saved, enable Autoscale to make the rules active.

That's it! Azure will now monitor the specified metrics and automatically adjust the number of instances based on the conditions you've set. Autoscale ensures that your application can handle varying workloads efficiently while optimizing costs.

Please note that the steps might vary slightly depending on the specific resource type you're configuring Autoscale for. Always refer to Azure's official documentation for the most up-to-date and detailed instructions.

1. **Azure Load Balancer**: This service distributes incoming traffic across multiple resources for better availability and responsiveness. Azure provides both internal and external load balancers.

2. **Azure Kubernetes Service (AKS)**: AKS helps automate the deployment, scaling, and management of containerized applications using Kubernetes, ensuring efficient resource usage and availability.

GCP:

Google Cloud Autoscaling: GCP's Autoscaling allows users to adjust the number of instances in managed instance groups based on traffic, usage, and other factors, ensuring optimal performance.

Google Cloud Autoscaling allows you to automatically adjust the number of instances in a managed instance group based on factors such as CPU utilization, request rate, and custom metrics. It helps ensure that your applications run smoothly under varying workloads while optimizing resource utilization and cost efficiency.

With Google Cloud Autoscaling, you can do the following:

- Scale out during high traffic periods to maintain performance

- Scale in during low traffic times to save costs

- Handle unexpected traffic spikes without manual intervention

- Utilize Google's expertise in optimizing scaling decisions

Let's learn how to set up Google Cloud Autoscaling for a managed instance group:

1. **Sign into the Google Cloud console**: Log in to the Google Cloud Console (`https://console.cloud.google.com/`) using your credentials.

   - **Create a managed instance group**: Create a managed instance group that contains the instances you want to scale. You can use Google Compute Engine instances or instance templates.

   - **Configure an Autoscaler**: Inside the instance group's settings, navigate to **Autoscaling** from the left menu.

   - **Create an Autoscaler**: Click the + **Create an autoscaler** button.

   - **Configure your Autoscaler's settings**:

     - **Name**: Give your Autoscaler a descriptive name.

     - **Target utilization**: Choose the metric you want to optimize for (CPU utilization, request rate, and so on) and set the target utilization level.

     - Scaling policy: Define how autoscaling behaves when the target utilization is exceeded. Choose from **Off**, **On**, or **Only scale out**.

   - **Set scaling limits**:

     - Minimum and maximum number of instances: Set the minimum and maximum number of instances allowed by the Autoscaler

   - **Create a custom metric (optional)**: If you want to use a custom metric, create it beforehand and select it in the Autoscaler settings.

   - **Health check configuration**: Configure health checks to determine instance health and readiness.

   - **Cooldown period**: Set a cooldown period to avoid rapid scaling up or down.

   - **Review and create**: Review your settings and then click the **Create** button.

   - **Apply the Autoscaler to the managed instance group**: After creating the Autoscaler instance, associate it with the managed instance group.

   - **Monitoring and testing**: Monitor the autoscaler's behavior using Google Cloud Monitoring. Test your setup by simulating traffic and observing how the Autoscaler responds.

   By following these steps, Google Cloud Autoscaling will automatically adjust the number of instances in your managed instance group based on the defined criteria. This ensures your applications have the right amount of resources to handle workload variations efficiently.

2. **Google Cloud Load Balancing**: This service distributes incoming traffic across multiple instances, ensuring high availability and providing both internal and external load balancers.

3. **Google Kubernetes Engine (GKE)**: GKE automates container deployment, scaling, and management using Kubernetes, making it easy to manage resources for containerized applications.

IBM Cloud:

- **IBM Auto-Scaling**: IBM Cloud Auto-Scaling automatically adjusts the number of running instances based on predefined conditions, optimizing performance and cost

- **IBM Load Balancer**: This service ensures an even distribution of incoming traffic across multiple resources, enhancing availability and responsiveness

- **IBM Kubernetes Service**: It provides a managed Kubernetes environment to deploy, manage, and scale containerized applications effectively

Alibaba Cloud:

- **Alibaba Cloud Auto Scaling**: This service adjusts the number of ECS instances automatically based on user-defined policies, optimizing performance and cost-efficiency

- **Alibaba Cloud Server Load Balancer**: This service distributes incoming traffic across multiple instances, ensuring high availability and performance for applications

- **Alibaba Cloud Container Service for Kubernetes (ACK)**: ACK simplifies Kubernetes cluster management, helping with efficient scaling and resource management for containerized applications

Each of these cloud providers offers a range of tools and services designed to make resource management and scaling easier for users, catering to various workload types and application architectures.

The next section, *Updates and patching*, focuses on the critical process of keeping your software, applications, and systems up to date with the latest patches and updates. It explores the importance of regular updates in maintaining security, fixing vulnerabilities, and enhancing overall system performance. This section discusses strategies for managing updates, testing procedures, and how to handle updates in cloud environments. It also covers cloud-specific tools and services that help automate and streamline the update and patching process. By the end of this section, you will understand the significance of updates, the challenges involved, and how to effectively manage and implement them in various cloud environments.

Updates and patching

Updates and patching are critical aspects of maintaining the security, stability, and functionality of your software and systems. This process involves applying the latest updates, bug fixes, and security patches to your applications, operating systems, and other software components. This section delves into the details of updates and patching, highlighting their significance and best practices.

First, let's look at the importance of updates and patching:

- **Security**: Regular updates are crucial for addressing security vulnerabilities. Hackers often exploit known vulnerabilities, so patching them is vital to prevent breaches.

- **Bug fixes**: Updates fix software bugs that could lead to crashes, data corruption, or incorrect functioning.

- **Performance enhancement**: Updates can include performance improvements that optimize the software's efficiency.

- **Compatibility**: Updates ensure compatibility with new hardware, software, or platforms.

Here are its challenges and considerations:

- **Testing**: Before deploying updates, thorough testing is essential to avoid unforeseen issues

- **Downtime**: Some updates may require system downtime, which should be scheduled strategically to minimize disruptions

- **Rollback strategy**: Always have a rollback plan in case an update causes unexpected problems

- **Customizations**: Updates can overwrite custom configurations, so plan for reconfiguration if necessary

- **Dependency management**: Updates might affect other software components or dependencies, requiring adjustments

The following are some cloud-specific update considerations:

- For **Infrastructure-as-a-Service** (**IaaS**), you need to manage updates for both the operating system and software installed on the virtual machines

- With **Platform-as-a-Service** (**PaaS**), the cloud provider often handles the underlying infrastructure updates, while you manage application updates

- **Software-as-a-Service** (**SaaS**) providers automatically update their software, reducing your responsibility

Now, let's cover some best practices:

- **Regular reviews**: Keep track of software vendors' release notes and security bulletins to identify critical updates

- **Segment updates**: Prioritize critical security updates, and test non-critical updates in a controlled environment first

- **Backups**: Always back up your systems before applying updates to ensure data recovery

- **Testing environment**: Use a testing environment to validate updates' impact before deploying to production

- **Scheduled downtime**: If required, schedule maintenance windows during off-peak hours

- **Automation**: Automate updates where possible, using tools provided by your cloud provider

The following are some cloud provider tools we can use for updates and patching:

- **AWS**: AWS Systems Manager automates patch management across your Amazon EC2 instances
- **Azure**: Azure Update Management allows you to assess and apply updates across your Azure virtual machines
- **GCP**: Google Cloud's Operations Suite offers monitoring, logging, and alerting to track update-related issues

By following best practices and leveraging cloud-specific tools, you can ensure that your systems are kept up to date, secure, and functioning optimally. Updates and patching require a balance between security and continuity, and a well-planned approach helps you achieve both effectively.

Let's understand patching for one of the key components of the cloud: databases.

Updates and patching are crucial tasks in maintaining the security, performance, and reliability of your databases. Keeping your databases up to date with the latest software versions, security patches, and bug fixes is essential to mitigate vulnerabilities and ensure optimal functionality. This section covers various aspects of database updates and patching, including methodologies, best practices, and cloud-specific tools.

Here are some key aspects and considerations:

- **The importance of updates**: Regular updates and patching are necessary to address security vulnerabilities, fix bugs, and introduce new features. Neglecting updates can expose your databases to security risks.
- **Testing**: Before applying updates to production databases, thorough testing is essential. Create a testing environment to ensure that updates don't disrupt your application's functionality.
- **Backup and recovery**: Always back up your databases before applying updates. This ensures that you can revert to a known state in case an update causes unexpected issues.
- **High availability**: Maintain high availability during updates to minimize downtime. Strategies such as database replication, failover, and using standby instances can help ensure uninterrupted service.
- **Cloud provider tools**: Different cloud providers offer tools and services to assist in database updates and patching:
  - **AWS**: Amazon RDS provides automated backups and automated software patching for supported database engines
  - **Azure**: Azure SQL Database offers automatic patching and updates, allowing you to set the maintenance window
  - **GCP**: Google Cloud SQL offers automatic updates, and you can specify a maintenance window for minimal impact

- **Manual versus automated**: Some updates can be done manually, but for large-scale deployments, automated update processes are preferred to save time and ensure consistency.

- **Rolling updates**: Implement rolling updates where updates are applied gradually to different parts of your infrastructure to avoid sudden downtime.

- **Database life cycle management**: Consider the entire database life cycle, from provisioning to updates and retirement, to maintain a healthy database environment.

Here are some best practices:

- **Stay informed**: Regularly check for updates and security patches provided by the database vendor or cloud provider

- **Plan updates**: Develop a plan for applying updates, including a schedule and a strategy for testing

- **Back up data**: Always create backups before applying updates to ensure data recovery in case of issues

- **Test in staging**: Test updates in a staging environment to identify and address potential problems before updating production databases

- **Monitor and validate**: Monitor the performance of updated databases to validate that there are no adverse effects

- **Automate where possible**: Utilize cloud provider tools for automated updates and patching to simplify the process and reduce manual effort

- **Rollback plan**: Prepare a rollback plan in case an update causes unforeseen issues, ensuring you can revert to the previous state

Database updates and patching are ongoing responsibilities for maintaining a secure and well-functioning database environment. By following best practices and leveraging cloud-specific tools, you can ensure that your databases remain up to date, secure, and efficient while minimizing potential disruptions.

Now, let's understand patching for one of the key components of the cloud: operating systems and virtual machines.

Keeping your operating system and virtual machines up to date with the latest patches and updates is crucial for maintaining security, stability, and performance. This involves applying updates to both the operating system and any software installed on the virtual machines. Let's take a detailed look at how to manage updates and patching for operating systems and virtual machines.

Operating system updates are as follows:

- **The importance of operating system updates**: Operating system updates include security patches, bug fixes, and enhancements. They address vulnerabilities that could be exploited by attackers.

- **Patch management tools**: Cloud providers offer tools to manage operating system updates. Here are some examples:

  - **AWS**: AWS Systems Manager provides Patch Manager to automate patching
  - **Azure**: Azure Update Management centrally manages operating system updates
  - **GCP**: Google Compute Engine instances can use managed instance groups with rolling updates

- **Testing**: Before applying operating system updates to production, test them in a staging environment to ensure compatibility with your applications.

VM updates and patching are as follows:

- **Software dependencies**: Virtual machines often host various software applications. Updates should cover both the operating system and these applications to ensure security and functionality.

- **Virtual machine image management**: Create virtual machine images with the latest operating system updates and software configurations to streamline deployment.

- **Automated updates**: Most cloud providers offer automated operating system updates for virtual machine instances. This helps ensure security without manual intervention.

Here are some best practices:

- **Regular review**: Stay informed about operating system and software vendor updates through release notes, security advisories, and notifications.

- **Segment updates**: Prioritize updates based on their criticality. Apply critical security updates promptly and test non-critical updates before deployment.

- **Backup and recovery**: Always take virtual machine snapshots or backups before applying updates so that you have a recovery point in case of issues.

- **Testing environment**: Utilize testing environments to evaluate the impact of updates on your applications and configurations.

- **Automation**: Automate updates where possible to ensure consistency and timely application of patches.

Now, let's consider some challenges:

- **Compatibility**: Updates may affect software dependencies or configurations. Test to avoid disruptions.

- **Downtime:** Some updates require virtual machine restarts, which can cause temporary service disruptions.

- **Rollback planning**: Have a plan to revert to previous states if updates cause unforeseen problems.

Managing updates and patching for operating systems and virtual machines is a fundamental practice in ensuring the security and reliability of your cloud infrastructure. By following best practices and leveraging the tools provided by your cloud provider, you can maintain a robust and up-to-date environment while minimizing potential risks.

Let's discuss an example of applying a patch to a cloud component.

In Azure, you can apply patches to the operating system of your virtual machines using Azure Update Management. This service allows you to automate the patching process for your Azure virtual machines, ensuring they remain up to date and secure. Here's how you can apply patches to the operating system in Azure:

1. **Enable update management**:

    A. Go to the Azure portal (`https://portal.azure.com/`).

    B. Navigate to the virtual machine you want to patch.

    C. Under the **Operations** section, select **Update management**.

2. **Create an update deployment**:

    A. In the **Update management** blade, click **Schedule update deployment**.

    B. Configure the deployment settings:

        a. Select the target VMs or VM groups.

        b. Choose a patching schedule (one-time or recurring).

        c. Set maintenance windows to control when patches are installed.

        d. Define patch classifications and severity levels.

3. **Review and deploy patches**:

    A. Review the settings and click **Review + Create**.

    B. Once reviewed, click **Create** to start the deployment.

4. **Monitor progress**:

    A. In the **Update management** blade, you can monitor the progress of the deployment.

    B. You'll see details about the status of patches being downloaded and installed.

5. **Verify patching**:

    -   After the deployment is complete, you can verify the patching status by checking the update compliance report.

Azure Update Management provides a centralized and automated way to manage patching across your Azure VMs. It helps streamline the patching process, ensures timely application of security updates, and provides visibility into the compliance status of your virtual machines. This approach helps you maintain a secure and up-to-date operating system environment without manual intervention.

With this, we can conclude this chapter.

Summary

This chapter, *Monitoring and Management*, offered an in-depth exploration of the critical practices that are essential for successfully managing cloud environments. It started by underscoring the significance of real-time monitoring and alerts, elucidating how continuous monitoring aids in early issue detection and rapid response, thus ensuring system stability and user satisfaction. The subsequent focus on cloud-specific monitoring tools unveiled a range of sophisticated solutions tailored to each major cloud provider. These tools empower users with insights into resource utilization, performance metrics, and operational trends, enabling informed decision-making.

Transitioning to the concept of automated scaling and resource management, this chapter emphasized the dynamic nature of cloud computing. Automated scaling mechanisms, powered by advanced algorithms and rules, dynamically adjust resources to match varying workloads. This optimization ensures cost-efficiency, eliminates the risk of under or overprovisioning, and guarantees consistent performance under fluctuating demand scenarios.

This chapter then delved into the crucial area of updates and patching. This section spotlighted strategies for maintaining the health and security of cloud environments through regular updates and patches. The explanation encompassed the significance of staying up to date, considerations when planning updates, and best practices to minimize disruptions.

By dissecting these pivotal topics, this chapter provided you with comprehensive insights and skills for proficiently managing cloud environments. From real-time monitoring to automated scaling, from cloud-specific tools to updates and patching strategies, you gained a comprehensive toolkit to ensure optimal performance, scalability, security, and resilience in your cloud endeavors. The integration of cloud-native tools and methodologies not only streamlines management but also empowers users to harness the full potential of cloud computing for their organizational success.

In the upcoming chapter, *Backup and Restore Mechanisms*, you will explore essential practices surrounding data protection and recovery within cloud environments. This chapter will provide an in-depth examination of various backup strategies, restoration mechanisms, and optimal practices customized for cloud infrastructures. By delving into topics such as data backup methodologies, retention policies, disaster recovery planning, and efficient restoration protocols, you will acquire a comprehensive understanding of how to ensure data safety and availability in cloud settings. Through practical examples and insights specific to cloud operations, you will grasp the skills required to choose the right backup solutions, design robust disaster recovery strategies, navigate data retention policies, and expertly manage data recovery processes. This chapter will equip you with the knowledge to establish robust data protection measures, respond effectively to data loss situations, and bolster overall business continuity and resilience in the cloud.

11

Backup and Restore Mechanisms

This chapter, *Backup and Restore Mechanisms*, delves into the critical aspects of data protection and recovery in cloud computing. In this chapter, you can expect a thorough exploration of various backup and restoration strategies, techniques, and best practices tailored to the cloud environment. Key topics that will be covered in this chapter include the following:

- **Data backup strategies**: An in-depth look at different backup strategies, such as full backups, incremental backups, and differential backups, and when to use each

- **Retention policies**: Understanding how to define and implement data retention policies to meet compliance requirements and business needs

- **Disaster recovery (DR) planning**: Strategies for DR planning, including backup storage locations, data redundancy, **recovery time objectives (RTOs)**, and **recovery point objectives (RPOs)**

By the end of this chapter, you will have a comprehensive understanding of how to protect your data assets in the cloud and be able to create effective DRPs, meet compliance requirements, and confidently perform backup and restoration operations using cloud-native tools and best practices.

Technical requirements

To fully engage with the content of this chapter on cloud computing architecture, you should have a basic understanding of computer systems, networking concepts, and information technology.

Additionally, the following technical requirements are recommended:

- **Internet access**: You should have a reliable internet connection to access online resources, references, and examples related to cloud computing.

- **Computing device**: A desktop computer, laptop, tablet, or smartphone with a modern web browser is necessary to read the chapter content and access any online materials.

- **Web browser**: The latest version of a modern web browser such as Google Chrome, Mozilla Firefox, Microsoft Edge, or Safari is recommended. This ensures compatibility and optimal viewing experience of web-based resources and interactive content.

- **Familiarity with cloud services**: Some familiarity with cloud services and their basic functionalities will enhance the understanding of the chapter. This includes knowledge of basic backup and restore operations, basic database and networking concepts, OS, and servers.

Data backup strategies

The section on data backup strategies is a fundamental exploration of various approaches to safeguarding data in cloud environments. You will gain a deep understanding of the different backup strategies available, including full backups, incremental backups, and differential backups. You will learn when to employ each strategy, depending on your data protection needs, recovery goals, and resource constraints. By comprehending these strategies, you will be well equipped to make informed decisions on how to effectively and efficiently back up your critical data in the cloud, ensuring its availability and recoverability in case of unforeseen incidents or data loss scenarios.

Data backup strategies are essential components of any robust data protection plan, especially in cloud computing, where data is the lifeblood of digital operations. This section explores various backup strategies and provides an in-depth understanding of each.

Full backups

A full backup involves copying all data in a system or dataset to a backup location. While this ensures comprehensive data recovery, it can be resource-intensive and time-consuming, making it ideal for critical data that doesn't change frequently.

Here, I'll provide a detailed overview of full backups, their characteristics, advantages, and considerations.

The characteristics of full backups include the following:

- **Comprehensive data capture**: A full backup captures all the data in a given system or dataset, leaving no file or piece of information behind. This includes both active and archived data.

- **Independent restore point**: Full backups create an independent restore point. This means that you can restore data from a full backup without the need for any previous backup files. It stands alone as a complete snapshot of your data.

- **Resource-intensive**: Creating full backups can be resource-intensive in terms of storage space, network bandwidth, and time. This is because every piece of data is copied in its entirety, regardless of whether it has changed since the last backup.

Advantages of full backups include:

- **Simplicity and reliability**: Full backups are straightforward to create and restore from. There's no need to track multiple backup versions or worry about the order of restore operations. This simplicity can be advantageous, especially for critical data.

- **Complete data recovery**: Full backups offer the highest level of data recovery assurance. In the event of data loss, you can restore your entire dataset to a specific point in time, ensuring no data is left behind.

- **Independence**: Each full backup is independent of previous backups. If one full backup becomes corrupt or unavailable, you can still rely on others to restore your data.

The considerations for full backups include the following:

- **Resource usage**: Due to their comprehensive nature, full backups consume significant storage space and can strain network resources during backup operations. This makes them less suitable for frequent backups of large datasets.

- **Backup window**: The time required to perform a full backup can be substantial. Organizations need to plan for backup windows that won't disrupt regular operations.

- **Retention and cost**: Storing multiple full backups over time can lead to higher storage costs compared to incremental or differential backups.

The use cases include the following:

- **Critical data**: Full backups are often used for critical data that requires the highest level of protection and assurance in case of data loss

- **DR**: They are a key component of **DR plans** (**DRPs**), ensuring a complete dataset can be restored in the event of catastrophic data loss

Full backups are a reliable and straightforward data protection strategy, ideal for safeguarding critical data and ensuring comprehensive recovery capabilities. However, their resource-intensive nature and storage requirements should be carefully considered when implementing backup strategies in a cloud or an on-premises environment.

Incremental backups

Incremental backups only copy data that has changed since the last backup, reducing storage and bandwidth requirements. These backups are faster and more efficient, but restoring data requires the most recent full backup and all subsequent incremental backups. Incremental backups are a data protection strategy that captures and stores only data that has changed since the last backup, whether it's a full backup or a previous incremental backup. This approach offers efficiency in terms of storage space and backup duration. Next, I'll provide a detailed overview of incremental backups, including their characteristics, advantages, and considerations.

The characteristics of incremental backups include the following:

- **Capturing changes**: Incremental backups focus on changes made to data since the last backup. This can include newly created files, modified files, or deleted files (as deletion is considered a change).

- **Dependency on previous backups**: To restore data from an incremental backup, you need the most recent full backup and all subsequent incremental backups in the correct order. Each incremental backup relies on the previous backup for a complete dataset.

- **Reduced resource usage**: Compared to full backups, incremental backups are more resource-efficient. They require less storage space and less time to execute since they capture only changed data.

The advantages of incremental backups include the following:

- **Efficiency**: Incremental backups are efficient in terms of storage and bandwidth usage. They reduce the amount of data that needs to be transferred and stored since only changes are captured.

- **Faster backup operations**: Since only changed data is backed up, incremental backups are quicker to perform than full backups. This reduces the impact on network resources and minimizes the backup window.

- **Lower storage costs**: Storing incremental backups generally requires less storage space compared to full backups, making it a cost-effective strategy for long-term data retention.

The considerations for incremental backups include:

- **Dependency on chain**: Incremental backups are dependent on the entire backup chain. If any part of the chain becomes corrupted or unavailable, it can affect the ability to restore data.

- **Restore complexity**: Restoring data from incremental backups can be more complex, as you need to ensure that all necessary incremental backups are available and in the correct order.

- **Resource efficiency versus full recovery**: While incremental backups are resource-efficient, they may not provide the same level of data recovery assurance as full backups in certain scenarios.

The use cases include:

- **Frequent backups**: Incremental backups are ideal for situations where frequent backups are necessary, such as backing up data multiple times a day

- **Balancing resources**: They help balance resource usage (storage, bandwidth, and processing) by capturing only the most recent changes

- **Backup window reduction**: Organizations with limited backup windows can benefit from the faster execution of incremental backups

Incremental backups offer a balance between resource efficiency and data recovery capabilities. They are particularly suitable for scenarios where frequent backups are needed and resource constraints must be managed effectively. However, their dependency on previous backups requires careful management to ensure reliable data restoration.

Differential backups

Differential backups are another approach to data protection, distinct from both full and incremental backups. These backups capture all changes made to data since the last full backup, providing a middle ground between the comprehensive nature of full backups and the efficiency of incremental backups. Here's a detailed overview of differential backups.

The characteristics of differential backups include:

- **Capturing changes since the last full backup**: A differential backup captures all changes made to data since the last full backup. Unlike incremental backups, it doesn't rely on the previous backup in the chain; instead, it captures changes since the last full backup.

- **Independent restore point**: Similar to a full backup, a differential backup creates an independent restore point. It can be used alone to restore data to a specific point in time without the need for other differential backups.

- **Cumulative changes**: Differential backups accumulate changes made to the data over time. For example, the second differential backup captures changes since the first differential backup, and so on.

The advantages of differential backups include:

- **Simplicity of restoration**: Restoring data from differential backups is simpler compared to incremental backups. To restore to a specific point in time, you only need the last full backup and the most recent differential backup.

- **Less dependency**: Differential backups are less dependent on the backup chain compared to incremental backups. You only need the most recent full backup and the latest differential backup for restoration.

- **Faster restoration than incremental backups**: While differential backups capture more data than incremental backups, they usually require fewer backup files for restoration, making the process faster.

The considerations for differential backups include:

- **Increasing size over time**: Since a differential backup captures all changes since the last full backup, its size tends to increase over time. This can impact storage requirements.

- **Backup window**: Depending on the frequency of full backups, the backup window might be longer for differential backups compared to incremental backups.

The use cases include:

- **Balancing between full and incremental**: Differential backups provide a balance between the comprehensive nature of full backups and the efficiency of incremental backups

- **Simplified restoration**: They are suitable for scenarios where a simplified restoration process is preferred over the more complex restoration process of incremental backups

In summary, differential backups offer a middle ground between the simplicity of full backups and the efficiency of incremental backups. They provide a compromise in terms of storage efficiency and ease of restoration, making them suitable for certain backup strategies and data protection requirements.

Synthetic full backups

Synthetic full backups are a strategy in data protection that creates a full backup by combining a previous full backup with subsequent incremental or differential backups. This process is performed without the need to read all data from the source, providing efficiency in terms of time and resource usage. Here's a detailed overview of synthetic full backups.

The characteristics of synthetic full backups include:

- **Combining incremental or differential backups**: Instead of creating a new full backup by reading all data from the source, a synthetic full backup combines a previous full backup with subsequent incremental or differential backups.

- **Reduced source impact**: Since synthetic full backups don't involve reading data directly from the source, they reduce the impact on the source system. This is particularly beneficial when the source system experiences high workloads or performance constraints.

- **Creation at the backup location**: Synthetic full backups are typically created at the backup location or storage repository rather than at the source system. This can be performed by the backup software or appliance.

The advantages of synthetic full backups include:

- **Reduced source load**: By not directly accessing the source system, synthetic full backups minimize the impact on the source system's performance during backup operations

- **Time and resource efficiency**: Creating a synthetic full backup is often faster and more resource-efficient than reading all data from the source, especially in scenarios with large datasets

- **Storage efficiency**: Synthetic full backups contribute to storage efficiency by consolidating changes from incremental or differential backups into a new full backup without duplicating unchanged data

The considerations for synthetic full backups include:

- **Dependency on previous backups**: Similar to incremental and differential backups, synthetic full backups depend on the availability of the previous full backup and subsequent incremental or differential backups

- **Storage impact**: While synthetic full backups contribute to storage efficiency, they still require sufficient storage space to store the consolidated full backup

The use cases include:

- **Reducing backup window**: Synthetic full backups are suitable for scenarios where reducing the backup window is critical, as they can be created faster than traditional full backups

- **Minimizing source impact**: Organizations with source systems that are sensitive to performance impact during backup operations can benefit from synthetic full backups

- **Storage optimization**: Synthetic full backups contribute to storage optimization by creating consolidated full backups without duplicating unchanged data

In summary, synthetic full backups offer a strategy to create efficient full backups by combining previous full backups with incremental or differential backups. They provide advantages in terms of reduced source impact, time efficiency, and storage optimization, making them a valuable component of a comprehensive backup strategy.

Mirror backups

Mirror backups, also known as copy backups, involve creating an exact copy of the source data in a separate location without any form of compression or incremental changes. Here's a detailed discussion of mirror backups.

The characteristics of mirror backups include:

- **Full copy of source data**: Mirror backups involve copying the entire dataset, creating an identical, uncompressed replica of the source data

- **Independent of incremental changes**: Unlike incremental or differential backups that capture changes made since the last backup, mirror backups are standalone copies, independent of previous backups

- **Not storage-efficient**: Mirror backups are not storage-efficient because they replicate the entire dataset every time, even if only a small portion has changed

The advantages of mirror backups include:

- **Simplicity**: Mirror backups are straightforward and easy to understand. They involve a direct, full copy of the source data without complex algorithms for tracking changes.

- **Independence:** Each mirror backup is independent, making it suitable for scenarios where you might want a standalone copy of the data, unaffected by the history of incremental changes.

- **Quick recovery:** Since each mirror backup is a complete copy of the data, the recovery process is straightforward and quick.

The considerations for mirror backups include:

- **Storage requirements:** Mirror backups consume a significant amount of storage space, as they duplicate the entire dataset

- **Time and resources:** Creating mirror backups can be time-consuming and resource-intensive, especially when dealing with large datasets

The use cases include:

- **Data archiving:** Mirror backups can be used for archiving purposes when you need a complete, independent copy of the data at a specific point in time

- **Data duplication:** In scenarios where maintaining an exact replica is crucial, such as for regulatory compliance or data validation, mirror backups can be useful

Here's a comparison with other backup types:

- **Differential and incremental backups:** Mirror backups contrast with differential and incremental backups, which focus on capturing changes since the last backup, making them more storage-efficient but potentially complex

- **Synthetic full backups:** Unlike synthetic full backups that consolidate changes into a new full backup, mirror backups create standalone, complete copies

In summary, mirror backups offer a straightforward approach to data protection by creating full, independent copies of the source data. While they may not be as storage-efficient as incremental or differential backups, they are valuable in scenarios where maintaining exact replicas or creating independent copies is a priority.

Continuous data protection

Continuous data protection (CDP) is a backup and recovery technique that enables the real-time or near-real-time capture of every change made to data. This approach ensures that the backup is a mirror image of the production system at any point in time, providing a comprehensive and granular backup strategy. Here's a detailed discussion of CDP.

The characteristics of CDP include:

- **Real-time or near-real-time:** CDP captures changes to data as they occur or at very short intervals, ensuring that the backup is almost in sync with the production system.

- **Granular recovery points**: CDP allows for granular recovery points, meaning that you can restore data to any specific point in time, not just predefined intervals.

- **Minimal RPO**: CDP aims to minimize the RPO, representing the amount of data loss in the event of a failure. With near-real-time capture, the data loss is typically minimal.

- **Continuous monitoring**: CDP systems continuously monitor changes at the block or file level, depending on the implementation, to ensure that every modification is captured.

The advantages of CDP include:

- **Minimized data loss**: CDP significantly reduces data loss in the event of a failure because changes are captured almost instantly

- **Granular recovery**: The ability to restore to any specific point in time provides granularity in recovery, allowing for precise restoration of data

- **Reduced backup windows**: Since CDP operates continuously, there is no need for large backup windows that may impact production systems

- **Less impact on production systems**: CDP systems often have minimal impact on the performance of production systems since they capture changes at a low level

The considerations for CDP include:

- **Resource intensiveness**: CDP systems can be resource-intensive, especially if changes are captured at a very fine level of granularity

- **Storage requirements**: Continuous capture of changes can lead to significant storage requirements, especially for systems with high transaction rates

The use cases include:

- **Mission-critical systems**: CDP is often employed for mission-critical systems where minimizing data loss is crucial

- **Regulatory compliance**: In industries with stringent regulatory requirements, CDP ensures that data is continuously protected and recoverable

Here's a comparison with other backup types:

- **Incremental backups**: CDP differs from traditional incremental backups by capturing changes continuously rather than at predefined intervals

- **Snapshot-based backups**: While both CDP and snapshots capture changes, CDP provides a more continuous and granular approach

In summary, CDP is a backup strategy that aims to minimize data loss by capturing changes in near real time. It offers granular recovery options and is particularly valuable for mission-critical systems where minimizing downtime and data loss is essential. However, it's important to consider resource requirements and storage implications when implementing CDP.

Snapshot backups

Snapshot backups are a method of capturing the state of a system or data at a specific point in time. Unlike traditional backups that copy data to a separate location, snapshots create a **point-in-time (PIT)** reference or *snapshot* of the data in its current state. Here's a detailed discussion of snapshot backups.

The characteristics of snapshot backups include:

- **PIT capture**: Snapshots capture the state of data at a specific moment, creating a reference point for recovery.

- **Incremental changes**: Subsequent snapshots only capture changes made since the last snapshot. This is achieved through the use of pointers or copy-on-write mechanisms, making snapshots more storage-efficient.

- **Fast and efficient**: Creating a snapshot is generally fast and efficient, as it involves recording differences rather than copying the entire dataset.

- **Read-only reference**: Snapshots are typically read-only references to the data. They allow users to view or revert to the state of the data at the time of the snapshot.

The advantages of snapshot backups include:

- **Fast recovery**: Snapshots enable fast recovery by providing a PIT reference that can be used to roll back data to a specific state.

- **Storage efficiency**: Since snapshots capture incremental changes, they are more storage-efficient compared to full backups. Only changes since the last snapshot need to be stored.

- **Low impact**: Snapshot creation has a minimal impact on system performance, making them suitable for environments where downtime must be minimized.

The considerations for snapshot backups include:

- **Dependency on storage technology**: The effectiveness of snapshot backups depends on the underlying storage technology. Some storage systems may not support efficient snapshot creation or may have limitations.

- **Limited retention**: Snapshots are typically retained for a limited duration due to storage constraints. Long-term retention may require additional storage resources.

The use cases include:

- **Quick rollback**: Snapshots are useful for quickly rolling back data to a known good state in case of errors or data corruption

- **Testing and development**: Snapshots provide a convenient way to create a baseline for testing and development environments

Here's a comparison with other backup types:

- **CDP**: CDP captures changes continuously, while snapshots provide PIT references. CDP may offer more granularity in recovery.

- **Incremental backups**: Snapshots are similar to incremental backups in that they capture changes, but snapshots are typically more space-efficient.

In summary, snapshot backups provide a fast and efficient way to capture the state of data at specific points in time. They are useful for quick recovery and are particularly effective when storage efficiency is a priority. However, the effectiveness of snapshots may depend on the underlying storage technology and the specific requirements of the environment.

Cloud-native backup solutions

Cloud-native backup solutions are specifically designed to address the unique challenges and opportunities presented by cloud environments. These solutions leverage the characteristics of cloud platforms to provide efficient, scalable, and cost-effective backup and recovery capabilities. Here's a detailed discussion of cloud-native backup solutions.

The characteristics of cloud-native backup solutions include:

- **Scalability**: Cloud-native backup solutions can scale dynamically to accommodate the growing volume of data in cloud environments. They leverage the elastic nature of cloud resources.

- **Cost efficiency**: These solutions are often designed to optimize costs by taking advantage of cloud storage tiers, which offer different performance and cost characteristics.

- **Automation**: Cloud-native backup solutions incorporate automation features for scheduling, policy management, and life-cycle management of backups. This reduces the need for manual intervention.

- **Integration with cloud services**: They seamlessly integrate with native cloud services, such as object storage, **identity and access management** (**IAM**), and monitoring tools.

- **Security**: Cloud-native backup solutions are built with a focus on security, incorporating encryption, access controls, and compliance features to ensure the protection of backup data.

The advantages of cloud-native backup solutions include:

- **Flexibility**: Cloud-native solutions are flexible and can adapt to various cloud architectures and deployment models

- **Reduced management overhead**: Automation and integration with cloud services reduce the operational burden on IT teams, allowing them to focus on higher-value tasks

- **Cost optimization**: These solutions often leverage cloud-native storage options, such as object storage with different storage classes, optimizing costs based on the access patterns of backup data.

- **Global accessibility**: Cloud-native solutions enable data to be backed up and recovered from anywhere with internet connectivity, supporting the global nature of cloud environments.

The considerations for cloud-native backup solutions include:

- **Vendor lock-in**: Depending on the specific solution, there might be considerations related to vendor lock-in if the backup solution is tightly coupled with a particular cloud provider

- **Data transfer costs**: Consideration should be given to data transfer costs associated with moving backup data between cloud regions or between on-premises and the cloud

The use cases include:

- **Cloud-native applications**: Organizations running applications designed for the cloud can benefit from backup solutions that seamlessly integrate with their cloud architecture

- **Hybrid cloud environments**: Cloud-native backup solutions are suitable for environments that span both on-premises and cloud infrastructure

Here's a comparison with other backup types:

- **Traditional backup solutions**: Cloud-native solutions differ from traditional solutions in their design for cloud environments, leveraging cloud services and optimizing for scalability and cost-effectiveness

- **Legacy on-premises backup solutions**: Cloud-native solutions offer advantages over on-premises solutions in terms of flexibility, scalability, and cost efficiency, particularly in cloud-centric or hybrid environments

Cloud-native backup solutions are tailored to the characteristics of cloud environments, offering flexibility, scalability, and cost-effectiveness. They play a crucial role in ensuring the availability and recoverability of data in modern, cloud-centric IT architectures.

The *Data backup strategies* section comprehensively covered a spectrum of methodologies crucial for effective data protection. It began by dissecting the concept of full backups, providing you with insights into creating complete snapshots of data at specific intervals. Incremental backups were explored, shedding light on their efficiency in capturing changes since the last backup and optimizing storage usage. The discussion extended to the benefits of differential backups, offering a balance between storage efficiency and simplified restoration processes. Synthetic full backups were introduced, illustrating how combining full and incremental backups enhances restore operations. Mirror backups were examined for their redundancy benefits, providing an exact duplicate of critical data. CDP was elucidated as a method for real-time change capture, ensuring high granularity for recovery. Snapshot backups, creating read-only references at specific moments, were also explored. The section concluded with an exploration of cloud-native backup solutions, emphasizing scalability, automation, and cost-effectiveness in cloud environments. You, therefore, gained a nuanced understanding of each strategy's advantages, considerations, and optimal use cases, and you are now empowered to implement tailored and resilient data backup approaches.

The next section, *Retention policies*, focuses on the crucial aspect of determining how long different data backups should be retained. Retention policies play a pivotal role in data management, addressing questions of compliance, storage optimization, and the need for historical data. This section will delve into considerations involved in setting retention periods for various types of backups, exploring best practices to strike a balance between regulatory requirements and operational efficiency. Additionally, it will discuss how retention policies align with broader data governance strategies, ensuring that organizations retain data for as long as necessary while avoiding unnecessary storage costs and compliance risks. You can expect to gain insights into crafting effective retention policies that align with your specific business needs and compliance obligations.

Retention policies

Retention policies are a critical component of data management, dictating how long different types of data, particularly backups, should be retained. The establishment of effective retention policies is vital for regulatory compliance, optimizing storage resources, and ensuring the availability of historical data when needed. Here's a detailed exploration of the topic.

Regulatory compliance

Retention policies are often influenced by legal and regulatory requirements governing data storage. Industries such as finance, healthcare, and others may have specific mandates on how long certain types of data must be retained. Regulatory compliance refers to the adherence of an organization's processes, policies, and practices to laws and regulations relevant to its industry and geographical location. In the context of data management, including backups, regulatory compliance is crucial for ensuring that organizations meet legal obligations regarding the handling, storage, and protection of sensitive information. Here's a detailed exploration of the topic:

- **Data protection laws**: Compliance often starts with adherence to data protection laws, such as the **General Data Protection Regulation (GDPR)** in Europe, the **Health Insurance Portability and Accountability Act (HIPAA)** in the US healthcare sector, or the **Personal Information Protection and Electronic Documents Act (PIPEDA)** in Canada. Understanding the specific requirements of these laws is fundamental to compliance.

- **Industry-specific regulations**: Different industries may have specific regulations. For example, financial institutions need to comply with regulations such as the **Sarbanes-Oxley Act (SOX)** or the **Payment Card Industry Data Security Standard (PCI DSS)**. Healthcare organizations must adhere to regulations such as HIPAA. Compliance requires a deep understanding of these industry-specific laws.

- **Data handling and storage standards**: Regulatory compliance often involves following specific standards for data handling and storage. This can include encryption requirements, access controls, and secure transmission protocols. Compliance ensures that sensitive data is treated according to established best practices.

- **Data retention requirements**: Many regulations specify the duration for which certain types of data should be retained. For instance, financial records may need to be retained for a minimum number of years. Compliance involves establishing and adhering to these retention periods.

- **Data security measures**: Compliance often mandates specific security measures, such as encryption of sensitive data, regular security audits, and the implementation of access controls. Organizations need to ensure that their data management practices align with these security requirements.

- **Data breach notification**: Some regulations require organizations to notify authorities and affected individuals in the event of a data breach. Compliance involves having mechanisms in place to detect and respond to breaches promptly.

- **Documentation and auditing**: Compliance is not only about implementing measures but also about documenting those measures and being able to demonstrate compliance through audits. This involves maintaining detailed records of data management practices, security measures, and compliance efforts.

- **International considerations**: In a globalized world, organizations may need to consider compliance with regulations from different jurisdictions. Understanding the extraterritorial reach of certain laws is crucial for multinational organizations.

- **Adaptability to regulatory changes**: Regulatory landscapes are dynamic, and laws can change. Compliance involves not only meeting current regulations but also having processes in place to adapt to changes in the legal environment.

- **Legal consequences of non-compliance**: Non-compliance can lead to severe consequences, including fines, legal actions, and damage to reputation. Understanding potential legal ramifications is essential for prioritizing compliance efforts.

Regulatory compliance in the context of data management ensures that organizations operate within the legal frameworks that govern the handling of sensitive information. It involves a proactive approach to understanding and adhering to applicable laws and standards, implementing robust security measures, and being prepared to adapt to changes in the regulatory landscape. Compliance is not just a legal requirement; it is a fundamental aspect of responsible and ethical business practices.

Business continuity

Retention policies should align with the organization's continuity and DR strategies. This involves determining the duration for which backup data needs to be stored to facilitate effective recovery in the event of data loss or system failures. **Business continuity (BC)** is a comprehensive strategy that encompasses the processes, procedures, and resources an organization puts in place to ensure that essential business functions can continue during and after a disaster or disruptive event. The goal of BC planning is to maintain operations, minimize downtime, and recover quickly from disruptions. Here's a detailed exploration of the topic:

- **Risk assessment**: BC planning begins with a thorough risk assessment. This involves identifying potential risks and understanding their potential impact on business operations. Risks can include natural disasters, cyber-attacks, supply chain disruptions, and more.

- **Business impact analysis (BIA)**: BIA is a crucial step in understanding critical processes and functions within an organization. It helps identify the resources required to support these functions and assess the potential financial and operational impact of disruptions.

- **Development of BC strategies**: Based on the risk assessment and BIA, organizations develop strategies to ensure the continuity of critical functions. This involves creating plans for alternate work locations, data backup and recovery, communication strategies, and more.

- **Data backup and recovery**: BC relies heavily on the ability to back up and recover data. This includes regular backups of critical information and systems, offsite storage, and a robust recovery plan to restore data and operations quickly.

- **Alternate work locations**: Organizations must have plans for alternate work locations in case the primary workplace becomes unusable. This can involve having backup offices, allowing employees to work remotely, or establishing agreements with co-working spaces.

- **Communication plans**: Effective communication is vital during a crisis. **BC plans (BCPs)** include detailed communication strategies for internal and external stakeholders. This ensures that everyone is informed and knows which steps to take.

- **Employee training and awareness**: Employees play a crucial role in BC. Training programs ensure that employees are aware of BCPs, their roles during a crisis, and the steps they need to take to ensure a smooth recovery. The following are key areas:

  - **Testing and exercising**: BCPs are not effective unless they are regularly tested and updated. Organizations conduct drills and exercises to simulate various scenarios, identify weaknesses, and improve the overall effectiveness of the plan.

  - **Supply chain resilience**: Organizations are often interconnected with suppliers and partners. BCPs extend beyond the immediate organization to include strategies for ensuring the resilience of the entire supply chain.

- **Insurance and financial strategies**: In addition to operational strategies, BC planning involves financial considerations. This includes having appropriate insurance coverage to mitigate financial losses and having financial strategies for sustaining operations during a crisis.

- **Regulatory compliance**: Depending on the industry, there may be regulatory requirements regarding BC planning. Compliance with these regulations is a critical aspect of overall business resilience.

- **Continuous improvement**: BC planning is an iterative process. Organizations continuously review and improve their plans based on feedback from exercises, changes in the business environment, and emerging threats.

BC is a holistic approach to ensuring that organizations can withstand and recover from disruptions. It involves a combination of strategic planning, technological solutions, employee training, and ongoing evaluation to create a resilient and adaptive organization. A robust BCP is a key element of risk management and ensures that an organization can continue to deliver its products or services even in the face of adversity.

Data life cycle

Different types of data have varied life cycles. Retention policies take into account the relevance and usefulness of data over time. For instance, customer transaction data may have a shorter retention period than historical financial records. The data life cycle refers to the stages that data goes through from its creation to its eventual deletion or archival. Understanding the data life cycle is crucial for organizations to manage and derive value from their data effectively. Here's a detailed exploration of the data life cycle:

- **Data creation**: The life cycle begins with the creation of data. This can occur through various means such as user input, sensor readings, system logs, or other data sources. The format and structure of the data are established at this stage.

- **Data ingestion**: Once created, data needs to be ingested into storage or processing systems. This involves moving data from its source to a centralized repository, which could be a database, data warehouse, or data lake. Ingestion methods may vary depending on the type and volume of data.

- **Data storage**: Data is stored in a structured or unstructured format depending on the storage system. This stage involves decisions about where and how data is stored, considering factors such as accessibility, performance, and cost. Storage solutions range from traditional databases to cloud-based storage services.

- **Data processing and analysis**: Data is often processed and analyzed to derive insights or support decision-making. This stage involves the use of analytics tools, **machine learning** (**ML**) algorithms, and other processing methods. The goal is to transform raw data into meaningful information.

- **Data usage:** The processed data is used for various purposes, such as generating reports, making business decisions, or training ML models. Different stakeholders across an organization may use the data for their specific needs.

- **Data sharing:** Organizations often share data internally between departments or externally with partners and customers. Data sharing involves ensuring that the right people have access to the right data while maintaining security and compliance.

- **Data archiving:** As data ages, it may move to an archival state. Archiving involves storing data that is no longer actively used but may be needed for compliance, historical analysis, or other purposes. Archival systems should provide efficient retrieval when needed.

- **Data deletion:** Data that is no longer needed or has reached the end of its life cycle should be securely deleted. This is crucial for compliance with data protection regulations and helps organizations manage storage costs.

- **Data retention policies:** Organizations define data retention policies to govern how long different types of data should be retained. These policies are influenced by regulatory requirements, business needs, and data value over time.

- **Data governance:** Data governance encompasses policies, procedures, and standards for managing data throughout its life cycle. This includes data quality, security, and compliance measures to ensure that data is used responsibly and ethically.

- **Data security:** Ensuring the security of data at every stage is critical. This involves implementing access controls, encryption, and other security measures to protect data from unauthorized access or breaches.

- **Data backup and recovery:** Regularly backing up critical data is essential to ensure its availability in case of data loss or system failures. Data recovery plans are crucial for restoring data to a consistent state after an incident.

- **Data retirement:** Data that is no longer of value or relevance to the organization may be retired. This involves a formal process of identifying and decommissioning datasets that are no longer needed.

Understanding and effectively managing the data life cycle contributes to better data governance, improved decision-making, and compliance with data protection regulations. Organizations that implement robust data life-cycle management practices can derive more value from their data assets while mitigating risks associated with data misuse, loss, or unauthorized access.

Storage optimization

Balancing the need for data availability with storage costs is crucial. Retention policies help in optimizing storage resources by defining when data can be safely purged without compromising compliance or operational needs. Storage optimization is a crucial aspect of managing data efficiently, ensuring cost-effectiveness, and maintaining performance. It involves strategies and techniques to make the most of storage resources, whether they are on-premises or in the cloud. Here's a detailed exploration of storage optimization:

- **Data compression**:
    - *Definition*: Compression reduces the size of files or datasets, saving storage space
    - *Benefits*: It lowers storage costs and speeds up data transfer

- **Data deduplication**:
    - *Definition*: Deduplication eliminates duplicate copies of the same data, storing only one instance
    - *Benefits*: Reduces storage requirements and improves data management

- **Tiered storage**:
    - *Definition*: Data is categorized based on access frequency, and different storage tiers are used accordingly
    - *Benefits*: Frequently accessed data is stored on faster, more expensive storage, while less accessed data is moved to cost-effective storage

- **Archiving**:
    - *Definition*: Archiving involves moving inactive or infrequently accessed data to long-term storage
    - *Benefits*: Frees up primary storage for active data and reduces costs

- **Life-cycle management**:
    - *Definition*: Data life-cycle policies automate the movement of data through different storage tiers based on predefined criteria
    - *Benefits*: Ensures that data is stored on the most suitable storage class at each stage of its life cycle

- **Storage virtualization**:
    - *Definition*: Virtualization abstracts physical storage resources, making them easier to manage
    - *Benefits*: Improves flexibility and simplifies storage management

- **Thin provisioning**:
    - *Definition*: Allocates storage space on demand rather than pre-allocating the full amount
    - *Benefits*: Reduces wasted space and delays the need for additional storage purchases

- **Object storage**:

  - *Definition*: Object storage organizes data as objects, each with a unique identifier

  - *Benefits*: Scalable and cost-effective for large-scale data storage

- **Efficient filesystems**:

  - *Definition*: Optimized filesystems reduce overhead and increase storage efficiency

  - *Benefits*: Improve performance and maximize storage utilization

- **Storage analytics**:

  - *Definition*: Analyzing storage usage helps identify patterns, optimize configurations, and plan for future needs

  - *Benefits*: Informed decision-making for storage allocation and optimization

- **Cloud storage optimization**:

  - *Definition*: Leveraging cloud-native features, such as life-cycle policies and auto-tiering, to optimize storage in cloud environments

  - *Benefits*: Maximizes the cost-effectiveness of cloud storage solutions

- **Data replication strategies**:

  - *Definition*: Replicating data across different storage locations for redundancy and DR

  - *Benefits*: Enhances data availability and ensures BC

- **Storage performance tuning**:

  - *Definition*: Fine-tuning storage systems to optimize performance for specific workloads

  - *Benefits*: Improves application responsiveness and user experience

- **Data archiving best practices**:

  - *Definition*: Following best practices for archiving data, including defining retention policies and ensuring easy retrieval when needed

  - *Benefits*: Maintains compliance, reduces costs, and streamlines data management

- **Monitoring and reporting**:

  - *Definition*: Implementing tools and processes to monitor storage usage, performance, and trends

  - *Benefits*: Enables proactive management and optimization based on real-time insights

Storage optimization is an ongoing process that requires a combination of technology, policies, and best practices. By implementing these strategies, organizations can effectively manage their storage infrastructure, reduce costs, and ensure that storage resources align with business needs.

Data governance

Effective data governance involves not only retaining data for the required duration but also ensuring secure deletion when data is no longer needed. This aligns with the principles of data minimization and privacy. Data governance refers to the overall management of the availability, usability, integrity, and security of the data employed in an enterprise. It involves the orchestration of people, processes, and technology to ensure high data quality, compliance with regulations, and alignment with business goals. Here's a detailed exploration of data governance:

- **Data quality management**:
  - *Objective*: Ensuring that data is accurate, consistent, and meets predefined standards
  - *Activities*: Implementing validation rules, conducting data profiling, and establishing data quality metrics

- **Metadata management**:
  - *Objective*: Managing metadata to provide context and understanding of data
  - *Activities*: Creating a metadata repository, documenting data lineage, and defining data dictionaries

- **Data classification and categorization**:
  - *Objective*: Classifying data based on its sensitivity, criticality, and usage
  - *Activities*: Defining data classification policies, labeling sensitive data, and enforcing access controls accordingly

- **Data security and privacy**:
  - *Objective*: Ensuring the confidentiality, integrity, and availability of data, especially sensitive information
  - *Activities*: Implementing access controls, encryption, and auditing mechanisms to safeguard data

- **Compliance management**:
  - *Objective*: Ensuring that data management practices adhere to regulatory requirements and industry standards
  - *Activities*: Conducting regular compliance audits, implementing necessary controls, and staying informed about relevant regulations

- **Data stewardship**:

  - *Objective*: Assigning responsibility for the oversight and management of specific sets of data

  - *Activities*: Appointing data stewards, defining their roles and responsibilities, and establishing communication channels

- **Master data management (MDM)**:

  - *Objective*: Managing critical business data entities in a centralized and consistent manner.

  - *Activities*: Creating a master data repository, defining data governance policies for master data, and ensuring synchronization across systems

- **Data life-cycle management**:

  - *Objective*: Managing data from its creation to deletion in a structured and efficient manner

  - *Activities*: Defining data retention policies, archiving strategies, and ensuring proper disposal of data

- **Data ownership**:

  - *Objective*: Assigning accountability for specific datasets to individuals or **business units (BUs)**

  - *Activities*: Defining data ownership roles, establishing communication channels between data owners and users, and ensuring data accountability

- **Data governance framework**:

  - *Objective*: Providing a structured approach to data governance that aligns with organizational goals

  - *Activities*: Developing a governance framework that includes policies, processes, and technologies, and ensuring its adoption across the organization

- **Data governance council**:

  - *Objective*: Establishing a governing body responsible for making decisions regarding data governance policies and practices

  - *Activities*: Forming a cross-functional council, defining its charter, and conducting regular meetings to address data governance issues

- **Data quality monitoring and reporting**:

  - *Objective*: Continuously monitoring data quality and providing reports to relevant stakeholders

  - *Activities*: Implementing data quality monitoring tools, defining **key performance indicators (KPIs)**, and generating regular reports

- **Change management**:

  - *Objective*: Managing changes to data-related processes and technologies to minimize risks and ensure compliance

  - *Activities*: Implementing change management processes, conducting impact assessments, and ensuring communication about changes

The benefits of effective data governance include the following:

- **Improved decision-making**: Reliable and high-quality data enhances the accuracy of business decisions

- **Compliance**: Ensures that data practices align with legal and regulatory requirements

- **Efficiency**: Streamlines data-related processes and reduces redundancies

- **Risk mitigation**: Minimizes the risks associated with data breaches, errors, and non-compliance

- **Data transparency**: Provides a clear understanding of data assets and their usage

- **Accountability**: Assigns responsibility for data quality and security, fostering a culture of accountability

Effective data governance is a cornerstone of data management, contributing to organizational success by ensuring that data is a valuable and trusted asset.

Granularity of retention

Different categories of data might have different retention requirements. For instance, critical business transaction data might have a longer retention period compared to routine operational logs. Retention policies should be granular enough to accommodate these variations. The granularity of retention refers to the level of detail at which data is preserved and retained over time. It involves making decisions about how long different categories or types of data should be retained based on their importance, regulatory requirements, and business needs.

The key aspects and considerations include:

- **Data classification**:

  - *Importance of data*: Not all data holds the same level of significance. Critical data may have longer retention periods than less critical data.

  - *Regulatory requirements*: Different data types may be subject to various regulatory mandates specifying retention periods.

- **Business requirements**:

  - *Usage patterns*: The frequency and manner in which data is accessed can influence retention policies. Frequently accessed data might have different retention needs than seldom-used data.

  - *Operational necessities*: The operational requirements of the business, including historical analysis and reporting, can dictate the retention of certain data.

- **Legal and compliance considerations**:

  - *Industry regulations*: Different industries have specific regulations that prescribe how long certain types of data must be retained.

  - *Data privacy laws*: Compliance with data privacy laws, such as GDPR, may necessitate specific retention periods for personal data.

- **Data life cycle**:

  - *Creation to deletion*: Understanding the entire life cycle of data is crucial. This involves not only how data is created and used but also how and when it should be safely deleted or archived.

- **Risk management**:

  - *Data security*: Retaining data for extended periods can pose security risks. Decisions about retention must consider the potential security implications of holding onto data longer than necessary.

  - *Data breach implications*: Retaining sensitive data for longer than needed increases the potential impact in case of a data breach.

- **Operational efficiency**:

  - *Storage costs*: Retaining vast amounts of data can lead to increased storage costs. Optimizing the granularity of retention helps manage storage expenses.

  - *Access and retrieval*: Efficient access to data is essential. Keeping data with varying access patterns in a manner that aligns with business needs can enhance operational efficiency.

- **Technology considerations**:

  - *Archiving solutions*: Implementing effective archiving solutions can allow organizations to retain data at a lower cost, making it feasible to retain certain data for longer periods.

  - *Data aging*: Some data might lose its relevance or accuracy over time. Establishing policies to identify and address aging data is essential.

- **Communication and documentation**:

  - *Clear policies*: Organizations should establish clear policies regarding the granularity of retention. This includes communicating these policies to relevant stakeholders.

  - *Documentation*: Maintaining documentation regarding retention decisions, especially for compliance purposes, is crucial.

The benefits of a well-defined granularity of retention include:

- **Cost efficiency**: Efficiently managing data retention reduces storage costs
- **Compliance**: Helps in meeting regulatory and legal compliance requirements
- **Risk mitigation**: Reduces risk associated with retaining unnecessary or outdated data
- **Operational optimization**: Enhances operational efficiency by aligning data retention with business needs
- **Data security**: Limits the exposure of sensitive information, contributing to improved data security

The challenges include:

- **Balancing act**: Striking the right balance between retaining valuable data and minimizing risk and costs can be challenging
- **Changing requirements**: Keeping policies flexible to adapt to changing regulatory and business requirements

Establishing a granularity of retention involves a strategic approach that considers legal, regulatory, operational, and technological aspects. It's an essential component of effective data governance and management.

Legal discovery and litigation

In the event of legal proceedings, having well-defined retention policies is crucial. These policies guide the preservation and retrieval of relevant data, ensuring the organization is well prepared for legal discovery. Legal discovery, also known as e-discovery, refers to the process of identifying, collecting, and producing **electronically stored information** (**ESI**) as evidence in legal cases. In the context of data management, legal discovery and litigation involve ensuring that an organization's data is properly managed and can be retrieved in compliance with legal requirements.

The key aspects and considerations include:

- **Data identification and preservation**:

  - *Identification of relevant data*: Organizations must have mechanisms in place to identify and preserve data that may be relevant to legal proceedings

- *Preservation protocols*: Implementing protocols to ensure that potentially relevant data is preserved and not altered is critical

- **Data accessibility and retrieval**:

  - *Searchability*: The ability to search and retrieve specific data quickly is crucial during legal discovery

  - *Metadata management*: Effective management of metadata facilitates the efficient retrieval of relevant information

- **Legal hold policies**:

  - *Implementation*: Organizations should have clear policies and procedures for placing legal holds on data, ensuring that relevant information is not deleted or modified during legal proceedings

  - *Communication*: Proper communication of legal holds to relevant personnel is essential

- **Compliance with regulations**:

  - *Data privacy laws*: Adhering to data privacy regulations becomes crucial during legal discovery to avoid potential legal consequences

  - *Industry-specific regulations*: Different industries may have specific regulations regarding the handling and disclosure of data during legal proceedings

- **Collaboration with legal teams**:

  - *Communication channels*: Establishing effective communication channels between IT, data management teams, and legal teams is vital

  - *Understanding legal requirements*: Ensuring that data management teams understand legal requirements and can collaborate seamlessly with legal professionals

- **Technology solutions**:

  - *E-discovery tools*: Implementing e-discovery tools and technologies that aid in the identification, collection, and review of relevant data

  - *Data classification*: Using data classification tools to categorize information and streamline the identification of relevant data

- **Data privacy and redaction**:

  - *Sensitive information*: Identification and redaction of sensitive information to comply with privacy laws and protect individuals' privacy during legal proceedings

- *Consistent practices*: Ensuring consistent practices across different types of data to avoid accidental disclosures

- **Documentation and auditing**:

  - *Audit trails*: Maintaining detailed audit trails of data access and changes to demonstrate compliance with legal requirements

  - *Documentation*: Thorough documentation of the entire legal discovery process, including actions taken and decisions made

The benefits include:

- **Compliance**: Ensures compliance with legal and regulatory requirements

- **Efficiency**: Streamlines the legal discovery process, reducing time and costs

- **Risk mitigation**: Minimizes the risk of legal consequences for non-compliance or mishandling of data

The challenges include:

- **Volume and complexity**: Dealing with large volumes of data and complex data structures can pose challenges

- **Changing regulations**: Adapting to evolving legal and regulatory landscapes

In summary, effective management of legal discovery and litigation involves a strategic combination of technology, policies, and collaboration between legal and data management teams. It is a crucial aspect of data governance, ensuring that organizations can meet their legal obligations while efficiently managing their data.

Communication and documentation

Clear communication and documentation of retention policies are essential. This includes informing relevant stakeholders, training staff, and maintaining records of policy changes. Effective communication in data management involves collaborative efforts, stakeholder engagement, alignment with legal and compliance teams, clear policies, and transparent **incident response** (**IR**) communication. These practices foster a culture of understanding, compliance, and efficient response to data-related challenges. Let's understand what the key components of this piece are:

- **Interdepartmental collaboration**:

  - *Cross-functional teams*: Effective data management requires collaboration between IT, data management, legal, compliance, and other relevant departments

  - *Clear channels*: Establishing clear communication channels ensures that all stakeholders are informed about data policies, procedures, and changes

- **Stakeholder engagement**:

  - *Training programs*: Conducting regular training sessions to educate employees about data management practices

  - *Feedback mechanisms*: Encouraging feedback from employees helps in addressing concerns and improving data management processes

- **Legal and compliance teams**:

  - *Alignment*: Ensuring that legal and compliance teams are aware of data management practices and any changes in regulations

  - *Collaboration*: Collaboration between legal and data management teams is crucial for addressing legal and regulatory requirements

- **Clear policies and guidelines**:

  - *Accessible documentation*: Making data management policies and guidelines easily accessible to all employees

  - *Regular updates*: Communicating updates to policies and guidelines promptly

- **IR communication**:

  - *Preparedness*: Establishing communication protocols for data incidents, ensuring that response teams are well prepared

  - *Transparency*: Communicating transparently with stakeholders during and after data incidents

Documentation includes the following:

- **Policy documentation**:

  - *Data management policies*: Documenting clear and comprehensive data management policies to guide employees

  - *Version control*: Maintaining version control to track changes in policies over time

- **Procedure manuals**:

  - *Step-by-step guides*: Creating manuals that provide step-by-step guidance on data management procedures

  - *Visual aids*: Including visual aids to enhance understanding and adherence to procedures

- **Data catalogs**:

  - *Metadata documentation*: Maintaining documentation on metadata for datasets to aid in data discovery

  - *Usage information*: Including information on how data is used and any restrictions on usage

- **Training materials**:

  - *Training modules*: Developing training materials, including presentations, videos, and interactive content

  - *Certification programs*: Establishing certification programs for employees to validate their understanding of data management practices

- **Audit trails**:

  - *Activity logs*: Keeping detailed audit trails of data-related activities for compliance and security purposes

  - *Documentation of changes*: Documenting changes made to databases, applications, or data structures

- **Communication during the data life cycle**:

  - *Data creation*: Documenting the purpose and context of data at its creation

  - *Data archiving and deletion*: Clearly documenting the archiving and deletion processes at the end of the data life cycle

- **IR documentation**:

  - *Incident reports*: Creating comprehensive incident reports detailing the nature of the incident, its impact, and the steps taken for resolution

  - *Post-incident analysis*: Documenting lessons learned and improvements made after a data incident

The benefits include:

- **Clarity and consistency**: Clear communication and documentation promote consistency in data management practices

- **Compliance**: Well-documented policies and procedures help in demonstrating compliance with legal and regulatory requirements

- **Training effectiveness**: Comprehensive training materials contribute to the effectiveness of employee training programs

- **Efficient IR**: Detailed documentation aids in efficient IR and recovery

The challenges include:

- **Maintaining updated documentation**: Keeping documentation up to date can be challenging, especially in rapidly evolving technological environments
- **Ensuring accessibility**: Ensuring that documentation is easily accessible to all relevant stakeholders

In summary, effective communication and documentation are essential components of successful data management. They ensure that everyone involved understands their roles and responsibilities, contribute to a culture of transparency, and support compliance with regulations and best practices.

Automation and monitoring

Automation tools can assist in enforcing retention policies and automating the process of data deletion when it reaches the end of its defined retention period. Regular monitoring ensures compliance and identifies deviations. Automation plays a crucial role in enhancing the efficiency, accuracy, and reliability of data management processes. Let's discuss key components of automation and monitoring:

- **Data ingestion and integration**:
  - Automated tools facilitate the seamless ingestion and integration of data from various sources into a central repository
  - **Extract, Transform, Load** (**ETL**) processes are often automated to ensure timely and error-free data movement

- **Data cleansing and quality**:
  - Automation tools identify and rectify data quality issues through predefined rules, minimizing manual intervention
  - Regular automated data cleansing processes maintain the integrity of the database

- **Backup and replication**:
  - Automated backup processes ensure regular and consistent data backups, reducing the risk of data loss
  - Replication tasks, particularly in distributed systems, are often automated for data redundancy

- **Security and access control**:
  - Automated security measures, such as **role-based access control** (**RBAC**), help manage user permissions and ensure data confidentiality
  - Security patches and updates are automatically applied to safeguard against vulnerabilities

- **Data archiving and deletion**:
  - Automated archiving mechanisms move older or less frequently accessed data to long-term storage, optimizing resources
  - Scheduled data deletion processes ensure compliance with data retention policies

- **Workflow orchestration**:
  - Automated workflows streamline complex data processing tasks, ensuring a smooth and orchestrated data pipeline
  - Conditional triggers and alerts automate responses to specific events or data conditions

Monitoring

Monitoring is essential for maintaining data integrity, performance, and security. Automated monitoring tools provide real-time insights into the health of data systems. Let's discuss the key components of monitoring:

- **Performance monitoring**:
  - Continuous monitoring of database performance metrics, such as response times and query execution, identifies bottlenecks
  - Automated alerts notify administrators of performance degradation or potential issues

- **Security monitoring**:
  - Real-time monitoring of security events, such as unauthorized access attempts, helps in identifying and responding to potential threats
  - Automated **security information and event management** (**SIEM**) systems enhance threat detection

- **Data quality monitoring**:
  - Automated checks and validations ensure ongoing data quality by identifying anomalies or inconsistencies
  - Monitoring tools generate alerts when data quality thresholds are not met

- **Resource utilization monitoring**:
  - Monitoring system resources, such as CPU, memory, and storage, helps optimize resource allocation
  - Automated scaling based on resource usage ensures efficient resource utilization

- **Compliance monitoring**:

  - Automated tools track and audit data-related activities to ensure compliance with regulatory requirements

  - Regular compliance reports provide documentation for regulatory purposes

- **Backup and recovery monitoring**:

  - Continuous monitoring of backup processes ensures that backups are completed successfully

  - Alerts are generated for any failures or deviations from the backup schedule

The benefits of automation and monitoring include:

- **Efficiency**: Automation reduces manual intervention, leading to faster and more consistent processes

- **Accuracy**: Automated processes minimize the risk of human errors in data management tasks

- **Proactivity**: Monitoring tools enable proactive identification and resolution of issues before they impact operations

- **Compliance**: Automated tracking and reporting support adherence to regulatory and compliance standards

- **Resource optimization**: Automation and monitoring help optimize resource usage and prevent resource bottlenecks

The challenges include:

- **Complexity**: Implementing automation and monitoring solutions can be complex, requiring careful planning

- **Integration**: Ensuring seamless integration of automated processes with existing systems may pose challenges

- **Cost**: Initial setup costs and ongoing maintenance costs of automation and monitoring tools should be considered

Automation and monitoring are integral components of modern data management strategies, ensuring operational efficiency, data integrity, and compliance with regulatory requirements.

In conclusion, retention policies form the backbone of a robust data management strategy, addressing legal, operational, and cost considerations. Crafting effective policies requires a nuanced understanding of the organization's regulatory landscape, business needs, and the inherent life cycle of diverse data types. Implementing and enforcing these policies ensures that data is retained appropriately, supporting compliance, operational efficiency, and strategic decision-making.

The next section delves into DR planning, focusing on comprehensive strategies for safeguarding data assets. This includes the strategic selection of backup storage locations, establishing data redundancy measures, and defining crucial metrics such as RTOs and RPOs. DR planning ensures organizations are well prepared to navigate unforeseen disruptions, minimizing downtime and maintaining data integrity. Let's explore the intricacies of crafting robust strategies to fortify data against the unexpected.

DR planning

Disasters, whether natural or technological, can severely disrupt business operations and jeopardize data integrity. Cloud computing offers a robust platform for DR planning, providing scalable, flexible, and cost-effective solutions. Here's a detailed exploration of key elements in DR planning from a cloud perspective:

- **Cloud-based backup and storage**:

  - *Objective*: Safeguarding data against loss by utilizing cloud storage for backups.

  - *Implementation*: Regularly back up critical data to remote cloud servers. Services such as Amazon **Simple Storage Service (S3)**, Azure Blob Storage, and Google Cloud Storage offer secure, scalable options.

Next is an example using the **Amazon Web Services (AWS)** Management Console. Setting up a cloud-based backup on Amazon S3 involves several steps:

1. **Create an Amazon S3 bucket**:

   - *Go to the AWS Management Console*: Navigate to the Amazon S3 service.

   - *Create a bucket*: Click **Create bucket** and follow the prompts. Choose a globally unique name and specify a region for your bucket.

2. **Configure bucket permissions**:

   - *Access control*: In the bucket properties, configure access control. This includes setting permissions for who can access and modify objects in the bucket.

3. **Enable versioning**:

   - *Versioning settings*: Enable versioning to keep multiple versions of an object in the same bucket. This helps in recovering from accidental deletions or modifications.

4. **Set up cross-region replication (CRR) (optional)**:

   - *Replication configuration*: If you want to replicate your data across different regions for additional redundancy, configure CRR.

5. **Configure life-cycle policies**:

- *Life-cycle management*: Define rules for object life-cycle management. For example, you can automatically transition older versions of objects to Glacier for cost savings.

6. **Back up data to the S3 bucket**:

- *Upload files*: Use the AWS Management Console, the AWS CLI, or SDKs to upload files to your S3 bucket. You can organize your data using folders within the bucket.

7. **Automate backups with AWS Backup (optional)**:

- *AWS Backup*: For a more centralized and automated approach, you can use AWS Backup. Configure backup plans, set retention periods, and monitor backups from the AWS Backup console.

8. **Monitoring and logging**:

- *Amazon CloudWatch*: Set up CloudWatch for monitoring. You can configure alarms based on specific metrics and receive notifications for any anomalies.

9. **Testing and recovery**:

- *Regular testing*: Periodically test your backup and recovery processes to ensure that data can be restored successfully.
- *Restore options*: Amazon S3 provides multiple options for restoring data, including restoring previous versions, bulk restores, and using AWS Backup for orchestrated recoveries.

10. **Security measures**:

- *Encryption*: Implement server-side encryption to secure your data. Amazon S3 supports various encryption methods, including SSE-S3, SSE-KMS, and SSE-C.

Important considerations include:

- **Cost management**: Understand the cost structure of Amazon S3, including storage costs, data transfer costs, and costs associated with additional features

- **Access controls**: Configure proper access controls and authentication mechanisms to ensure data security

- **Data transfer speeds**: Consider the data transfer speeds based on your region and internet connectivity

Let's take another example and understand how we can back up a database to Amazon S3 with the following **Transact-SQL (T-SQL)** commands:

```
-- Single bucket backup
BACKUP DATABASE db1
TO URL = 's3://sql-backups-2023DG.s3.us-east-1.amazonaws.com/backups/
db1.bak'
WITH FORMAT, COMPRESSION, MAXTRANSFERSIZE = 20971520;
```

This T-SQL command backs up the db1 database to an Amazon S3 bucket. The backup includes formatting, compression for storage savings, and a specified maximum transfer size:

```
-- Striped backup across multiple files
BACKUP DATABASE db1
TO URL = 's3://sql-backups-2023DG.s3.us-east-1.amazonaws.com/backups/
db1-part1.bak',
    URL = 's3://sql-backups-2023DG.s3.us-east-1.amazonaws.com/backups/
db1-part2.bak',
    URL = 's3://sql-backups-2023DG.s3.us-east-1.amazonaws.com/backups/
db1-part3.bak',
    URL = 's3://sql-backups-2023DG.s3.us-east-1.amazonaws.com/backups/
db1-part4.bak',
    URL = 's3://sql-backups-2023DG.s3.us-east-1.amazonaws.com/backups/
db1-part5.bak'
WITH FORMAT, COMPRESSION, MAXTRANSFERSIZE = 20971520;
```

This example shows striping the backup across five URLs for improved performance. You can adjust the number of URLs up to a maximum of 64:

```
-- Mirrored backup to a second bucket
BACKUP DATABASE db1
TO URL = 's3://sql-backups-2023DG.s3.us-east-1.amazonaws.com/backups/
db1-part1.bak',
    URL = 's3://sql-backups-2023DG.s3.us-east-1.amazonaws.com/backups/
db1-part2.bak',
    URL = 's3://sql-backups-2023DG.s3.us-east-1.amazonaws.com/backups/
db1-part3.bak',
    URL = 's3://sql-backups-2023DG.s3.us-east-1.amazonaws.com/backups/
db1-part4.bak',
    URL = 's3://sql-backups-2023DG.s3.us-east-1.amazonaws.com/backups/
db1-part5.bak'
MIRROR TO URL = 's3://sql-backups-2023DG-ohio.s3.us-east-2.amazonaws.
com/backups/db1-part1.bak',
    URL = 's3://sql-backups-2023DG-ohio.s3.us-east-2.amazonaws.com/
backups/db1-part2.bak',
    URL = 's3://sql-backups-2023DG-ohio.s3.us-east-2.amazonaws.com/
backups/db1-part3.bak',
```

```
    URL = 's3://sql-backups-2023DG-ohio.s3.us-east-2.amazonaws.com/
backups/db1-part4.bak',
    URL = 's3://sql-backups-2023DG-ohio.s3.us-east-2.amazonaws.com/
backups/db1-part5.bak'
WITH FORMAT, COMPRESSION, MAXTRANSFERSIZE = 20971520;
```

This command mirrors the backup to a second Amazon S3 bucket for added redundancy. Adjust bucket names in the T-SQL command as needed.

Data redundancy and replication

- *Objective*: Ensuring data availability and resilience through redundancy.

- *Implementation*: Employ multi-region or multi-zone replication. Cloud providers often offer built-in redundancy features, automatically duplicating data across geographically distributed centers.

Data redundancy and replication are crucial aspects of ensuring data availability, durability, and resilience in cloud computing. Here's a detailed discussion:

- **Redundancy defined**: Data redundancy involves duplicating critical data to safeguard against data loss due to hardware failures, accidental deletion, or other unforeseen issues. Redundancy ensures that there are multiple copies of the same data stored in different locations or systems.

- **Importance of data redundancy**:

  - **Fault tolerance (FT)**: Redundancy enhances FT by providing alternative data sources in case of hardware failures or other disruptions.

  - **Continuous operations**: It enables uninterrupted operations even when one or more components fail.

The types of data redundancy include:

- **Hardware redundancy**: Involves duplicating critical hardware components to eliminate **single points of failure (SPOFs)**

- **Data redundancy**: Duplicate storage of critical data to prevent data loss

Replication strategies include:

- **Synchronous replication**: Updates are mirrored to multiple locations simultaneously. While this ensures data consistency, it might introduce latency.

- **Asynchronous replication**: Updates are copied to other locations with a delay. It reduces latency but may lead to temporary inconsistencies.

Cloud storage redundancy models include:

- **AWS S3 replication**: Amazon S3 offers CRR and **same-region replication** (**SRR**). It allows automatic and asynchronous replication of objects across buckets.
- **Azure Storage redundancy**: Azure provides options such as **Locally Redundant Storage** (**LRS**), **Geo-Redundant Storage** (**GRS**), and **Zone-Redundant Storage** (**ZRS**) to replicate data across different locations.
- **Google Cloud Storage**: Google Cloud offers multi-region, dual-region, and regional storage classes, allowing users to choose redundancy options based on their needs.

The benefits of data replication in the cloud include:

- **High availability (HA)**: Replication ensures data is available even if one or more components fail
- **DR**: Copies of data in different regions provide protection against regional outages or disasters
- **Scalability**: Replication facilitates load balancing and scaling operations by distributing data across multiple servers

The challenges and considerations include:

- **Consistency**: Maintaining data consistency across replicas can be challenging, especially in asynchronous replication models
- **Cost**: Replicating data across multiple regions may incur additional costs

Best practices include:

- **Choose an appropriate redundancy level**: Assess the criticality of data and choose redundancy options accordingly
- **Regular testing**: Periodically test data recovery and failover mechanisms to ensure effectiveness
- **Security measures**: Implement encryption for data in transit and at rest to enhance security

The compliance and legal considerations include:

- **Data residency laws**: Understand and comply with data residency and sovereignty laws when replicating data across regions or countries
- **Data privacy**: Ensure that replicated data adheres to privacy regulations and user consent requirements

Data redundancy and replication strategies should align with the specific requirements and objectives of the organization, considering factors such as cost, performance, and regulatory compliance. Always refer to the latest documentation from **cloud service providers** (**CSPs**) for specific implementation details and updates.

RTOs and RPOs

- *Objective*: Defining acceptable downtime and data loss thresholds.

- *Implementation*: Cloud-based DR services allow organizations to set and meet specific RTOs and RPOs. Solutions such as **AWS Elastic Disaster Recovery (AWS DRS)**, **Azure Site Recovery (ASR)**, and Google Cloud's **Disaster Recovery as a Service (DRaaS)** streamline this process.

- *Definition*:

  - **RTO**: RTO represents the targeted duration within which a business process must be restored after a disaster to avoid unacceptable consequences. It defines the acceptable downtime for an organization.

  - **RPO**: RPO indicates the maximum tolerable period during which data might be lost due to a significant incident. It defines the allowable data loss in terms of time.

- *Significance*:

  - **BC**: RTOs and RPOs are crucial elements in ensuring BC after a disruptive event. They guide the planning and execution of recovery strategies.

  - **Risk mitigation**: Understanding acceptable downtime and data loss helps organizations mitigate risks and align their DR strategies with business priorities.

The factors influencing RTO and RPO include:

- **Nature of business**: Different industries and businesses may have varying tolerance for downtime and data loss. For example, financial institutions often require minimal downtime and data loss.

- **Application criticality**: Critical applications may demand shorter RTOs and RPOs compared to less critical ones.

- **Regulatory requirements**: Compliance standards often dictate the maximum allowable downtime and data loss for specific industries.

Here are some guidelines for implementing RTOs and RPOs in the cloud:

- **Cloud-based DR solutions**: Cloud services provide scalable and flexible DR solutions. Organizations can leverage **Infrastructure as a Service (IaaS)** or DraaS to meet their RTO and RPO goals.

- **Automation and orchestration**: Cloud platforms offer automation tools to streamline the recovery process, reducing manual intervention and minimizing downtime.

- **Data replication**: Implementing continuous data replication across geographically dispersed regions helps achieve low RPOs, ensuring minimal data loss.

The challenges and considerations include:

- **Cost versus objectives**: Achieving aggressive RTOs and RPOs might entail higher costs. Organizations need to strike a balance between cost considerations and desired recovery objectives.

- **Technology limitations**: The technology used for data replication and recovery may impose limitations on how low RTOs and RPOs can realistically be set.

Best practices include:

- **Regular testing**: Periodically test DRPs to ensure that RTOs and RPOs can be met effectively.

- **Documentation**: Clearly document and communicate RTOs and RPOs across the organization. Ensure that stakeholders are aware of recovery expectations.

- **Continuous improvement**: Regularly review and update recovery objectives based on changes in business requirements, technology advancements, and lessons learned from testing.

The legal and compliance considerations include:

- **Regulatory compliance**: Ensure that the chosen recovery objectives comply with industry regulations and legal requirements

- **Contractual obligations**: Align RTOs and RPOs with contractual obligations, especially when using third-party DR services

RTOs and RPOs are integral components of a comprehensive DR strategy, and their effective implementation is crucial for maintaining business resilience in the face of unexpected disruptions. Organizations should tailor their recovery objectives based on their unique business needs, industry regulations, and the technology landscape.

Cloud-based DR services

- *Objective*: Leveraging specialized services for rapid recovery in case of a disaster.

- *Implementation*: Cloud providers offer DRaaS solutions with automated failover, allowing seamless transitions to backup environments. These services minimize downtime and ensure BC.

Cloud-based DR services are a critical component of modern BC strategies, offering scalable, flexible, and cost-effective solutions for organizations to recover their IT infrastructure and data in the event of a disaster. Here's an in-depth exploration of key aspects:

- **Definition and purpose**:

  - **Cloud DRaaS**: A cloud DRaaS is a service model that uses cloud resources to back up data and applications and provide system failover in the event of a disaster. It enables organizations to maintain BC without the need for significant on-premises infrastructure.

- **Advantages**:

  - **Cost-effectiveness**: Cloud-based solutions eliminate the need for extensive physical infrastructure, reducing capital expenses. Organizations pay for the resources they consume during actual recovery scenarios.

  - **Scalability**: A cloud DRaaS scales resources dynamically, accommodating the changing needs of an organization. This flexibility ensures that the IT environment can adapt to evolving requirements.

  - **Accessibility**: Cloud-based solutions provide remote access to critical applications and data, allowing employees to work from virtually anywhere, enhancing business resilience.

  - **Automated recovery**: Many cloud DRaaS solutions offer automation, enabling swift recovery with minimal manual intervention. This automation reduces downtime and human error during recovery processes.

The key features of a cloud DraaS include:

- **Data replication**: Continuous replication of data to a cloud environment ensures up-to-date copies are available for recovery

- **Failover and failback**: A cloud DRaaS allows for seamless failover to the cloud during a disaster and subsequent failback to on-premises infrastructure when conditions stabilize

- **Testing capabilities**: Regular testing of DRPs is facilitated in the cloud, ensuring that recovery processes are well understood and effective

- **Monitoring and reporting**: Cloud DRaaS solutions often include monitoring tools that provide real-time insights into the status of replicated systems, helping organizations meet their RTOs and RPOs

1. Here are the implementation steps:

2. **Assessment**: Conduct a thorough assessment of critical applications and data to determine their recovery priorities and dependencies.

3. **Selection of cloud provider**: Choose a reliable CSP that aligns with organizational requirements, compliance standards, and recovery objectives.

4. **Data replication configuration**: Set up continuous data replication to the cloud, ensuring that critical data is mirrored in real time.

5. **Testing and training**: Regularly test the DRP to ensure its effectiveness and train relevant personnel on their roles during a recovery event.

6. The challenges and considerations include:

   - Security concerns: Organizations must address security concerns associated with transmitting and storing sensitive data in the cloud

- Bandwidth requirements: Continuous data replication may require substantial bandwidth, especially for organizations with large datasets

- Integration with existing systems: Seamless integration with existing on-premises systems and applications is crucial for a successful cloud-based DR strategy

7. Industry use cases include:

- E-commerce: Online retailers rely on cloud-based DR to ensure uninterrupted service during peak times and critical shopping seasons

- Financial services: Financial institutions leverage cloud DRaaS to meet stringent regulatory requirements and maintain continuous operations

8. Regulatory compliance includes:

- HIPAA, GDPR, and so on: Organizations must ensure that their cloud DR strategies comply with industry-specific regulations regarding data privacy and protection

Cloud-based DR services have become integral for organizations aiming to enhance their resilience against unforeseen disruptions. By leveraging the cloud's agility, scalability, and automation capabilities, businesses can design robust DRPs that align with their specific needs and regulatory obligations.

In the realm of cloud computing, both AWS and Microsoft Azure offer robust DRaaS solutions. Let's delve into an example scenario for each cloud provider.

AWS – AWS DR solution

Scenario: Consider a multinational e-commerce company that relies on AWS for hosting its critical applications and databases. The company operates across multiple regions, ensuring a global reach for its customers. To safeguard against unforeseen disasters and ensure BC, the company implements an AWS DRaaS solution.

Here are the implementation steps:

1. **Region selection**: The company selects a secondary AWS region strategically located geographically distant from its primary region. This ensures redundancy in the event of a regional outage.

2. **Data replication**: AWS provides services such as AWS Storage Gateway and **AWS Database Migration Service** (**AWS DMS**) for continuous replication of critical data to the secondary region. This ensures that data is synchronized in near real time.

3. **Automated failover**: AWS offers tools such as AWS Elastic Beanstalk, AWS CloudFormation, and AWS Lambda for automated application deployment and failover orchestration. In the event of a disaster impacting the primary region, these tools automate the failover process to the secondary region.

4. **Testing and compliance**:

   - AWS enables organizations to regularly test their DRPs using services such as AWS CloudFormation. This ensures that failover mechanisms work as expected. The solution also helps in meeting compliance requirements by providing audit logs and reporting.

   - Cost efficiency: AWS allows organizations to optimize costs by paying only for resources consumed during actual failover events. The use of reserved instances and AWS Budgets helps in cost management.

Setting up a DR solution in AWS involves several steps, and the specifics may vary based on the complexity of your architecture. Next is a general guide for setting up a basic AWS DR solution:

Prerequisites:

1. **AWS accounts**:

   - Ensure you have two AWS accounts: one for the primary environment and one for the DR environment.

2. **Regions**:

   - Choose AWS regions for your primary and DR environments. They should be geographically distant to minimize the risk of regional outages affecting both environments.

Here are the implementation steps:

1. **Identify critical resources**: Identify critical resources that need to be included in the DRP. This includes **Elastic Compute Cloud** (**EC2**) instances, databases, storage, and other essential components.

2. **AWS IAM**: Set up IAM roles and permissions for the DR environment, allowing necessary access to resources. This includes permissions for EC2, S3, and other services.

3. **Amazon Virtual Private Cloud** (**VPC**): Set up a VPC in the DR region mirroring the configuration of the primary VPC. Ensure connectivity between the VPCs in both regions.

4. **Data replication**: Use AWS services such as AWS Storage Gateway, AWS DMS, or Amazon S3 CRR for continuous data replication. Choose the service based on the type of data you're replicating.

5. **Automated scripting**: Leverage AWS SDKs or the CLI to automate the setup process. This is especially useful for scripting resource creation, ensuring consistency, and reducing manual errors.

6. **Failover testing**: Regularly conduct failover testing to ensure that the DR environment functions as expected. AWS services such as AWS CloudFormation can be used for automated failover testing.

7. **Monitoring and alerts**: Implement monitoring using Amazon CloudWatch. Set up alarms for critical metrics to be notified of any issues. Amazon CloudWatch Events can trigger automated responses.

8. **Documentation**: Create detailed documentation outlining the DRP, including steps for failover, contact information, and any additional procedures. This documentation is critical for a swift and efficient response during an actual disaster.

9. **Cost management**: Implement cost management strategies. AWS Budgets can be used to set cost thresholds, and AWS Cost Explorer can provide insights into resource costs.

10. **Security considerations**: Implement security best practices, including encryption of data in transit and at rest. Ensure that security groups and network ACLs are configured correctly.

11. **Compliance**: If your organization operates in a regulated industry, ensure that the DR setup complies with relevant regulatory requirements. AWS Artifact provides compliance reports.

12. **Regular updates**: Regularly review and update the DRP as your architecture evolves. This includes incorporating changes in resources and AWS service offerings.

Azure – ASR

Scenario: Now, let's consider a global financial institution heavily invested in Microsoft Azure for its infrastructure. The institution wants a comprehensive DRaaS solution to protect its critical financial systems and ensure compliance with regulatory standards.

Here are the implementation steps:

1. **Configuration**: ASR provides a simple setup through the Azure portal. The financial institution configures ASR to replicate **virtual machines (VMs)** and data from its primary Azure region to a secondary region.

2. **Application-aware replication**: ASR supports application-aware replication, ensuring that dependencies between different applications are considered during the replication process. This is crucial for maintaining consistency in complex application environments.

3. **Failover orchestration**: Azure provides tools such as ASR Planner and Azure Automation for orchestrating failovers. These tools help in defining and testing failover plans to meet specific RTOs and RPOs.

4. **Integration with Azure services**: ASR seamlessly integrates with other Azure services, such as Azure Virtual Network, ensuring that the network configuration is replicated along with the VMs. This simplifies the failover process.

5. **Monitoring and reporting**: Azure Monitor and Azure Security Center provide monitoring and reporting capabilities. The financial institution can gain insights into the health of its replicated infrastructure and receive alerts for any issues.

Setting up ASR for DR in Microsoft Azure involves a series of steps. Next is a general guide:

Prerequisites:

1. **Azure subscription**: Ensure you have an active Azure subscription. If you don't have one, you can create a free account.

2. **Azure Recovery Services vault**: Set up an Azure Recovery Services vault. This vault acts as a management and orchestration entity for ASR.

3. **Source and target regions**: Choose an Azure region for your primary environment and another region for the DR environment.

Here are the implementation steps:

1. **Create a Recovery Services vault**: In the Azure portal, create a new Recovery Services vault.

2. **Configure the vault**: Within the Recovery Services vault, configure settings such as the region and replication storage account.

3. **Register resources**: Register the Azure VMs and other resources that you want to protect in the Recovery Services vault.

4. **Site recovery infrastructure**: Set up the necessary infrastructure components, including a configuration server and process server. These components play a crucial role in managing replication.

5. **Replication policy**: Define a replication policy specifying replication frequency, RPOs, and retention settings.

6. **Protection groups**: Organize VMs into protection groups based on their dependencies and recovery objectives.

7. **Enable replication**: Enable replication for the VMs in the protection groups. ASR will start replicating data to the designated target region.

8. **Network mapping**: Configure network mapping to ensure that VMs can communicate appropriately after failover. This includes mapping source and target networks.

9. **Recovery plans**: Create recovery plans that define the sequence of actions to be taken during failover. This includes orchestrating the recovery of multiple VMs.

10. **Testing failover**: Perform regular testing of failover scenarios to validate that the DR setup works as expected. ASR provides a **Test Failover** feature for this purpose.

11. **Failover**: In the event of a disaster, initiate failover to the DR region. This can be a planned failover or an unplanned failover, depending on the situation.

12. **Monitoring and alerts**: Leverage Azure Monitor and Azure Security Center for monitoring and alerts. Set up alerts for critical metrics and events.

13. **Security considerations**: Implement security best practices, including encryption of data, secure access controls, and compliance with regulatory requirements.

14. **Cost management**: Use Azure Cost Management tools to monitor and manage costs associated with the DR setup.

15. **Documentation**: Maintain comprehensive documentation of the ASR setup, including recovery plans, failover procedures, and contact information.

In both examples, AWS and Azure offer comprehensive DRaaS solutions with features such as automated failover, application-aware replication, cost efficiency, and integration with other cloud services. These solutions empower organizations to create resilient IT environments and ensure minimal disruption in the face of disasters.

Automated orchestration and testing

- *Objective*: Streamlining recovery processes and ensuring their effectiveness through regular testing.

- *Implementation*: Cloud platforms facilitate the automated orchestration of recovery workflows. Regularly simulate disaster scenarios to validate recovery plans and identify areas for improvement.

Automated orchestration and testing are critical components of a comprehensive DR strategy in cloud environments. These processes ensure that in the event of a disaster, applications and services can be efficiently and reliably recovered, meeting predefined recovery objectives. Here are some key aspects to consider:

1. **Failover automation**: Automated orchestration involves scripting or defining workflows that automate the failover process. This includes stopping production workloads in the primary environment and initiating the failover of replicated resources in the secondary environment.

2. **Recovery plans**: Orchestration tools allow the creation of detailed recovery plans. These plans outline the sequence of steps to be taken during a failover, including the order in which services are brought online.

3. **Dependency management**: Orchestration tools understand dependencies between different components. For example, a database server might need to be started before an application server. Orchestration ensures that these dependencies are honored during recovery.

4. **Cross-platform orchestration**: In heterogeneous environments where multiple platforms or cloud providers are involved, orchestration tools provide a unified way to manage failover processes.

5. **Scripting and automation languages**: Orchestration tools often support scripting languages or automation frameworks, allowing customization of recovery workflows based on specific organizational needs.

Testing

1. **Regular testing**: Automated testing is crucial to validate the effectiveness of the DRP. Regularly scheduled tests simulate failover scenarios without impacting production environments.

2. **Non-disruptive testing**: Testing should be non-disruptive to ongoing operations. Automated tools enable the creation of isolated testing environments that mirror the production setup.

3. **Scenario-based testing**: Testing should cover various disaster scenarios, including infrastructure failures, data corruption, and application-level issues. This ensures that the DRP is robust and can handle different types of disasters.

4. **Performance testing**: Evaluate the performance of applications and services during simulated failover scenarios. This helps identify potential bottlenecks and optimize the recovery process.

5. **Logging and reporting**: Automated testing tools provide detailed logs and reports, allowing organizations to assess the outcome of tests, identify any issues, and make necessary adjustments to the DRP.

- **Continuous improvement**: Automated testing is an iterative process. The results of each test should inform improvements to the DRP. This could include refining recovery procedures, optimizing resource allocation, or updating dependencies.

The benefits include:

- **Reduced recovery time**: Automation minimizes the manual steps involved in recovery, leading to faster recovery times

- **Reliability**: Automated processes are consistent and reliable, reducing the risk of errors during recovery

- **Adaptability**: Orchestration tools can adapt to changes in the IT environment, making them suitable for dynamic cloud landscapes

- **Documentation**: Automated processes contribute to comprehensive documentation of recovery workflows and procedures

Geo-diversity for resilience

- *Objective*: Ensuring resilience by spreading resources across different geographic regions.

- *Implementation*: Distribute critical components across multiple regions to mitigate the impact of regional disasters. Cloud providers offer global infrastructure for geo-diversification.

Geo-diversity for resilience is a strategy aimed at enhancing the availability and resilience of IT systems by distributing infrastructure across geographically diverse locations. This approach is particularly important for DR and BC planning. Here's an in-depth discussion.

The key concepts include:

1. **Geographical distribution**: Geo-diversity involves spreading IT resources, including data centers, servers, and other critical components, across different geographic locations. This distribution reduces the risk of a SPOF due to a regional disaster.

2. **DR and BC**: The primary goal of geo-diversity is to ensure continuity of operations even in the face of regional disasters, such as earthquakes, floods, or other events that might impact an entire geographical area.

3. **Reducing risk exposure**: By having infrastructure in multiple locations, organizations mitigate the risk of a catastrophic event affecting all their operations simultaneously. This enhances the overall resilience of the IT ecosystem.

4. **Data replication**: Geo-diversity often involves replicating data and applications across different geographical regions. In the event of a failure in one region, operations can seamlessly switch to a backup located in another region.

5. **Load balancing and redundancy**: Beyond DR, geo-diversity supports load balancing and redundancy. Traffic can be distributed across multiple data centers to ensure optimal performance and minimize the impact of localized outages.

6. **Latency optimization**: Geo-diversity allows organizations to position resources closer to end users, reducing latency and improving the overall user experience. **Content delivery networks (CDNs)** are an example of this, distributing content across global points of presence.

Implementation strategies include:

1. **Multi-cloud deployments**: Leveraging multiple CSPs across different regions provides an additional layer of redundancy. In case of an issue with one cloud provider, operations can seamlessly transition to another.

2. **Global content delivery**: Content, applications, and services can be distributed globally through CDN services. This ensures fast and reliable access to resources regardless of the user's location.

3. **Active-active data centers**: Maintaining active-active data centers in different regions allows for continuous operations. Both data centers actively handle traffic, providing redundancy and load distribution.

4. **Hybrid cloud configurations**: Hybrid cloud setups, combining on-premises infrastructure with cloud resources, can be strategically distributed for geo-diversity. This approach offers flexibility and resilience.

5. **Cross-region data replication**: Critical data and databases can be replicated across regions to ensure that, in the event of a disaster or outage, the data remains accessible from an alternate location.

The benefits include:

- **HA**: Geo-diversity ensures HA by reducing the impact of regional failures

- **Resilience to disasters**: Organizations can continue operations even if an entire region is affected by a disaster

- **Optimized performance**: By distributing resources closer to end users, organizations can optimize performance and reduce latency

- **BC**: Geo-diversity is a key component of robust BC planning, ensuring that operations can continue in various circumstances

- **Risk mitigation**: It mitigates the risk associated with localized events, providing a more robust and secure IT infrastructure

In summary, geo-diversity is a fundamental principle for building resilient IT systems that can withstand disruptions and maintain operational integrity. It's a crucial element of DR and BC strategies in the context of modern, distributed, and cloud-based computing environments.

Cross-cloud and hybrid solutions

- *Objective*: Avoiding reliance on a single cloud provider for added resilience.

- *Implementation*: Consider hybrid or multi-cloud architectures. This involves distributing workloads across multiple cloud providers or combining on-premises infrastructure with cloud resources for added redundancy.

Cross-cloud and hybrid solutions refer to IT architectures that incorporate elements from multiple cloud providers (cross-cloud) or combine on-premises infrastructure with cloud resources (hybrid). These approaches offer organizations flexibility, resilience, and the ability to leverage the strengths of different cloud providers. Here's a detailed discussion.

Let's look at cross-cloud solutions first:

1. **Definition**: Cross-cloud solutions involve deploying and managing applications, services, or infrastructure across multiple cloud environments. This could include using services from different cloud providers simultaneously.

2. **Flexibility and vendor neutrality**: Organizations opt for cross-cloud solutions to avoid vendor lock-in and take advantage of the unique features or cost structures offered by different cloud providers. This flexibility allows them to choose the best services for their specific needs.

3. **Risk mitigation**: Distributing workloads across multiple cloud providers can mitigate the risk of service outages or disruptions from a single provider. It enhances resilience and ensures BC even if one cloud provider experiences issues.

4. **Optimizing costs**: Organizations can optimize costs by selecting cloud providers based on pricing models and features that align with specific workloads. This approach enables cost savings and efficient resource utilization.

5. **Best-of-breed services**: Leveraging the strengths of different cloud providers allows organizations to access best-of-breed services for specific requirements. For instance, using one cloud provider for data analytics and another for ML.

6. **Geographical considerations**: Cross-cloud solutions provide the flexibility to host resources in data centers located in different regions or countries, ensuring compliance with data residency and sovereignty requirements.

Now, let's look at hybrid cloud solutions:

1. **Definition**: Hybrid cloud solutions combine on-premises infrastructure with cloud resources. This model provides a seamless extension of existing data centers into the cloud.

2. **Scalability and flexibility**: Hybrid clouds allow organizations to scale their infrastructure dynamically by utilizing cloud resources during peak demand while retaining on-premises infrastructure for baseline workloads.

Data sovereignty and compliance

Certain industries and regions have strict data sovereignty and compliance requirements. Hybrid solutions enable organizations to keep sensitive data on-premises while leveraging the cloud for other services. Let's look at this in more detail:

*   **Legacy system integration**: Many organizations have legacy systems that may not be easily migrated to the cloud. Hybrid solutions enable the integration of on-premises legacy systems with modern cloud services.

*   **Gradual cloud adoption**: Hybrid cloud facilitates a gradual transition to the cloud. Organizations can move specific workloads or applications to the cloud while maintaining critical infrastructure on-premises.

*   **Cost efficiency**: Hybrid models offer cost advantages by allowing organizations to use on-premises infrastructure for certain workloads, avoiding the need to fully invest in cloud resources.

The challenges and considerations include:

*   **Interoperability**: Ensuring seamless interoperability between different cloud providers or between on-premises and cloud environments can be a challenge

*   **Data integration**: Integrating and synchronizing data across hybrid or multi-cloud environments requires robust data integration strategies

- **Security concerns**: Managing security consistently across diverse environments is crucial. IAM, data encryption, and network security must be well coordinated

- **Operational complexity**: Operating in a multi-cloud or hybrid environment introduces additional complexity in terms of management, monitoring, and troubleshooting

The benefits include:

- **Flexibility and choice**: Organizations have the flexibility to choose the right cloud services for specific needs

- **Risk mitigation**: Reduced risk of service disruptions or outages affecting a single cloud provider

- **Scalability**: Scalability is enhanced by leveraging cloud resources for variable workloads

- **Data sovereignty compliance**: Hybrid solutions enable compliance with data sovereignty regulations

- **Cost optimization**: Optimization of costs by selecting the most cost-effective services from different providers

- **Gradual cloud adoption**: Allows organizations to adopt cloud technologies at their own pace

Cost efficiency and scalability

- *Objective*: Ensuring that DR solutions are both scalable and cost-effective.

- *Implementation*: Cloud platforms offer pay-as-you-go models, enabling organizations to scale resources based on needs. This ensures cost efficiency while maintaining the ability to rapidly scale during a disaster.

Cost efficiency and scalability are two critical aspects of cloud computing, and organizations strive to strike a balance between these factors to optimize their operations. Let's discuss each of these aspects in detail.

First, let's look at cost efficiency:

- **Pay-as-you-go model**: Cloud computing typically follows a pay-as-you-go model, where organizations pay for the resources they consume. This helps in cost optimization as organizations only pay for the computing power, storage, and services they actually use.

- **Resource optimization**: Cloud providers offer tools and services to monitor resource usage. Organizations can analyze this data to optimize resource allocation, ensuring that they are not over-provisioning or under-provisioning resources.

- **Elasticity**: The ability to scale resources up or down based on demand is a key feature of the cloud. This elasticity ensures that organizations can dynamically adjust their resource allocation, saving costs during periods of low demand.

- **Managed services**: Cloud providers offer a variety of managed services, eliminating the need for organizations to manage the underlying infrastructure. This not only reduces operational overhead but also ensures efficient use of resources.

- **Spot instances and reserved capacity**: Cloud providers offer options such as spot instances (temporary compute capacity) and reserved capacity (long-term commitments) at discounted rates. Organizations can leverage these options for cost savings based on their workload characteristics.

- **Cost monitoring and optimization tools**: Cloud providers offer tools that help organizations monitor and optimize costs. These tools provide insights into spending patterns, identify idle resources, and suggest ways to optimize resource usage.

- **Serverless computing**: Serverless computing allows organizations to run applications without provisioning or managing servers. This model is highly cost-efficient as organizations pay only for the actual compute time consumed by their applications.

Now, let's look at scalability:

- **Horizontal and vertical scaling**: Cloud environments support both horizontal and vertical scaling. Horizontal scaling involves adding more instances of resources (for example, adding more servers), while vertical scaling involves increasing the capacity of individual resources (for example, adding more CPU or memory).

- **Auto-scaling**: Auto-scaling enables automatic adjustment of resources based on demand. Organizations can set up policies to dynamically scale resources up or down, ensuring that they meet performance requirements while minimizing costs.

- **Global reach**: Cloud providers have data centers distributed globally. This enables organizations to deploy applications and services close to their users, reducing latency and improving performance.

- **Load balancing**: Load balancing distributes incoming network traffic across multiple servers. This ensures that no single server bears too much load, and it optimizes resource utilization.

- **Serverless architecture**: In a serverless architecture, scalability is inherent. Functions are executed in response to events, and the cloud provider automatically scales resources based on demand.

- **Database scalability**: Cloud databases offer scalable solutions. Organizations can dynamically adjust the capacity of their databases to handle varying workloads efficiently.

The challenges and considerations include:

- **Cost monitoring**: While the cloud offers cost efficiency, organizations must actively monitor and manage costs to avoid unexpected expenses.

- **Scalability planning**: Effective scalability requires planning. Organizations must understand their workloads and design scalable architectures accordingly.

- **Application design**: Applications must be designed to take advantage of cloud scalability. This may involve breaking down monolithic applications into microservices or adopting serverless architectures.

- **Data management**: Scalability in data management requires careful consideration. Distributed databases and caching mechanisms may be necessary for large-scale applications.

The benefits include:

- **Optimized costs**: Pay-as-you-go and resource optimization lead to cost savings

- **Efficient resource utilization**: Scalability ensures that resources are utilized efficiently based on demand

- **Global presence**: The cloud's global infrastructure enables organizations to scale globally, reaching users in different regions

- **Agility and innovation**: Scalability and cost efficiency provide the agility needed for innovation and rapid development

Summary

This chapter is a pivotal guide for readers navigating the complexities of safeguarding data within cloud environments. We meticulously explored a range of backup strategies, from the comprehensive nature of full backups to the efficiency of incremental and differential backups, enabling you to discern the optimal approach for your unique requirements. The discussion of retention policies equipped you with the expertise to craft nuanced data management strategies that align with both compliance standards and business goals, striking a delicate balance. Moving beyond, the chapter delved into DR planning, offering profound insights into critical elements such as backup storage locations and the intricacies of defining RTOs and RPOs. You not only acquired theoretical knowledge but also gained practical, actionable insights, empowering you to establish resilient and effective backup and recovery frameworks in the dynamic landscape of cloud computing.

The upcoming chapter, *Backup and Restore Procedures*, is a practical guide, offering step-by-step instructions on executing data backup and restoration operations in the landscape of cloud environments. You can anticipate comprehensive insights into the intricacies of each procedural step, ensuring a nuanced understanding of the entire process. Furthermore, the chapter delves into the realm of automated backup solutions, providing an exploration of cloud-native tools and services. Focused on major cloud providers such as AWS, Azure, and Google Cloud, this chapter equips you with the knowledge to leverage cutting-edge technologies for seamless and efficient backup and recovery within your cloud infrastructure.

12

Backup and Restore Procedures

This chapter, *Backup and Restore Procedures*, delves into the critical aspects of data protection and recovery in cloud computing. In this chapter, you can expect a thorough exploration of various backup and restoration strategies, techniques, and best practices tailored to any cloud environment. The key topic that will be covered in this chapter is the following:

- *Backup and restore procedures*: Step-by-step guidance on how to perform data backup and restoration operations within a cloud environment

By the end of this chapter, you will have gained a comprehensive understanding of the intricacies involved in safeguarding and recovering data within cloud environments. The step-by-step guidance provided will ensure that you acquire practical skills, enabling you to proficiently execute data backup and restoration operations. Furthermore, exploring automated backup solutions from major cloud providers such as AWS, Azure, and Google Cloud will empower you with knowledge of cutting-edge tools and services. This will equip you not only to navigate the complexities of contemporary backup procedures but also to leverage cloud-native technologies for efficient and resilient data management. Whether you're new to cloud computing or seeking to enhance your expertise, this chapter offers valuable insights and practical skills to fortify your data management strategies in the cloud.

Technical requirements

To fully engage with the content in this chapter on cloud computing architecture, you should have a basic understanding of computer systems, networking concepts, and information technology.

Additionally, the following technical requirements are recommended:

- **Internet access**: You should have a reliable internet connection to access online resources, references, and examples related to cloud computing.

- **A computing device**: A desktop computer, laptop, tablet, or smartphone with a modern web browser is necessary to read this chapter's content and access any online materials.

- **A web browser**: The latest version of a modern web browser such as Google Chrome, Mozilla Firefox, Microsoft Edge, or Safari is recommended. This ensures compatibility and an optimal viewing experience for web-based resources and interactive content.

- **Familiarity with cloud services**: Some familiarity with cloud services and their basic functionalities will enhance your understanding of this chapter. This includes knowledge of basic backup and restore operations, basic database and networking concepts, operating systems, and servers.

Backup and restore procedures

This section delves into the practical intricacies of safeguarding and recovering data within a cloud environment. It offers step-by-step guidance on executing data backup and restoration operations. Additionally, we'll explore automated backup solutions, shedding light on cloud-native tools and services provided by major cloud platforms such as AWS, Azure, and Google Cloud. You can expect to gain a comprehensive understanding of the procedures involved in securing and restoring data, complemented by insights into the specific tools and features offered by leading cloud service providers.

Backup and restore procedures are foundational components that ensure the integrity, availability, and recoverability of data. The cloud environment introduces unique challenges and opportunities, shaping these procedures to align with the dynamic nature of distributed systems. Backup procedures involve creating redundant copies of data, often leveraging snapshots or incremental methods to minimize storage and optimize efficiency. Cloud-based backups are flexible, allowing for automation and scheduling to ensure regular snapshots without manual intervention.

Restore procedures, which are equally as critical, must be swift and reliable in terms of the cloud. Cloud platforms typically offer scalable storage and efficient retrieval mechanisms, enabling rapid recovery in case of data loss or system failures. A key advantage of the cloud is the ability to restore not only the data but also the entire environment through services such as **Infrastructure as Code (IaC)** or container orchestration tools.

Cloud-native databases often come with built-in backup and restore functionalities, seamlessly integrating these procedures into the overall data management strategy. Additionally, versioning and access controls in the cloud contribute to more granular control over the backup and restoration processes.

Importantly, adherence to compliance standards and data governance is integral to these procedures in the cloud. Encryption, both in transit and at rest, ensures that backup data remains secure, addressing the paramount concern of data protection.

In the landscape of cloud computing, the paradigm of *backup and restore procedures* undergoes nuanced transformations across various cloud service providers, each offering its unique set of tools and methodologies.

Amazon Web Services (AWS)

In AWS, the cornerstone is Amazon **Simple Storage Service** (**S3**), which provides a highly durable and scalable object storage solution. Backup procedures often involve utilizing AWS Backup, a fully managed backup service that centralizes and automates the backup process for a variety of AWS resources. For databases, AWS offers services such as Amazon **Relational Database Service** (**RDS**) with automated backup and restore features. Restoration can be initiated through the AWS Management Console or programmatically using the AWS **Command-Line Interface** (**CLI**).

Amazon Web Services (**AWS**) provides robust backup and restore services for its RDS, ensuring data durability and recovery capabilities. Here's an overview:

- *Automated backups*: AWS RDS offers automated backups as a fundamental feature. These backups are automatically taken daily during the maintenance window. They capture the entire database instance, including the database instance's entire storage volume. Automated backups are retained for a specified retention period, and during a restore, you can choose any point within this retention period.

- *Database snapshots*: Database snapshots are user-initiated backups that you can create at any time. Unlike automated backups, database snapshots are retained even if you delete the original database instance. They are stored until you explicitly choose to delete them. This feature is handy for creating backups before making significant changes to your database.

Let's walk through an example of creating a database snapshot in AWS for an RDS instance using the AWS Management Console.

Example: *Creating a database snapshot in AWS RDS*:

1. *AWS Management Console*:

    A. Log in to the AWS Management Console.

    B. Navigate to the Amazon RDS service.

2. *Choose an RDS instance*:

    - Select the RDS instance for which you want to create a database snapshot.

3. *Create a database snapshot*:

    A. In the RDS dashboard, locate the **Snapshots** section in the navigation pane.

    B. Click on the **Create Snapshot** button.

4. *Configure the snapshot*:

    A. Provide a meaningful name for your snapshot in the **DB Snapshot Identifier** field.

    B. Optionally, add a description to help identify the snapshot's purpose.

5. *Advanced options (optional)*:

   - You can specify additional settings such as enabling encryption for the snapshot, or you can add tags for better organization.

6. *Create a snapshot*:

   - Click on the **Create Snapshot** button to initiate the snapshot creation process.

7. *Monitor the snapshot creation process*:

   - You can monitor the progress of the snapshot's creation in the RDS console. Once completed, your new database snapshot will be listed.

AWS CLI command

If you prefer to use the AWS CLI, you can achieve the same using the following command:

```
aws rds create-db-snapshot --db-snapshot-identifier your-snapshot-name
--db-instance-identifier your-db-instance-name
```

Replace your-snapshot-name with a unique identifier for your snapshot and your-db-instance-name with the name of your RDS instance.

Here are some important considerations:

- Ensure that your AWS **Identity and Access Management** (**IAM**) user has the necessary permissions to create snapshots
- Regularly review and manage your snapshots, as they contribute to storage costs

This example demonstrates the simplicity of creating a database snapshot through the AWS Management Console or CLI, providing a **point-in-time recovery** (**PITR**) option for your RDS instance.

PITR

PITR allows you to restore a database instance to any specific second during your retention period. This feature uses both automated backups and database snapshots to provide granular control over the recovery point. PITR is particularly useful for recovering from user errors or database corruption.

In AWS, PITR allows you to restore a database to any specific time, down to a fraction of a second, within your specified retention period. Let's look at an example of setting up PITR for an Amazon RDS instance.

Example: *PITR in AWS RDS*:

1. *Navigate to the AWS Management Console*: Log in to the AWS Management Console and navigate to the Amazon RDS dashboard.

2. *Select the RDS instance*: Choose the RDS instance for which you want to enable PITR.

3. *Enable PITR*: In the RDS dashboard, select the target RDS instance and, under the **Backup** tab, find the **Backup retention period** setting. Set an appropriate retention period.

4. *Apply changes*: Click on the **Modify** button to apply the changes. AWS will start taking automatic backups, retaining them according to the specified period.

5. *Restore to a point in time*: Once the backups have been created, you can restore the database to any specific point in time within the retention period. Go to the **Databases** section, select your instance, and click on **Restore to a point in time**.

6. *Specify a time*: Choose the desired time for recovery; AWS will handle the restoration process, creating a new instance.

7. *Confirm and restore*: Confirm your settings and click **Restore DB Instance**. AWS will initiate the process of creating a new RDS instance based on the selected point in time.

8. *Access the restored database*: Once the restoration is complete, you'll have a new RDS instance representing the database at the specified point in time.

This process provides a powerful mechanism to recover from accidental data loss or database corruption by reverting to a specific point in time.

Now, let's learn how to enable PITR for an Amazon RDS instance using the AWS CLI.

Example: *Enabling PITR with the AWS CLI*:

1. *Set the backup retention period*: Use the modify-db-instance command to set the backup retention period:

   ```
   aws rds modify-db-instance --db-instance-identifier
   YourDBInstanceIdentifier --backup-retention-period 7
   ```

   This command sets the retention period to 7 days. Adjust the value based on your requirements.

2. *Enable automatic backups*: Ensure that automatic backups are enabled. This is often the default setting, but you can explicitly set it using the following command:

   ```
   aws rds modify-db-instance --db-instance-identifier
   YourDBInstanceIdentifier --backup-retention-period 7
   --preferred-backup-window "08:00-08:30"
   ```

   Here, we're also setting a preferred backup window, though it's optional.

3. *Monitor the modifications*: Monitor the modifications using the following command:

```
aws rds describe-db-instances --db-instance-identifier
YourDBInstanceIdentifier
```

Check `LatestRestorableTime` in the output to confirm that the changes have been applied.

4. *Restore to a point in time*: To restore the database to a specific point in time, use the `restore-db-instance-to-point-in-time` command:

```
aws rds restore-db-instance-to-point-in-time --source-db-
instance-identifier YourDBInstanceIdentifier --target-db-
instance-identifier YourRestoredDBInstanceIdentifier --restore-
time 2023-09-28T12:30:00
```

5. Adjust the `--restore-time` parameter to the desired point in time.

6. *Monitor the restoration*: Monitor the status of the restoration:

```
aws rds describe-db-instances --db-instance-identifier
YourRestoredDBInstanceIdentifier
```

Wait for the status to become **available**.

These commands leverage the AWS CLI for managing Amazon RDS instances and illustrate the process of enabling PITR and restoring to a specific point in time. Adjust the identifiers and timestamps accordingly for your use case.

AWS Backup integration

AWS Backup is a centralized, fully managed backup service that allows you to back up data across AWS services, including RDS. It provides a unified backup solution, enabling you to manage and monitor backups across multiple AWS resources.

AWS Backup is a centralized backup service that makes it easy to manage and automate backups across various AWS services. Let's look at an example of how to integrate AWS Backup with an Amazon RDS instance.

Example: *AWS Backup integration for Amazon RDS*:

1. *Create an AWS Backup plan*: First, create an AWS Backup plan using the `create-backup-plan` command. Specify the resources to be backed up, such as the Amazon RDS instance:

```
aws backup create-backup-plan --backup-plan-name
YourBackupPlan --rule-name YourBackupRule --resource-arn-list
arn:aws:rds:region:account-id:db:YourDBInstance
```

This will create a backup plan named `YourBackupPlan` with a rule named `YourBackupRule` for the specified RDS instance.

2. *Assign the backup plan*: Assign the backup plan to the RDS instance:

```
aws backup start-backup-job --backup-vault-name default
--resource-arn arn:aws:rds:region:account-id:db:YourDBInstance
--iam-role-arn arn:aws:iam::account-id:role/service-role/
AWSBackupDefaultServiceRole
```

This command starts a backup job for the RDS instance using the specified backup plan.

3. *Monitor backup jobs*: Monitor the status of backup jobs:

```
aws backup list-backup-jobs --by-backup-vault-name default
--resource-arn arn:aws:rds:region:account-id:db:YourDBInstance
```

Check for the completion of backup jobs.

4. *Restore from a backup*: If needed, restore the RDS instance from a backup using the restore-db-instance-from-aws-backup command:

```
aws rds restore-db-instance-from-aws-backup --db-instance-
identifier YourRestoredDBInstance --backup-arn
arn:aws:rds:region:account-id:backup:backup-id
```

Specify the backup ARN you obtained from the AWS Backup console.

This example demonstrates how to integrate AWS Backup with Amazon RDS, allowing you to manage and monitor backups centrally. Adjust the identifiers and parameters based on your setup.

Cross-region automated backups

For additional redundancy and disaster recovery, you can enable cross-region automated backups. This feature creates a copy of your automated backups in a different AWS region, enhancing data resilience.

Multi-Availability Zone (AZ) deployments

In **multi-Availability Zone** (**AZ**) deployments, AWS RDS automatically replicates your database to a standby instance in a different availability zone. In the event of a failure, AWS automatically switches to the standby instance, providing high availability and reducing the risk of data loss.

These backup and restore mechanisms in AWS RDS empower users with comprehensive data protection and recovery options, ensuring the integrity and availability of their databases.

Microsoft Azure

Azure employs Azure Backup as a comprehensive solution for data protection. Azure Backup supports various workloads, including virtual machines, databases, and files. For instance, Azure Virtual Machines can be backed up using Azure Backup Vaults, and the restore process is facilitated through the Azure portal. Azure's SQL Database service also integrates automatic backups with point-in-time restore capabilities.

Azure Backup is Microsoft Azure's cloud-based backup solution and provides scalable, secure, and cost-effective backup services for various Azure services as well as on-premises data. Here's an overview of the backup and restore services offered by Azure:

- **Azure Backup for Azure Virtual Machines**:

  - *Backup*: Azure Backup enables you to create backup policies for Azure Virtual Machines. You can schedule daily, weekly, or custom backup frequencies:

    - Backups can include the entire virtual machine or specific disks

    - Backups are stored in recovery services vaults, which can be geo-redundant for enhanced durability

  - *Restore*:

    - You can restore the entire virtual machine or individual files and folders

    - Azure Backup supports instant restores for virtual machines

Example: *Azure Backup for Azure Virtual Machines*:

1. *Create a Recovery Services Vault*:

   I.   In the Azure portal, navigate to **All services** and select **Recovery Services Vaults**.

   II.   Click on + **Add** to create a new Recovery Services Vault.

   III. Provide the required details, select your subscription, resource group, and region, and then click **Review + create**.

2. *Configure Azure Backup for Azure Virtual Machines*:

   I.   Within the newly created vault, click on **Backup** and then + **Backup**.

   II.   Set the workload to **Virtual Machine**.

   III. Choose the virtual machine you want to back up.

   IV.   Configure the backup policy, including the backup frequency, retention range, and time.

3. *Review and create the backup*:

   I.   Review your settings and click **Enable Backup** to start the initial backup.

4. *Trigger a backup restore*:

   I.   To trigger a restore, go to the **Backup items** section in the vault.

   II.   Select the virtual machine and click on **Restore VM**.

III.   Choose the restore point you want to recover.

IV.   Configure the restore settings, such as target resource group, virtual network, and so on.

5.   *Monitor and manage backups*:

I.   Monitor the backup jobs and their status in the **Backup items** section.

II.   Review recovery points, backup jobs, and related metrics in the vault.

Using the Azure CLI

Here's a simplified example of using the Azure CLI to initiate a backup:

```
# Create a Recovery Services Vault
az backup vault create --resource-group YourResourceGroup --name
YourRecoveryServicesVault --location YourLocation
# Enable backup for a VM
az backup protection enable-for-vm --vm YourVMName --policy-name
DefaultPolicy --vault-name YourRecoveryServicesVault --resource-group
YourResourceGroup
```

> **Note**
>
> Ensure you replace placeholders such as `YourResourceGroup`,
> `YourRecoveryServicesVault`, `YourVMName`, and so on with your actual resource
> group, vault name, virtual machine name, and so on.

This example illustrates the basic steps of setting up Azure Backup for Azure Virtual Machines through the Azure portal and using the Azure CLI for automation. The service provides flexibility in managing backup policies and restoring virtual machines based on specific recovery points:

- **Azure Backup for databases**:

  - *Backup*:

    - Azure Backup supports backup for various databases, including Azure SQL Database, MySQL, PostgreSQL, and more

    - Backup policies can be configured for automatic backups

  - *Restore*:

    - PITRs are supported for databases

    - Cross-region restores for geo-redundancy are available

Let's walk through an example of using Azure Backup for databases, focusing on Microsoft Azure SQL Database, and demonstrate using the Azure CLI.

Example: *Azure Backup for databases (Azure SQL Database)*:

1. *Create a Recovery Services Vault*:

   I.   In the Azure portal, navigate to **All services** and select **Recovery Services Vaults**.

   II.   Click on + **Add** to create a new Recovery Services Vault.

   III. Provide the required details, select your subscription, resource group, and region, and then click **Review + create**.

2. *Configure Azure Backup for Azure SQL Database*:

   I.   Within the newly created vault, click on **Backup** and then + **Backup**.

   II.   Set the workload to **Azure SQL Database**.

   III. Choose the Azure SQL Database you want to back up.

   IV.   Configure the backup policy, including the backup frequency, retention range, and time.

3. *Review and create a backup*:

   I.   Review your settings and click **Enable Backup** to start the initial backup.

Using the Azure CLI

Here's a simplified example of using the Azure CLI to initiate a backup for an Azure SQL Database instance:

```
# Create a Recovery Services Vault
az backup vault create --resource-group YourResourceGroup --name
YourRecoveryServicesVault --location YourLocation
# Enable backup for an Azure SQL Database
az backup protection enable-for-azurewl --policy-name DefaultPolicy
--workload-type AzureSQL --item-name YourSQLDatabase --vault-name
YourRecoveryServicesVault --resource-group YourResourceGroup
```

> **Note**
> Ensure you replace placeholders such as `YourResourceGroup`,
> `YourRecoveryServicesVault`, `YourSQLDatabase`, and so on, with your actual
> resource group, vault name, Azure SQL Database name, and so on.

This example illustrates the basic steps of setting up Azure Backup for an Azure SQL Database through the Azure portal and using the Azure CLI for automation. The service provides flexibility in managing backup policies and restoring databases based on specific recovery points.

Restoring a database using Azure Backup in Azure SQL Database

Prerequisites:

- Ensure you have a Recovery Services Vault in your Azure subscription
- A backup of the Azure SQL Database should already exist in the vault

1. *Access the Azure portal*:

    I.   Navigate to the Azure portal (`https://portal.azure.com/`).

2. *Open the Recovery Services Vault*:

    I.   In the left navigation pane, click on **All services**, and then search for `Recovery Services Vaults`.

    II.   Select your recovery services vault.

3. *Access Backup Items*:

    I.   Inside the vault, click on **Backup Items** in the left menu.

    II.   Choose the SQL Database backup item associated with your database.

4. *Initiate a restore*:

    I.   Under the **Items** tab, select the SQL database for which you want to initiate the restore.

    II.   Click on the **Restore** button in the top menu.

5. *Configure restore options*:

    I.   Choose a restore point from the available backups.

    II.   Configure additional restore options, such as the target server, database name, and other settings.

    III. Click **OK** to confirm the restore configuration.

6. *Monitor the restore's progress*:

    I.   Navigate to the **Jobs** tab to monitor the progress of the restore operation.

    II.   Once the restore job has been completed, the database will be restored to the specified point.

7. *Access the restored database*:

    I.   Verify the restored database in the Azure SQL Database service.

> **Note**
>
> These steps provide a high-level overview. Depending on your specific requirements, the restore process might involve additional configurations.

Using the Azure CLI

If you prefer using the Azure CLI, you can achieve similar steps programmatically. Here's a simplified example:

```
# Set variables
resourceGroup="YourResourceGroup"
vaultName="YourRecoveryServicesVault"
itemName="YourSQLDatabaseBackupItem"
restorePoint="YourRestorePoint"

# Restore database
az backup restore restore-azurewl --resource-group $resourceGroup
--vault-name $vaultName --container-name SqlServers --item-name
$itemName --rp-name $restorePoint
```

Remember to replace placeholders with your actual values.

This example demonstrates how to restore an Azure SQL Database using Azure Backup, ensuring that you have control over the PITR of your databases.

1. **Azure Backup for files and folders**:

   - *Backup*:

     + You can back up files and folders from Azure Virtual Machines
     + Granular file-level recovery is supported

   - *Restore*:

     + You can restore files and folders to the original or a different location

Let's walk through an example of using Azure Backup for files and folders, focusing on protecting files from an Azure Virtual Machine, and demonstrate using the Azure CLI.

Example: *Azure Backup for files and folders (Azure Virtual Machine)*:

1. *Configure Azure Backup for files and folders*:

   I.   In the Azure portal, navigate to your virtual machine.

   II.   Under the **Settings** menu, select **Backup**.

   III.   Click on **+Backup** to create a new backup policy.

Define the backup policy settings, including the frequency, retention, and storage redundancy.

2. *Enable a backup for files and folders*:

Using the Azure CLI, do the following:

```
# Set variables
resourceGroup="YourResourceGroup"
vaultName="YourRecoveryServicesVault"
policyName="YourBackupPolicy"
vmName="YourVMName"

# Enable backup for files and folders
az backup protection enable-for-vm --policy-name $policyName
--vm $vmName --vault-name $vaultName --resource-group
$resourceGroup
```

3. *Trigger a backup for files and folders*:

Using the Azure CLI, this is done as follows:

```
# Trigger an on-demand backup for the specified files and
folders
az backup protection backup-now --item-name /var/www --vault-
name $vaultName --container-name $vmName --resource-group
$resourceGroup
```

> **Note**
>
> Replace placeholders such as YourResourceGroup, YourRecoveryServicesVault, YourBackupPolicy, YourVMName, and so on, with your actual values.

This example illustrates the basic steps of setting up Azure Backup for files and folders from an Azure Virtual Machine through the Azure portal and using the Azure CLI for automation. The service protects critical files and folders with flexible backup policies and on-demand backup capabilities:

- **Azure Backup for on-premises data**:

    - *Backup*:

        - Azure Backup can be used to back up on-premises servers, files, and folders

        - Azure Backup Server is an on-premises solution for backing up to Azure

    - *Restore*:

        - You can restore on-premises data to Azure or on-premises servers

- **Azure Site Recovery (ASR)**:

  - *Disaster Recovery*:

    - ASR provides **Disaster Recovery as a Service (DRaaS)**

    - It allows replication of on-premises servers to Azure for disaster recovery purposes

  - *Failover and failback*:

    - ASR supports failover to Azure and failback to on-premises

- **Long-term retention**:

  - Azure Backup provides long-term retention capabilities, allowing you to store backup data for extended durations

- **Monitoring and reporting**:

  - Azure Backup offers monitoring and reporting features to track backup jobs, storage usage, and compliance

To use Azure Backup, you typically create a Recovery Services Vault and configure backup policies based on your requirements. The integration is designed to be user-friendly, allowing for both on-demand and scheduled backups. Restores can be initiated through the Azure portal or using PowerShell commands.

Google Cloud Platform (GCP)

In GCP, **Google Cloud Storage (GCS)** acts as a robust platform for backup storage. Google Cloud's snapshot feature is widely used for creating point-in-time backups of persistent disks. Google Cloud SQL, the managed database service, incorporates automatic daily backups that can be restored with a few clicks through the Google Cloud Console. GCP's IaC tool, Deployment Manager, allows you to restore entire environments.

GCP provides several services for backup and restore, each designed to cater to different data types and use cases. Here are some key services:

- **Google Cloud Storage (GCS)**:

  - *Backup*: GCS is a highly durable and available object storage service. You can use it to back up and store various types of data, including images, videos, and other unstructured data.

  - *Restore*: Data stored in GCS can be easily restored through the GCP console, the `gsutil` command-line tool, or programmatically using APIs.

Let's consider a scenario where you want to back up a local file to GCS using the `gsutil` command-line tool. Here are the steps:

1. *Install gsutil*:

    I.   Ensure that you have the `gsutil` command-line tool installed.

2. *Authenticate with Google Cloud*:

    I.   Run the following command to authenticate and configure the `gsutil` tool with your Google Cloud project:

    ```
    gcloud auth login
    ```

    Follow the instructions to log in and set the appropriate configurations.

3. *Create a bucket*:

    If you don't have a GCS bucket, create one using the following command:

    ```
    Replace [BUCKET_NAME] with your desired bucket name:
    gsutil mb -c regional -l us-central1 gs://[BUCKET_NAME]
    ```

4. *Perform the backup*:

    Now, you can back up a local file to your GCS bucket. Replace `[LOCAL_FILE]` with the path to your local file and `[BUCKET_NAME]` with your GCS bucket:

    ```
    gsutil cp [LOCAL_FILE] gs://[BUCKET_NAME]/
    ```

    For example, let's say you want to back up a file named `example.txt` located in your home directory to a bucket named `my-backups`. The commands would be as follows:

    ```
    gsutil mb -c regional -l us-central1 gs://my-backups
    gsutil cp ~/example.txt gs://my-backups/
    ```

    This example creates a bucket named `my-backups` and then copies the local file, `example.txt`, to that bucket.

    Here are some notes:

    *   Ensure that you have the necessary permissions to perform these operations

    *   Customize the bucket name, file path, and other parameters based on your requirements

Now, let's go through the process of restoring a file from GCS to your local machine using the `gsutil` command-line tool.

For this, you must make sure you have the `gsutil` command-line tool installed and that you've authenticated with your Google Cloud account (as explained previously).

Restoring a file

Follow these steps:

1. *List objects in the bucket*:

    You need to identify the object (file) you want to restore. List the objects in your bucket using the following command:

    ```
    gsutil ls gs://[BUCKET_NAME]/
    ```

    Replace [BUCKET_NAME] with the name of your GCS bucket. This command will display a list of objects in the bucket.

2. *Restore the file*:

    Now, you can restore the file from GCS to your local machine. Use the following command:

    ```
    gsutil cp gs://[BUCKET_NAME]/[OBJECT_NAME] [LOCAL_DESTINATION]
    ```

    Replace [BUCKET_NAME] with your bucket name, [OBJECT_NAME] with the name of the object you want to restore (obtained from the list command), and [LOCAL_DESTINATION] with the path where you want to restore the file locally.

    For example, let's say you want to restore the example.txt file from the my-backups bucket to your home directory.

    This command copies the specified object from the bucket to your local machine.

    Here are some notes:

    - Ensure that you have the necessary permissions to perform these operations
    - Customize the bucket name, object name, local destination, and other parameters based on your requirements

3. **Google Cloud SQL**:

    - *Backup*: Cloud SQL provides automated daily backups for MySQL, PostgreSQL, and SQL Server databases. You can also create on-demand backups.
    - *Restore*: You can restore from automated backups to a point in time or a specific backup.

    Let's go through the process of backing up a Google Cloud SQL database using the gcloud command-line tool.

    For this, make sure you have the gcloud command-line tool installed and that you've authenticated with your Google Cloud account.

Backing up a Cloud SQL database

Follow these steps:

1. *List your Cloud SQL instances*:

   First, list your Cloud SQL instances to get the name of the instance you want to back up. Use the following command:

   ```
   gcloud sql instances list
   ```

2. *Start a backup*:

   Now, initiate a backup for your Cloud SQL instance. Use the following command:

   ```
   gcloud sql backups create --instance=[INSTANCE_NAME]
   ```

   Replace [INSTANCE_NAME] with the name of your Cloud SQL instance that you obtained from the list command.

   For example, let's say your Cloud SQL instance is named my-instance. The command would be as follows:

   ```
   gcloud sql backups create --instance=my-instance
   ```

   This command triggers a backup for the specified Cloud SQL instance.

3. *Monitor the backup's status*:

   You can monitor the status of your backup using the following command:

   ```
   gcloud sql backups list --instance=[INSTANCE_NAME]
   ```

   Replace [INSTANCE_NAME] with your Cloud SQL instance's name. This command shows a list of backups and their statuses.

   Here are some notes:

   • Ensure that you have the necessary permissions to perform these operations

   • Customize the instance's name and other parameters based on your requirements

Restoring a Google Cloud SQL database involves selecting a specific backup and restoring it to your Cloud SQL instance. The following subsection walks through the steps to restore a Cloud SQL database using the gcloud command-line tool:

Prerequisites:

Make sure you have the gcloud command-line tool installed, and you've authenticated with your Google Cloud account.

Restoring a Cloud SQL database

Follow these steps:

1. *List the available backups*:

   List the available backups for your Cloud SQL instance. Use the following command:

   ```bash
   gcloud sql backups list --instance=[INSTANCE_NAME]
   ```

   Replace `[INSTANCE_NAME]` with the name of your Cloud SQL instance.

   Here's an example:

   ```bash
   gcloud sql backups list --instance=my-instance
   ```

   This command shows a list of backups and their statuses.

2. *Restore the database*:

   Choose a specific backup from the list and use the following command to restore it:

   ```bash
   gcloud sql backups restore [BACKUP_ID] --restore-instance=[NEW_
   INSTANCE_NAME]
   ```

   Replace `[BACKUP_ID]` with the ID of the backup you want to restore.

   Replace `[NEW_INSTANCE_NAME]` with the name you want to give to the restored instance.

   Here's an example:

   ```bash
   gcloud sql backups restore my-instance-20210901-123456
   --restore-instance=my-restored-instance
   ```

   This command restores the selected backup to a new Cloud SQL instance.

3. *Monitor the restore status*:

   You can monitor the status of the restore operation using the following command:

   ```bash
   gcloud sql operations list --instance=[NEW_INSTANCE_NAME]
   ```

   Replace `[NEW_INSTANCE_NAME]` with the name of your newly restored Cloud SQL instance.

Here's an example:

```bash
gcloud sql operations list --instance=my-restored-instance
```

This command shows the status of the restore operation.

Here are some notes:

- Ensure that you have the necessary permissions to perform these operations
- Customize the instance names, backup IDs, and other parameters based on your requirements

4. **Google Cloud Spanner**:

   - *Backup*: Cloud Spanner offers continuous, incremental backups, allowing you to restore your database to any point in time within the backup retention window
   - *Restore*: PITR is supported, and you can choose a specific timestamp or a transaction to restore to

   Google Cloud Spanner provides an automated, continuous backup and restore process, making it easier for users to manage and restore their databases. Here, we will provide a detailed explanation of the backup and restore process for Google Cloud Spanner.

   Backup process:

   I. **Automated backups**:

   - Google Cloud Spanner automatically performs continuous backups of the entire database
   - Backups are incremental, and only changes since the last backup are stored, minimizing storage costs

   II. **Retention policy**:

   - Backups are retained for 7 days by default, but users can configure a custom retention period
   - Users can also create on-demand backups as needed

   Restore process:

   III. **Selecting a backup**:

   - Identify the specific backup you want to restore. You can view available backups and their timestamps

   IV. **Restoring a backup**:

   - Use the Google Cloud Console, the `gcloud` command-line tool, or the API to initiate the restore process

- Specify the timestamp or version of the backup you want to restore

Here's an example of using `gcloud`:

```bash
gcloud spanner databases create [DATABASE_ID]
--instance=[INSTANCE_ID] --ddl='[SCHEMA_DEFINITION]' --from-
backup='[BACKUP_TIMESTAMP]'
```

Replace `[DATABASE_ID]`, `[INSTANCE_ID]`, `[SCHEMA_DEFINITION]`, and `[BACKUP_TIMESTAMP]` with your specific values.

V.   **Monitoring the restore**:

Monitor the restore operation's progress using the Google Cloud console or the `gcloud` command-line tool.

Here's an example of using `gcloud`:

```bash
gcloud spanner operations list --instance=[INSTANCE_ID]
```

Replace `[INSTANCE_ID]` with your Spanner instance ID.

VI.   **Verification and testing**:

- After the restore operation is complete, verify the database's integrity and functionality
- Optionally, test the restored database to ensure it meets your requirements

Here are some notes:

- The automated backup and restore process simplifies database management, but users should understand their specific RPOs and RTOs
- Remember to follow best practices and consider your specific business requirements when managing backups and restores in Google Cloud Spanner

5. **Google Cloud Bigtable**:

- *Backup*: Bigtable supports online backups, allowing you to create a backup of your data while it is still online and accessible
- *Restore*: You can restore a table to a specific backup, creating a new table with the same schema and data

6. **Google Cloud Dataproc**:

- *Backup*: While Dataproc is primarily for processing large datasets, you can use Cloud Storage to back up any critical data

- *Restore*: Data stored in Cloud Storage can be used to restore or recreate a Dataproc environment

7. **Google Cloud Filestore**:

- *Backup*: Filestore provides backups for its file shares, allowing you to create a backup at any time

- *Restore*: You can restore a file share to a specific backup, effectively rolling back to that point in time

8. **Google Cloud Pub/Sub**:

- *Backup*: Pub/Sub doesn't provide a direct backup service. However, you can use Dataflow to process and store messages in other Google Cloud services such as Cloud Storage or BigQuery.

- *Restore*: Restoration would involve reprocessing stored data in other services.

9. **Google Cloud Firestore**:

- *Backup*: Firestore automatically backs up your data, and you can also manually export data to Cloud Storage

- *Restore*: You can import data from Cloud Storage back into Firestore

Each of these services comes with its own set of features and considerations. When implementing a backup and restore strategy, it's crucial to consider factors such as data consistency, RTOs, and cost implications.

Cross-cloud solutions

For users employing a multi-cloud strategy, solutions such as Veeam and Commvault offer cross-cloud backup and recovery services. These tools provide a unified approach to backup procedures, allowing users to manage and restore data across different cloud environments seamlessly.

In essence, these examples showcase the diversity of approaches and tools available for backup and restore procedures in the cloud, emphasizing the adaptability and richness of each cloud service provider's ecosystem.

Cross-cloud solutions refer to strategies and tools that enable data management, including backup and restore services, across multiple cloud providers. Let's look at some key considerations and services related to cross-cloud backup and restore.

Multi-cloud data management platforms

Platforms such as Rubrik, Cohesity, and Veeam offer solutions that can manage data across various cloud providers.

They provide features such as a unified management interface for backups and restores, support for various cloud storage options, and automation for backup policies and scheduling.

Multi-cloud data management platforms provide a unified and centralized approach to data operations, including backup, recovery, migration, and analytics. They aim to simplify data management in complex, multi-cloud scenarios.

Let's look at their key features:

- **Unified management interface**:
- Example: *Rubrik*:

  - Rubrik provides a single dashboard for managing data across on-premises and multiple cloud environments
  - Users can define policies, monitor activities, and perform operations seamlessly

- **Multi-cloud backup and recovery**:
- Example: *Cohesity*:

  - Cohesity offers backup and recovery solutions that support various cloud providers
  - It enables organizations to have a consistent backup strategy across their multi-cloud architecture

- **Automation and orchestration**:
- Example: *Veeam*:

  - Veeam orchestrates backup and recovery workflows across different cloud platforms
  - Automation features enhance efficiency and reduce manual intervention

- **Cloud storage integration**:
- Example: *NetApp Cloud Volumes ONTAP*:

  - NetApp Cloud Volumes ONTAP integrates with various cloud storage services
  - It allows seamless movement of data between on-premises and cloud environments

- **Scalability and flexibility**:
- Example: *Druva*:

  - Druva provides scalable data protection across multiple clouds
  - It adjusts to the dynamic nature of cloud environments, supporting the growth of data

- **Comprehensive data management**:
- Example: *Commvault*:

  - Commvault offers a complete data management platform for multi-cloud environments
  - It covers backup, recovery, archiving, and compliance requirements

- **Cloud-native backup services**:
- Overview: Major cloud providers (AWS, Azure, and GCP) offer native backup services for their respective cloud platforms.
- Features:

  - AWS Backup, Azure Backup, and Google Cloud's Cloud Storage provide scalable and integrated backup solutions
  - Automated snapshots, incremental backups, and life cycle management

Cloud-native backup services refer to backup solutions that are specifically designed to operate seamlessly within cloud environments. These services leverage the native capabilities of the cloud provider, providing efficient and scalable backup and recovery solutions. Here, we'll provide a detailed discussion with examples.

Here are the key characteristics:

- **Integration with cloud platforms**:
- Example: *AWS Backup*:
  - AWS Backup is a fully managed backup service that centralizes and automates the backup of data across AWS services
  - It supports services such as Amazon EBS, Amazon RDS, and more

- **Automated policies and scheduling**:
- Example: *Azure Backup*:

  - Azure Backup offers automated backup policies and scheduling for various Azure services
  - Users can define policies to back up virtual machines, databases, and files

- **Snapshot-based backups**:
- Example: *Google Cloud Snapshot*:

  - Google Cloud's snapshot feature allows you to create point-in-time snapshots of persistent disks
  - It's an efficient way to back up data for Google Cloud instances

- **Incremental backups**:
- Example: *Alibaba Cloud Backup*:

  - Alibaba Cloud Backup supports incremental backup for ECS instances, reducing backup time and storage costs
  - It efficiently captures changes since the last backup

- **Serverless architectures**:
- Example: *AWS Backup for AWS Lambda*:

  - AWS Backup supports serverless architectures, allowing users to back up and restore AWS Lambda functions
  - It integrates with AWS Lambda's native features

  Here are its benefits:

  - **Native integration**: Cloud-native backup services seamlessly integrate with the cloud provider's ecosystem
  - **Scalability**: These services scale with the growing data and workload demands
  - **Automation**: Automated policies simplify the backup and recovery process
  - **Cost-efficiency**: Many cloud-native services offer cost-effective pricing models

  Here are some considerations:

  - **Service compatibility**: Ensure compatibility with the specific cloud services your organization uses
  - **Security**: Adhere to security best practices and compliance standards
  - **RTOs and PITR**: Assess the service's capabilities in meeting recovery objectives

Now, let's recap the examples:

1. **AWS Backup**:

   - **Use case**: Centralized backup for various AWS services
   - **Key feature**: Integration with a wide range of AWS services

2. **Azure Backup**:

   - **Use case**: Automated backup for Azure VMs, databases, and files
   - **Key feature**: Incremental backups and scheduling

3. **Google Cloud Snapshot**:

   - **Use case**: Snapshot-based backups for Google Cloud persistent disks
   - **Key feature**: Efficient point-in-time backups

4. **Alibaba Cloud Backup**:

   - **Use case**: Incremental backup for Alibaba Cloud ECS instances
   - **Key feature**: Captures changes since the last backup

5. **AWS Backup for AWS Lambda**:

   - **Use case**: Serverless backup and restore for AWS Lambda functions
   - **Key feature**: Integration with serverless architectures

Third-party cloud backup solutions

Companies such as Commvault and Druva provide cloud-agnostic backup solutions that support multiple cloud providers.

Their features include backup and restore capabilities for various cloud services and support for compliance and data governance.

Third-party cloud backup solutions are independent services or tools provided by external vendors to perform data backup and recovery in cloud environments. These solutions offer features beyond the native capabilities of cloud providers and cater to a wide range of cloud platforms. Let's consider an in-depth discussion with examples.

The following are their key characteristics:

- **Cross-cloud compatibility**:
- Example: *Veeam Backup & Replication*:

  - Veeam supports backup and recovery across various cloud platforms, including AWS, Azure, Google Cloud, and others
  - It provides a unified solution for multi-cloud data protection

- **Comprehensive data protection**:
- Example: *Commvault*:

  - Commvault is a comprehensive data management platform that includes backup, recovery, and other data protection features
  - It supports a variety of cloud providers and on-premises environments

- **Hybrid cloud support**:
- Example: *Druva*:

  - Druva's cloud data protection platform extends support to hybrid environments, providing backup for both on-premises and cloud-based data

  - It integrates with major cloud platforms

- **Security and compliance**:
- Example: *Acronis Cyber Protect Cloud*:

  - Acronis combines backup with cybersecurity features, ensuring data security in the backup process

  - It's designed to meet security and compliance requirements

- **Flexible deployment models**:
- Example: *Rubrik*:

  - Rubrik offers a cloud data management platform with flexibility in deployment, supporting both on-premises and cloud environments

  - It provides a unified solution for data backup and management

Here are the benefits:

- **Platform-agnosticism**: Third-party solutions often support multiple cloud platforms, providing flexibility

- **Advanced features**: Many third-party tools offer advanced features such as deduplication, compression, and granular recovery options

- **Unified management**: Backups are managed centrally across different clouds and on-premises infrastructure

- **Customization**: Additional features are provided for security, compliance, and customization based on organizational needs

Here are some considerations:

- **Compatibility**: Ensure compatibility with the specific cloud platforms and services your organization uses

- **Scalability**: Assess the scalability of the solution with growing data volumes

- **Cost model**: Understand the pricing model and ensure it aligns with your budget and usage patterns

Now, let's recap the examples:

- **Veeam Backup & Replication**:

  - **Key feature**: Cross-cloud compatibility that supports AWS, Azure, and other platforms

- **Commvault**:

  - **Key feature**: A comprehensive data management platform with support for various cloud providers

- **Druva**:

  - **Key feature**: Hybrid cloud support, providing backups for both on-premises and cloud-based data

- **Acronis Cyber Protect Cloud**:

  - **Key feature**: A security-focused backup solution with compliance features

- **Rubrik**:

  - **Key feature**: Flexible deployment models, supporting both on-premises and cloud environments

Cloud-integrated backup appliances

Some solutions, such as NetApp Cloud Volumes ONTAP, offer backup appliances with integration across different cloud environments.

Their features include providing unified backup and restore capabilities for on-premises and cloud environments, as well as snapshot management and replication between clouds.

Cloud-integrated backup appliances are purpose-built hardware or virtual appliances designed to seamlessly integrate with cloud storage and backup services. These appliances offer a combination of on-premises data storage and backup capabilities with cloud storage for extended data retention and disaster recovery. Here, we will provide a detailed discussion with examples.

First, let's look at the key characteristics:

- **Hybrid architecture**:
- Example: *Barracuda Backup*:

  - Barracuda Backup appliances provide on-premises backup and recovery capabilities

  - They seamlessly integrate with Barracuda Cloud for off-site storage and disaster recovery

- **Unified management**:
- Example: *Dell EMC Data Domain Cloud Tier*:

  - Dell EMC Data Domain appliances integrate with cloud storage, extending on-premises backup to the cloud
  - Unified management allows users to manage on-premises and cloud backups through a single interface

- **Scalability**:
- Example: *HPE StoreOnce*:

  - HPE StoreOnce integrates with cloud storage to provide scalable backup solutions
  - It supports various deployment models, including on-premises and hybrid cloud environments

- **Data deduplication**:
- Example: *Nutanix Mine*:

  - Nutanix Mine is an integrated data protection solution that includes backup appliances
  - It integrates with cloud storage, and its features include data deduplication for efficient storage use

- **Security features**:
- Example: *Cohesity DataPlatform*:

  - Cohesity DataPlatform offers a hyper-converged infrastructure with integrated backup capabilities
  - It supports cloud integration for data archival and disaster recovery

Now, let's consider the benefits:

- **Data retention**: Appliances provide local backups for fast restores and leverage cloud storage for extended data retention
- **Cost-efficiency**: Cloud storage integration allows organizations to benefit from scalable and cost-effective cloud storage
- **Simplified management**: Unified interfaces for managing both on-premises and cloud-based backups simplify administration
- **Disaster recovery**: Cloud-integrated appliances support disaster recovery strategies with off-site copies in the cloud

Here are some considerations:

- **Bandwidth**: Uploading data to the cloud may impact network bandwidth, especially for large datasets

- **Security**: Ensure that data is encrypted during transmission and at rest in the cloud

- **Compatibility**: Check compatibility with cloud providers and services to ensure seamless integration

Now, let's recap the examples:

1. **Barracuda Backup**:

   - **Key feature**: A hybrid architecture with on-premises backup appliances integrated with Barracuda Cloud.

2. **Dell EMC Data Domain Cloud Tier**:

   - **Key feature**: Unified management of on-premises and cloud backups, with data stored in the cloud tier

3. **HPE StoreOnce**:

   - **Key feature**: Scalable backup solutions with support for various deployment models, including on-premises and hybrid cloud

4. **Nutanix Mine**:

   - **Key feature**: An integrated data protection solution with backup appliances and cloud integration, featuring data deduplication

5. **Cohesity DataPlatform**:

   - **Key feature**: A hyper-converged infrastructure with integrated backup capabilities, supporting cloud integration for data archival

Organizations should evaluate their specific backup and recovery needs, scalability requirements, and cloud integration preferences when considering a cloud-integrated backup appliance. Always refer to the official documentation of these solutions for the latest and most accurate information. The examples provided are based on information available up to September 2021.

Data replication tools

Solutions such as Dell EMC RecoverPoint and AWS Storage Gateway provide replication services for disaster recovery across clouds.

Their features include continuous data protection and replication between cloud regions or providers, as well as support for hybrid cloud architectures.

Data replication involves creating and maintaining a copy of data across different locations or systems. This is crucial for ensuring data availability, disaster recovery, and enabling data access in distributed environments. Here, we'll discuss this topic in detail and provide examples of data replication tools.

First, let's look at the key characteristics:

- **Synchronous versus asynchronous replication**:
- Example: *EMC Symmetrix Remote Data Facility (SRDF)*:

  - EMC SRDF offers both synchronous and asynchronous replication

  - Synchronous replication ensures data consistency but may introduce latency, while asynchronous replication provides more flexibility but might have some data lag

- **Multi-platform and cloud support**:
- Example: *AWS Database Migration Service (DMS)*:

  - AWS DMS supports the migration and replication of databases, including on-premises databases to the cloud

  - It supports various database engines, making it versatile for heterogeneous environments

- **Real-time replication**:
- Example: *GoldenGate by Oracle*:

  - Oracle GoldenGate provides real-time data replication for heterogeneous databases

  - It supports continuous availability by capturing and delivering changes in real time

- **Change data capture (CDC)**:
- Example: *Attunity Replicate*:

  - Attunity Replicate is known for CDC, capturing changes in source systems and replicating them to target systems

  - This is particularly useful for minimizing the amount of data transferred

- **Global distribution**:
- Example: *Microsoft Azure Cosmos DB*:

  - Azure Cosmos DB is a globally distributed, multi-model database service with built-in replication

  - It ensures low-latency access to data for users around the world

- **Automated failover and recovery**:
- Example: *MySQL Group Replication*:
  - MySQL Group Replication provides a built-in, synchronous replication mechanism
  - It supports automated failover and recovery, enhancing high availability

- **Data consistency models**:
- Example: *Couchbase Cross Data Center Replication* (*XDCR*):
  - Couchbase XDCR supports bidirectional data replication between clusters
  - It provides flexibility in choosing eventual consistency or strong consistency models

Here are the benefits:

- **High availability**: Replication ensures data availability, reducing the risk of data loss in case of system failures
- **Disaster recovery**: Distributed copies of data enable quick recovery in the event of a disaster
- **Data migration**: Replication tools facilitate seamless migration of data between databases or environments
- **Load balancing**: Replicating data across multiple nodes helps balance the load and improves performance

The following are some considerations:

- **Latency**: Synchronous replication may introduce latency, impacting performance.
- **Conflict resolution**: Tools should provide mechanisms for resolving conflicts when changes occur simultaneously in multiple locations.
- **Scalability**: Evaluate the scalability of the replication solution to accommodate growing data volumes.

Now, let's recap the examples:

- **EMC SRDF**:
  - **Key feature**: Synchronous and asynchronous replication for EMC Symmetrix storage systems
- **AWS DMS**:
  - **Key feature**: Supports migration and replication of databases with multi-platform and cloud support
- **Oracle GoldenGate**:
  - **Key feature**: Real-time data replication for heterogeneous databases with support for continuous availability

- **Attunity Replicate**:

  - **Key feature**: Known for CDC to minimize the amount of data transferred during replication

- **Azure Cosmos DB**:

  - **Key feature**: A globally distributed, multi-model database service with built-in replication for low-latency access

- **MySQL Group Replication**:

  - **Key feature**: Built-in, synchronous replication for MySQL with automated failover and recovery

- **Couchbase XDCR**:

  - **Key feature**: Bidirectional data replication supporting various consistency models

Choosing the right data replication tool depends on specific use cases, database systems in use, and the desired level of consistency and availability.

Here are some things you should consider while backing up and restoring data:

- **Interoperability**: Ensure compatibility and seamless integration between on-premises infrastructure and various cloud environments

- **Security and compliance**: Cross-cloud solutions must comply with security standards and regulations governing data storage and transfer

- **Cost management**: Evaluate the cost implications of storing and transferring data across different clouds

Summary

This chapter comprehensively covered the intricacies of safeguarding and restoring data in a cloud environment. You gained insights into diverse backup strategies such as full, incremental, and differential backups, understanding when to employ each method effectively. Exploring such retention policies equipped you with the knowledge to define and implement data retention policies that align with your compliance and business requirements. The strategies for disaster recovery planning, inclusive of backup storage locations, data redundancy, and understanding RTOs and RPOs, provided a holistic view of ensuring data resilience. This chapter delved into cloud-native backup solutions, exemplifying major cloud providers such as AWS, Azure, and Google Cloud, offering automated backup services. Overall, you obtained a nuanced understanding of backup and restoration processes within a cloud context, empowering you with the expertise to devise robust data protection strategies tailored to your specific needs.

Index

S

www.packtpub.com

Subscribe to our online digital library for full access to over 7,000 books and videos, as well as industry leading tools to help you plan your personal development and advance your career. For more information, please visit our website.

Why subscribe?

- Spend less time learning and more time coding with practical eBooks and Videos from over 4,000 industry professionals

- Improve your learning with Skill Plans built especially for you

- Get a free eBook or video every month

- Fully searchable for easy access to vital information

- Copy and paste, print, and bookmark content

Did you know that Packt offers eBook versions of every book published, with PDF and ePub files available? You can upgrade to the eBook version at packtpub.com and as a print book customer, you are entitled to a discount on the eBook copy. Get in touch with us at customercare@packtpub.com for more details.

At www.packtpub.com, you can also read a collection of free technical articles, sign up for a range of free newsletters, and receive exclusive discounts and offers on Packt books and eBooks.

Other Books You May Enjoy

If you enjoyed this book, you may be interested in these other books by Packt:

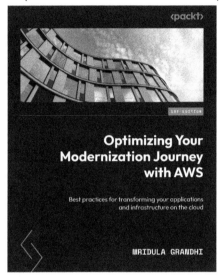

Optimizing Your Modernization Journey with AWS

Mridula Grandhi

ISBN: 978-1-80323-454-0

- Strategize approaches for cloud adoption and digital transformation
- Understand the catalysts for business reinvention
- Select the right tools for cloud migration and modernization processes
- Leverage the potential of AWS to maximize the value of cloud investments
- Understand the importance of implementing secure workloads on the cloud
- Explore AWS services such as computation, databases, security, and networking
- Implement various real-life use cases and technology case studies for modernization
- Discover the benefits of operational excellence on the cloud

Azure Cloud Adoption Framework Handbook

Sasa Kovacevic, Darren Dempsey

ISBN: 978-1-80324-452-5

- Understand cloud adoption and digital transformation generally
- Get to grips with the real-world, day-to-day running of a cloud platform
- Discover how to plan and execute the cloud adoption journey
- Guide all levels of the organization through cloud adoption
- Innovate with the business goals in mind in a fast and agile way
- Become familiar with advanced topics such as cloud governance, security, and reliability

Packt is searching for authors like you

If you're interested in becoming an author for Packt, please visit `authors.packtpub.com` and apply today. We have worked with thousands of developers and tech professionals, just like you, to help them share their insight with the global tech community. You can make a general application, apply for a specific hot topic that we are recruiting an author for, or submit your own idea.

Share Your Thoughts

Now you've finished *The Cloud Computing Journey*, we'd love to hear your thoughts! Scan the QR code below to go straight to the Amazon review page for this book and share your feedback or leave a review on the site that you purchased it from.

`https://packt.link/r/1-805-12228-2`

Your review is important to us and the tech community and will help us make sure we're delivering excellent quality content.

Download a free PDF copy of this book

Thanks for purchasing this book!

Do you like to read on the go but are unable to carry your print books everywhere? Is your eBook purchase not compatible with the device of your choice?

Don't worry, now with every Packt book you get a DRM-free PDF version of that book at no cost.

Read anywhere, any place, on any device. Search, copy, and paste code from your favorite technical books directly into your application.

The perks don't stop there, you can get exclusive access to discounts, newsletters, and great free content in your inbox daily

Follow these simple steps to get the benefits:

1. Scan the QR code or visit the link below

https://packt.link/free-ebook/9781805122289

2. Submit your proof of purchase
3. That's it! We'll send your free PDF and other benefits to your email directly

www.ingramcontent.com/pod-product-compliance
Lightning Source LLC
LaVergne TN
LVHW081511050326
832903LV00025B/1439